Chromebook®

2nd Edition

by Peter H. Gregory and Mark LaFay

for
dummies®
A Wiley Brand

Chromebook® For Dummies®, 2nd Edition

Published by: **John Wiley & Sons, Inc.**, 111 River Street, Hoboken, NJ 07030-5774, www.wiley.com

Copyright © 2020 by John Wiley & Sons, Inc., Hoboken, New Jersey

Published simultaneously in Canada

For general information on our other products and services, please contact our Customer Care Department within the U.S. at 877-762-2974, outside the U.S. at 317-572-3993, or fax 317-572-4002. For technical support, please visit https://hub.wiley.com/community/support/dummies.

Wiley publishes in a variety of print and electronic formats and by print-on-demand. Some material included with standard print versions of this book may not be included in e-books or in print-on-demand. If this book refers to media such as a CD or DVD that is not included in the version you purchased, you may download this material at http://booksupport.wiley.com. For more information about Wiley products, visit www.wiley.com.

Library of Congress Control Number: 2020902717

ISBN: 978-1-119-65171-0; ISBN 978-1-119-65172-7 (ebk); ISBN 978-1-119-65174-1 (ebk)

Manufactured in the United States of America

10 9 8 7 6 5 4 3 2 1

Contents at a Glance

Table of Contents

Introduction

Laptop sales have been declining for years. This decline is mainly due to the rise in popularity of smartphones and tablets in the consumer market. Technology is getting smaller, faster, and more portable, so the world's dependence on full-size, full-featured computers with fixed connections has begun to decrease.

However, in this declining market, the rising star is the *Chromebook* — a low-cost portable computer powered by Google's Chrome OS, the first popular operating system inspired by and designed specifically for the Internet. Unlike Windows PCs and the Mac, which were designed for general computer use with lots of big applications, Chromebooks are designed *primarily* for Internet use. Instead of a gigantic hard drive, Chromebook relies mainly on cloud-based storage. Instead of lots of expensive memory, Chromebook uses the Chrome browser that doesn't use a lot of memory. And instead of resident applications, Chromebook uses mainly web-based applications that are accessed and bookmarked through the Chrome Web Store and the Google Play store.

By offloading the bulk of the functionality to the cloud, Google made it possible for hardware manufacturers to create computers with hardware configurations designed specifically for life on the web. The result is an accessible, user-friendly computer with a much lower price point, making it an excellent option for schools, students, companies, and budget-conscious people in need of modern computing power.

It's paying off. Chromebooks make up almost two-thirds of all computers sold to K–12 schools in the U.S., and they're gaining traction worldwide. This market share means that the future of Chromebooks is bright. What students use in school today, they'll use at home and at work tomorrow.

Similarly, more corporations are offering Chromebooks to employees for their corporate workstations. Chromebooks have a lower price point, are easier to manage, and don't have the security problems experienced by Windows (mostly), and Macs (a little, and growing).

Although Chromebooks use Google's Chrome OS operating system, by no means are Chromebooks "Google only" computers. Tools from Microsoft (Office 365, Word, Excel, and Skype), Apple, and Amazon work on Chromebooks, too. And because Chromebooks are browser-centric, the entire world of the Internet is your oyster!

About This Book

Sometimes the greatest obstacle with new technology is the fear that you won't be able to learn it fast enough for it to be of use. The good news is that this book is designed to remove all the guesswork. *Chromebook For Dummies*, 2nd Edition is designed to give you all the tips and tools you need to excel with your Chromebook.

You don't need to have any preexisting experience with Chromebooks, Chrome OS, Android, or the Chrome browser to be able to use *Chromebook For Dummies*, 2nd Edition. You don't even have to own a Chromebook: This book can help you choose the Chromebook that's right for you! (See Chapter 1 for an overview of features and Chapter 20 for details on selecting the right Chromebook for your needs.) If you do have a Chromebook, this book guides you from the initial setup phase to the features that make Chromebooks unique and easy to use. Later sections of the book give you step-by-step instructions on installing popular apps that can make you productive (or entertained) on day one. By the time you hit the advanced settings and features section of the book, you'll probably consider yourself an advanced Chromebook user.

Many computer books get bogged down with technical jargon and mumbo jumbo. This book, however, isn't written for the technical elite; it's written for the 99.9 percent of the population who just want a no-nonsense approach to using an easy-to-use computer.

Currently, several hardware manufacturers make Chromebooks. You've probably heard of many of them: HP, Samsung, Lenovo, Dell, Acer, and Asus, to name a few. Google even has its own branded Chromebook, known as the Chromebook Pixel and the Pixelbook. The only difference between these different devices is the hardware — not the operating system. For that reason, *Chromebook For Dummies*, 2nd Edition doesn't reference any specific device or manufacturer.

Chromebooks are great devices, and their intuitive design makes for a very short learning curve. This book can help ensure that you have all the info you need to use your Chromebook like a rock star.

Foolish Assumptions

Chromebook For Dummies, 2nd Edition requires no prior computer knowledge or experience. Of course, if you do have experience using PCs or Macs, you'll already be very familiar with many of the Chromebook's features. If you've never used a laptop before but have used smartphones, you'll find that many of the concepts carry over. You'll be fine!

This book makes no assumptions about your skill level. Although this book is primarily an introductory guide to the Chromebook and Chrome OS, you can also consider it to be an introductory guide on personal computing.

Icons Used in This Book

As you read this book, you see icons in the margins that indicate material of interest (or not, as the case may be). This section briefly describes each icon in this book.

TIP

Tips are nice because they help you save time or perform some task without a lot of extra work. The tips in this book are timesaving techniques or pointers to resources that you should try so that you can get the maximum benefit from your Chromebook.

WARNING

At the risk of sounding like an alarmist, I use a warning icon to point out something you should pay close attention to. Proceed with caution if you must proceed at all.

TECHNICAL STUFF

Whenever you see this icon, think *advanced* tip or technique. You might find these tidbits of useful information to be just too boring for words, or they could contain the solution you need to get your Chromebook working just the way you want. Skip these bits of information whenever you like.

REMEMBER

If you don't get anything else out of a particular chapter or section, remember the material marked by this icon. This text reminds you of meaningful content that you should file away. This icon might also draw your attention to something I already covered that's useful again.

Beyond the Book

A lot of extra content that you won't find in this book is available at www.dummies. com. There, search this book's title and then click More on This Book on the page that appears. You can find the Cheat Sheet for this book, which contains quick-reference information that might come in handy when you're in a pinch. You can also find updates to this book, if we have any.

Where to Go from Here

The time has come to dive into the world of Chromebooks and Chrome OS. If you're entirely new to computers or maybe just a little timid with new computers, start with Chapter 1. The first chapters of the book are designed to guide you through the process of powering on your device, logging in, navigating your new computing environment, and even getting familiar with some keyboard and touchpad features unique to the Chromebook.

If you're a little more daring than others, you may consider skipping the first few chapters of the book and heading directly to the chapter on the Chrome browser. If you already have a Chromebook, you can read this book from cover to cover to pick up knowledge here and there, or go to the Table of Contents or the Index to look up specific information you need. Regardless of how you fancy yourself, this book can serve as an excellent primer for life with a Chromebook. And what a great life it can be!

1

Getting Started with Chromebook

Chapter **1**

Choosing and Setting Up Your Chromebook

With the world entrenched in Windows and Mac laptops, it was gutsy of Google to introduce a brand new concept in laptops — the Chromebook. In 2014, Google captured 1 percent of the laptop market in the U.S., which equates to roughly 5.3 million units sold, a number expected to grow. In 2016, Chromebooks captured 3.6 percent of the overall U.S. laptop market. And in late 2017, nearly 60 percent of all computers sold into K–12 education in the U.S. were Chromebooks. This growth means that a lot more people will be using Chromebooks in the future.

In this chapter, I discuss what makes the Chromebook unique when compared to other personal computers on the market. I also take an in-depth look at how to set up your Chromebook and prepare you to transition to Chromebook from Windows or Mac.

But I can tell you right up front: A Chromebook is very easy to use and learn. Easier, I'd say, than a Windows computer or even a Mac. In fact, a Chromebook is about as easy to use as an iPhone or an iPad. I've used Windows and Macs professionally and personally for more than 25 years, so believe me when I tell you this.

Checking Under the Hood of the Chromebook

But what is a Chromebook? In short, a Chromebook is a laptop computer running Google's proprietary operating system, Chrome OS.

TECHNICAL STUFF

The *operating system (OS)* is the software that manages and schedules the basic tasks and functions of your computer. You might have a little experience with other popular operating systems like Microsoft Windows, Linux, or Apple's Mac OS. Smartphones and tablets have operating systems, too; Apple's iphone OS is called iOS, iPadOS runs on Apple iPads, and the OS that runs on Android tablets and phones is called, um, Android.

Chrome OS is an operating system developed by Google to work primarily with web-based software on laptop computers. Your experience using your Chromebook will be very similar to previous experiences you might have had surfing the web with the Chrome web browser (or any browser). The Chrome web browser shares many similarities with other web browsers on the market like Firefox, Internet Explorer, and Safari. (See Figure 1-1.)

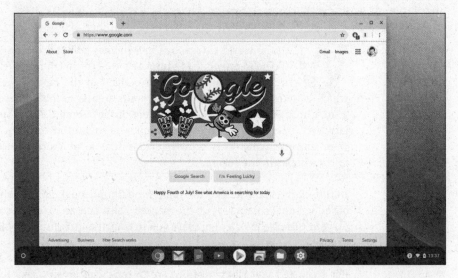

FIGURE 1-1:
The Google Chrome web browser.

Except for the Chromebook Pixel, Google isn't manufacturing Chromebooks directly. Instead, Google has licensed several major laptop manufacturers to create them. Manufacturers such as Acer, ASUS, HP, Lenovo, Dell, Toshiba, and Samsung are all making their own Chromebooks with their own technical specifications.

The software

Much of what you will do on your Chromebook happens in the Chrome web browser. This is because many of the applications you will use on your Chromebook actually reside on the Internet. This is one of the things that sets Chromebook apart from other computers: You don't install applications on a Chromebook; instead, you access them from the Internet. You find applications through the Chrome Web Store (dubbed CWS) and add them to your Launcher, which, in many cases, means nothing more than creating a bookmark for quick access through your Chrome web browser. This approach can be limiting in some cases, but these cases are rare. Thanks to the vast nature of Google's global computing ecosystem, thousands of great applications are at your fingertips.

REMEMBER

Although some Chromebook applications offer offline features and functionality, you will need an Internet connection to initially set up your Chromebook and be able to take advantage of everything your Chromebook has to offer. You could say that Chromebooks are designed for an "always online" lifestyle, but you can definitely do things with your Chromebook while offline as well.

The hardware

Unlike all other computers on the market that run Mac OS or Windows, not much software is installed on your Chromebook, which means that your Chromebook doesn't need to have vast amounts of hard drive space, memory, or processing power. Most Chromebooks have 2–4 gigabytes (GB) of memory, less than 64GB of hard drive space, and a low-power processor.

The reduced technical features mean that Chromebooks use less power, which means longer battery life. It also means that Chromebooks come with a drastically lower price tag compared to other computers available today. This explains why Google is gaining such a large share of the laptop market. For the things that most people do, a Chromebook is more than adequate.

If you prefer a desktop computer running Chrome OS, plenty are available. These computers are called *Chromeboxes*. If you own or are thinking about getting a Chromebox instead of a Chromebook, 99 percent of everything you will read in this book will still apply to you, because most of what's in this book is about Chrome OS— the same OS that runs on Chromebooks and Chromeboxes.

Choosing a Chromebook

Given the nature of Chrome OS, Chromebooks do not require extremely high-powered hardware to provide an excellent user experience. Even so, the great variety of manufacturers and hardware specifications available can make choosing a Chromebook somewhat tricky.

If you are not yet familiar with computer things like hard drives, RAM, SD card slots, or HDMI ports, you don't really need to understand any of these things to buy a Chromebook that will work for you. If you are shopping for your first Chromebook (even if it's the first computer you have ever purchased), go to a store with a good selection (three or more models) of Chromebooks and knowledgeable salespeople. If you buy the least expensive model with a screen size you can live with, you probably won't be disappointed. If this is you, you can read about RAM, hard drives, HDMI, and other things later — or never! If you *do* want to understand the inner details of Chromebooks and make your purchase decision based on RAM, hard drive size, and ports, flip over to Chapter 21 for all those details.

TIP

Another useful way to decide which Chromebook to purchase is to research them online. Amazon.com has a good article from *Consumer Reports* on Chromebooks (just search for Chromebooks). *PC Magazine* and other well-known publications also have good reviews on Chromebook models.

Setting Up Your Chromebook

TIP

You really should have a wireless Internet service available when you first set up your Chromebook. (If you don't know about the Internet service, it's time to bring in the person who does.) If you're using a stationary (home or public) wireless Internet network or a portable device with an Internet *hotspot*, you probably need to know

>> The network name (like Smith Family Wi-Fi or ATT034)

>> The network password (usually a bunch of random letters and numbers)

If you don't already have a Google Account, you'll also need a phone handy to verify your new account while you set up your Chromebook.

Turning on your device

Regardless of the brand you choose, the Chromebook is built for speed — and you'll notice this speed the first time you turn on your device! To turn on your device, you may simply need to plug in the power cord and open the laptop. If your Chromebook doesn't turn on automatically, locate the Power button, which may be found on the top-right corner of the keyboard itself, or on the side or back of the Chromebook. Look for the familiar "0-1" logo. Figure 1-2 shows the Power button on the Lenovo C330 and on the Samsung 303C. The Power button on your Chromebook is probably similar to one of these.

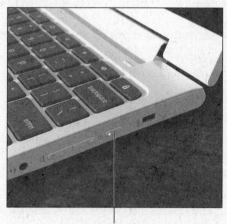 

FIGURE 1-2:
The Power button on two different Chromebook models.

Power button   Power button

When you turn on the device for the first time, a Chrome logo pops up on the screen, and within seconds, the computer powers on and displays the Welcome window. Click Let's Go to begin setup.

Selecting a language

When the Welcome window appears, it will most likely say Welcome in your language. If it's not in your language, click Country Language at the lower-left corner of the Welcome window and then find and select your language. (I wish it had an option for Pirate English. *"Select your languaaaarge, matey!"*)

If you needed to change your language, you might also need to select the keyboard layout. If you're living in the United States, you likely want to select the defaults here, which are English (United States) and US Keyboard.

Most people will not need to change the language, country, or keyboard options.

Connecting to the Internet

Next, you need to select a network to connect to the Internet. If no network is available, I suggest holding off on attempting to set up your Chromebook until you can connect to an Internet source.

If you're using a mobile device that can provide an Internet hotspot, it's time to turn on the hotspot and find the network name and password, which you use in the following steps to connect your Chromebook to the Internet for the first time:

1. **Click the Open the Network drop-down list and select your network name.**

Your Chromebook may detect and display several other nearby home or business networks. You can ignore them.

2. **If your Chromebook requests it, enter your network password.**

After you select the network and enter a password, if applicable, the Wi-Fi bars onscreen fluctuate as your computer tries to connect. (Figure 1-3 shows the Wi-Fi signal icon.) After the connection is successfully established, the Continue button at the bottom of the dialog window becomes active.

If your Chromebook does not successfully connect to the Wi-Fi network, you'll see the error message bad password and you can try entering the password again. You can also select a different Wi-Fi network if you wish.

You can view the Wi-Fi password you are typing by clicking the little eye symbol to the right of where you are typing in your password.

3. **Click the Continue button.**

FIGURE 1-3:
The Wi-Fi
signal icon.

Wi-Fi Signal Indicator

Agreeing to the Terms of Service

You might see a message that says `Your Connection is Not Private`. This issue is not something to worry about at this point.

If you've installed software or activated a device within the last 10 years, you've likely seen a terms-of-service agreement. You can accept it by following these steps:

1. **Review the Terms of Service.**

2. **(Optional) When you're satisfied that you understand and agree to the terms, select or deselect the check box that sends usage stats back to Google.**

   TIP

   I recommend that you leave this box selected. The data is useful for identifying and fixing bugs, creating new features, and otherwise making the Chromebook better for everyone! (Google and the NSA have all our information anyway, so why not?)

3. **Click Accept and Continue to move to the next step.**

Logging In for the First Time

To unlock all the features that your Chromebook has to offer, you must first log in with a Google username and password. You can use your existing Google Account or create a new account at this time.

Logging in using an existing Google Account

You can log in by using your Google Account username and password:

1. **Enter your Google Account username into the Username field.**

2. **Enter your Google Account password into the Password field.**

3. **Click Login.**

   The option to select a profile picture appears.

4. **Select your profile picture.**

   Pick one of the default pictures, use your existing Google profile picture, or take a new picture.

5. **Click OK.**

   This completes the initial login process.

REMEMBER

If your Google account uses Google Authenticator or Google Advanced Protection for logging in to Google, you need to log in to your Chromebook using those services for the first time. If this is your situation, your first login to your new Chromebook will be like logins you've done in the past on other computers.

Creating a new Google Account

You can create a Google Account by following these steps:

1. **On the login screen, click the Create a Google Account Now option.**

   The Chrome web browser launches and takes you to a page where you can create your account.

2. **Complete the form and click Next.**

   On this screen, Google wants to verify that you are a real human being. I assume that you are!

3. **Enter your phone number and whether you'd rather be called or texted, and click Next.**

   Google will contact you in the manner you selected to provide you with a verification code.

4. **Enter the verification code and click Continue.**

5. **Close the browser by clicking the X in the upper-right corner of the browser window.**

6. **On the bottom-right of the screen, click the word Guest.**

   A pop-up menu appears with several options.

7. **Select Exit Guest from the list.**

   This step takes you back to the login screen.

8. **Log in to your Chromebook with your new Google Account.**

Using Chromebook as a guest

Logging in to your Google Account allows you to use all of Chromebook's functionality, but you can still access many of these functions without logging in. Chromebook allows you to use the device as a guest by selecting the Browse as Guest option.

TIP

Letting a friend or family member use your Chromebook for a while is a great use of Chromebook's Guest feature.

If you browse the Chromebook as a guest and then later decide to register or log in as a user, you first need to exit Guest mode. You can log out by clicking the status area (on the bottom-right of your screen, where you see the time, battery, and Wi-Fi status) and then selecting Exit Guest from the top of the list. (See Figure 1-4.) Exit Guest takes you back to the login screen.

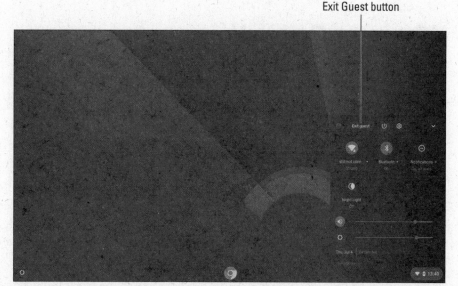

Exit Guest button

FIGURE 1-4:
The Exit Guest button.

Transitioning to a Chromebook from Mac, Linux, or Windows

Transitioning from a Mac, Linux, or Windows computer requires a few easy steps outlined in the following list. All these items are covered later in this book:

>> **Get a Google Account.** The section "Creating a new Google Account," earlier in this chapter, shows you how to get a Google Account. Your Google Account is the key to nearly everything you do on your Chromebook moving forward.

>> **Move your files.** In Chapter 6, you can find out how to access your Chromebook hard drive, external storage, and Google Drive (which is where the bulk of your files will reside after you make the leap to Chromebook).

>> **Get your Chrome bookmarks.** If you've signed in while using the Chrome web browser on other devices, your bookmarks, apps, and extensions will come with you to your new Chromebook! I cover bookmarks in Chapter 3.

>> **Find new apps.** Your Chromebook comes with several applications in your Launcher by default. You can, however, add new apps by navigating to the Chrome Web Store and adding them to your menu. In Chapter 5, you can look at some of the existing apps on your Chromebook, as well as discover ways to locate and add new apps that are useful to you.

Where to Go Next

Now that you've completed the basics of setting up your Chromebook and logging in, what would you like to do next? Here are a few ideas:

>> Learn more about using your Chromebook. Go to Chapter 2.

>> Learn more about the Chrome browser. Go to Chapter 3.

>> Download and use other Chromebook apps. Go to Chapter 5.

>> Use office tools to create documents and worksheets. Go to Part 2 (Chapters 7–11).

>> Start working with photos, videos, and ebooks. Go to Part 3 (Chapters 12–16).

>> Explore advanced features (are you ready?). Go to Part 4 (Chapters 17–20).

A last word: If you're finding your initial Chromebook experience to be difficult or frustrating, don't give up! You'll soon develop "muscle memory" for common functions and before long, you'll love the sheer simplicity and ease of use of your Chromebook.

Chapter **2**

Working with the Chromebook Desktop

The Chromebook desktop is displayed after you turn on and log in to your Chromebook. The desktop is a visual interface that uses a system of windows to control, organize, and manage applications, data, and files. You interact with the desktop by using a mouse, touchpad, keyboard, touch screen, or your voice. Your desktop has a launching point from which you can manually navigate your computer's apps and files. Other operating systems have similar launching points: Microsoft Windows uses the *taskbar,* and Macs have the *dock.* On your Chromebook, this launching button is called the Launcher, and the region on your screen is called the *shelf.*

In this chapter, you explore the Chromebook desktop, Launcher, status area, and shelf. You learn how to find, add, and organize apps, as well as how to modify basic Chromebook settings and navigate the Chromebook window system.

If you're learning Chrome OS for the first time, remember to be patient. Soon, your Chromebook will feel as comfortable as your favorite shoes!

Accessing the Chromebook Shelf

The *shelf* is where all the magic happens on your Chromebook. Your shelf is customized specifically to you. To access it, however, you must first log in to your Chromebook with your Google username and password (refer to Chapter 1 for instructions on creating a Google account and logging in).

REMEMBER

Logging in takes you out of Guest mode. When you're in Guest mode, you can't install apps or permanently customize your Chromebook, so it's of limited use. However, Guest mode is a great way to give your friends and family access to your Chromebook without fear of them changing or manipulating your data or your settings in any way.

Okay, now that you're logged in, you find a row of icons lined up along the bottom of the screen. This is the *shelf.* The shelf appears by default at the bottom of the screen. You *can* change the location of your shelf, as described in Chapter 17, but for now, leave it on the bottom of the screen. A quick tour of the shelf reveals two key groupings of icons: one on the left and one on the right (see Figure 2-1):

» The icons on the left include

- **The Launcher (on the far lower left of the screen):** This icon looks like a white circle and functions in a manner similar to the Start button in Windows or the Apple key on Macs. Click the Launcher icon, and a collection of app icons appears, arranged in a grid. Click any icon to launch the app. Click the up-arrow on the screen and you'll see the entire Launcher as it fills the screen. Click the Launcher once again to close it entirely.

- **App shortcut icons (immediately to the right of the Launcher):** For convenience, you can place any of the apps you see in the Launcher on your shelf. By default, your Chromebook comes with a few popular app shortcuts already installed on the shelf. You can add or remove any of these as you like.

» The group of icons on the right is referred to as the *status area.* These icons include

- Clock

- Wi-Fi signal indicator

- Battery icon (indicates battery charge)

- Notifications (if any)

REMEMBER

The appearance of the figures on your Chromebook is likely to differ a bit from the illustrations from my Chromebooks in this book. Don't worry if yours are not exactly like mine. In most cases, the differences won't matter at all.

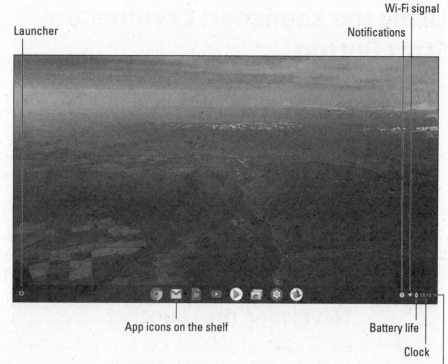

Launcher

Wi-Fi signal

Notifications

App icons on the shelf

Battery life

Clock

Status area

FIGURE 2-1:
The Chromebook
shelf.

THE CONQUERING DESKTOP

With your desktop, you can run programs and create, edit, and otherwise manipulate files by dragging, dropping, and clicking filenames or icons. However, this type of functionality wasn't always the case. Did you know that the first desktop — the graphical user interface (GUI) kind of desktop, not the physical kind — was actually created back in 1973 by Xerox? This version of the desktop, known first as the Xerox Alto and then later as the Xerox Star, never really took off because the devices and software were too expensive. Apple and Microsoft took note of the innovation, and in the 1980s both companies rolled out their own versions — Windows and MacOS. A parallel effort at MIT resulted in the functionally similar X-Windows system used on Unix computers.

The desktop was a revolutionary approach to interacting with a computer because it simplified things (for most people, anyway) by making things visual. These days, of course, the desktop is a staple of all major operating systems, but in the early days of computing, users could interface with computers only by typing obscure commands in a command line. (Remember DOS and CP/M, if you're not too young?) The desktop was a quantum leap in accessibility, and it made possible the digital future we're all living in today.

Using the Launcher: Chromebook's Start Button

Among the icons on the left side of the screen is one icon that looks like a white circle. This is your Launcher icon, comparable to the Start button on Windows or the Apple key on Macs. When you click the Launcher icon, you reveal the *Launcher*, a pop-up window containing a number of applications. Until you add applications yourself, the only apps that appear here are the default ones that come with your Chromebook and any apps already associated with your Google Account.

If you click the Launcher once, you see a search field along with a little up-arrow above it. If you click the arrow, the Launcher fills the entire screen, displaying up to 20 Google apps, including Chrome (your browser), Web Store, Play Store, and many more. These are all Chrome apps that run if you click them. If you click the Launcher button again, the Launcher closes the full screen you're viewing.

Navigating the Launcher

The Launcher window can display up to 20 apps. As you install applications, Chrome OS adds more windows to contain your applications. When you have more than 20 applications, little buttons shaped like tiny dots appear to the right of the application icons. These buttons indicate the presence of additional applications. The color of the button indicates which window is active. You can navigate among windows by clicking these buttons. (See Figure 2-2.)

Buttons indicate two or more pages with icons.

FIGURE 2-2:
The Chromebook
Launcher.

Organizing Launcher Icons

If you like to keep things in a particular order, like the way you can arrange glasses and dishes in your cupboard, then you will appreciate being able to organize the icons on your Launcher as you see fit. Simply click applications and drag them around inside the Launcher window until they are in the order you desire. You can move the app icons in the Launcher by following these steps:

1. Open the Launcher and then click the little up-arrow in the top-middle of the Launcher window to expand the view of application icons to full screen.

2. Click and hold the application icon that you want to move.

3. Drag the icon to the place in which you would like to place your selected application.

Wait patiently until the window shifts.

4. Drop the app icon in the desired location.

When you are done moving app icons around, you can close the Launcher by clicking the Launcher icon on your shelf.

Setting Up App Shortcuts

Next to the Launcher icon, you see several additional application icons. These are shortcuts to frequently used applications on your Chromebook. If you find yourself frequently using applications like Gmail, Calendar, Docs, or Drive, adding shortcuts to these apps on your shelf is a great way to streamline your user experience.

Pinning app shortcuts to your shelf

You can add application icons to your shelf by following these steps:

1. Click the Launcher icon.

The Launcher appears.

2. Navigate to the application that you want to add directly to your shelf.

Finding the application may require moving among Launcher windows.

3. **While holding down the Alt key, click the application icon.**

A menu with several options appears.

4. **Select Pin to Shelf from the list.**

Your application shortcut has been added to your shelf (see Figure 2-3).

FIGURE 2-3:
Pinning
application
shortcuts to
your shelf.

A second option for pinning apps to your shelf is the drag-and-drop method. Simply click and hold the icon for any application you want to pin and drag it down to the shelf. You can easily move the icon to any position you desire. Then, just release the click to drop it in place.

Don't worry, pinning icons to your shelf doesn't remove the application from the Launcher. It simply creates an additional way for you to use the application so that you can quickly move among your frequently used applications.

After you pin an application to your shelf, you can place your icons in the order that you desire by clicking and dragging icons left or right along the shelf.

TIP

If you've never performed a drag-and-drop action before, it can take a little practice. Although it tends to be a bit easier to do using a mouse, you can do it with your trackpad as well. Move the pointer to the object you want to move; at the lower-left corner of the trackpad, use your thumb to click and hold the object; keeping your thumb down, press your finger on the trackpad and keep pressing while moving it to drag the object to another part of the screen, drop the object by lifting your thumb to release the click. Practice makes perfect!

Removing app shortcuts from your shelf

If you want to remove an application shortcut from your shelf, you have a few options. Here's one easy method:

1. **Hold the Alt key and click the application icon on the shelf.**

   You see a pop-up menu with several options.

2. **Select Unpin to remove the icon from the shelf.**

   Selecting Unpin doesn't delete the application from your machine; it just removes the shortcut from your shelf. You can still find it if you click the up-arrow in the Launcher.

Another easy method: Just click and drag the icon you wish to remove from the shelf. (If you have a touchscreen, you can just tap and drag the icon off the shelf.)

Getting the Scoop in the Status Area

On the right side of your screen is a bunch of icons. This set of icons is called your *status area.* The leftmost icon in this group is nothing more than a circle with a number in it, and your number may be zero (or it may not appear at all). This icon is the *notification panel* (see Figure 2-4). If you click this icon, your notification window appears. Notifications can be many things, including

>> Calendar event reminders

>> Stock tickers

>> Sports scores

>> Weather

>> Email

>> Application updates

>> Chrome OS updates

Google selects its notifications by learning from your behavior. By using Google for repeated searches, Google starts to learn your common searches and automatically funnels those search results into your notification panel.

For instance, say you're a huge Washington Huskies fan and you keep up with the scores by conducting Google searches. Google will learn your search habits and begin sending scores automatically to your notification panel.

FIGURE 2-4:
The Chromebook
notification panel.

TIP

The notification icon disappears if you have no new unread notifications.

Next to your notifications is the *Settings area*. This area contains the current time, a Wi-Fi signal indicator, and a battery indicator. Click anywhere in this area to reveal your Settings page. In your Settings page, you can make some basic settings tweaks that include

>> **Wi-Fi:** Click the Wi-Fi symbol to turn Wi-Fi on and off. When Wi-Fi is turned on, the icon is blue; when it is off, it's gray. Click below the Wi-Fi icon to view available wireless networks. If you're already connected to a network and you want to view information specific to that connection, simply click the network, and a window will pop up revealing additional and advanced information.

>> **Bluetooth:** In the Bluetooth section of the page, you can enable or disable your Bluetooth signal. In this section, you can browse Bluetooth devices and manage your connections.

>> **Notifications:** Click here to configure which applications are permitted to show notifications and which ones you don't want to hear from. You can also turn off all notifications by clicking Do Not Disturb.

>> **Night Light:** This feature dims the blue parts of the display, making it appear more reddish. You can turn this feature off and on, or set up a schedule such as "sunset to sunrise." I talk more about using Night Light in Chapter 17.

>> **Cast:** If you have a Google Chromecast device or a television or monitor with a built-in casting feature, you can use the device or television as an additional monitor to play a movie, for instance.

>> **Volume:** Easily control volume levels by dragging the slider to the right to increase and to the left to decrease the volume level.

>> **Brightness:** Control the brightness of the Chromebook display. (Your Chromebook's keyboard likely also has screen brightness keys.)

As you navigate through the different basic settings windows, you always have the option to navigate back to the main Settings page by clicking the left-pointing arrow at the top of the settings window. If you're in the Wi-Fi window, for example, the button at the bottom will look like < Network. If you're in the Bluetooth window, the button will be < Bluetooth. If you want to get into the advanced settings, you can do so by clicking Settings in the settings panel window.

Taking Charge of Window Controls

The other main feature of your Chromebook desktop is the window system. When opened, almost all applications will load into a system of windows, much as they would on a Windows or Apple computer.

The following list describes the window controls (shown in Figure 2-5) on your Chromebook. Each window has a little set of controls in the upper-right corner of the window.

>> **Close:** You can close a window by clicking the *X*, which is the right-most window control. Closing a window causes the app to exit.

>> **Maximize:** You can maximize a window (so that it fills the entire screen) by clicking the middle button that looks like a little box. To return a window to its original size, click the middle control again (which now looks like one box over another).

>> **Minimize:** You can minimize a window by clicking the little "underline" button, which is the leftmost of the three controls. Minimizing a window sets it aside, metaphorically; the app is still running. To get it back, click its icon on the shelf and the window reappears just as it was before.

Maximize window

Minimize window   Close window

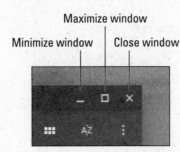

FIGURE 2-5:
Controls to minimize, maximize, and close a window.

Multitasking with Multiple Windows

Sometimes you may want to multitask. You can multitask by activating several application windows at one time. You can quickly switch from one window to another using one of two methods:

>> **Alt+Tab:** While holding down the Alt key, press the Tab key. A bar appears across the screen with a smaller version of each window. Each time you press Tab, the selection moves to the next window. You can press Tab repeatedly and view all the active windows. When you reach the window you want to view, release both the Alt and Tab keys (see Figure 2-6).

>> **Select from the shelf:** Look on the shelf at the application icons. Each one that is currently running has a small white dot beneath it. Just click the icon whose window you want to view. It's that simple!

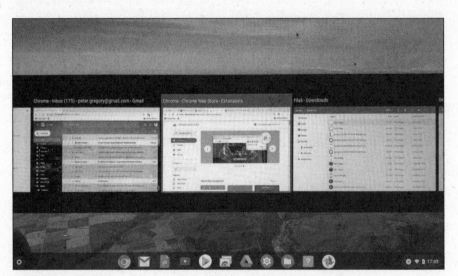

FIGURE 2-6: Navigating among applications using Alt+Tab.

Your Chrome browser can have two or more tabs. If you want to make a browser tab into a stand-alone window, you can do so by following these steps:

1. **Locate the tab that you want to break out.**

2. **Click and hold the desired tab.**

   This brings the tab to the front and makes it active.

3. **Drag the tab in any direction until it pops out into its own window, as shown in Figure 2-7.**

4. **Release the click.**

Tab dragged out to its own window

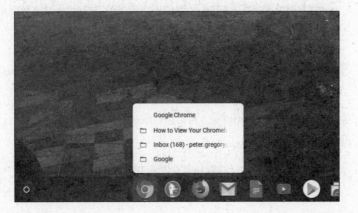

While on the subject of window controls, I need to cover one more topic. If, for any given application, you have several windows open, you have an additional way to identify those windows and navigate to the one you want. For example, if you have three different windows for the Chrome browser and you want to open one of them, /click the Chrome browser icon on the shelf. If only one window is active in the app, the Chrome browser window opens. If, however, two or more windows are active, your Chromebook displays a list of them, as shown in Figure 2-8. Click the one you want to open, and voilà!

Setting Up a Printer

The world is not quite paperless; sometimes you need a hard copy. For example, you may need to print and sign a legal agreement, or you might want to print a recipe to jot notes on.

Many kinds of printers are available, and you have several ways to set them up. I cover the basics here.

TIP

When you shop for a new printer to work with your Chromebook, if you stick with major brands (Brother, Canon, Epson, HP, and Lexmark, for example), chances are your printer and your Chromebook will get along just fine. Still, it's probably wise to ensure that any new printer you are thinking of buying will work with your Chromebook with no fuss. It's a good idea to ask a salesperson, read the specs, and read reviews.

Direct connect printing

Direct connect, which is the easiest type of printing to set up, involves connecting a USB cable from your printer to your Chromebook. You need to follow the instructions that came with your printer, and if they vary from the steps here, definitely go with the printer's instructions! Otherwise, follow these steps:

1. **Turn on the printer and connect the USB cable from your printer to a USB plug on your Chromebook.**

2. **On your Chromebook screen, click the status area to open the Settings view and then click the Settings icon, which looks like a tiny gear near the top-right corner.**

    The Settings window opens.

3. **Scroll all the way down in the Settings window and click Advanced.**

    You see the Advanced settings section in the Settings window.

4. **Keep scrolling until you find Printing; then click Printers. (See Figure 2-9.)**

5. **Click Add Printer.**

    The Add a Nearby Printer window appears and your printer should appear in a list. (Your printer might be the only one in the list.)

6. Click the printer that is shown.

It should match the make and model of printer that your Chromebook is connected to.

7. Click Save.

That's all you should need to do.

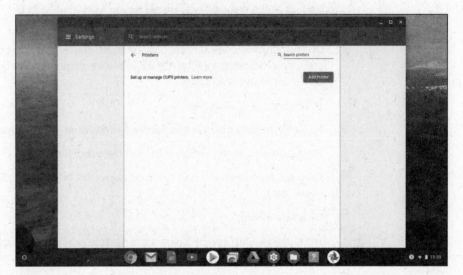

FIGURE 2-9:
Setting up a local printer.

You can rename your printer if you want. For example, I wanted to change my printer's name from "HP Officejet 4630 Series (USB)" to something more useful for me, so I called mine "Office Printer." To change your printer's name, click the three little dots to the right of the printer and then, in the little window that appears, click Edit to open the Edit Printer window. In the Printer Name field, enter your printer's new name and click Save. (You should not need to change anything else in the Edit Printer window.)

Here's a bit of trivia: The symbol with the three little dots is sometimes called a Twinkie. If you're not sure why this is, go buy a Twinkie and look at it from underneath. You will find three little holes there, which is where the manufacturer injects a whipped-cream-like substance into the bread-like substance. Enjoy!

Wi-Fi printing

Several brands of printers support Wi-Fi printing so that you don't have to connect a USB cable to your printer. One great advantage of having a Wi-Fi–supported printer is that you can print from anyplace in your home or office.

Be sure to follow your printer's setup instructions for this type of printing, in case they vary from the procedure outlined in this section. Here are the basics of setting up Wi-Fi printing on your Chromebook:

1. Turn on your printer and follow its setup instructions to connect it to your Wi-Fi network.

Have your Wi-Fi network identifier and password handy. Your Wi-Fi network identifier is the name of the network to which you connect your Chromebook, in the "Connecting to the Internet" section in Chapter 1.

2. On your Chromebook screen, click the status area to open the Settings view and then click the Settings icon (which looks like a tiny gear near the top right corner of the status window).

The Settings window appears.

3. Scroll all the way down in the Settings window, and click Advanced.

The Advanced settings section in the Settings window appears.

4. Keep scrolling until you find Printing; then click Printers. (Refer to Figure 2-9.)

5. Click Add Printer.

The Add a Nearby Printer window appears. Your printer should appear in a list. If you don't see it, check to see whether the printer is still turned on.

6. Click the printer that matches the make and model of printer that your Chromebook is connected to.

7. Click Save.

That's all you should need to do.

Cloud printing

Part of what makes the Chromebook operating system so fast is that it offers only limited support for the vast assortment of peripheral devices on the market, including printers. But what does that mean for Chromebook users who need to print? Thankfully, Google has rolled out a way to print over the web called *cloud printing*. Cloud printing allows you to connect a printer to the Internet and access it using your Google Account. Several printers on the market are cloud-printing enabled, but in the event your printer isn't, don't fret: You can still set it up for printing. (See the previous two sections for help with setting up a printer.)

TIP

If you haven't yet purchased a printer and, after reading this section, you're interested in having a printer that is made for Google Cloud printing, you can go to this website to see printer makes and models that are compatible: `https://www.google.com/cloudprint/learn/printers`.

Setting up a Google Cloud Print–enabled printer

Depending on your cloud-print-enabled printer, there are two ways to set it up. Follow these instructions:

1. **Turn on the printer.**

2. **Connect the printer to your Wi-Fi network per the printer's instructions.**

   You need to know your Wi-Fi network ID and password because one of the early steps is to connect your computer to your Wi-Fi network so that it can work with Google Cloud Print.

3. **Find your printer on this page:** `https://www.google.com/cloudprint/learn/printers/`.

4. **See whether "v2" appears next to your printer's make and model.**

   If you see "v2," do the following:

   a. **On your Chromebook, open the Chrome browser.**

   b. **Type** chrome://devices **in the address bar and press Enter.**

   c. **Find your printer under New Devices.**

   d. **Click Manage next to your printer's name.**

   e. **Click Register in the Confirm Registration box that appears.**

   f. **Follow any instructions on the printer to complete registration.**

   Your printer is all set up. It should appear when you manage your printers. See the "Managing Google Cloud Printers" section, later in this chapter.

   If you don't see "v2 next to your printer's make and model, do the following:

   a. **Go to** `https://www.google.com/cloudprint/learn/printers/` **using your Chrome browser.**

   b. **Click your printer manufacturer.**

   c. **Scroll to the bottom of the section.**

   d. **Find and click the link to go to the printer manufacturer's website.**

   e. **Follow the instructions there to set up your printer for Google Cloud Print.**

When I set up my own Wi-Fi printer, it wasn't in the list of supported printers. However, I found instructions online on the manufacturer's website. After completing the instructions, the printer printed a confirmation page containing a URL that I entered on my Chromebook to complete registration (see Figure 2-10). Moral of the story: Several methods are used to set up printers with Google Cloud Printing!

After your printer has been registered, you see a message in your browser confirming that setup has been completed. (See Figure 2-11.)

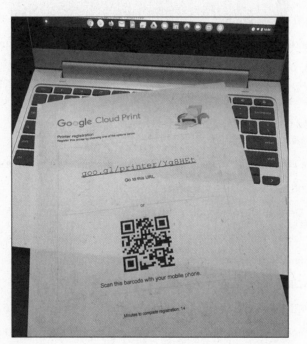

FIGURE 2-10:
Some printers print a page with a URL to complete Google Cloud Print setup.

FIGURE 2-11:
Completion of Google Cloud Print setup on your printer.

Google Cloud Print

Thanks, you're ready to go!

Your printer is now registered with Google Cloud Print.

Manage your printers

Setting up a non-Google Cloud Print–enabled printer

To set up cloud printing with a classic (that is, *not* cloud-printing–enabled) printer, you need a computer that's not a Chromebook (in other words, a Windows, Linux, or Mac computer) and an Internet connection. Then follow these steps:

1. **Plug your printer into your non-Chromebook computer and power it on.**

2. **Open the Chrome browser on the computer.**

REMEMBER

Ensure that you're logged into Chrome with the same Google Account that you use to access your Chromebook. If you're not, click the Disconnect your Google Account button and then log in with the correct credentials before proceeding!

3. **After the Chrome browser loads, click the Settings button in the top-right corner of the browser.**

A menu appears.

4. **Click Settings.**

Your Chrome browser settings load into the Chrome browser.

5. **Click Show Advanced Settings.**

6. **Click Printing.**

Several additional options appear.

7. **In the Print section, choose Google Cloud Print.**

8. **In the Google Cloud Print window, click Manage Cloud Print devices.**

A list appears, displaying the devices on your network that are available to be registered with Google Cloud Print.

9. **Locate the Classic Printers section and click Add Printers.**

A page loads, giving you the option to add every printer installed on your device.

10. **Deselect every printer except for the printer you just connected to your non-Chromebook computer; then click Add Printer.**

A confirmation page appears.

At this point, you can print from your Chromebook as long as the computer to which your classic printer is connected is on and connected to the Internet.

To test that you successfully set up your printer for cloud printing, follow these steps:

1. **With your Chromebook, open a Chrome web browser.**

2. **Click the Settings button in the top-right corner.**

   A menu appears.

3. **Click Print.**

   Print options appear in a window.

4. **Click the printer in the Destination section on the left side of the screen.**

   The Select a Destination window appears, as shown in Figure 2-12.

5. **Select your cloud printer.**

   The window disappears, and your selection is indicated in the Destination area of the print window.

6. **Click Print.**

   Your document prints to the selected printer.

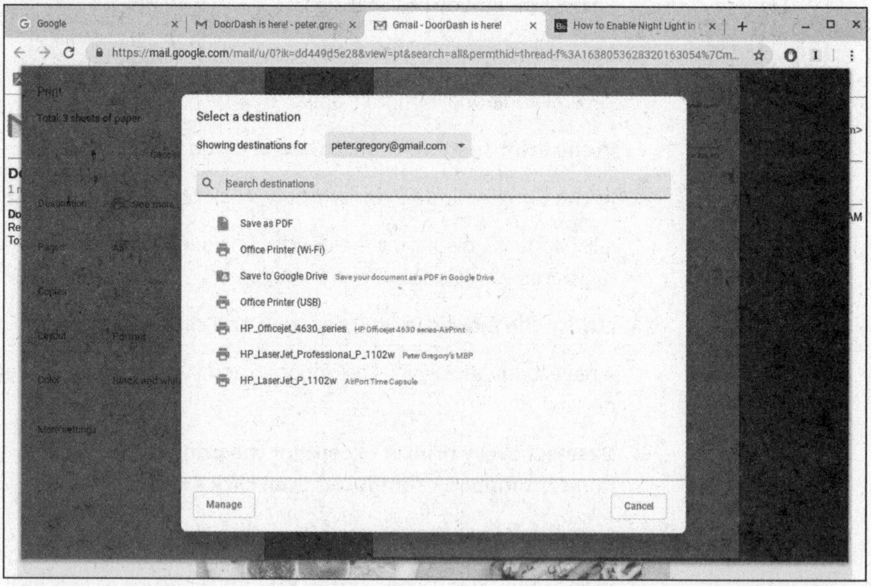

FIGURE 2-12: Selecting your cloud printer.

TIP

If your document didn't print, ensure the following:

» The printer to which you're printing is turned on.

» The computer that's connected to your printer is turned on.

» The computer that's connected to your printer is connected to the Internet.

» Chrome is open on the computer that's connected to your printer.

Managing Google Cloud Print printers

After you have set up one or more printers in Google Cloud Print, you can manage these printers and your printing. Follow these steps:

1. Open your browser and go to https://www.google.com/cloudprint/.

If you have any current printing jobs, they appear in the display. (See Figure 2-13.)

2. To view your Google Cloud Print printers, click the Printers link.

Your Google Cloud Print printers appear. (See Figure 2-14.)

3. View and edit the configuration of each Google Cloud Print printer, view print jobs, or remove the printer from your list of Google Cloud Print–managed printers.

FIGURE 2-13:
The Google Cloud Print print jobs display.

TIP

I suspect that Google will continue to improve Google Cloud Print. If you get lost, go to `https://support.google.com/cloudprint/`, where you can find up-to-date instructions for setting up and managing printers in Google Cloud Print.

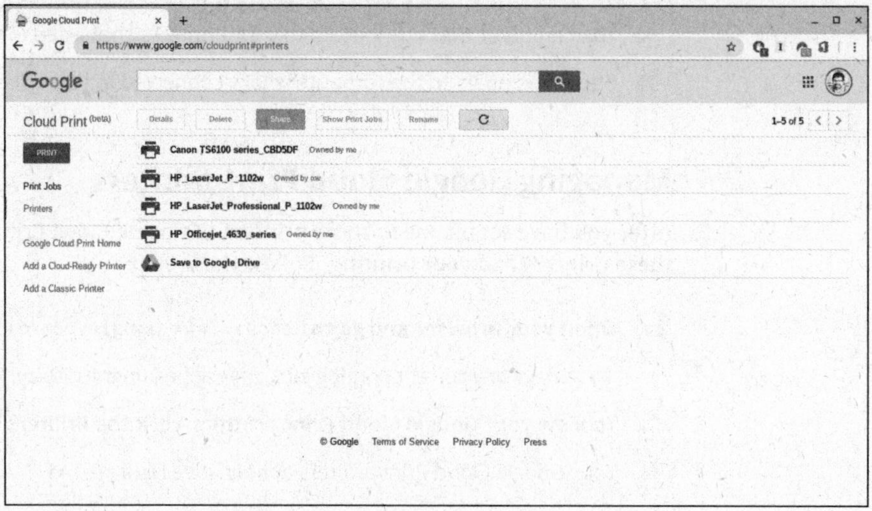

FIGURE 2-14:
List of printers managed by Google Cloud Print.

Chapter **3**

Surveying the Chrome Browser

I n late 2008, after a brief beta run, Google released the first consumer-ready version of its Chrome web browser. Google's goal was to create an alternative to popular existing web browsers such as Internet Explorer, Safari, and Firefox. The application was launched globally in 43 languages, and Chrome quickly gained about 1 percent of the web-browser market.

Chrome's stripped-down approach, and its speed and extensibility, proved to be popular with a wide range of users, from dabblers to the technologically savvy. It was quickly developed for other operating systems like MacOS, Linux, as well as mobile platforms Android and iOS. Today, Chrome accounts for over 60 percent of all web browsing on the Internet.

At their core, web browsers are nothing more than vehicles for surfing the web. In this chapter, you take an in-depth look at the Chrome browser for Chromebook. Learn how to create and manage your bookmarks, manage your browser history, and surf without leaving a record in your browser history. Finally, in case you prefer other browsers like Firefox or DuckDuckGo, I show you how to find, install, and run these browsers.

Navigating the Chrome Browser

Before breaking down the Chrome browser into its different pieces, let me give you a quick tour. Figure 3-1 shows an open Chrome browser window. At the top-left corner is the tab — in this figure, the only tab — featuring the word *Google* and the Google icon; below the tab are the navigation buttons. To the right is the navigation bar, also referred to as the *Omnibox*.

On the far right of the Omnibox is an icon that looks like three little dots — the Settings button. Below the Omnibox is the bookmark bar, and below the bookmark bar is where web pages are loaded.

Navigation Buttons · Navigation Bar (Omnibox) · Add to bookmarks · Settings

Tab · Bookmark bar · Window controls

Chrome icon

FIGURE 3-1:
The layout of the Chrome browser.

Sizing the Chrome window

To launch Google Chrome on your Chromebook, just click the Chrome icon in the bottom left of your screen. (Refer to Figure 3-1.)

The first time you use Chrome, it opens only one browser window, which contains one tab. You can launch additional windows by holding the Ctrl key and clicking the Chrome icon again or by pressing Ctrl+N.

TIP

Instead of opening additional windows, consider using multiple tabs within a single window to achieve the same effect. (I introduce tabs in the next section.)

You can close an open Chrome browser window by clicking the *X*-shaped Close button in the top-right corner of the browser window (as I discuss in Chapter 2) or by pressing Ctrl+W.

When a window is maximized, it takes up the entire screen of your Chromebook. If you want Chrome to take up only a portion of your screen, however, you have a few options. These include

>> **Restoring a window to a nonmaximized size:** You can de-maximize a window by clicking the box-shaped Maximize icon at the top-right of the browser window, or by clicking the header space between the tab and the Maximize button. Either method shrinks your window, allowing you to move it around on the screen.

>> **Minimizing a window:** *Minimizing* shrinks the active window so that it's hidden from the screen but not closed. Minimizing is helpful when you want to open a different application or perform some function on your Chromebook without having the Chrome window in the way. To minimize a window, hover your cursor over the Minimize button until a drop-down menu of options appears, and then click the button in the middle.

TIP

If you have only one Chrome window open, you can also minimize it by clicking the Chrome icon in your shelf.

Working with tabs

More often than not, you find that using Chrome window tabs is much easier and more efficient than opening and managing multiple windows. The tab system is a lot like tabs on folders in your filing cabinet. Take a look at Figure 3-2 to see what Chrome tabs look like. You can have one website open per tab and almost a limitless number of tabs open in one Chrome window.

By default, when you launch Chrome or open a new Chrome window, one tab is opened. To open additional tabs, click the New Tab button located to the right of the last tab in your browser window.

REMEMBER

Multiple tabs make it easier to surf the web without losing your place. You can also open additional tabs by pressing Ctrl+T. You can close a tab by clicking the *X* in the right corner of the tab or by pressing Ctrl+W.

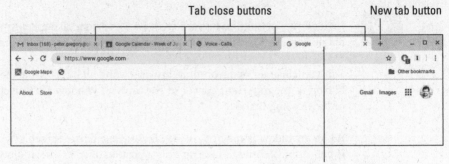

Tab close buttons   New tab button

The current tab is white

FIGURE 3-2:
Chrome
browser tabs.

Using the Omnibox and the navigation buttons

Chrome's Omnibox and navigation buttons allow you to surf the web. They're located at the top of the Chrome browser window. (Refer to Figure 3-1.) In the Omnibox, you can enter a URL (such as www.bbc.com) or a search term or phrase (such as "hardware stores in Seattle"). Chrome and other browsers work in this way.

From left to right, the navigation buttons found to the left of the Omnibox are

» **Back:** Allows you to navigate to the web page that you were on previous to the current page.

» **Forward:** Takes you forward one page in your browser history. Chrome isn't psychic, however; this button remains grayed-out and inaccessible until you've used the Back button. Go backward one page, and clicking the Forward button returns you to your original page.

» **Refresh:** Reloads your current page. Sometimes you might want to use the Refresh button to load new information that may be in the process of launching. Have you ever been tracking a package in shipment? You might click the Refresh button repeatedly to view updates on the progress of your shipment. (We are all guilty of this.)

Saving your place with the bookmark bar

Just as a bookmark helps you remember your place in a book you're reading, so Chrome's bookmarks allow you to quickly pick up where you left off. If you find a place on the Internet to which you want to return in the future, you can create a bookmark so that you can get there with a click of the mouse. With Chrome book-marks, you don't have to write down a URL or record it somewhere else (like a document or worksheet); let Chrome remember it for you!

To create a bookmark in Chrome, first navigate to the web page you want to save and then click the star icon on the right side of the Omnibox. This action auto-matically adds the name and address of the site to your list of bookmarks in the Bookmark Manager. If your bookmark bar is enabled, and if you have space avail-able, your new bookmark also appears there.

TIP

You can also bookmark a page simply by pressing Ctrl+D while you're on the page that you want to bookmark.

Chrome can store an almost unlimited number of bookmarks in your Bookmark Manager. Chrome also gives you the option of saving a small number of bookmarks in the bookmark bar in the browser window. The bookmark bar is located directly under the navigation buttons and Omnibox. As you can see in Figure 3-3, the bookmark bar has limited space. Keep your best bookmarks — the places you visit most frequently — in the bookmark bar.

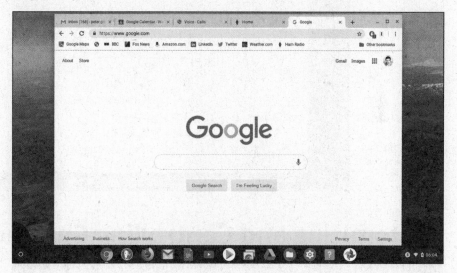

FIGURE 3-3:
The bookmark bar has limited space.

If you can't see the bookmark bar, it may not be turned on. To turn it on, follow these steps:

1. **Click the Settings button on the right side of the Omnibox.**

The Settings menu appears.

2. **Hover your cursor over the Bookmarks option in the Settings menu.**

   A submenu appears.

3. **Select the Show Bookmarks Bar option.**

   The bookmark bar appears in your browser window.

Now your favorite places on the Internet are only one click away!

The Chrome browser also remembers where you visit, and Chrome helps you in yet another way. To see how, click the + (plus sign) icon in the Chrome browser to add another tab. In the window that appears, Chrome displays icons for up to eight recent or frequently visited sites. Just click one of those to visit the page. (See Figure 3-4.) You can also hover over any of the icons and click the x in the top-right corner of the box that appears around it to remove it from the list.

FIGURE 3-4:
Chrome shows recent sites in a new blank tab.

Customizing and Controlling Chrome

You can access many of Chrome's functions and advanced settings in the Settings menu. The Settings menu contains quite a bit of general-purpose functionality. Within the Settings menu, you can

- >> Launch a new tab

- >> Open a new window

- >> Open a new incognito window (more on this in the section "Going incognito," later in the chapter)

- >> View your browser history to find a page you visited in the past

- >> View files you have downloaded in the past

- >> Access and manage bookmarks

- >> Zoom in to make web pages appear larger or smaller

- >> Print the current page you are viewing

- >> Cast the page to another device, such as a television

- >> Find text on a page

- >> Copy and paste text

- >> View and change Chrome and Chromebook settings

- >> Get help

The Settings menu also has features and settings for advanced users and developers alike. With these options, you can

- >> View or save the HTML source of a web page

- >> Clear browsing data

- >> Manage Chrome browser extensions

- >> Inspect web page elements

- >> Debug JavaScript

REMEMBER

If you're not sure how to go about doing something in the Chrome browser, the Help page is a good place to start looking.

You can access the Help page by clicking the Settings button on the right side of the Omnibox, clicking Help, and then clicking Get Help. The Settings button looks like a vertical stack of three lines, as shown in Figure 3-5.

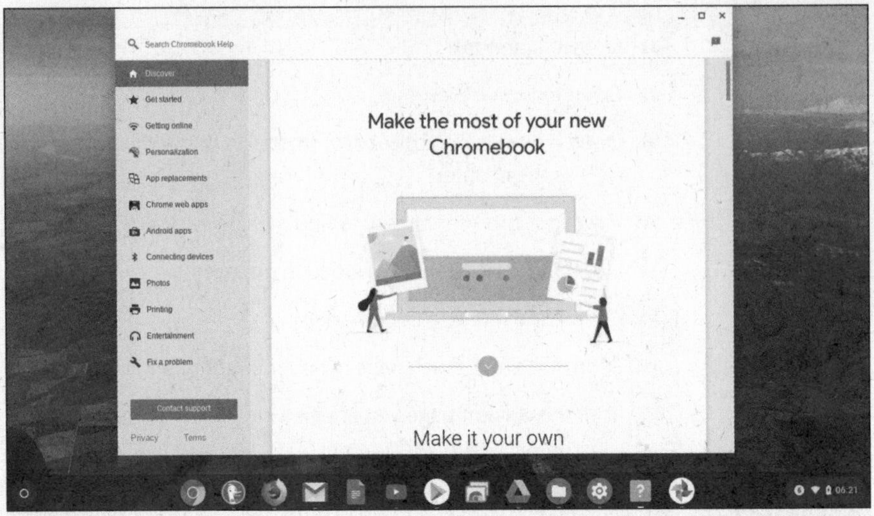

FIGURE 3-5:
The Help page.

Managing bookmarks

The Bookmark Manager is a tool in the Chrome browser used to manage your bookmarks. To access the Bookmark Manager, click the Settings button to the right of the Omnibox and then hover your cursor over the Bookmarks option in the menu that appears. In the resulting submenu, select Bookmark Manager, as shown in Figure 3-6.

In the Bookmark Manager, you can perform the following actions:

>> Add or edit bookmarks

>> Delete bookmarks

>> Organize bookmarks into folders

>> Add or remove bookmarks to the bookmarks bar

>> Search for saved bookmarks

The Bookmark Manager window is divided into two main sections: folders for organizing bookmarks on the left and the bookmarks themselves on the right.

You can add new folders to the section on the left by following these steps:

1. **In the Bookmark Manager, click the Organize button to the right of the Search field, as shown in Figure 3-6.**

   A menu of options appears.

2. **Click Add new folder.**

A new folder is added to your folder list.

3. **Type in the desired name for your folder and click Save.**

Your new folder is saved in the Bookmark Manager.

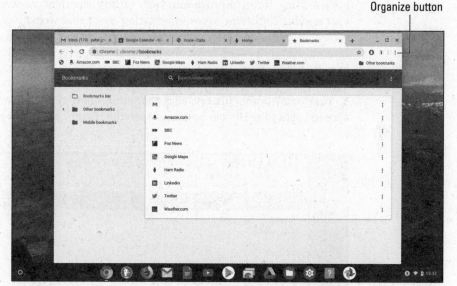

Organize button

FIGURE 3-6:
The Chrome
browser
Bookmark
Manager.

On the right side of your Bookmark Manager window is the bookmark folder contents pane. In this pane, you see bookmarks and subfolders. You can organize your bookmarks in this pane by dragging the bookmarks to any position you want. If you want to add a bookmark to one of the folders in the leftmost pane, just click and drag the bookmark to the desired folder.

To delete a bookmark, simply select it and hit the Delete key.

Managing your history and downloads

As you surf the Internet, you create a breadcrumb trail of activity, otherwise known as your Internet history. The Chrome browser stores your history so that you can go back to a page that you may not have bookmarked. Because the sites you visit are stored in your history, in the event your Chrome browser window unexpectedly closes while you're surfing the web, Chrome remembers all the websites that were loaded into tabs and windows prior to closing.

In addition to tracking the websites you visit, Chrome manages the files downloaded with your Chrome browser. The Download Manager keeps track of files downloaded and logs where they reside on your Chromebook. The Download Manager also gives you options for re-downloading lost files and for pausing large downloads for resuming at a later time.

There are advantages to keeping track of your Internet and download history. For one thing, it can improve your web-surfing experience: Sometimes when you visit a website, Chrome saves information about that website on your computer so that it will load faster the next time you visit it. Also, many parents use Internet history to keep track of their children's web-surfing habits in order to keep their kids safe.

To view your Internet history, click the Settings button. In the Settings menu that appears, select the History option to open the History page, shown in Figure 3-7.

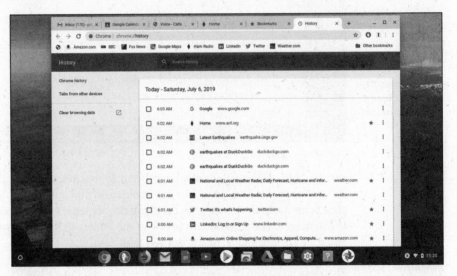

FIGURE 3-7:
The Chrome browser History page.

The Chrome History page is broken up into three distinct sections:

» **The Search History box:** The top of the page contains the search box for quickly searching through your browsing history.

» **Device-specific history:** The section below the search box contains the recent web history grouped by the browsing device.

As noted earlier in the book, when you log in to your Chromebook, Chrome imports all your browsing data, bookmarks, and plug-ins to your device. If you use the Chrome browser on your smartphone or another computer, Google tracks your web history and makes it accessible wherever you log in to a Chrome browser.

>> **Complete browsing history:** Below the device-specific section of the History page is your complete browsing history from each of your devices, combined into one list and organized by date and time.

On the right side of each history entry is a menu icon that looks like three little dots. Clicking this icon gives you the option to remove the site from your history.

Erasing your browsing history

Before you sell your computer (or loan it to someone else), you may want to remove any personal information first. Your browsing history certainly qualifies as personal information. To erase your entire browser history, just follow these steps:

1. **In the History page, click the Clear Browsing Data link.**

A window with several options appears, as shown in Figure 3-8.

FIGURE 3-8:
The Clear
Browsing Data
window.

2. **(Optional) Click All Time to select from the drop-down list a period of time in your history that you want to delete.**

   All Time is typically the default.

3. **Select the Browsing History check box.**

   Deselect all remaining boxes, unless you want to remove those items as well.

TECHNICAL STUFF

   In addition to clearing your browsing history, you can clear out several other items by selecting their associated boxes. These items include

   - **Download history:** A list of files you have downloaded from Internet sites

   - **Cookies and other site data:** Small files that keep track of your login status and other preferences on websites

   - **Cached images and files:** Images and other files that remain in your Chromebook, helping web pages you've visited before load faster if any of the large image files are unchanged

   If you click the Advanced button in the Clear Browsing Data window, several more items appear that you can also clear, including

   - **Passwords:** If you instructed the Chrome browser to save any passwords you entered when logging in to various web sites, you can clear them here.

   - **Auto-fill form data:** This is data such as your email address and home address, which Chrome can remember to make filling out forms easier and faster.

   - **Site data:** This data includes HTML5-enabled storage types such as application caches and application data associated with some websites.

   If you're browsing the web quite a bit, these collections of information can get rather large and begin eating up your available storage space. For this reason, try to periodically clear out that information.

4. **Click Clear Browsing Data.**

Going incognito

Sometimes you may want to browse without the worry of creating a trail of crumbs for someone to follow. You may be using a public computer or a computer that's not yours. Or maybe you're planning to surprise someone and you don't want him to stumble across your surprise when he uses the Chrome browser on your computer. Whatever your reason for wanting to not leave a history trail, Chrome gives you the option to go incognito.

For Chrome, going incognito means opening an *incognito browser window*. This window is separate from any other open browser windows, and it functions differently. In an incognito browser, Chrome doesn't keep a record of the sites you visit or any files you download, and any cookies sent to an incognito browser are deleted when the browser is closed. The browser goes incognito only up to a point, however. Although Chrome doesn't keep records of your history in an incognito browser, your Internet service provider, employer, or anyone else monitoring web traffic still can. An incognito browser window is simply a good way to surf the web without needing to manually clear the history from your account.

Follow these steps to open an incognito window in the Google Chrome browser:

1. **In Google Chrome, click the Settings button to the right of the Omnibox (search field).**

   The Launcher opens.

2. **Click New Incognito Window.**

   Your incognito browser window opens.

You can also type Ctrl+Shift+N to open a new incognito window.

TIP

You know you're incognito if you see the silhouette of a person wearing a hat and sunglasses in the top-left corner of your Chrome browser window, as shown in Figure 3-9.

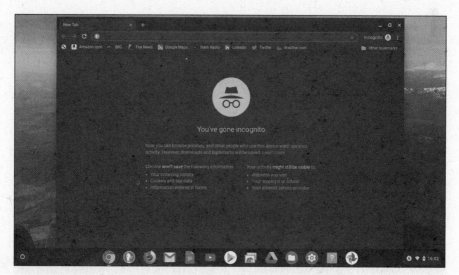

FIGURE 3-9: The Incognito window.

Changing Search Engine Providers

By default, Google is the search engine used when you type any search term in the Omnibox (search field) in your Chrome browser. For a variety of reasons, you might prefer to use another search engine, such as Yahoo!, Bing, About.com, and hundreds of others. There are choices associated with many different retail stores, for instance, and setting your browser search engine to one of these if you are a frequent shopper might be handy.

To manage and change your Chrome browser search engine, follow these steps:

1. **Click the Settings button to the right of the Chrome browser Omnibox (search field).**

2. **Click Settings.**

3. **Scroll down until you see the Search Engine section.**

4. **Click Manage Search Engines.**

    The Manage Search Engines window appears, as shown in Figure 3-10. The Default search engines are those that are most often used. The Other search engines are additional search engines that you can also use.

5. **To select any of these search engines as your new default, click the More Actions button (three little dots to the right of the search engine name), and select Make Default.**

FIGURE 3-10: Selecting a new default search engine.

TIP

In your browser, the search engine used when you type searches into the Omnibox is identified by a small icon at the left of the Omnibox.

TIP

If the site you want to use as your default search engine does not appear in the list, you can bookmark the site and use the site directly for searching.

Using Other Browsers

Other browsers exist besides Chrome, and they're available for your Chromebook.

Some people just prefer other browsers. For me, it's Firefox. I won't judge you, and I doubt anyone else will, either. Firefox has a great reputation, and so does DuckDuckGo.

To install the Firefox browser, follow these easy steps:

1. Open the Google Play app.

2. In the search window, type Firefox.

You see a result that resembles Figure 3-11. Remember, Firefox is from Mozilla, and you should see that company name showing as the source for Firefox.

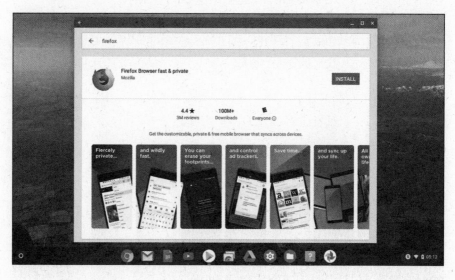

FIGURE 3-11:
Installing the Firefox browser.

3. Click Install.

4. When the installation is complete, click Open.

The Firefox browser starts.

5. If you think you will want to use Firefox often, go to the shelf and Alt-click and then click Pin to pin Firefox to the shelf.

This way, it's always there when you want to use it.

Installing the DuckDuckGo privacy web browser is just as simple as installing Firefox. Search for DuckDuckGo in the Google Play app, click Install, and then click Open. Pin it to the shelf if you like.

TIP

The DuckDuckGo web browser is popular with people who don't like to be tracked. Unlike Google Chrome, which sends a lot of information about your web surfing history to Google, DuckDuckGo performs no tracking at all. However, the use of any browser (even in incognito mode) does not stop websites you visit from tracking your visits.

Chapter **4**

Getting Your Hands on the Keyboard and Touchpad

t's hard telling whether Christopher Latham Sholes thought that his design and letter layout of the keyboard would still be in use well into the 21st century. Regardless of what his original intent was, his legacy is alive and well in the world today. When Sholes devised the layout and functionality of the keyboard that we use today, his intent was to reduce typewriter jams and thereby speed up the typist. ("Glass half empty" people argue that the arrangement of letters was really to slow down the typist and thus also reduce typewriter jams.)

Over the last 140 years, the keyboard has evolved very little. The basic layout of letters and numbers is the same; the only major additions have been multipurpose keys like the ?/ key or the :; key. Additionally, with the advent of word processors and computers, keys like Alt, Caps Lock, Num Lock, and Shift appeared, as well as function keys (you know, the F keys located at the top of some keyboards).

Several other modifications came about as computer manufacturers and software developers like Microsoft and Apple fought to differentiate themselves within the marketplace. For instance, Windows computers have a Start key and rely heavily on the function keys. Apple keyboards ditched the Alt key for the Apple key (now the Command key) and the Fn key. Vive la différence!

Each computer manufacturer created nuances designed to improve users' experiences while typing and otherwise operating their computers. The Chromebook is no different! In this chapter, you explore the Chromebook keyboard and touchpad in all their glory. You learn how to customize the language of your keyboard, adjust the function of some keys, and save time with keyboard shortcuts. You also learn how to add an external mouse or keyboard and how to customize external devices.

The Chromebook Keyboard at a Glance

Google didn't stray too far from the norm when it created the keyboard for the Chromebook. Figure 4-1 shows the keyboard on the Lenovo C330. Check out the top row: If you've done much work on a Mac or a PC, you probably remember the function keys (F1 through F12), used as shortcuts for various operating-system-specific functions. On Chromebook, the function keys are gone, replaced by a series of more intuitive keys, called *shortcut keys*.

FIGURE 4-1:
The Chromebook keyboard on the author's Lenovo C330.

Moving left to right, the top row of keys are

>> **Esc:** The "get me out of here" key. Often used to stop something you're doing. In the web browser, it stops a page from loading.

>> **Back (indicated by a left arrow):** Navigates to the previous web page.

>> **Forward (indicated by a right arrow):** If you navigated back a page, use forward to navigate forward.

>> **Refresh/Reload (indicated by a circular arrow):** Reloads your current web page.

>> **Full Screen (indicated by a box with little arrows in two corners):** Makes the current window full screen, without the menu bar or other ancillary window controls.

>> **Reveal All Windows (indicated by a box with two bars to the right):** If you have multiple windows open, clicking this key reveals them all on the screen at one time so that you can quickly click and navigate between windows.

>> **Dim (indicated by a small sun):** If you're in a dark environment, you may want to reduce the screen's brightness so that the light emitted isn't a disturbance to others. This feature is also a great way to extend battery life if you're using your Chromebook with its internal battery, away from electric power.

>> **Brighten (indicated by a bigger sun):** If you're in a bright environment, you may want to brighten your screen because the screen may be too dim to see.

>> **Mute (indicated by a speaker with a slash through it):** Quickly eliminates all sound coming from your machine.

>> **Volume Down (indicated by a speaker with a single sound wave):** Decrease your machine's volume incrementally.

>> **Volume Up (indicated by a speaker with two sound waves):** It's time to party. Turn up the volume!

>> **Lock:** Locks your Chromebook if you are stepping away and don't want others to tamper with it (requires that you have your screen lock setting turned on).

The remaining keys on the keyboard are more or less what you'd expect — with the exception of the Search key, as shown in Figure 4-2.

REMEMBER

As is typical of laptop manufacturers, you can find some minor variation in the layout of keys among various makes and models of Chromebooks. The two Chromebooks in our home differ a bit, and you might notice that the keyboard of yours varies slightly from what I show in Figure 4-1.

FIGURE 4-2:
The Chromebook
Search key.

Pushing the Search key opens the Launcher and puts your cursor in the search bar so that you can quickly submit a search query. If you're searching for an application, like Gmail, simply type in **gmail**, press Enter, and your Chromebook opens the Chrome web browser and loads your Gmail. Maybe you want to quickly do a Google search. This search can even find one of your Google Docs documents. To do a Google search, enter your query in the search bar and press Enter. Chromebook opens a Chrome browser and loads Google.com (or your default search engine, if it's something else) with your search results teed up.

The last thing you should notice about the keyboard is that the bottom row of keys includes no Start key, Fn key, or Command/Apple key. Instead, it simply has a Ctrl and Alt key on both sides of the spacebar. Ctrl and Alt are used quite a bit in shortcut combinations, so you might as well get used to having them there!

Using Shortcut Key Combinations

In addition to shortcut keys, several key combinations perform a litany of tasks on your Chromebook without making you navigate and click your way through the Chrome OS menu system. Tables 4-1, 4-2, and 4-3 show several different shortcut key combinations that will make your experience on a Chromebook more intuitive and efficient. (You can find a full list in the Cheat Sheet for this book at www.dummies.com.)

TIP

When you see a keyboard shortcut like Ctrl+N, it means you should press the Ctrl and N keys at the same time. When you see a keyboard shortcut like Ctrl+Shift+N, press the Ctrl, Shift, and N keys at the same time.

TABLE 4-1 ## Shortcuts for Chromebook and Chromebook Apps

Shortcut	Function
Ctrl+Alt+/	Open the list of available keyboard shortcuts.
Ctrl+/	Open Help center.
Ctrl+O	Open a file.
Ctrl+Shift+W	Close the current application window.
Alt+=	Maximize the application window.
Alt+-	Minimize the application window.
Shift+Search+Esc	Unpin an app from the shelf.
Ctrl+Shift+T	Reopen the last tab or window you've closed. Google Chrome remembers the last ten tabs you've closed.
Search+1 through Search+=	Use F1 to F12.
Alt+Tab	Go to the next window you have open.
Alt+Shift+Tab	Go to the previous window you have open.
Ctrl+Shift+=	Zoom in entire screen.
Ctrl+Chift+-	Zoom out entire screen.
Ctrl+Shift+0 (zero)	Reset screen zoom level.
Ctrl+Alt+(Reveal All Windows key)	Take a screen shot of the current window.
Ctrl+(Reveal All Windows key)	Take a screen shot of the entire screen.
Full Screen key	Toggle full screen.
Ctrl+Full Screen key (confirm)	Configure one or more monitors.
Speaker Off key	Mute sound.
Alt+Shift+M	Open the Files app.
Alt+Shift+S	Open the Status area.
Alt+Shift+N	Display notifications.
Search key	Open/Close the Launcher.
Search+L	Lock your Chromebook (requires your Chromebook password or PIN to unlock).
Ctrl+Shift+Q	Log out of the Chromebook.
Shift+Search+L	Put your Chromebook in sleep mode.
Brightness Up key	Make the display brighter.
Brightness Down key	Make the display dimmer.

TABLE 4-2   ## Shortcuts for Chrome Browser Pages

Shortcut	Function
Windows and Tabs	
Ctrl+N	Open a new Chrome browser window.
Ctrl+Shift+N	Open a new Chrome browser window in incognito mode.
Ctrl+T	Open a new Chrome browser tab.
Ctrl+W	Close the current Chrome browser tab.
Ctrl+9	Go to the last Chrome browser tab in the window.
Ctrl+Tab	Go to the next Chrome browser tab in the window.
Ctrl+Shift+Tab	Go to the previous Chrome browser tab in the window.
Ctrl+click a link	Open the link in a new Chrome browser tab in the background.
Ctrl+Shift+click a link	Open the link in a new Chrome browser tab and switch to the newly opened tab.
Shift+click a link	Open the link in a new Chrome browser window.
Type a URL in the address bar, then press Alt+Enter	Open the URL in a new Chrome browser tab.
Browsing History	
Ctrl+H	Open the History page.
Alt+left arrow	Go to previous page in your Chrome browser browsing history.
Alt+right arrow	Go to the next page in your Chrome browser browsing history.
Viewing Web Pages	
Alt+up arrow	Scroll up.
Alt+down arrow	Scroll down.
Alt+left arrow	Go to previous page.
Alt+right arrow	Go to next page.
Spacebar	Scroll down the web page.
Ctrl+Alt+up arrow	Go to top of page.
Ctrl+Alt+down arrow	Go to bottom of page.

Shortcut	Function
Ctrl+Enter	Add www. and .com to your input in the address bar and open the resulting URL.
Alt+Home (the Home icon in the Chrome browser if you have made it visible)	Go to the home page.
Ctrl+P	Print your current page.
Ctrl+R	Reload your current page.
Ctrl+Shift+R	Reload your current page without using cached content. This forces a reload of all content from the website.
Ctrl++ (plus sign)	Zoom in on the page.
Ctrl+- (dash)	Zoom out on the page.
Ctrl+0	Reset zoom level to original setting.
Ctrl+F	Open the find bar to search for text in the current tab.
Ctrl+G	Go to the next match in your search.
Ctrl+Shift+G	Go to the previous match in your search.
Bookmarks	
Ctrl+D	Save your current web page as a bookmark.
Ctrl+Shift+D	Save all open pages in your current window as bookmarks in a new folder.
Drag link to Bookmarks bar	Save link as a bookmark.
Configuring the Chrome Browser	
Alt+E or Alt+F	Open the Chrome menu.
Ctrl+K or Ctrl+E	Places focus on the Chrome browser Omnibox. Press Esc to revert.
Ctrl+Shift+Backspace	Clear browsing data
Ctrl+J	Open the Downloads page.

TIP

When using external keyboards: If you are using a Windows keyboard, use the Windows key when Chromebook specifies the Search key. If you are using a Mac keyboard, use the Command key for Chromebook's Search key.

TABLE 4-3   ## Shortcuts for Text Editing

Shortcut	Function
Selecting Text	
Ctrl+A	Select everything on the page.
Ctrl+Shift+right arrow	Select the next word or letter.
Ctrl+Shift+left arrow	Select the previous word or letter.
Navigating in the Document	
Ctrl+right arrow	Go to the end of the next word.
Ctrl+left arrow	Go to the start of the previous word.
Ctrl+Search+left arrow	Go to the beginning of document.
Ctrl+Search+right arrow	Go to the end of document.
Alt+up arrow	Page up.
Alt+down arrow	Page down.
Ctrl+Search+up arrow	Home.
Ctrl+Search+down arrow	End.
Changing Content	
Ctrl+C	Copy selected content to the Clipboard.
Ctrl+V	Paste content from the Clipboard.
Ctrl+X	Cut. Copies selected content to the Clipboard and deletes the content.
Ctrl+Backspace	Delete the previous word.
Search+Backspace	Delete the next letter (forward delete).
Alt+Search	Turn Caps Lock on and off.

The good news is that when you don't have your copy of *Chromebook For Dummies*, 2nd Edition nearby, you can use Google's built-in Help tool for quick reference. To access the visual helper, press Ctrl+Alt+/. The Keyboard Shortcuts window appears. The main categories of keyboard shortcuts appear on the left; select one and view the individual shortcuts on the right. (See Figure 4-3.) Use the Keyboard Shortcuts screen for a quick reminder as you use your Chromebook.

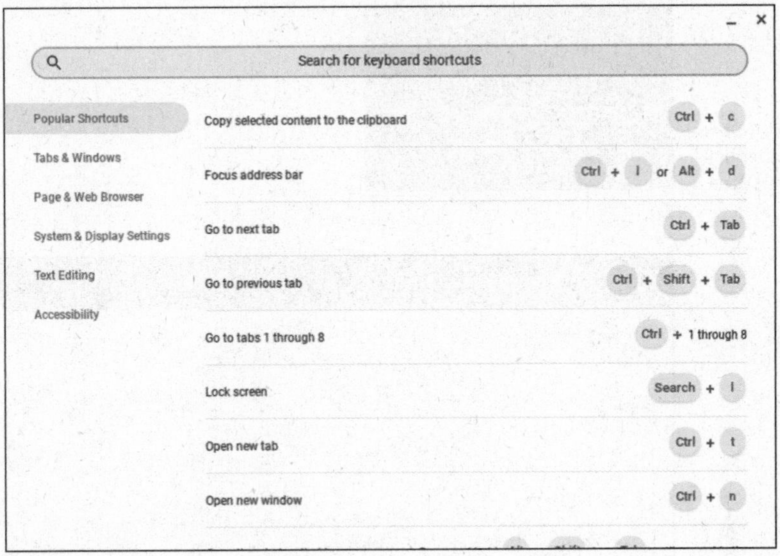

FIGURE 4-3:
The Keyboard
Shortcut Help
page.

The screenshot shows a keyboard shortcut help window with a search bar labeled "Search for keyboard shortcuts." The left navigation includes: Popular Shortcuts, Tabs & Windows, Page & Web Browser, System & Display Settings, Text Editing, Accessibility. The right side lists shortcuts:

Copy selected content to the clipboard	Ctrl + c
Focus address bar	Ctrl + l or Alt + d
Go to next tab	Ctrl + Tab
Go to previous tab	Ctrl + Shift + Tab
Go to tabs 1 through 8	Ctrl + 1 through 8
Lock screen	Search + l
Open new tab	Ctrl + t
Open new window	Ctrl + n

TIP

Don't be intimidated by the long list of keyboard shortcuts. You are not obligated to memorize them! Even every-day Chromebook experts use a small number of these shortcuts.

Configuring Keyboard Settings

The first time you turn on your Chromebook, you have to complete a basic setup process that includes selecting your language and desired keyboard language layout. You can edit this setting, among other keyboard settings, after the fact. To access your keyboard settings, follow these steps:

1. **Click the status area located in the bottom-right corner of your desktop.**

   You might recall that the status area contains your clock, Wi-Fi indicator, and battery charge level indicator. It is also pictured in Figure 4-4.

   Your settings panel appears.

2. **Select Settings.**

   A window launches and loads your Chromebook Settings page.

3. **Scroll down to the Device section and select Keyboard Settings.**

   A Keyboard Settings window appears, as shown in Figure 4-5.

FIGURE 4-4:
The Chromebook
status area.

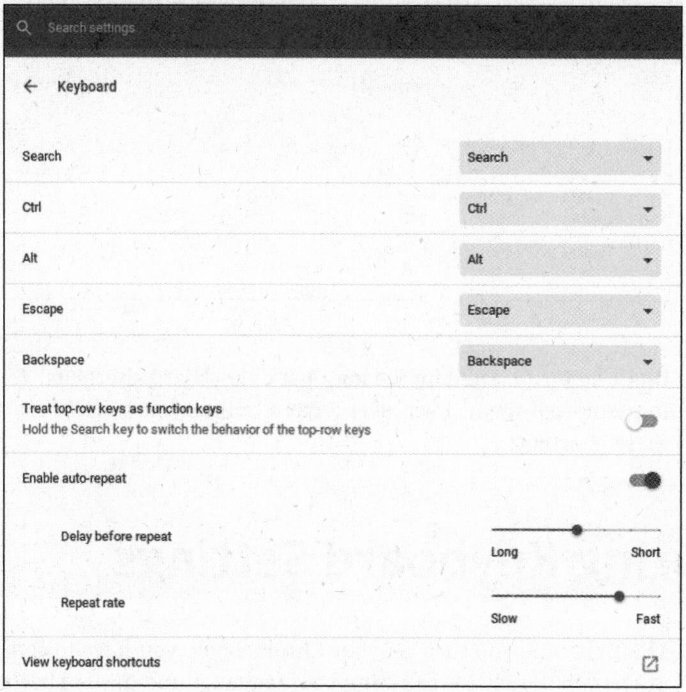

FIGURE 4-5:
The Keyboard
Settings
dialog box.

In the Keyboard Settings dialog box, you can

>> Reconfigure your Search, Alt, Ctrl, Esc, and Backspace keys.

>> Turn your shortcut keys into function keys (F keys).

>> Change your keyboard language configuration.

I discuss these options more fully in the next few sections.

Reconfiguring keyboard keys

By default, the Alt, Ctrl, Search, Esc, and Backspace keys perform their intended tasks: You use the Alt and Ctrl keys in combination with other keys (and the mouse) to access additional functionality, and you use the Search key to quickly access the search function in the Launcher, as well as to unlock additional functionality when used in combination with other keys. The Esc key is the "get me out of here" key that has somewhat different meanings, depending on what you're doing at the time. You use the Backspace key to delete characters to the left of the cursor.

You can modify these keys so that they serve different purposes. For instance, you can change your Search key to behave like a Caps Lock or set your Ctrl key to act like the Alt key. To change the function of the Alt, Ctrl, and Search keys, follow these steps:

1. **Click the status area in the bottom-right of your desktop.**

   The settings panel appears.

2. **Click Settings.**

   Your Chromebook Settings page loads the Chrome browser.

3. **Scroll down to the Device section and select Keyboard Settings.**

   The Keyboard Settings dialog box appears.

   Another way to quickly open the Keyboard Settings dialog box is to press your Search key, type **chrome://settings/keyboard-overlay**, and then press Enter.

4. **Click the corresponding box for the key you want to reconfigure.**

   A drop-down list appears with options for changing the selected key's function, as shown in Figure 4-6.

5. **Make your desired changes and click OK.**

This feature allows you to configure your keyboard in a manner that is convenient to you. You can reconfigure your keys as many times as you like.

The reason that the Search, Ctrl, Alt, and other keys can be modified is that these keys appear in slightly different positions on different kinds of keyboards. As advanced users move between different computers and keyboards, this helps give everything the same feel.

Turning shortcut keys into function keys

On most Chromebooks, the function keys (F1 to F10) common to Macs and PCs have been replaced by shortcut keys. Few Chromebook models come with F11 or F12, and depending on your model, you may not even have a reference to the function key on each shortcut key.

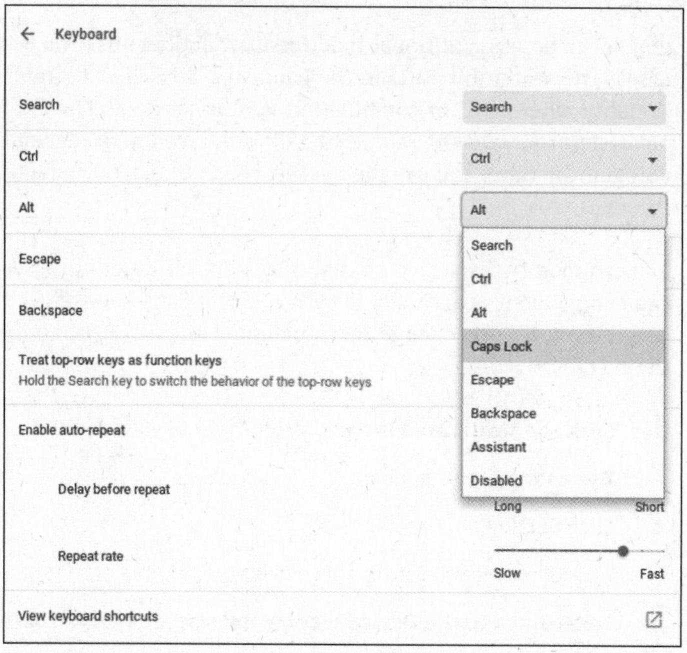

FIGURE 4-6:
Reconfiguring
the Alt key.

If you have a need for function keys, don't fret; you can disable the shortcut keys and enable function keys in your keyboard settings by following these steps:

1. **Click the status area in the bottom-right of your desktop.**

The settings panel opens.

2. **Select Settings.**

Your Chromebook Settings page appears in the Chrome browser.

3. **Scroll down to the Device section and select Keyboard Settings.**

The Keyboard Settings dialog box appears.

4. **Deselect the Treat Top-Row Keys as Function Keys setting.**

This disables the shortcut functionality of the shortcut keys and enables their functions as function keys.

To re-enable shortcut keys and disable function keys, simply deselect the setting.

TIP

Changing your keyboard language

Your keyboard language configuration is set the first time you log into your Chromebook. If you're in America, you probably set your language to English (United States) and your keyboard to US Keyboard. If you would like to change your keyboard language, you can do so by following these steps:

1. **Click the status area in the bottom-right of your desktop.**

   The settings panel appears.

2. **Select Settings.**

   Your Chromebook Settings page loads in the Chrome browser.

3. **Scroll down to the bottom and click Advanced.**

4. **In the Languages and Input section, select Language.**

5. **Select the desired language.**

   If you don't see your language, click Add Languages. When you find the desired language, click Add.

6. **Next to your desired language, click More (three dots) and select how you want to use the language.**

   You find two settings here. The first indicates the language used by your Chromebook; the second indicates the language that Google will translate web page content into.

   The Languages and Input page appears, as shown in Figure 4-7.

   The language you selected when setting up your device appears in the Languages pane on the left side of the dialog box.

7. **To change the language, click the Add Languages button.**

   The Add Languages dialog box appears. (See Figure 4-8.)

8. **Select the language you want from the drop-down list of available languages.**

9. **Click OK.**

   The language you selected is added to the list of languages in the Languages pane.

10. **Click the newly added language to highlight it.**

    A list of options appears in the right pane of the Languages and Input dialog box.

11. **In the Input Method section, select the box for the desired keyboard(s).**

12. **Click Done.**

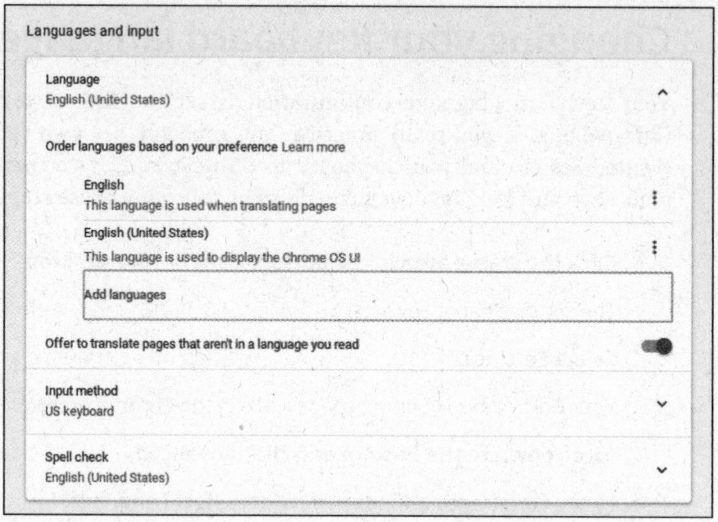

FIGURE 4-7:
The Languages and Input dialog box.

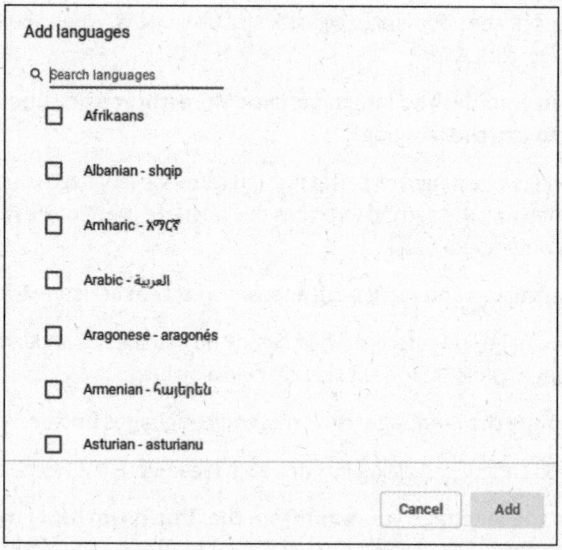

Languages and input

Language
English (United States)

Order languages based on your preference Learn more

English
This language is used when translating pages

English (United States)
This language is used to display the Chrome OS UI

Add languages

Offer to translate pages that aren't in a language you read

Input method
US keyboard

Spell check
English (United States)

FIGURE 4-8:
The Add Languages dialog box.

Add languages

Search languages

☐ Afrikaans

☐ Albanian - shqip

☐ Amharic - አማርኛ

☐ Arabic - العربية

☐ Aragonese - aragonés

☐ Armenian - հայերեն

☐ Asturian - asturianu

Cancel   Add

You can activate your newly added keyboard by following these steps:

1. **Click the status area in the lower-right of your desktop.**

The settings panel opens.

2. **Click the keyboard option located at the top of the panel.**

A menu of available keyboards appears.

3. **Click the desired keyboard language.**

After you switch your keyboard, you'll notice as you type that your keys have changed to the standard for the language and country you selected. Change your language by repeating the preceding steps.

Using the Touchpad

Over the years, numerous different laptop mouse controllers have appeared. The trackball was cool until you got too much of your lunch stuck under the ball. The pointing stick was nice if you didn't mind that it was the size of a pencil eraser. Then came the touchpad. The touchpad on the Chromebook is a lot like most touchpads that are used on Windows, Linux, and Mac computers. Here are some basic gestures to get you going:

>> To move the cursor across the screen, simply place one finger on the touchpad and move it in any direction.

>> Click buttons and links by pressing down on the bottom half of the touchpad until you feel or hear a click. Or, if you like *tap-to-click* instead, just tap the touchpad to click.

>> Right-click by tapping with two fingers.

>> Scroll vertically by placing two fingers on the touchpad and moving them up and down; scroll horizontally by moving them left and right.

>> Drag items or highlight text by simultaneously pressing (and holding down) with one finger and moving the pointer using another finger.

Finger gestures

Google aimed to make Chromebook one of the easiest and most intuitive devices on the laptop market. Naturally, Google has built in several advanced features for the touchpad to make using the Chromebook fluid and intuitive. Some of these features include the following:

>> You can reveal all available windows by placing three fingers on the touchpad and swiping up simultaneously. You can then click the desired window to make it active and bring it to the front.

>> While you are in the Chrome browser, use two fingers to swipe from left to right across the touchpad to go backward in your browsing history.

>> In the Chrome browser, use two fingers to swipe right to left across the touchpad to go forward in your browsing history.

Touchpad and keyboard combinations

Google has implemented several different ways to perform the same function, mainly to accommodate users transitioning from other devices. Some quick ways to use the touchpad and keyboard together are

» **Right-click:** Hold down the Alt key and click the touchpad. Right-clicking is useful in revealing common functions without having use a menu or shortcut keys.

» **Highlight content:** Click one side of the content you want to highlight. Then, holding down the Shift key, click the other side of the content. The text is highlighted. This feature is particularly useful when you want to copy a body of text. Alt+click the highlighted text to reveal options like Copy or Cut.

Customizing Touchpad Settings

The touchpad is not without customization capability. You can make changes to the touchpad settings from within the Chromebook Settings page. To open the touchpad settings, follow these steps:

1. **Click the status area in the bottom-right of your desktop.**

   The settings panel opens.

2. **Select Settings.**

   Your Chromebook Settings page opens in the Chrome browser.

3. **Scroll down to the Device section and select Touchpad Settings.**

   The Touchpad dialog box appears, as shown in Figure 4-9.

In the Touchpad dialog box, you can make the following customizations:

» Change the touchpad speed.

» Adjust your click settings.

» Change scroll directions.

I discuss these settings in the next few sections.

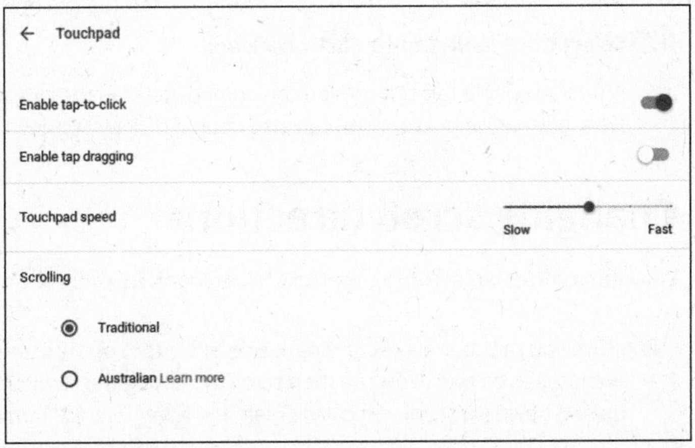

← Touchpad	
Enable tap-to-click	⬤
Enable tap dragging	◯
Touchpad speed	Slow ⬤ Fast
Scrolling	
⦿ Traditional	
◯ Australian Learn more	

FIGURE 4-9:
Configuring the
Touchpad.

Changing the touchpad speed

Found in the Device section of your Chromebook Settings page, the Touchpad Speed slider allows you to adjust the speed of your touchpad — that is, the distance your cursor moves onscreen in relation to the distance your finger travels on the touchpad. To move the cursor faster, move the slider to the right. To move it slower, move the slider to the left. Figure 4-9 shows the Touchpad Speed control.

Adjusting the touchpad click settings

Clicking the touchpad requires you to press down on the bottom half of the touchpad until you hear a click. If you want to use less effort to click, you can also turn on the Tap to Click feature. After you engage this feature, your touchpad treats any quick tap or touch of the touchpad as a click. To enable this feature, follow these steps:

1. **Click the status area in the bottom-right of your desktop.**

The settings panel opens.

2. **Select Settings.**

Your Chromebook Settings page opens in the Chrome browser.

3. **Scroll down to the Device section and select Touchpad Settings.**

The Touchpad dialog box appears.

4. Select the Enable Tap-to-Click check box.

After you enable this option, you can immediately tap the touchpad to click links, buttons, and so on. You can also double-click by tapping twice.

Changing scroll directions

You can accomplish scrolling on the Chromebook in a few ways:

» Move your pointer over to the right side or bottom of the screen to reveal the available scroll bars. You can then scroll by clicking the scroll bar and dragging up and down (to scroll vertically) or left and right (to scroll horizontally).

» Place two fingers on the touchpad and move them up and down to scroll vertically, or left and right to scroll horizontally.

By default, the Chromebook is set up to scroll traditionally, meaning that swiping your fingers up on the touchpad makes the window scroll up and swiping your fingers down makes it scroll down.

You may, however, be more familiar with the opposite action, meaning that when you swipe up, it's as if you're pushing your finger on the screen and pulling more content from the bottom of the screen, and vice versa if you swipe down. On Chromebook, this scrolling style is referred to as *Australian scrolling* (remember that Australia is "down under," where everything, including scrolling, apparently, is upside-down). You can activate this feature by taking these steps:

1. Click the status area in the bottom-right of your desktop.

The settings panel appears.

2. Select Settings.

Your Chromebook Settings page opens in the Chrome browser.

3. Scroll down to the Device section and select Touchpad Settings.

The Touchpad dialog box appears.

4. Select the Australian Scrolling radio button.

5. Click OK.

Your scroll has now been changed, mate!

Connecting a Mouse or Keyboard

Sometimes when duty calls, you have to work on your computer for hours on end. Spending hours upon hours using a laptop keyboard and touchpad may make your mobile-computing experience a bit of a grind. To make things easier, it's sometimes nice to have a separate keyboard or mouse that you can plug in and use with your laptop. With your Chromebook, you can add a physical keyboard or mouse by using USB or Bluetooth.

To connect a USB keyboard or mouse to your Chromebook, you just need to locate the USB port on the side of your computer and insert the USB connector for your device into the port. (Your USB connector can go in only one way, so don't force it.) Your Chromebook automatically detects the new keyboard or mouse and applies all existing settings to it. You might not see any messages as you would on a Windows computer; instead, it will just begin to work automatically.

If your keyboard or mouse and your Chromebook are Bluetooth enabled, no cable is necessary! Connect your Bluetooth keyboard or mouse by following these steps:

1. **Click the status area in the bottom-right of the desktop and then click the Settings icon.**

   The settings panel opens.

2. **Select Bluetooth.**

3. **If your Bluetooth is disabled, click to enable it.**

   Chromebook begins searching for available Bluetooth devices.

4. **Ensure that your Bluetooth keyboard or mouse is enabled and wait for it to appear in the Bluetooth list.**

5. **Select your keyboard or mouse from the list and follow any instructions for "pairing" them to your Chromebook that appear.**

6a. **When connecting a keyboard, enter the randomized pin on the keyboard to ensure that it's the correct device.**

   Upon successfully pairing your keyboard with your Chromebook, your Bluetooth keyboard assumes all existing keyboard settings, and you can start typing immediately.

6b. When connecting a mouse (optional): After your mouse has been plugged in or paired and Chromebook has identified it, you can configure it to be a "left-handed" mouse — that is, to swap the functionality of the left and right mouse buttons — by following these steps:

a. Open the settings panel and choose Settings.

b. Scroll down to the Device section and select Touchpad Settings.

The Mouse and Touchpad dialog box appears. (See Figure 4-10.)

c. Select the Swap Primary Mouse control.

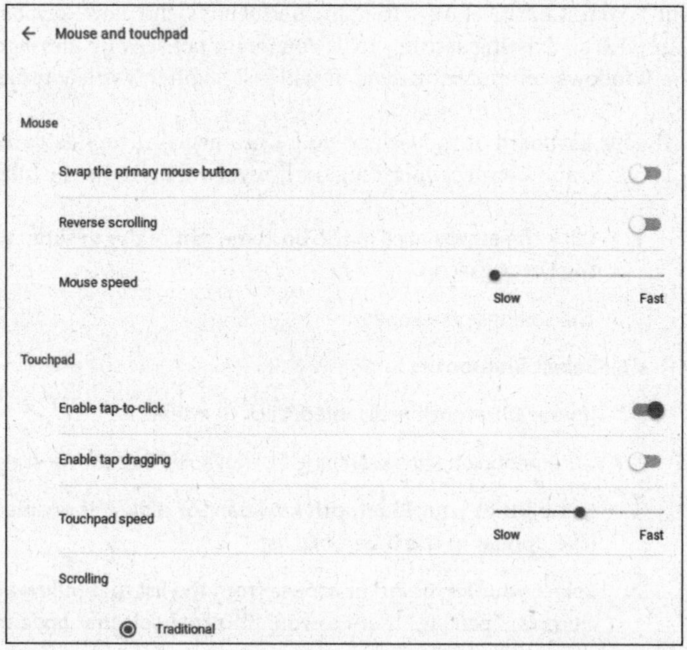

← Mouse and touchpad

Mouse

Swap the primary mouse button

Reverse scrolling

Mouse speed   Slow   Fast

Touchpad

Enable tap-to-click

Enable tap dragging

Touchpad speed   Slow   Fast

Scrolling

⊙ Traditional

FIGURE 4-10: Configuring a mouse.

Chapter **5**

Finding and Exploring Chromebook Apps

Because Google's original vision for Chromebook was to create a computer that did most of its work over the Internet, a lot of a Chromebook's func-tionality is achieved through the Chrome web browser. Unlike Windows or Mac computers, few applications are installed on the Chromebook; instead, they're stored on remote computers and accessed over the Internet. Google has numerous applications to help you with work, school, personal development, entertainment, and more. This concept — using online applications and reducing the need to install, store, and run software locally — reduces costs for both Google and for the consumer because the Chromebook doesn't require expensive hard-ware to run the applications.

In this chapter, you get a brief overview of the applications that come with your Chromebook, as well as the lowdown on how to find and add new applications to your Launcher. Keep in mind that adding apps to your Chromebook requires little more than adding a shortcut to your menu and adjusting a few settings.

TIP

Your Chromebook holds many built-in apps, and more are available in the Chrome Web Store, which means that you can do a lot with your Chromebook! But don't feel that you have to learn all these apps to get the most out of your Chromebook. If you just want to check Turner Classic Movies schedules with your browser and play Mahjong, that's fine!

Exploring Chromebook's Pre-Installed Apps

Apps, short for *applications,* are computer programs made for some purpose. For people using laptop computers, including Chromebooks, examples of apps are the Chrome browser, Gmail, Calendar, and Solitaire. Apps make computers useful and fun.

On a Chromebook, a few applications are pre-installed on the system. Many of the applications shown on your shelf are more like links that open web applications in the Chrome web browser. You can view the applications on your computer in a couple of different ways:

>> **Press the Search key.** This opens the Launcher and places a cursor in the search bar. You can then scroll through your windows in the Launcher by using two fingers to swipe up or down on the touchpad.

>> **Click the Launcher.** This is located on the bottom-left corner of your desktop on your Chromebook shelf.

Your Chromebook comes with shortcuts for several applications already in place. These shortcuts may differ slightly from Chromebook to Chromebook. If I cover an application not already existing on your Chromebook, you can easily add it through the Web Store. The next few sections give you a quick look at some of the more important applications.

Storing data in the cloud with Google Drive

Whether you're creating applications through the Google web-based office tools or you just want a place to store your important files, Google Drive is your hard drive in the cloud. Save your files to your Google Drive folder, and it will sync to every device you own that has Google Drive installed. You can even access your files through a web browser on any computer with a web connection. Google Drive is a necessity for any Chromebook user.

You can find a lot more detail about Google Drive in Chapter 6.

Word processing with Docs

Docs is Google's word-processing application. If you have done any work with Microsoft Word or Apple Pages, you'll be at home with Google Docs. Create text documents; format your text; add links, images, videos, tables, and more; use templates to quickly create preformatted documents; and save in numerous formats, including Microsoft Word, OpenDocument, Rich Text Format (RTF), or

Portable Document Format (PDF). Documents created with Google Docs are automatically saved to Google Drive and accessible from any device that can access the Internet. You can even invite others to collaborate on your Docs files without having to email files and worry about duplication of efforts or lost work. This feature means that two or more users can be working on a Google Doc at the same time.

More information on using Google Docs appears in Chapter 7.

Using spreadsheets with Sheets

Sheets is Google's spreadsheet application. Sheets is a lot like Microsoft Excel and Apple Numbers. With Sheets, you can build lists, keep track of personal finances, analyze data, and so much more. A templates library helps you by creating worksheets that are already formatted. Build formulas for performing complex calculations and data analysis. Filter, sort, and otherwise organize your data with ease. As with Docs, all spreadsheets are saved in Google Drive and easily shared with collaborators.

Starting a new business? You should consider using Sheets for your cash-flow projections. You and your business partners can work on it without fear of losing information or overwriting each other's work!

Learn more about Google Sheets in Chapter 8.

Making presentations with Slides

Slides is another of Google's web-based office products. With it, you can create beautiful slide presentations with all sorts of prebuilt or custom themes. Import images, videos, and other interactive content; link to web content like YouTube videos; and more. Slides is a powerful presentation tool that allows you to present through the web or export to PowerPoint, PDF, and other globally supported formats. If you've used Microsoft PowerPoint or Apple Keynote, Slides will be familiar to you. Collaboration is also made easy with Google Drive.

You can learn more about Google Slides in Chapter 9.

Taking notes with Keep

Whether you're a student, stay-at-home mom or dad, or in the workforce, note-taking is an important part of life. Google Keep is designed to make note-taking a breeze. Use Keep to take written notes or voice notes. Easily add pictures and videos. Save your notes to Google Drive to share with other users and collaborators.

You can even export your notes to services like Dropbox (www.dropbox.com), OneDrive, or Box.com, or you can download them to your computer or storage device. In the usual Google style, your Keep notes will be available on all of your devices. Google Keep's minimalist interface makes it fast and easy to use. Take notes more efficiently than paper and pen with Keep. Figure 5-1 shows a Google Keep session.

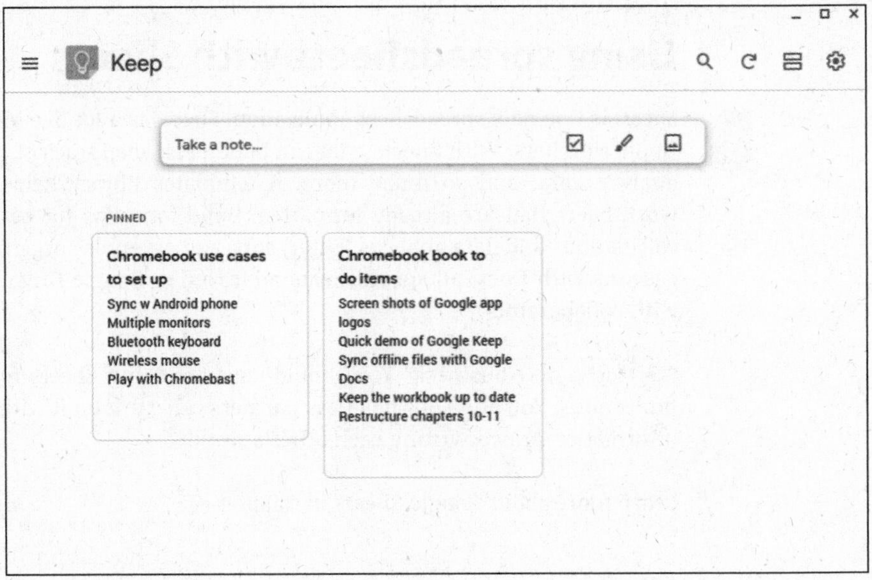

FIGURE 5-1: Take notes with Google Keep.

Organizing and playing music with Google Play Music

Google Play Music is the one-stop music service on your Chromebook. Move your music collection into Google Play Music and have it be accessible to you anywhere in the world. Organize your songs into playlists, share your playlists, or listen to your friends' playlists. Stream countless themed music channels for free. Shop through the Google Play Music database of songs to purchase and expand your collection. You can even subscribe to get access to stream more than 20 million songs at any time. Google Play Music syncs with all your devices. (See Figure 5-2.)

Explore Google Play Music in all its glory in Chapter 12.

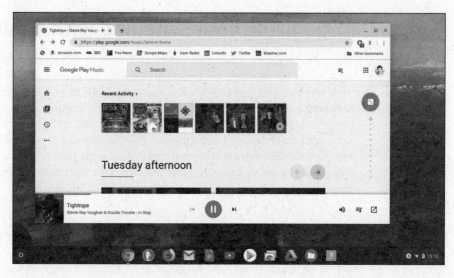

FIGURE 5-2:
Take your music
collection with
you on Google
Play Music.

Communicating with video, voice, and text with Voice and Duo

You don't need any fancy hardware or additional software to make calls using your Chromebook. Simply launch Google Voice, and you can quickly call any phone number in the world. Domestic calls are usually free, and international calls cost a fee, but you don't need a phone to call your family anywhere in the world! Chat via text, and take pictures and send them. With Duo, you can video chat with one, two, three, or more people all at the same time.

Chapter 14 explores Google Voice and Google Duo in a lot more detail, as well as the ever-popular Skype program.

Emailing with Gmail

Gmail is Google's powerful free email platform. With Gmail, you can send and receive emails; attach files, pictures, videos, and links; and quickly save attachments to your Google Drive cloud storage. Gmail for Chromebook also has an offline feature so that you can check emails, write emails, and queue them up to send the next time you get online. Native Gmail apps are also available for Android and iPhones, and available on all other laptop and desktop computers through their browsers. Google also offers Gmail for businesses so that you can have hosted email that comes from your company domain. Learn more about Gmail in Chapter 10.

Organizing your schedule with Calendar

Google Calendar is a versatile calendar system. You can easily create events on your calendar, set them to repeat periodically, set alarms, invite others to attend your events, and more. You can create multiple calendars within your Google Calendar and share the calendar with your family, friends, and coworkers. Organize your calendar and view it by day, week, month, or even agenda. You can also sync your calendar with any modern smartphone, and if you need to access your Google Calendar from a Mac, you can sync it with your Mac's Calendar. You can even bring your Google Calendar content into Microsoft Outlook on your PC. (See Figure 5-3.)

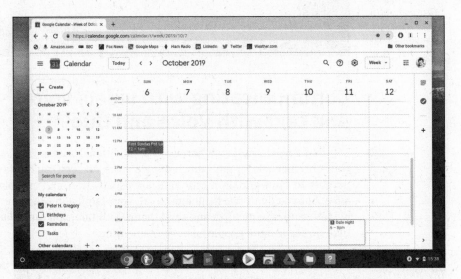

FIGURE 5-3: Organize your life with Google Calendar.

Remotely accessing with Remote Desktop

Google Remote Desktop is a handy tool for accessing your other computers, or for accessing your own Chromebook from anywhere. Install Remote Desktop on your Mac or Windows PC, and you can access them from your Chromebook anywhere in the world. Of course, the computers you want to access must be turned on and connected to the Internet. Other than that, accessing your files, running applications, and otherwise working remotely is a breeze with Remote Desktop.

Reading with Google Play Books

If you've used a Kindle or iBooks, you can probably imagine how easy and awesome Google Play Books would be. Shop for books at low cost and store them in your Google Play Books account. Easily sync your books to any device you own that has Google Play Books installed. Then you can read your favorite novel or business book on the beach, in bed, at the office, or anywhere else you like— and you can choose: from your phone, your tablet, or your Chromebook. (See Figure 5-4.)

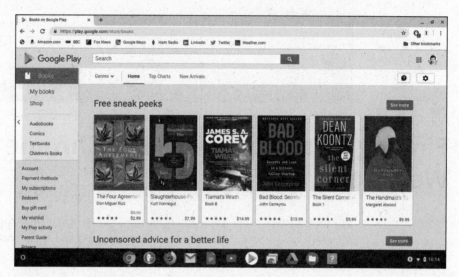

FIGURE 5-4:
Check out bestsellers at Google Play Books.

Getting directions with Maps

Google Maps is one of the most powerful map programs currently available. Look up point-to-point directions or route a road trip with multiple destinations. Wherever the wind takes you, Google can make sure you're on the right road. Search for businesses, locations, or popular destinations within Google Maps; share maps with friends; and even zoom all the way down to the street view. Switch your views to satellite view and see whether you recognize the cars parked near your dwelling. Google Maps isn't just functional, it's FUNctional. Figure 5-5 shows Google Maps at a favorite location.

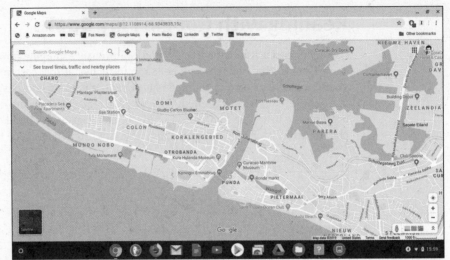

FIGURE 5-5:
Finding your
way with
Google Maps.

Finding More Apps with the Chrome Web Store

The Chrome Web Store has many more apps to offer than what appears by default on your Chromebook. You can search for apps and add them with great ease by taking these steps:

1. **Click the Launcher icon located in the bottom-right of your screen.**

   The Launcher, a window containing your applications, appears.

2. **Find and click the Web Store icon.**

   A Chrome browser window appears and loads the Web Store.

3. **Browse applications by category or search by name.**

4. **Click the desired application.**

   A window appears that contains information specific to the selected application.

5. **To add an application, click the Add to Chrome button located in the top-right of the application window.**

   The application is added to your Launcher. (See Figure 5-6.)

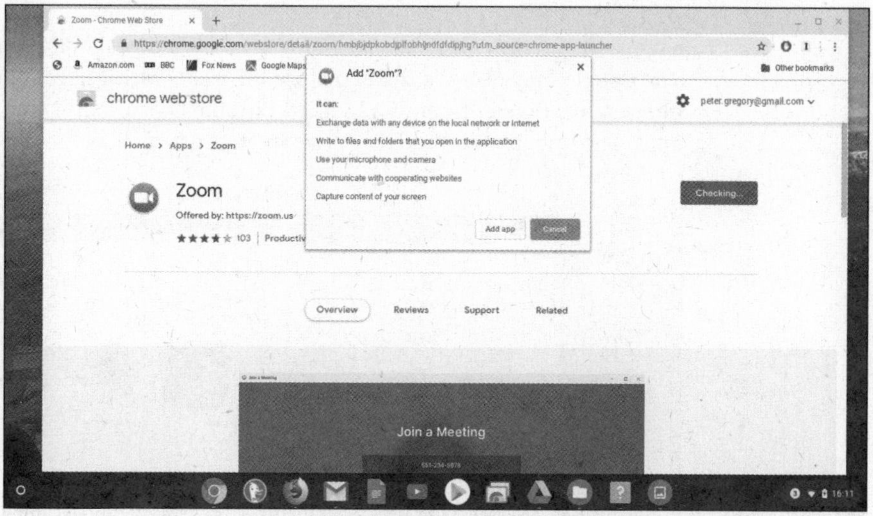

FIGURE 5-6:
Finding and installing apps at the Web Store.

Launching applications that you've added from the Web Store is the same as apps that come by default with your Chromebook. Just follow these steps:

1. **Click the Launcher icon located in the bottom-right corner of your screen.**

   The Launcher opens.

2. **Move between Launcher windows until you locate the icon of your recently installed application.**

3. **Click the application icon.**

   The application launches.

If you're curious about whether a particular app is useful or popular, you can read the customer reviews in the Web Store. These reviews, although public opinion, can be helpful in deciding between different apps. The majority of apps in the Web Store are free, so you take little risk in simply trying an application. If you don't like or use it, you can always uninstall it.

REMEMBER

The Google Play Store

If you have a newer Chromebook, or an older Chromebook with a current version of Chrome OS, you also find the Google Play Store on your shelf or in the Launcher. The Google Play Store is functionally similar to the Web Store, so why do you have two stores for getting apps? Originally, only the Web Store was available for Chromebook users; the Web Store has apps that run on Chromebooks, as well as extensions for the Google Chrome browser on Windows, MacOS, and Chromebooks. The Google Play Store is the app store for users with Android tablets and smartphones, but Google recently modified Chrome OS so that it, too, can run Android apps. The Google Play Store is shown in Figure 5-7.

FIGURE 5-7:
Exploring apps on the Google Play Store.

I tell you about Google Play Music earlier in this chapter. Yes, this same Google Play Store, which is Google's main distribution point for digital content, offers gazillions of Android apps as well as music.

Some of the apps available in the Google Play Store include Facebook, Instagram, Snapchat, Netflix, WhatsApp, Slack, Reddit, Adobe Reader, and more than I could list in this book.

TIP

Whenever you're looking for an app for your Chromebook, I recommend that you first search through the Web Store; if you don't find what you're looking for, consider the Google Play Store. And remember, you can always try an app from either source; if you don't like it, you can just remove it!

Installing apps

To install an app from the Google Play Store, just click the app's logo and then click the Install button. The app downloads and is automatically installed. You can open it right away by clicking Open. If it's an app that you want to run frequently, you can pin the app to the shelf, as discussed in Chapter 2.

Managing Installed Apps

You can use the Google Play Store app to manage all the apps that you have installed on your Chromebook. Just open the Google Play Store app (you probably know how to do this by now) and click the menu icon near the upper-left corner of the app (it looks like three little horizontal lines). A window slides out that contains your Google account name and a list of things you can do. Click My Apps & Games, which opens the window shown in Figure 5-8.

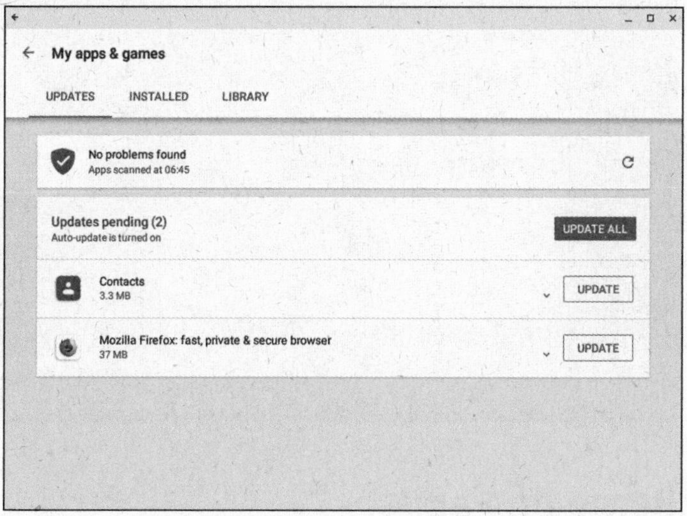

FIGURE 5-8:
Managing your installed apps with the Google Play Store.

Updating apps

The Updates function in the Google Play Store shows apps where software updates are available. You want to periodically check this feature and install any updates that are available because doing so is a good security practice. Chapter 18 provides more detail on Chromebook security.

One thing about updates: If you decide to update an app, checking first to see whether it is running is a good idea. The update will stop the app and install a new version. Depending on the app, you might get a warning that you have unsaved work, but to be on the safe side, just stop the app if you're not sure.

Finding out what apps you have installed

To see what apps are installed on your Chromebook, click the Installed button. Doing so shows the apps you've installed as well as how much storage you have used and how much remains. Figure 5-9 shows an example. Note that this list does not include the apps that were pre-installed on your Chromebook.

FIGURE 5-9:
Checking and removing installed apps using Launcher.

Removing apps

If you want to remove an app that you have installed, Google Play (interestingly enough) doesn't provide this feature. Instead, you go to the Launcher to do this. To remove an app, click the Launcher, and expand it to show all your apps. To delete an app, right-click or Alt-click the app and click Uninstall. (Refer to Figure 5-9.) It's that simple!

Chapter **6**

Working with Gmail and Google Calendar

In the beginning, Google was a search engine. Over time, however, Google has created or acquired hundreds of software tools and platforms and connected them together to make up what is commonly referred to as the Google ecosystem. Gmail was an early innovation that quickly took root and gained international appeal. At first, Gmail was nothing more than a free email platform that offered users 1GB of email storage. However, Inbox size, coupled with Gmail's easy-to-use interface, made the perfect recipe for growing a user base. Over the past 15 years, Gmail has acquired 1.4 billion users (yes, that's billion with a *b*), and it is still free. And now, users receive 15GB of free storage in Gmail.

In this chapter, you learn how to launch Gmail on your Chromebook, read emails, and sort your emails with labels. You can explore how to write emails, add multiple recipients who can be seen and unseen, and attach files to email messages. You learn how to use Gmail to access your other email accounts, even those outside of Google. Navigate your sent mail and save messages in your Drafts folder for editing at a later time. Write emails, even when you don't have Internet access, and send them when you're connected at a later time with Gmail Offline.

Gmail for Chromebook

Before you can access your Chromebook, you must log in using your Google Account username and password. Your Google Account gives you access to almost all of the Google platform, which includes Gmail. Your Chromebook came with a Gmail app icon that you can use to send and receive email.

TIP

If you have a non-Gmail email address that you've been using for a long time, you can still use it on your Chromebook. You can use the Gmail app to access it. If your non-Gmail email is a webmail service (such as Hotmail, Yahoo! Mail, or Pobox. com), you can simply use your Chrome browser to access any or all of those email services.

If you want to use the Gmail app for your Google account, or some non-Google account, you want to read and follow the steps in this section. If, on the other hand, you use your Chrome browser to access non-Google email services, you don't need to read this chapter at all.

Launching Gmail

Before you get started, have your Gmail username handy. Chances are, this is the account you used to initially set up and sign in to your Chromebook. You use that Gmail username (also known as your email address) in the procedures here.

To launch Gmail, just open the Launcher and click the Gmail icon. When you do so, Gmail launches in a Chrome browser window.

If you haven't created a Gmail email account, you're prompted to create an account, thus adding it to your Google Account. Gmail is free and perhaps always will be. Even if you don't intend to use Gmail as your preferred email application, you still need a Gmail account to send and receive message from other email apps on your Chromebook. To create your Gmail account, follow these steps:

1. **On the Add Gmail to Your Google Account page, shown in Figure 6-1, complete all the fields in the sign-up form on the right side of the screen.**

TIP

If you intend to use your Gmail account to send and receive email, make sure you select an email address that's easy to remember to avoid awkward conversations down the road. It's best if you write it down, along with your password.

2. **When you complete the form, click Submit.**

The Verify Your Account page appears, where you're requested to verify your identity.

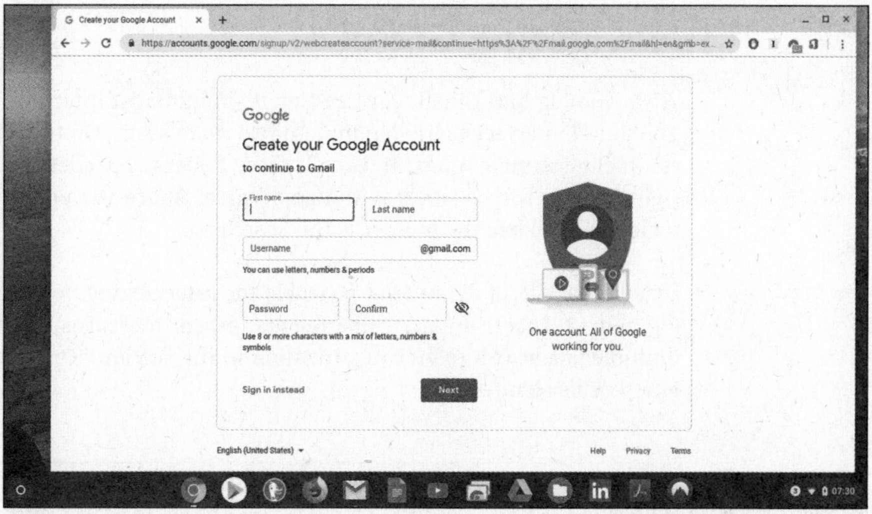

FIGURE 6-1:
The Google
account creation
page.

3. **Enter your phone number, or any phone number at which you can be reached.**

Google will call or text this number to give you a verification number. You should use a number at which you can be reached most of the time because you might need it in the future to verify your login.

4. **Using the radio buttons, select to receive a text message or a phone call.**

5. **Click Continue.**

The Verification page appears, on which you're prompted to enter the verification code that you received on your phone.

6. **Enter the verification code you received by phone call or text.**

7. **Click Continue.**

8. **When Google asks for a Recovery email address, enter the email address of another email account that you normally use.**

If you get locked out of the new account you are creating here, your recovery account can help you get this new email account unlocked.

9. **Enter your date of birth and gender.**

Google will not verify this now, but it may use your date of birth later to help you recover your account. It is important that you remember the date you use here.

10. **Review and agree to Google's privacy and terms.**

If you click More Options, you can opt out of various advertising and privacy features if you want.

After being verified, you're logged into your new Gmail account.

Navigating Gmail

When you log into Gmail, you see Gmail's minimalist interface. (See Figure 6-2.) The Gmail interface is broken up into two main areas. On the left is a list of folders, including your Inbox. In Gmail, these folders are called *labels*. Directly to the right of your list of labels is the email area. Above the email area is the Gmail toolbar, and above the toolbar is the Search bar.

Gmail gives you a default set of labels for categorizing your email, as shown in Figure 6-3. Labels are a lot like folders, except messages, unlike files, can have multiple labels. (More on categorization in the section "Organizing your Inbox," later in this chapter.)

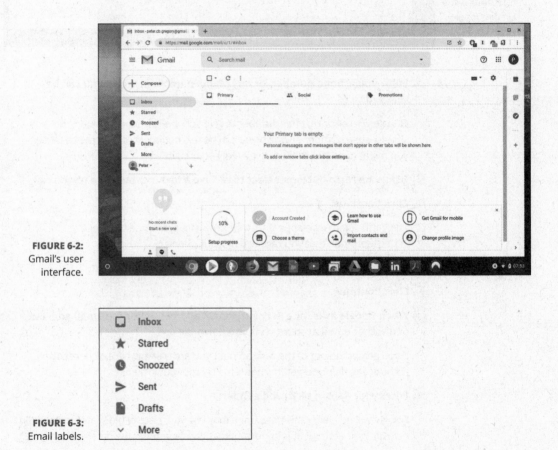

FIGURE 6-2:
Gmail's user
interface.

FIGURE 6-3:
Email labels.

The basic labels in Gmail are the following:

>> **Inbox:** Your Inbox is the location where your new mail is delivered. The Inbox doesn't include spam, trash, or sent mail.

>> **Starred:** Give your messages a special status by using a star so that you can more easily find them.

>> **Snoozed:** These are email messages that you don't want to be notified about at this time.

>> **Sent:** Any email you send to others is labeled Sent.

>> **Drafts:** Emails that you write but don't send are labeled Drafts.

>> **Spam:** Junk mail that Google automatically identifies as spam.

>> **Trash:** Email that you delete is labeled Trash and can be erased from existence.

Spam will not appear until either you or Gmail has marked an incoming email as spam. Similarly, Trash will not appear until you have deleted email messages.

Your Gmail view defaults to the Inbox label. When you have unread emails in your Inbox, a number appears directly to the right of the label. Both read and unread emails appear in the main email message area. Unread emails show up in bold, as shown in Figure 6-4. Directly above your email messages, by default, are three tabs — Primary, Social, and Promotions. Gmail automatically sorts the emails in your Inbox based on what it believes the incoming email to be. Google places emails from social outlets into your Social tab, emails judged to be advertisements into your Promotions tab, and the remainder into your Primary tab.

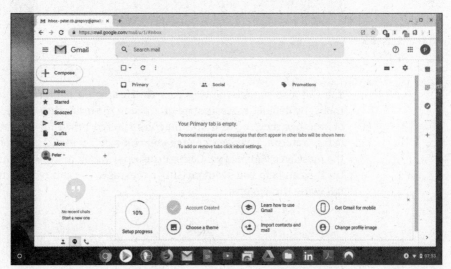

FIGURE 6-4:
The email area.

Customizing your view

You have several ways to customize the look and feel of Gmail. By default, Gmail leaves a good deal of space between lines, emails, and so on. However, if you prefer, you can condense this space to make room for more information on your screen. To compact the space, follow these steps:

1. **Click the Settings icon on the right side of the toolbar.**

   The Settings icon looks like a little gear.

   The Settings menu opens, as shown in Figure 6-5. The first option, Display Density, pertains to your Gmail display. If you click Display Density, a new window opens that shows the Default, Comfortable, and Compact options. Display Density options determine how close together messages in your folders appear, as shown in Figure 6-6.

2. **Pick a Display Density option and click OK.**

   Your Gmail display automatically reconfigures itself and refreshes the page.

Display density
Configure inbox
Settings
Themes
Get add-ons
Send feedback
Help
Gmail Setup (10%)

FIGURE 6-5:
Customizing your Gmail view.

You can also change the way your Gmail account handles the messages in your Inbox. By default, messages are grouped in the order they are received, regardless of whether they're read, and they are filtered based on the tab settings you're using. You can, however, change your Inbox view to assign different priorities to the messages you receive. Configuring your Inbox to keep all unread messages at the top can help you avoid missing a message. You can reconfigure your Inbox by following these steps:

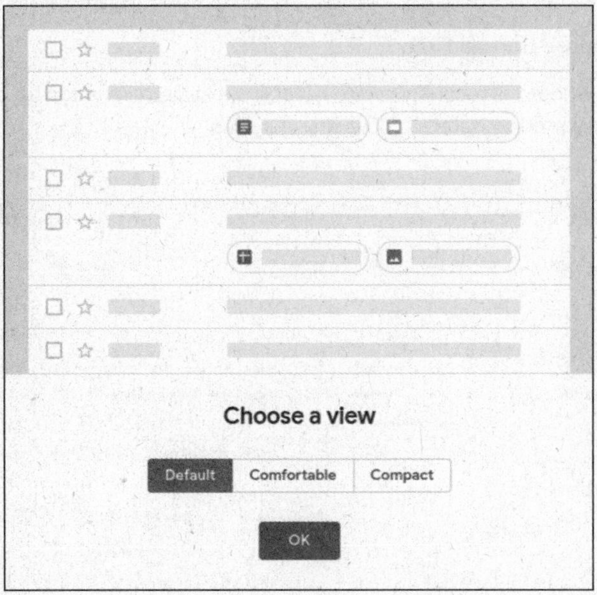

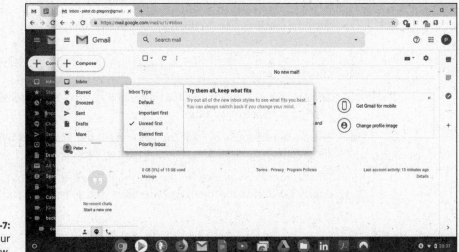

FIGURE 6-6:
Selecting the
density of display
of email
messages in
Gmail.

1. **Move your pointer over the Inbox label on the left side of your window and click the down-pointing arrow that appears.**

   A menu appears, as shown in Figure 6-7, revealing several options for configuring your Inbox.

2. **Mouse over each option to reveal a description of what the option will do to your Inbox.**

FIGURE 6-7:
Configuring your
Inbox view.

3. Choose Unread First.

Your Inbox is reconfigured to keep all unread emails at the top. All read emails are sorted by date, as shown in Figure 6-8.

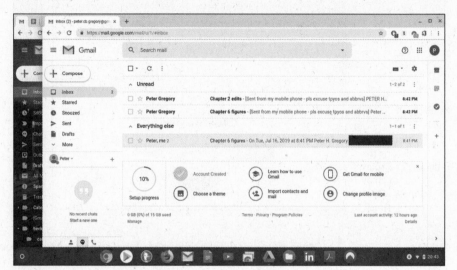

FIGURE 6-8:
Unread emails appear first.

Adding a theme

Gmail also comes with several different themes for adding color and images to your account screen. Add flavor to your Gmail with a theme by following these steps:

1. Click the Settings icon on the right side of the toolbar.

The Settings menu opens.

2. Choose Themes.

Gmail loads the Themes page that contains images of several themes. You can scroll down to see many more.

3. Browse the selection of color themes and HD themes. Select a theme by clicking the option, clicking Select, and then clicking Save.

Gmail automatically applies the theme to your Gmail, and returns to the Inbox display. Do you like the theme you selected? If not, go back and find another!

Sending Email with Gmail

All email consists of the same core elements — it must have a sender, a receiver, and a message — and email sent using Gmail is no different. The message is typically comprised of a subject line and a body of text. You can have multiple recipients and, in addition to text, your message can include documents, music, videos, archives, and more.

Navigating Gmail email

The New Message window has three main parts. The *header* of the email window is located at the top of the email message. The header contains the window controls for your email. The footer contains the editing tools for formatting and styling your email, and the middle portion is the email itself. Figure 6-9 shows a blank email message in Gmail. The email message is composed of the following parts:

» **To:** Specify the recipient(s) by entering an email address (or email addresses) here. You can add recipients using the carbon copy feature. Carbon copy is used to send a message to someone who isn't the primary intended recipient. You use a *carbon copy* (or *Cc*, as it's commonly referred to), to start dialogues among multiple people over email. You use a *blind carbon copy*, or *Bcc*, to send an email to one or many recipients, but none of the recipients know who any other Bcc recipients are (if any).

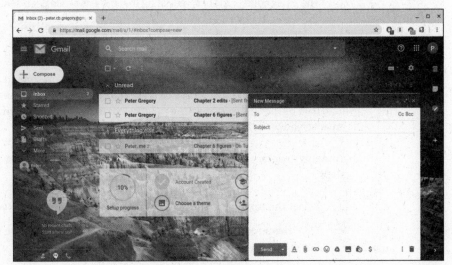

FIGURE 6-9:
Sending an email message in Gmail.

>> **Subject:** Add a subject line to your email. Subjects are usually 50 characters or fewer.

>> **Body:** You type your message in the body, which is the big, white, blank area below the Subject line.

Writing an email

Writing an email with Gmail is very similar to writing a letter using Google Docs or any other word processor. To write an email in Gmail, take the following steps:

1. **Click the Compose button at the top-left of your Gmail window.**

   A new, blank message appears on the bottom-right of the Gmail window.

2. **Click the To field at the top of the Email Editor and enter the email address of the person to whom you want to send your email.**

   Email addresses follow the format of *name@domain.something*; for instance, my email address is peter.cb.gregory@gmail.com.

3. **Click in the Subject field and enter a subject line for the message.**

   It's always good advice to keep your subject line short and to the point.

4. **Click in the Body of the email and type your message.**

5. **When you finish writing your email, click Send.**

   The Email Editor vanishes, indicating that the email has been sent.

Styling text

Gmail provides you with several advanced features for spicing up your emails, such as word-processor features to style your text. You can make your text bold or italicized by using the formatting palette located at the bottom of the composition area, as shown in Figure 6-10.

To apply boldface, italics, or underline to the text in your email, follow these steps:

1. **Select the text you want to format by clicking and dragging your pointer.**

2. **Click the underlined A button next to the Send button in the footer of the Email Editor.**

3. **Select the B button (to make the selected text bold), the I button (to make it italic), or the U button (to add an underline).**

    The selected text changes appropriately.

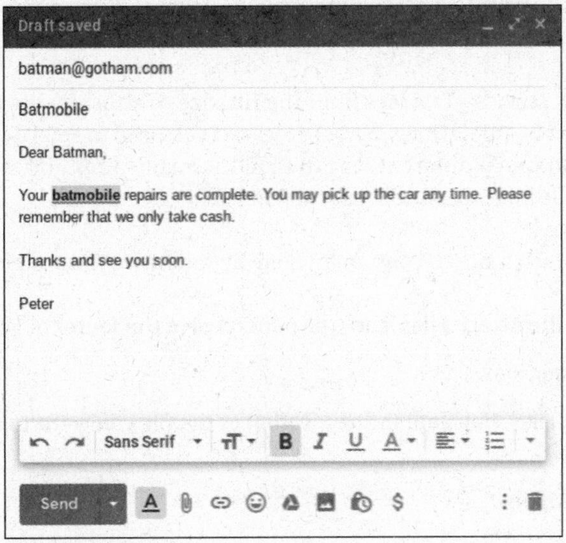

FIGURE 6-10:
The formatting palette in an email message.

> You can also use keyboard shortcuts to apply formatting to text in your emails. While your text is selected, use the following shortcuts to apply the associated style:
>
> **TIP**
>
> » **Bold:** Ctrl+B
>
> » **Italics:** Ctrl+I
>
> » **Underline:** Ctrl+U

To change the color of the text in your email, follow these steps:

1. **Select the text whose color you want to change by clicking and dragging your pointer.**

2. **Click the A button on the left side of the formatting toolbar.**

    A menu appears, giving you the option to select a color to apply to your text or to apply as a highlight on your text.

3. **Select your desired color from the available options.**

    Your text changes to the selected color.

Attaching files to an email

Email has come a long way since the early days of the Internet. Now you can send more than just a digital letter; you can also send files with your emails. Want to send pictures of your sister to Mom and Dad? Maybe you need to submit your homework to your teacher? Or maybe you're just swapping files with your friends. Email is a great way to do it.

WARNING

Most email service providers limit the file size of attachments that can be sent or received to 10–30MB (megabytes) or less. If you need to send a larger file, you may be forced to find a different way to send it. Gmail's limit, by the way, is 50MB — the total allowed size for all attachments.

You can attach a file to your email done by following these steps:

1. **Click the Attach Files icon (the paperclip) in the footer of your email.**

   Files launches.

2. **Using Files, navigate to the location of the file you want to attach. Select the file.**

3. **Click Open.**

   The file uploads and appears at the bottom of your email, as shown in Figure 6-11.

TIP

You can also attach files from your Chromebook by dragging and dropping the files directly from the Files app onto the body of the message.

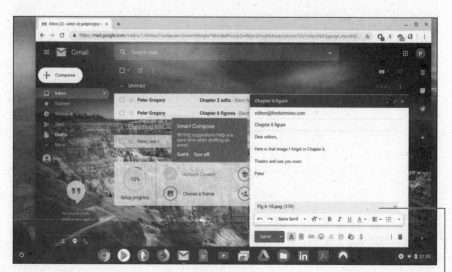

FIGURE 6-11:
The Uploaded File indicator in an email.

Attached file indicator

Customizing your email view

By default, the New Message window appears as a window on the bottom-right of your Chrome browser while you're in Gmail. You can, however, change the view so that the New Message window is full screen (actually, it's only three-quarters of a full screen, but who's counting?). Using the New Message window in Full Screen mode is helpful for writing emails that are longer in content. You can write emails in Full Screen mode by clicking the arrow icon in the top-right corner of your New Message window. To take your New Message window out of Full Screen mode, click the same arrow icon located in the top-right corner of the full-screen New Message window.

To tell Gmail to default to Full Screen mode every time, follow these steps:

1. **Click the Compose button on the top-left of the Gmail window.**

   A New Message window appears in the bottom-right corner of your window.

2. **Locate the More Options button in the bottom-right corner of the Email Editor (next to the little trash can) window and click it.**

   A menu appears, revealing several options.

3. **Click Default to Full Screen.**

   The menu disappears, and the Email Editor window remains the same size. New emails created from this point forward will automatically appear in Full Screen mode.

TIP

You can also set the default view of your New Message window to partial screen by following the preceding steps.

Creating an email signature

Every good letter deserves a great closing. As you write emails, you may find that your sign-off is the same for each email. Or you may find that it's helpful to include some contact details at the bottom of each of your emails, such as your email address or phone number. With Gmail, you can create a standard email *signature* so that every email you write contains a standardized closing. To create an email signature, follow these steps:

1. **With Gmail open, click the Settings icon (which looks like a cog or widget) at the top right of your screen.**

   The Settings menu appears, revealing several options. (Refer to Figure 6-5.)

2. **Choose Settings.**

The Gmail Settings window appears.

3. **To ensure that you're in the General tab, click General at the top left of the Settings window.**

4. **Scroll down to the Signature section and click the radio button located directly below the No Signature radio button.**

5. **Click in the text box, shown in Figure 6-12, and begin typing your signature.**

6. **When you finish typing your signature, scroll to the bottom of the Settings Editor and click Save Changes.**

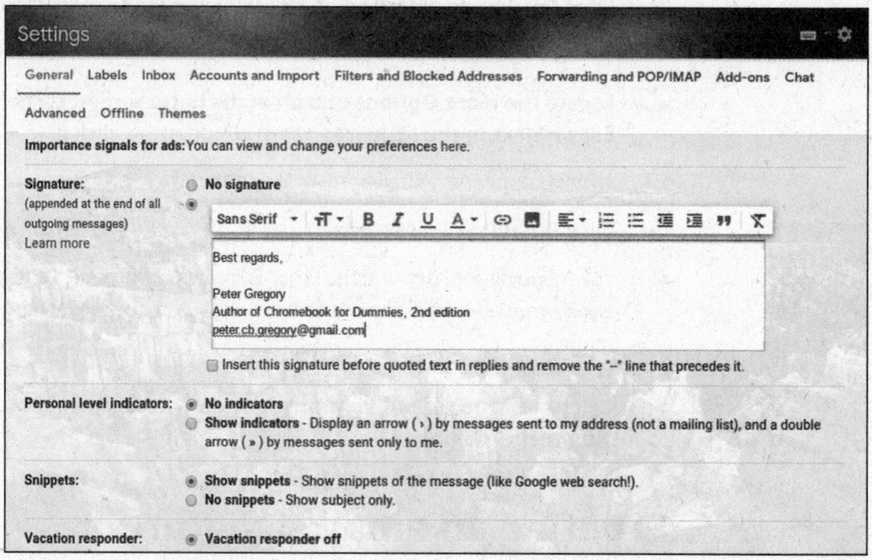

Settings

General Labels Inbox Accounts and Import Filters and Blocked Addresses Forwarding and POP/IMAP Add-ons Chat

Advanced Offline Themes

Importance signals for ads: You can view and change your preferences here.

Signature:
(appended at the end of all outgoing messages)
Learn more

○ No signature

⊙ Sans Serif ▾ T▾ B I U A▾ ⊖ 🖼 ☰▾ ⋮≣ ≣ ⫶ ⫷ " X̶

Best regards,

Peter Gregory
Author of Chromebook for Dummies, 2nd edition
peter.cb.gregory@gmail.com

☐ Insert this signature before quoted text in replies and remove the "–" line that precedes it.

Personal level indicators: ⊙ No indicators
○ Show indicators - Display an arrow (›) by messages sent to my address (not a mailing list), and a double arrow (») by messages sent only to me.

Snippets: ⊙ Show snippets - Show snippets of the message (like Google web search!).
○ No snippets - Show subject only.

Vacation responder: ⊙ Vacation responder off

FIGURE 6-12:
Adding an email signature that will appear at the end of every email message.

TIP

Place a line or two of blank space at the top of your email signature to ensure that you have enough space separating your signature from the body of your email. You can test your spacing by composing a new email to view your newly created, or edited, signature. If it doesn't look quite right, go back and modify your signature. Practice makes perfect!

Reading Email

All your incoming email is delivered to your Gmail Inbox. By default, the most current emails appear on top unless you changed your view to keep all unread emails on the top regardless of the date. Your Inbox gives you just enough information about the email for you to decide whether to read it. Each line starts with the name or address of the sender of the email, followed by the subject of the email. Gmail then previews the contents of the email with the remaining available space.

Unread emails appear with the sender's name and subject line in bold. After you read an email, the message appears unbolded in your Inbox, indicating that it has been viewed. To view an email, place your pointer over the email line and click. Gmail opens the email and loads it in the main email area, as shown in Figure 6-13.

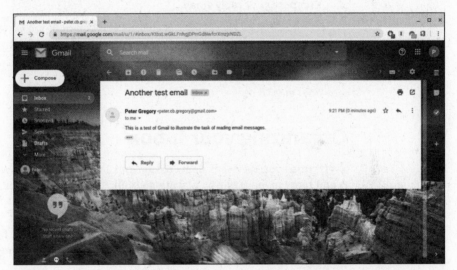

FIGURE 6-13:
Reading an email message.

When you finish reading the email, you can click the Inbox link in your labels list on the left side of the Gmail window to return to the list of messages in your Inbox. You can also click the Older and Newer email buttons located next to the Settings icon in the top-right corner of the Gmail window if you want to read other messages in your Inbox.

Replying to email

After you read an email, you may want to send a reply message to the sender. You can write a reply email by following these steps:

1. While viewing an email in your Inbox, click the Reply button at the bottom of the email message.

The message you were reading transforms into a window resembling a New Message window and containing a flashing cursor, which indicates that you can write an email. The only difference is that you can see the message you are replying to in the upper part of the window.

TIP

If you're replying to an email that was sent to multiple recipients, including yourself, you may want to send your reply to every person on the original email. This action is called Reply All. To reply to everyone, click Reply All in the email message. Reply All appears after you click More, to the right of the Reply button.

2. Compose your reply email.

Gmail automatically includes the original email message so that you have a history of your email dialogue in one place.

3. When you're satisfied with your reply, click Send.

Your email is sent.

Organizing your Inbox

Every email you receive is delivered to your Inbox. You can, however, make your Gmail more manageable by placing your emails into groups. Gmail allows you to organize your emails by applying labels.

REMEMBER

Gmail uses the term *labels* instead of *folders.* Labels act a lot like folders. However, you can apply multiple labels to an email, thus categorizing it in multiple locations.

By applying labels to your emails, you can quickly locate emails at a later date. Maybe you want to group all emails from your family members with a label you call Family. Or maybe you want to group all emails pertaining to work with the label Work. Whatever the case may be, labels are a helpful way to create order in your Inbox. Add a label to an email by following these steps:

1. With Gmail open, click the Inbox link in the list of labels to ensure that you're in your Inbox.

Your Inbox loads into the main email area.

2. **Locate the email you want to label and select the check box to the left of the email.**

   The selected email is highlighted.

3. **Click the Labels icon (which looks like a tag) directly above the main email area.**

   The Label menu appears, as shown in Figure 6-14.

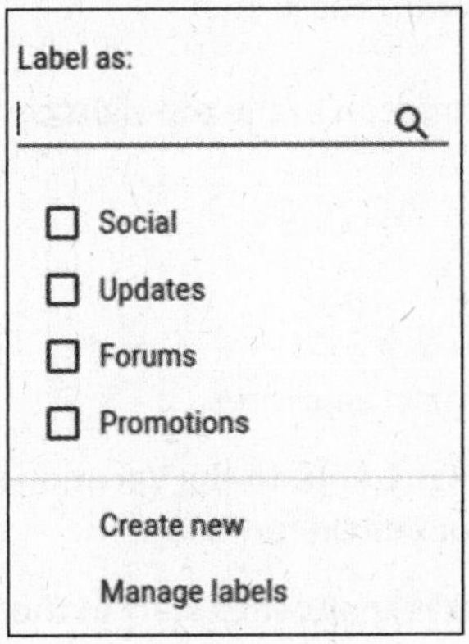

Label as:

| | 🔍

☐ Social

☐ Updates

☐ Forums

☐ Promotions

Create new

Manage labels

FIGURE 6-14:
Placing a label
on an email
message.

4. **You can either select the desired labels from the available options or click Create New to create a completely new label.**

   Clicking Create New opens the New Label pop-up window.

TIP

   You can also type the name of a label in the Search bar at the top of the Label menu and then click Create New.

5. **Enter the name of the new label.**

6. **(Optional) If you would like to make your label a subcategory of another label, click Nest Label Under and, from the drop-down list, select the label under which you want to create a subcategory.**

7. **Click Create.**

   After you apply a label to your email, that email appears in the associated group in the label list on the left side of the screen.

TIP

With the nested labels feature, you can manage a large volume of incoming email messages into a filing system arranged any way you choose.

Setting up a vacation responder

When you're ready to go on that monster vacation that you've been planning, you may want to totally unplug from technology. You don't have to worry about offending your family and coworkers by leaving them wondering and waiting for a reply. You can use the vacation responder to automatically send a message to every person who sends you a message. When you come home from your vacation, you can then get to the business of replying to the emails that you received while you were away, without needing to explain the delay to everyone who emailed you. To set up your vacation responder, follow these steps:

1. **With Gmail open, click the Settings icon in the top-right corner of the window.**

The Settings menu appears.

2. **Click Settings.**

The Settings Editor appears in the main email area.

3. **Scroll to the bottom of the Settings Editor, to the Vacation Responder section. Click the Vacation Responder On radio button.**

4. **Enter the first day you want your responder to start in the First Day field.**

If you know the last day you want your vacation responder on, enter it as well.

WARNING

If you don't set the last day for your vacation responder, you need to turn your vacation responder off manually. Otherwise, Gmail will continue to automatically send your message to each email you receive until someone reminds you that your vacation three months ago has probably ended by now.

5. **Enter the subject in the subject field and body in the body field for your vacation responder email. (See Figure 6-15.)**

6. **Don't forget to scroll down and click the Save Changes button.**

Anyone who sends you an email will receive an auto-response at least once while you're away.

TIP

Gmail reminds you that your vacation message has been set by displaying a yellow band across the top of your Gmail window with a reminder message. The reminder includes a link there where you can change your vacation responder settings.

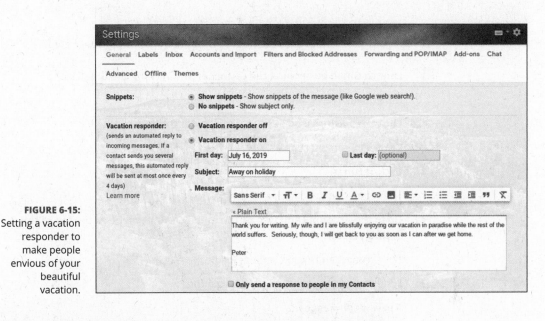

Use Gmail to Access Non-Gmail Accounts

If you already have an email address and it happens to not be a Gmail account, you may not want to create and use a new email address. That's understandable. Your contacts are likely quite familiar with your current contact info, and changing your details could prove to be frustrating. Gmail can work as an email client for up to five other email accounts.

Gmail can access your other email account, pulling in all your received emails and categorizing the messages by applying labels to them. You can then use Gmail to compose new email messages but have them appear to be sent from your other email account.

WARNING

Setting up Gmail to send and receive mail for a different account requires that you provide answers to several highly technical questions. Be prepared to enter your email address, password, POP3 or IMAP Server address, and security settings. Generally speaking, you should be able to find this information in either the Help, Support, or Settings sections provided by your other email provider. Don't proceed until you have been able to find this information.

Access your non-Gmail accounts through Gmail by following these steps:

1. Launch Gmail by opening the Launcher and clicking the Gmail icon.

Gmail loads in a Chrome web browser.

2. Click the Settings icon at the top right of the window.

The Settings menu appears.

3. Click Settings.

The Settings Editor loads into the main email area.

4. Open the Accounts and Import tab in the Settings menu at the top of the Settings Editor.

The Accounts and Import settings load.

5. Scroll down and click Add a Mail Account.

A new window appears.

6. Enter the full email address of your other account and then click Next.

7. On the next window, select Link Accounts with Gmailify or Import Emails from My Other Account (POP3).

Select each option to view the subsequent steps. This should help you decide how you want to access your other email account. With Gmailify, Gmail will try to figure out what your technical settings need to be. If Gmail can't figure this out, you need to select the Import Emails option instead. Figure 6-16 shows the Import window.

8. Complete the text boxes as indicated and click Add Account.

After your account has been added, you're asked if you want to be able to send email as this address.

9. Follow the prompts accordingly.

WARNING

Setting up Gmail to process emails for a non-Google account is not a simple task, even for experts. If you're trying to do this, be prepared for some trial and error. You'll want to use a pen or pencil and paper to write down all the settings you need to use to make it work.

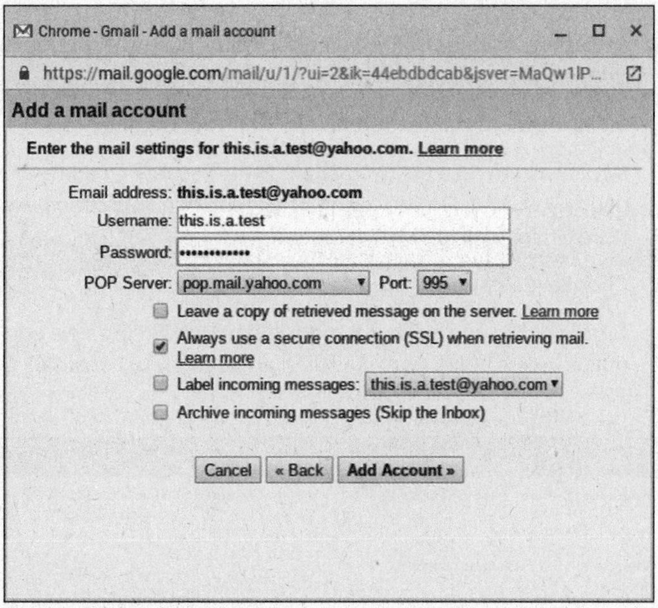

FIGURE 6-16:
Configuring Gmail to read email from a non-Google email service.

Using Gmail Offline

To send and receive email, you must be connected to the Internet. Gmail, however, has an Offline mode that allows you to write emails, even if you don't have an Internet connection, and Gmail will send those emails the next time you are online. To use Gmail offline, follow these steps:

1. **Launch Gmail by opening the Launcher and clicking the Gmail icon.**

   Gmail loads in a Chrome web browser.

2. **Click the Settings icon at the top right of the window.**

   The Settings menu appears.

3. **Click Settings.**

   The Settings Editor loads into the main email area.

4. **Click Offline.**

5. **Select the Enable Offline Mail check box, as shown in Figure 6-17.**

The window expands to show additional options. Select how many days of offline email you want to store locally on your Chromebook.

Scroll down to read the two options in the Security section and select the option you want. On your own Chromebook, you'll probably want to select Keep Offline Data on My Computer.

6. **Click Save Changes.**

Gmail reloads and displays a message that reads, "Create a bookmark for offline access." Click Got It and then press Ctrl+D to bookmark Gmail offline.

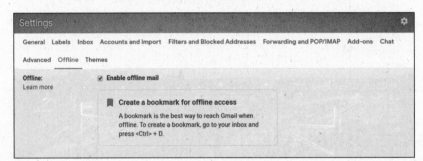

FIGURE 6-17:
Enabling Gmail
for offline use.

The Gmail Offline interface is essentially the same as the online Gmail interface. Everything appears as you are accustomed to seeing it. Your Inbox is displayed just as you remember, and the big white Compose button resides near the upper-right corner of the screen. After you click Send, a message appears at the bottom of the Gmail window that reads, "Offline. Message will be sent later." And remember: No new messages will arrive in your Inbox until you are back online.

Using Google Calendar

I have a calendar hanging in my office. Not to keep track of important dates, but because I like the pictures. For years, I've kept important dates of all kinds in my Google Calendar, from reminders for garbage and recycling day to important birthdates and anniversaries, and reminders to renew professional certifications and the like.

Google Calendar is a part of your Google account. The easiest way to start Google Calendar is to open a new browser window, and enter **calendar.google.com** in the Omnibox. If you're already logged in to Google, you can click the Google Apps button near the upper-right corner (next to your profile photo) and then click Calendar. See Figure 6-18 to view the features of Google Calendar.

Go to today

Settings

Create entry

Previous - Next

Search

View selection

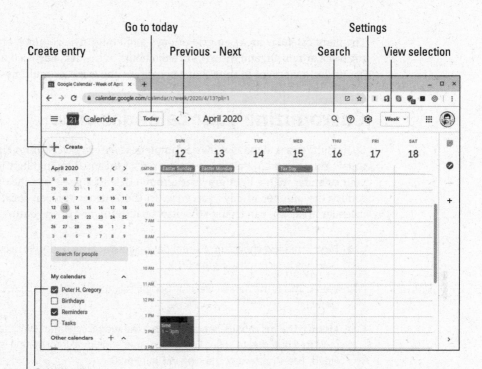

Calendar list

Mini calendar

Curiously, Google doesn't provide a shortcut for Google Calendar on a Chromebook. However, you can make one by following these steps:

1. **Open Google Calendar by navigating to calendar.google.com with your Chrome browser.**

2. **Click the menu button (three little dots) to the right of the address bar.**

3. **Click More Tools.**

4. **Click Create Shortcut.**

   You see Google Calendar appear on the shelf.

Your Calendar workspace has a few key areas: the left sidebar, controls at the top, and a calendar view taking most of the window. The left sidebar contains a mini-calendar that defaults to the current month. Below the mini-calendar is a collapsible list of all your calendars. Below your calendars is another collapsible list of calendars that have been shared with you. The top Settings bar contains buttons for changing your view, navigating through your calendar in the current view, and a Settings icon that can display several options for customizing and controlling your calendar.

The main calendar area is a grid of days and hours. The columns are the days of the week or month, and the rows are the hours of the day. Each cell in your calendar grid is a moment in time that can contain one event or multiple events.

Customizing your calendar view

By default, your calendar shows a complete seven-day week from Sunday to Saturday. Your calendar lets you know the day of the week by highlighting the day in your calendar with a light gray background Calendar gives you the option to customize the number of days you view. In the Settings toolbar, located above the calendar area, you can change the view by clicking one of the buttons, as follows:

>> **Day:** Your view shows the current day's calendar from midnight to midnight. Day view is pictured in Figure 6-19.

>> **Week:** This is the default view for Google calendar. Sunday to Saturday is shown.

>> **Month**: The full month view looks like a traditional calendar. Events are indicated but, due to space limitations, little additional information is provided. The Month view is shown in Figure 6-20.

>> **Schedule:** The Schedule view gives you a list of events across all days in your calendar, as seen in Figure 6-21. Find events by scrolling.

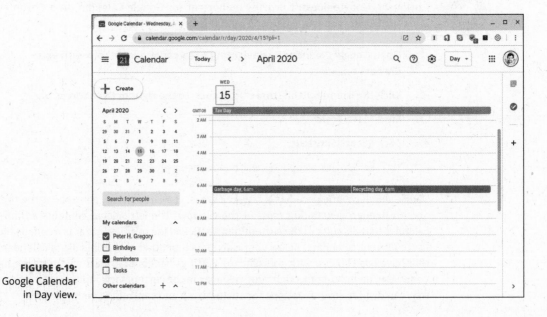

FIGURE 6-19:
Google Calendar
in Day view.

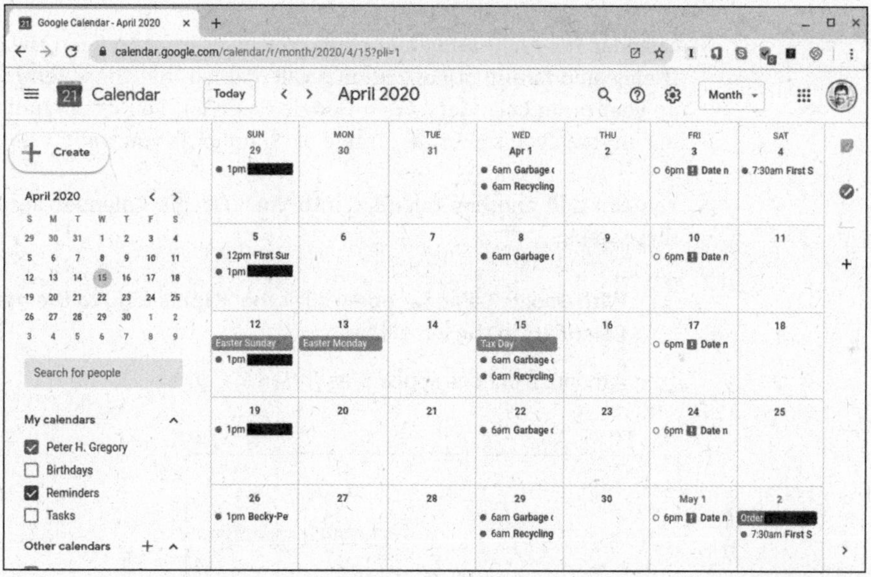

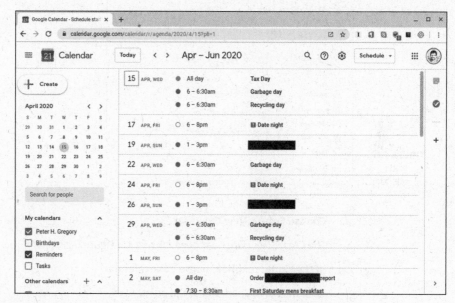

FIGURE 6-20:
Google Calendar
in Month view.

FIGURE 6-21:
Google Calendar
in Schedule view.

Creating additional calendars

Google Calendar gives you the option to have multiple calendars so that you can organize your events into groups. Use multiple calendars to keep your work, play, and other activities separate. If you're a parent trying to manage the activity schedules for each of your children, create a calendar for your children or a calendar for each individual child. You may want to keep the birthdays of your friends and family organized on a calendar so that those reminders don't clutter up your other calendars. With Google Calendar, you can organize the business of life any way you see fit, as simple or complex as you want.

You can add another calendar into your Google Calendar account by following these steps:

1. **With Google Calendar open, click the '+' (plus sign) to the right of Other Calendars in the left sidebar.**

A menu of options appears, as shown in Figure 6-22.

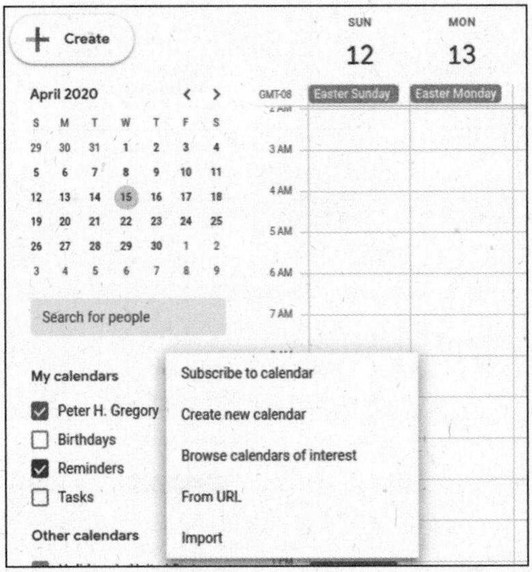

FIGURE 6-22:
Adding a
calendar.

2. **Choose Create New Calendar.**

The Create New Calendar page, pictured in Figure 6-23, opens.

3. **In the Name text box, name your calendar.**

Keep the name short and to the point.

4. **Enter a description for your calendar in the Description text box.**

5. **Choose a time zone for your calendar from the Now Select a Time Zone drop-down list.**

WARNING

The time zone for your calendar is important because Google Calendar will schedule all of your events with this time zone. When you travel to different time zones, Google maintains your calendar based on the default time zone of your calendar events.

6. **Scroll to the bottom of the screen and click Create Calendar.**

Calendar view reappears, and your newly created calendar appears in the My Calendars collapsible menu.

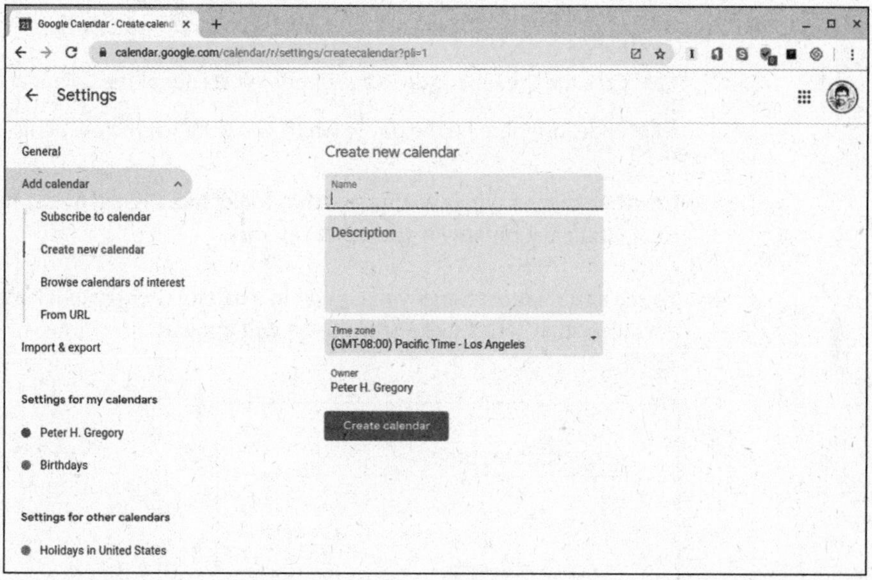

FIGURE 6-23:
Creating a new
calendar.

Creating a calendar event

Your Calendar is an organized collection of activities called events. Each event you create contains the following information that describes the event:

>> Event name

>> Date

>> Start and stop time

>> Time zone

>> Event location

>> Calendar

>> Event description

>> Reminders

>> Event guests

Aside from the date, you can create events with as little or as much of the remaining information outlined above as you want. However, the more information that you include, the more helpful your calendar becomes.

Creating a new calendar entry in Google Calendar is simple. In fact, you have at least two ways to do it:

>> Click the Create button in the upper-left corner of the Calendar window.

>> Click anywhere on the day in which you want to create an entry.

In either case, a window appears that looks like Figure 6-24. Just fill in the title, time, and click on any of the other options.

To see a full list of things you can do in a calendar entry, click More Options; then, a window that looks like Figure 6-25 will appear.

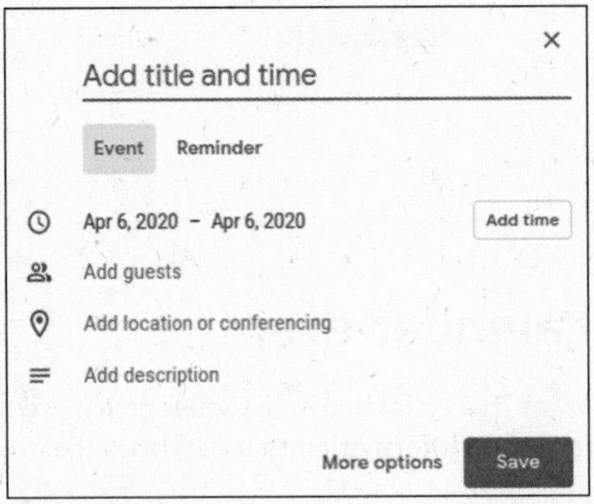

FIGURE 6-24: Adding a new event to your calendar.

The items you can add to a calendar entry include:

>> **Title:** This is the name of the event; for example, Bobby's Birthday.

>> **Date:** You can put in a single date, or a date range; if you're going on a five-day trip, your dates could read April 7, 2020 to April 12, 2020.

>> **All Day:** Select this box if this is an all-day event. If you deselect this, you can put in the time.

>> **Time:** The time of day of the event.

>> **Repeat:** This can be a one-time event, or one that occurs every N days, weeks, months, or years. Never forget an anniversary again!

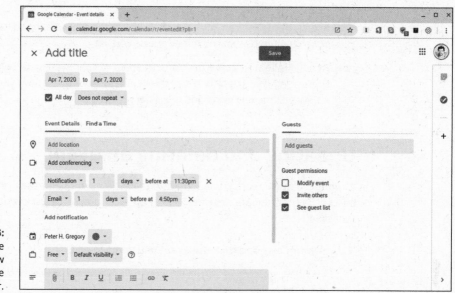

FIGURE 6-25:
Adding more details to a new event to Google Calendar.

>> **Location:** Put in the address or other information that will help you remember.

>> **Add Conferencing:** This can be a Hangouts call. Because Google is transitioning away from Hangouts to Duo (see Chapter 15 for more information), Duo might be your choice here.

>> **Notification:** You can put in a reminder that will pop up a notification on your Chromebook before the start of your event.

>> **Email:** You can have Google Calendar send you a reminder email at a set time before the start of the event.

>> **Calendar**. You can specify which calendar to put the event in.

>> **Free / Busy:** You can specify whether this event should block time on your calendar. This is handy if you are sharing your calendar with others and you want them to be able to see your busy and free times on your schedule.

>> **Guests:** You can enter the email address of one or more guests. Doing so causes an invitation to be sent to their email.

>> **Guest Permissions:** This item determines whether you will permit guests (people you invite) to be able to modify your calendar entry, invite others, or see the list of guests.

>> **Attachment:** You can add an attachment to the event. Doing so causes the attachment to be emailed to any guests you list.

>> **Save:** This item creates a permanent record of your event in Google Calendar. Don't worry if you don't know all the details for your event now; you can always edit the entry and add more details later.

Updating and deleting an event

After an event is created, you may find that you need to edit the event to add more notes, change the date or time, and so on. You can edit your events by following these steps:

1. **In your Calendar, click the event you want to edit.**

A window appears, as shown in Figure 6-26, showing the basic information about the event.

First Saturday mens breakfast
Saturday, May 2, 2020 · 7:30 – 8:30am
Monthly on the first Saturday

1 day before
2 days before

Peter H. Gregory

FIGURE 6-26: Editing an event in Google Calendar.

2. **Click the little pencil icon to edit the Event.**

The Event Details page, where you can edit the selected event, appears.

You can quickly remove events from your calendar by clicking Delete instead of Edit Event. The selected event is removed from your calendar.

Make sure you absolutely want to delete an event before you click Delete. There's no undo feature in Calendar, so you have to re-add any deleted events manually.

3. **When you've made your desired changes, click the Save button.**

TIP

WARNING

Inviting others to your event

Events often involve other people. You can make sure that other event participants don't forget about your scheduled events by adding those participants to your Calendar event. When you add someone to an event, Google Calendar sends each participant an invitation to the event via email. The email invitation contains a calendar entry so that your invitees can add the event to their own calendars, as well.

TIP

You can invite others to your events when you create a new event. Sometimes, though, you might want to complete the creation of your event first so you can be sure it contains all the necessary details, and then go back and add invitees to the event. Your invitees receive updates every time you modify the event, and that can become annoying. To invite participants to a calendar event, follow these steps:

1. **Click the calendar entry to which you would like to add invitees.**

A window containing the event appears.

2. **Click on the pencil icon to edit the event.**

The Event Details page loads, with the Add Guests text box on the right.

3. **Enter the email address of an event invitee in the Add Guests text box and click Add.**

4. **Repeat Step 3 for each invitee.**

The invitee appears below the Add Guests field when you enter him.

5. **Click the Save button at the top of the page.**

Upon saving, Google Calendar sends an event invitation to each invitee.

Later on, if you need to add or change event details, or cancel the event, all the invitees will be notified.

One cool feature of Google Calendar and other calendar tools is having some standard protocols at work under the surface. For example, you can invite others to your calendar event without needing to know whether they use Google Calendar, or a different tool such as Microsoft Outlook, Apple Calendar, or something else. Most of the time, people will be able to accept your invites, which places events on their calendar whether they use Google Calendar or something else.

Sharing Calendars

Whether your calendar is for work, home, or family, sharing a calendar can alleviate the need to have to constantly communicate your availability with other people. Share one of your calendars with your coworkers or your spouse so that they can see your events and even add events directly to your calendars. Share one of your calendars by following these steps:

1. **In the left sidebar, open the My Calendars collapsible menu.**

   All of your calendars appear.

2. **Move your pointer over the desired calendar.**

   A Settings icon appears to the right of the calendar name.

3. **Click the Settings icon.**

   A menu appears, revealing multiple options.

4. **Click Settings and Sharing.**

   The settings menu appears.

5. **Click Share with Specific People.**

6. **Click + Add People.**

7. **Enter the email address of the person with whom you wish to share your calendar in the Share with Specific People section. (See Figure 6-27.)**

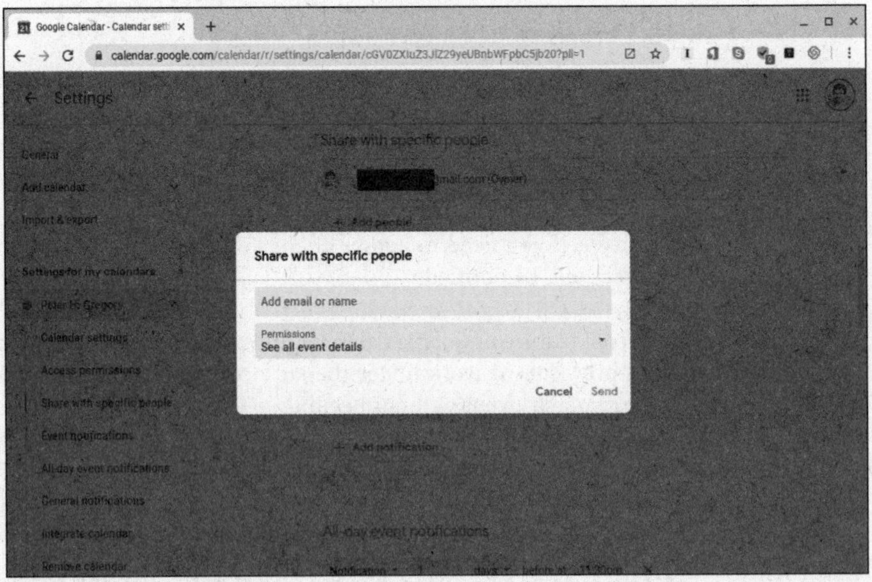

FIGURE 6-27: Sharing your calendar with specific people.

8. **Open the Permission Settings drop-down list.**

The following options are revealed:

- **See Only Free/Busy (Hide Other Details):** Allows others to see only your events and whether you're free or busy, but does not reveal any other event details.

- **See All Event Details:** Allows others to see your events but not make changes.

- **Make Changes to Events:** Allows others to view and make changes to your events only.

- **Make Changes AND Manage Sharing:** Allows others to make changes to your calendar and invites others to access your calendar.

9. **Select the desired permission setting and click Send.**

You can un-share your calendars by following the preceding Steps 1 through 7 and then clicking the *X* to the right of the person you want to delete.

If you have a calendar that you would like to make public — that is, so that the *entire world* can view it — follow these steps:

1. **In the left sidebar, open the My Calendars collapsible menu.**

All your calendars are displayed.

2. **Move your pointer over the desired calendar.**

A Settings icon appears to the right of the calendar name appears.

3. **Click the Settings icon.**

A menu appears, revealing multiple options.

4. **Click Settings and Sharing.**

The Calendar settings details load.

5. **Click Access Permissions.**

6. **Select the Make Available to Public check box.**

Your calendar is publicly accessible and completely visible in Google Search.

You can also link people to your calendar so that they can navigate to it and book-mark it. Locate the link by following these steps:

1. **In the left sidebar, open the My Calendars collapsible menu.**

All of your calendars appear.

2. **Move your pointer over the desired calendar.**

A Settings icon appears to the right of the calendar name.

3. **Click the Settings icon.**

A menu appears, revealing multiple options.

4. **Click Settings and Sharing.**

The Calendar settings details load.

5. **Click Access Permissions.**

6. **Click Get Shareable Link.**

A shareable link window appears, as shown in Figure 6-28, containing your calendar's web address (URL). Click on Copy Link and paste it wherever you wish to share it.

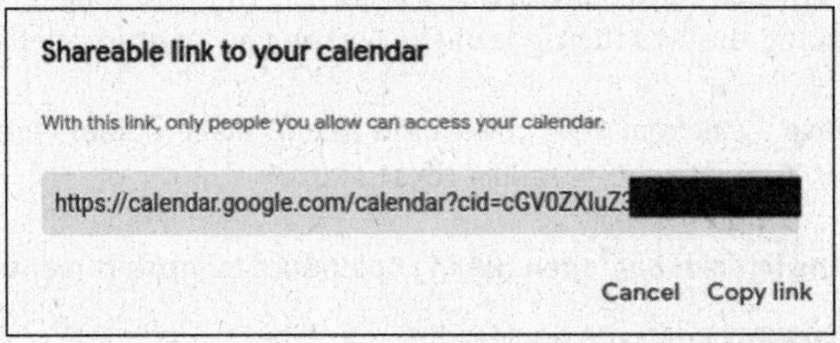

FIGURE 6-28: Your calendar has a publicly reachable URL.

Shareable link to your calendar

With this link, only people you allow can access your calendar.

https://calendar.google.com/calendar?cid=cGV0ZXIuZ3

Cancel   Copy link

Chapter **7**

Finding Your Files

A lthough you might not install many applications on the Chromebook itself, you will likely have a need for some storage. For instance, you might want to download a file attachment from an email, or take a screen shot or capture some video footage or stills with your Chromebook's camera. You need not only storage space for these files but also a way to gain access to them.

If you want to manage files on your Windows PC, you use Windows Explorer. If you use a Mac, you turn to the Finder. On a Chromebook, you use an app called Files. In this chapter, you learn how to navigate your Chromebook file system, how to add and use external storage, and how to set up and use Google Drive. Although you can consider the Chrome browser to be the gateway to the world of the Internet, Files is the gateway to your own content, wherever it may be on your Chromebook or in Google Drive.

Finding Files with the Files App

To launch Files, follow these steps:

1. **Click the Launcher icon in the bottom-left corner of your screen.**

The Launcher opens.

2. Locate the app icon for Files and click it.

Files opens in a new window. Note that the Files app runs separately from your Chrome browser. You'll see a separate icon on the Shelf just for Files.

Navigating Files

Figure 7-1 shows the open Files app window. On the left side of the window is a listing of storage locations. At first, you'll only have two options here:

» **Downloads:** Your Downloads folder is your hard drive (also referred to as *local storage*).

» **Google Drive:** This is Internet-based storage (also referred to as *cloud storage*). I discuss Google Drive in the section "Working with Google Drive," later in this chapter.

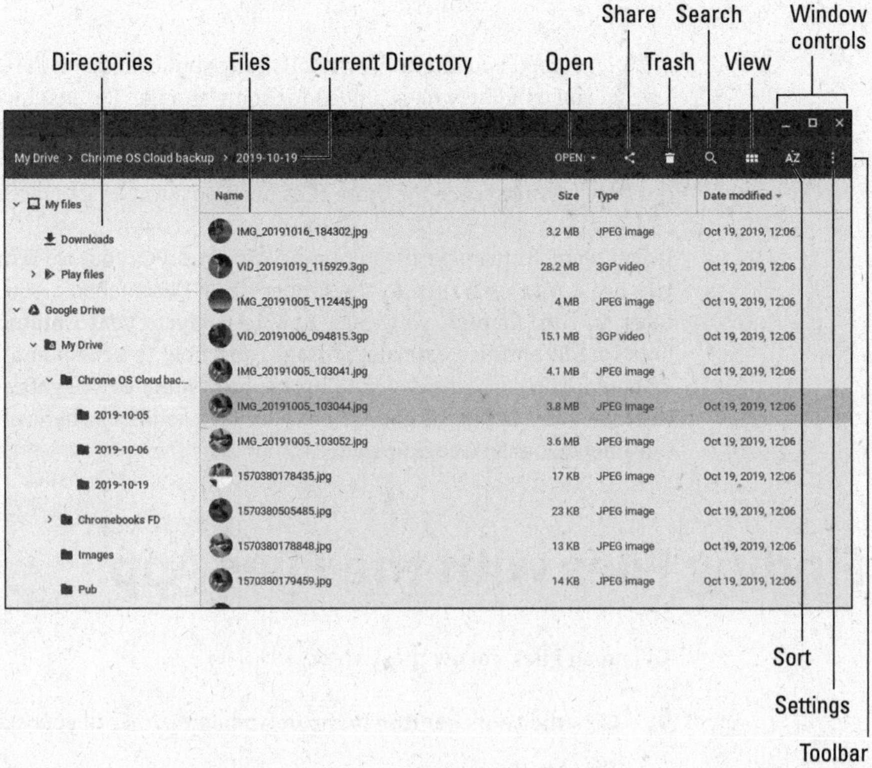

FIGURE 7-1:
Use the Chromebook Files app to access and manage files.

The toolbar spans the top of the Files app window. In the toolbar, you find the following:

>> Open button

>> Share

>> Trash can

>> Search

>> View button

>> Sort button

>> Settings button

>> Window controls

Click Settings to open the File Settings menu, as shown in Figure 7-2.

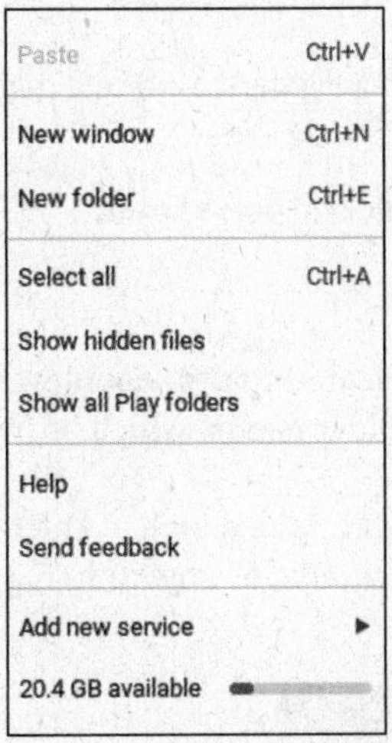

Paste	Ctrl+V
New window	Ctrl+N
New folder	Ctrl+E
Select all	Ctrl+A
Show hidden files	
Show all Play folders	
Help	
Send feedback	
Add new service	▶
20.4 GB available	

FIGURE 7-2:
The File Settings menu.

In this menu, you have the option to launch another Files window, create a new subfolder within the open folder, select all the files currently shown (presumably for some subsequent action), show hidden files, show Google Play files, get help, send feedback to Google, and add a new service.

REMEMBER

At the bottom of the Settings menu, a meter shows your available storage. This information is critical because your Chromebook does not offer much storage, so you want to periodically check to make sure you don't run out. Pictures, screen-shots, music, downloads, and the like add up the more you use your Chromebook, so beware! You can see the storage meter at the bottom of Figure 7-2. Never fear: You'll be storing most of your content in Google Drive, which I discuss later in this chapter, in "Working with Google Drive."

Beneath the Files toolbar is the file browser. This is where you can view, edit, move, or otherwise interact with your files.

Creating and navigating folders

Folders are helpful for organizing and sorting your files so that you can easily find them later. Create a new folder using the following steps. (In this example, you create a subfolder within the Downloads folder.)

1. **On the left side of the Files window, select the Downloads folder.**

2. **Click Settings in the top-right corner of the window.**

   The File Settings menu appears.

3. **Click New Folder.**

   A new folder appears with the name highlighted to indicate that it can be edited. Until you rename it, its name is "New folder."

4. **Type the desired name for the folder and press Enter.**

   The new folder name is saved.

If you would like to open your newly created folder, double-click or double-tap the new folder icon. A window for the folder opens, which at first will be empty.

While you are in your newly created folder, take a look at the top of the Files app window. You can see your *path*, or *breadcrumbs*, as shown in Figure 7-3.

FIGURE 7-3:
Following the Files breadcrumbs.

My files > Downloads > Test folder

TECHNICAL STUFF

On your Chromebook, folders are divided into *parent folders* and *child folders*. A parent folder contains a child folder or folders. In the path, the parent folder appears to the left of a child folder.

To return to the parent folder, click the parent folder's name in the path. In this case, doing so would take you back to the Downloads folder, which is the parent folder.

You can also click the folder name in the breadcrumbs to go to a folder.

If you need to make several folders, constantly clicking on Settings can get tedious. To create a folder quickly, you can type Ctrl+E. You can also rename a folder by following these steps:

1. **Click the desired folder.**

2. **Press Ctrl+E.**

   The folder name becomes editable.

3. **Type the newly desired name and press Enter.**

Moving files and folders

Use Files to move and otherwise organize your files. Creating several folders to group your files together and keep things in order is useful as you download and store files in your Chromebook's internal storage. You can move files and folders by following these steps:

1. **Click the Launcher icon in the bottom-left corner of your screen.**

   The Launcher appears.

2. **Locate the Files icon and click it.**

   Files opens in a new window.

3. **Click and hold the file that you want to move; then drag the file to the desired folder. (See Figure 7-4.)**

   When using the touchpad, after clicking and holding the file, use another finger to drag the file to the desired folder.

   Hovering the file over the folder highlights the folder.

4. **Release to drop the file into the target folder.**

To move multiple files and folders at one time, you can do so using the following steps:

1. **From within the Files application window, hold the Ctrl key and click the desired files.**

   The files you click are all highlighted. Each selected file's icon is replaced by a check mark, indicating that it has been selected. You can Ctrl+click a file again to deselect it.

My files > Downloads

Name	Size	Types	Date modified ⌄
📁 Chapter 6	—	Folder	Today 08:06
Fig 6-3.png	6 KB	PNG image	Today 07:59
Fig 6-2.png	618 KB	PNG image	Today 07:29
Fig 6	534 KB	PNG image	Today 07:22
Scree... 07-14 at 06.23.18.png	558 KB	PNG image	Today 06:23
Fig 5-9.png	280 KB	PNG image	Yesterday 07:22
Fig 5-8.png	492 KB	PNG image	Yesterday 07:16
Screenshot 2019-07-13 at 06.56.15.png	655 KB	PNG image	Yesterday 06:56
Fig 5-7.png	629 KB	PNG image	Yesterday 06:53
Screenshot 2019-07-11 at 04.32.00.png	321 KB	PNG image	11 Jul 2019, 04:32
Screenshot 2019-07-11 at 04.26.03.png	348 KB	PNG image	11 Jul 2019, 04:26
Screenshot 2019-07-11 at 04.25.47.png	308 KB	PNG image	11 Jul 2019, 04:25

Recent · Audio · Images · Videos · My files · Downloads · Chapter 6 · Play files · Google Drive

FIGURE 7-4:
Dragging a file to a new location.

2. **Click and hold any part of your selection; then, without releasing, drag the selection to the desired location.**

   Hovering the files over the destination folder highlights the folder.

3. **Release to drop the files into the target folder.**

To select an entire collection of files, follow these steps:

1. **Hold down the Shift key and then click with one finger or thumb and move the pointer with another finger to highlight several consecutive files at one time.**

2. **Click any part of your selection; then, without releasing, drag the selection to the desired location.**

   Holding the files over the destination folder highlights the folder, indicating that it is okay to release your finger from the touchpad.

3. **Release to drop the files into the target folder.**

REMEMBER

Don't be discouraged if selecting, dragging, and dropping doesn't work exactly right the first time. It takes a bit of coordination, like shifting gears on a manual transmission car (okay, maybe not *that* tricky). But with a bit of practice, it will soon become second nature.

Searching for files

If you want to search for a specific file, you can do so by following these steps:

1. **Click the magnifying glass icon on the far right of your Files toolbar.**

A cursor appears in the Search bar.

2. **Type in the word or words that are in the name of the file you desire.**

As you type, Chrome displays all files that fit your search term.

Deleting files and folders

Deleting files and folders can be accomplished with the following steps:

1. **Click the Launcher icon in the bottom-left corner.**

The Launcher appears.

2. **Locate the Files icon and click it.**

Files opens in a new window.

3. **Select the file that you want to delete by clicking or tapping the file once.**

4. **Click the trash can icon located in the toolbar of the Files app window.**

5. **When Chrome asks "Are you sure that you want to delete . . .?" click Delete to delete the file, or Cancel if you've changed your mind.**

REMEMBER

After you click the trash can icon, your file is gone forever. That's right. Unlike with Windows and Macs, which let you change your mind and get things out of the trash, the Chromebook allows no opportunity to change your mind. When you delete an item, it evaporates into the ether. Forever.

WARNING

Make sure you really don't need a file any longer before you delete it.

You can delete multiple files and folders: First, select them by holding down the Ctrl key and clicking the files (or tapping the files with your touchpad). Then press the trash can icon in the lower-right of the Files app window to delete all the selected files at one time. If your files are all in a row, you can select them more easily by pressing Shift+click and then moving the cursor to select the desired files.

Adding and Using External Storage

External storage in the form of a thumb drive (also known as a USB stick or jump drive), an external hard drive, or an SD card can easily be used on a Chromebook. You may have a number of reasons for using external storage, including to

>> Transfer pictures or video from a dashcam, GoPro, or digital camera

>> Copy pictures to a thumb drive or external hard drive to share with some-one else

>> Back up data to an external hard drive that you don't want to save to the cloud

If your jump drive or external hard drive has a USB connection, simply plug it into one of your available USB ports on your Chromebook. If your Chromebook has an available SD card slot, insert your card. Chromebook automatically detects your storage devices and makes them available to browse within Files, as shown in Figure 7-5.

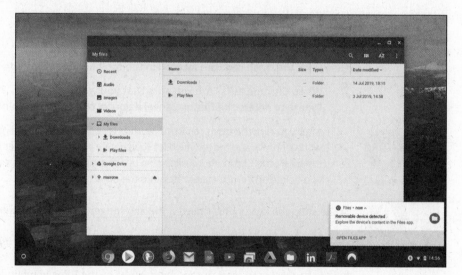

FIGURE 7-5:
Accessing external storage.

To navigate to your external storage, first select it on the left side of the Files window and then follow the directions outlined in the section "Creating and navigating folders," earlier in this chapter. Click and drag files or folders to the desired location. If you want to move them to your Chromebook hard drive, just drag them to the Downloads folder that appears under Files on the left side of the Files window. Hover over the Downloads folder long enough to open the folder and then drop the files or folders on the right side of the Files window.

To remove your external storage devices, you should click the Eject button, which is located next to the device name on the left side of the Files window. (Refer to Figure 7-5.) After you've clicked the Eject button, the device vanishes from your Files window, indicating that it is safe to remove from your Chromebook.

WARNING

If you do not click the Eject button before removing external storage, you take the chance of corrupting the data on the external storage device. If such a case, you might not be able to read data on the device.

Working with Google Drive

Google Drive (or just Drive) is Google's cloud-based storage service. *Cloud-based storage* is really just a fancy way of saying "your hard drive on the Internet." Users can create a Drive account at no cost and receive 15GB of storage space. Drive comes with every Chromebook, but you can also install the Google Drive app on your smartphone or on another computer like a Mac or a Windows PC. You can also access Google Drive from any web browser where you can add, change, or remove any of your files. Anything you put in your Drive folder is then be synced across all your devices. Pretty awesome, right?

As a Google account user, Google gives you access to Google Drive. Google has had a long-standing record of offering additional space on Google Drive at little or no cost. As of late 2019, Google was providing new Chromebook owners with a free one-year membership to Google One, which includes 100GB of free storage space for a year. That's a great value, because other companies charge a few dollars each month for that much storage. To take advantage of that discount, you need to first set up your Google Drive account. Read on.

Creating a Google Drive account

Account registration is required to use Google Drive. Registration protects your data so that only you can access it. The good news is that Drive access comes with every Google Account. You don't have to actually re-register to gain access to Drive from your Chromebook; however, if you want to take advantage of any free Google Drive upgrades or other offers that are made available to new Chromebook users, follow these steps:

1. **Click the Launcher icon in the bottom-left corner of your screen.**

   The Launcher opens.

2. **Locate the Chrome web browser icon and click it.**

   The Chrome web browser launches.

3. **In the Omnibox, enter the URL** www.google.com/chromebook/offers **and press Enter.**

4. **Read the page and find any offers that might be available; then click the Redeem Offer button.**

   You may be required to validate your eligibility.

5. **Click OK to allow Google to validate your eligibility.**

Figure 7-6 depicts an offer available in 2019.

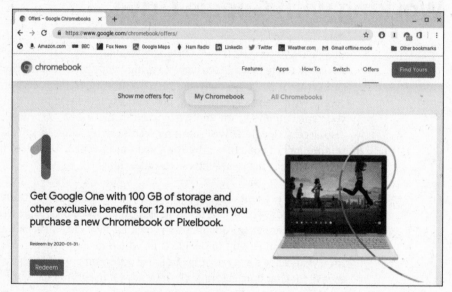

FIGURE 7-6:
Google often has promotions for new Chromebook users.

REMEMBER

After being approved, you may have additional Google Drive storage for free. The terms of any offer are specific to your particular device and any promotions that may be active when you purchase your Chromebook. Make sure you understand what the terms are by reading the documentation that came with your Chromebook.

Using Google Drive

You have a few different ways to use Google Drive. Google Drive has a web interface that you can access from any Internet-enabled device like a smartphone, tablet, PC, or Mac. To access the Drive web interface from your Chromebook, follow these steps:

1. **Click the Launcher icon in the lower-left side of your screen.**

   The Launcher appears.

2. **Locate the Chrome web browser icon and click it.**

   The Chrome web browser launches.

3. **In the Omnibox, enter the web address** `https://drive.google.com` **and press Enter.**

   You are directed to your Drive web interface, and you'll already be logged in thanks to Chromebook.

As you can see in Figure 7-7, the Google Drive web interface and Files on your Chromebook are somewhat dissimilar in appearance but similar in function.

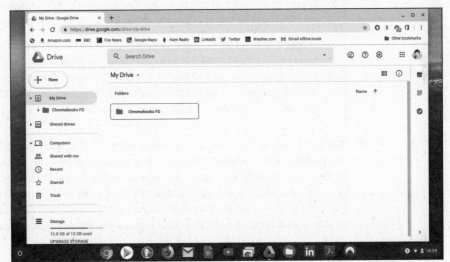

FIGURE 7-7:
The Google Drive web interface.

On the left side of the Drive interface, you have several options:

>> **My Drive:** This is your main Drive folder where you store all your files.

>> **Shared Drives:** These are directories in Google Drives that someone else has shared with you. If no one has shared a Google Drive with you, this will be empty or not appear at all.

>> **Computers:** This is a list of computers that are syncing their contents to Google Drive. If you have not set up any computers to sync with Google Drive, this will be empty.

>> **Shared With Me:** This folder contains all files and folders shared with you by other Drive users. Google Drive is a great tool for collaboration because it

simplifies sharing documents and managing versions of documents. When you work on a document, Drive updates the document for everyone who has access to it.

>> **Recent:** Documents that have been created, edited, or otherwise utilized recently appear in this folder. As your Drive gets more and more use, the Recent folder becomes increasingly useful because it allows you to quickly access files and folders that you use frequently, thus saving time looking for them.

>> **Starred:** You can "star" documents and folders in Drive to indicate them as important. Starred files and folders show up in the Starred folder.

>> **Trash:** Whenever you delete a file (or when a file is deleted automatically), that file is stored in the Trash folder before being removed permanently.

>> **Storage:** Beneath the options, you see a little graph that shows the total amount of storage available as well as how much you have used. Figure 7-7 shows that I have used 10.8GB out of the 15GB available storage. I took that screen shot before taking advantage of the free upgrade to 100GB that I discuss earlier in this section.

The right side of the Google Drive web interface is broken into two key parts. The top portion of the screen contains a Search bar that you can use to search for files by keyword. Next to the Search bar is the Settings area, which contains some buttons for customizing the appearance of your Drive, as well as a widget for accessing your Drive settings. You also find a button to launch Google apps, and your profile photo appears here, too, which gives you a quick link to your Google profile.

Directly below the Search bar, the My Drive label has a built-in menu that lets you create a folder, upload files, upload a folder, and open any of several Google apps. To the right of this menu, you can change how your files and folders are displayed. To the right of that, a lowercase letter *i* in a circle lets you view details about your contents.

Directly below the My Drive bar is your main work area. As you add files and folders, they populate this space.

Uploading files to Google Drive

Transitioning from a Mac or PC to your new Chromebook requires you to migrate your files to Google Drive. Use Google Drive for your file storage so that you can quickly access those files on your Chromebook anywhere you have an Internet connection. You have a few different ways to upload files to your Google Drive. Use the steps in the following sections to upload your files from your Mac or PC to your Google Drive.

Uploading files to Google Drive from a Mac, PC, or Linux system

If you are transitioning to a Chromebook from a Mac, PC, or Linux system, you can do so using the browser. Or you can install a Google Drive app on your Mac or PC and use the Google Drive app to migrate your files. If you want to use the Google Drive app, skip to the upcoming Mac or Windows sections. To use your browser instead, follow these steps:

1. **Launch your web browser on your Mac, PC, or Linux system.**

2. **In the navigation bar, enter the following URL and press Enter:** `https://drive.google.com`.

   Google Drive's website loads.

3. **Log in using your Google username and password — the same that you use to log in to your Chromebook.**

   You are taken to your Google Drive.

4. **Click the Upload button on the left side of the screen.**

   The Upload button is located next to the Create button.

   A menu appears, giving you the ability to select files for upload. (See Figure 7-8.)

5. **Select the files you want to upload to Drive and then click Open.**

   Drive begins uploading the files immediately. When uploading has completed, you can access your files from your Chromebook or any other device when you log in to Google Drive.

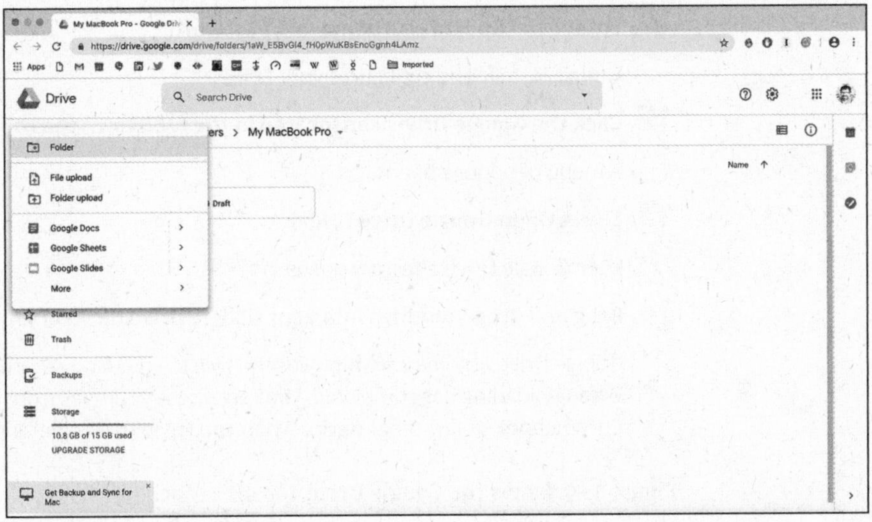

FIGURE 7-8:
Uploading files to Google Drive from a Mac using a browser.

Uploading files to Drive from your Mac with the Drive app

In this section, you are migrating your files on your Mac to Google Drive by using the Google Drive for Mac app. Proceed by following these steps:

1. **Open Safari or other web browser.**

2. **In the navigation bar, enter the following URL and press Enter:** `https://drive.google.com`

   Google Drive's website loads.

3. **Click Settings in the top-right corner of the screen.**

4. **Click Get Backup and Sync for Mac.**

5. **Click Download under Personal.**

   A window containing the Terms of Use loads.

6. **Read and accept the Terms of Use by clicking Agree and Download.**

   The application downloads.

7. **Navigate to your Download folder with Finder.**

8. **Click the InstallBackupAndSync.dmg file.**

   An Install window appears.

9. **In the Install window, click and drag the Google Drive logo to the Applications folder.**

10. **Follow the prompts until you are asked to enter your username and password.**

11. **Enter your Google username and password.**

    Google installs and configures your Drive.

12. **Click the Google Drive icon located in the toolbar at the top of your screen.**

    A menu of options opens.

13. **Select Open Google Drive Folder.**

    Your Google Drive directory opens.

14. **Drag and drop your files into your Google Drive directory.**

    Google Drive automatically uploads the files to your Google Drive account. When uploading has completed, you can access your files from your Chromebook or any other device when you log in to Google Drive.

Figure 7-9 shows the Google Drive app on a Mac.

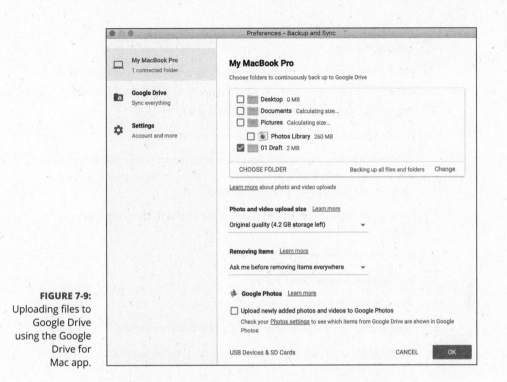

FIGURE 7-9:
Uploading files to
Google Drive
using the Google
Drive for
Mac app.

Uploading files to Drive from your PC with the Drive app

In this section, you are migrating your files on your Mac to Google Drive by using the Google Drive for Windows app. Proceed by following these steps:

1. **Open your favorite web browser on your PC.**

2. **In the navigation bar, enter the following URL and press Enter:** `https://drive.google.com`.

    Google Drive's website loads.

3. **Click Settings in the top-right corner of the screen.**

4. **Click Get Backup and Sync for Windows.**

5. **Click Download under Personal.**

    A window containing the Terms of Use loads.

6. **Read and accept the Terms of Use by clicking Agree and Download.**

    The application downloads.

7. **Install the app on your computer.**

8. Launch the app.

9. Follow the prompts until you are asked to enter your username and password.

10. Enter your Google username and password.

Google finishes installing and configuring your Drive.

You might need to sign in with the Chrome browser on your PC before you can sign in to Google Backup and Sync. If this is the case, open your Chrome browser and log in to your Google account.

11. Click the Google Drive icon in the toolbar at the bottom right of your screen.

A menu of options appears.

12. Select Open Google Drive Folder.

Your Google Drive directory opens.

13. Drag and drop your files into your Google Drive directory.

Google Drive automatically uploads the files to your Google Drive account.

Figure 7-10 shows the Google Drive for Windows app.

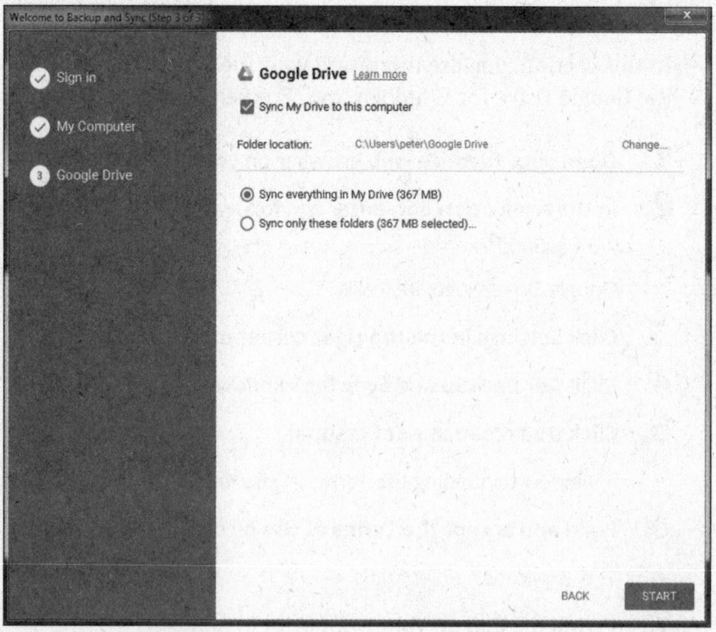

FIGURE 7-10:
Setting up Google Drive using the Google Drive for Windows app.

Using Google Drive with Your Smartphone or Tablet

Google Drive is also available on Android and Apple smartphones and tablets. For Android, go to the Google Play store and install Google Drive if it's not already installed. For Apple devices, go to the App Store and install Google Drive.

On either platform, after you log in to Google Drive, you have access to all the files you've stored there. But it goes beyond access: You can create directories, add files, and even update files. Figure 7-11 shows Google Drive on an Apple iPhone 8.

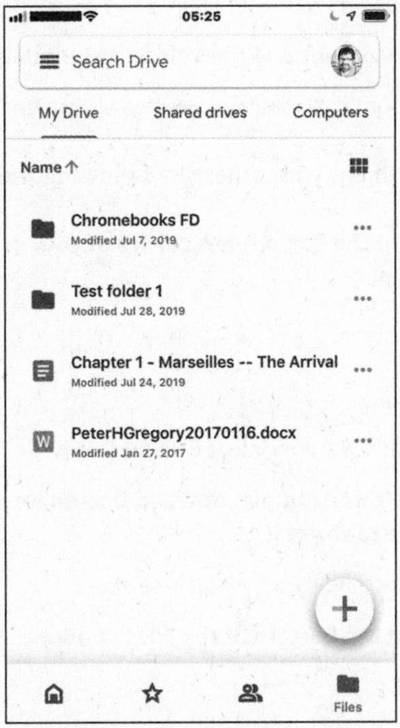

FIGURE 7-11: Google Drive on an Apple iPhone 8.

Collaborating with Drive

Google Drive makes sharing your work with others easy so that you can collaborate. Drive manages changes and controls versions so that your team is always working on the most current version of documents and worksheets. Before you can collaborate, you need a document, slide, or spreadsheet in your Drive folder.

If you do not have one of these file types in your Drive folder, create a sample Docs file by following these steps:

1. **Click the Launcher icon in the bottom-left corner of your screen.**

   The Launcher appears.

2. **Click the Docs icon.**

   Google Docs loads in a Chrome browser window.

3. **Click the colorful + (plus sign) in the lower-right corner of the Docs window to create a new document.**

   A new, blank document appears.

4. **Type some text in the document and then close the window.**

   The file now appears in your Drive folder as Untitled Document.

Now you can share your document with others by following these steps:

1. **Click the Launcher icon in the bottom-left corner of your screen.**

   The Launcher appears.

2. **Click the Files app icon.**

   Files load in a window.

3. **On the left side of the Files window, click Google Drive.**

4. **Locate the document (in this example, Untitled Document) that you want to share and click it once to select it.**

   The document is highlighted, indicating that it is selected.

5. **Click the Share button at the bottom of the Files window.**

   The Share window opens.

6. **At the bottom of the window in the Invite People box, enter the email address for each person you want to invite for collaboration. (See Figure 7-12.)**

7. **Click Done.**

   Everyone you invited receives an email with an invitation to collaborate. Upon clicking the link, each collaborator can access your file in her Drive folder. Any changes made by any of the collaborators will be reflected immediately in everyone's Drive folders.

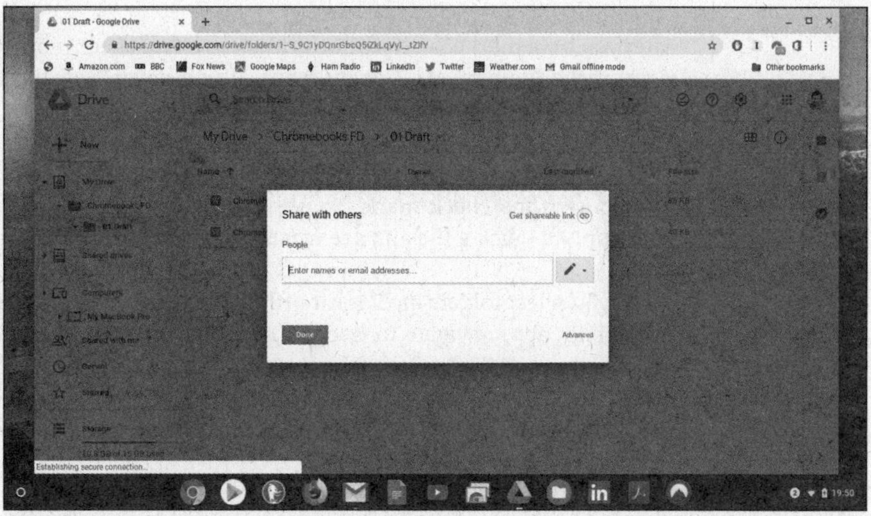

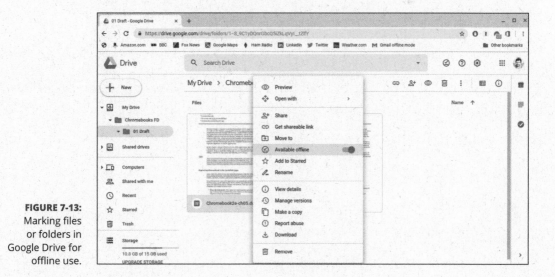

FIGURE 7-12:
Sharing a
document in
Google Drive.

Using Google Drive offline

Even though a Chromebook is designed for Internet access, you can't be online all
the time. If you want, you can tag a file or a directory as being available even when
you are not connected to the Internet. To configure a folder or file for offline use,
right-click or Alt-click the folder or file and change the Available Offline selector.
Figure 7-13 shows this selector.

FIGURE 7-13:
Marking files
or folders in
Google Drive for
offline use.

After you have marked a file for offline use, a small check mark icon appears to the right of the file name in Google Drive. If you hover over the icon, the message "Available Offline" appears.

TIP

The Google Drive app shows which files are available offline with the little Available Offline check mark. To see which files are available offline using the Files app, Alt-click a file and see whether the Available Offline option is selected.

When you select folders or files for offline use, you access them with the Files app. In the Files app, navigate to Google Drive and then to the file(s) or folder(s) you selected, as described previously. Here you will find synched copies of these files. You can edit these files while offline. When you are back online, the changes you made are synched with Google Drive and are available from all your devices.

2

Harnessing Business Power with the Chromebook

Chapter **8**

Writing with Word Processing

The Chromebook is not just for fun and games. It is a powerful tool for students and business users alike — even published authors! However, what makes the Chromebook powerful is not the hardware; it's the unrestricted access to — and complete integration with — the Google platform.

One key component of the Google platform is its web-based office tools. The name often used to describe the entire suite of these tools, however informally, is *Google Docs*. However, this name can be confusing: *Docs* is also the official name of Google's web-based word processing tool within that suite. For the purposes of this book, then, when I refer to Google Docs, I'm referring to Google's word processor.

Docs is a powerful word processor that offers an extensive amount of functionality. The goal of this chapter is not to dive into every nook and cranny of the Docs application – which would fill an entire book. Instead, I just cover the basics. By the end of this chapter, you should be able to open and create documents; write, format, and otherwise manipulate text; and save, export, and share your documents with anyone across the web for collaboration. This chapter describes the steps used to create documents such as resumes, recipes, and flyers. If this capability is interesting to you, read on!

Navigating Google Docs

Docs is Google's answer to Microsoft Word. If you've had any experience working with Word on a Mac or PC, you will find the interface quite similar. If you're using a word processor for the first time, don't worry: Docs is extremely intuitive. To get started, launch Google Docs by clicking the Docs icon in the Launcher. The Docs application opens in a Chrome browser window and creates a new, untitled document. Have a look at Figure 8-1.

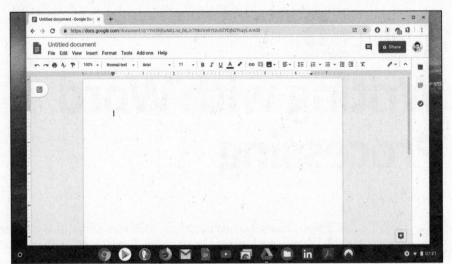

FIGURE 8-1:
Google Docs.

TIP

If you *really* want to (or must) use Microsoft Word, you can, by using Office 365, which works on your Chromebook. If this is you, skip over to Chapter 11, which talks about using Office 365 on a Chromebook.

TECHNICAL STUFF

Instead of displaying a new, empty document, *Docs* might instead show you a list of documents you have worked on before. When this is the case, and you want to start on a new document, press the + (plus sign) button near the lower-right corner of the Docs window.

Surveying the Docs workspace

The Docs workspace is broken into two main areas: The menu area and the main document area. The menu area, by default, is composed of the Applications menu and the Edit toolbar, as shown in Figure 8-2.

Menu area   Application menu   Edit toolbar

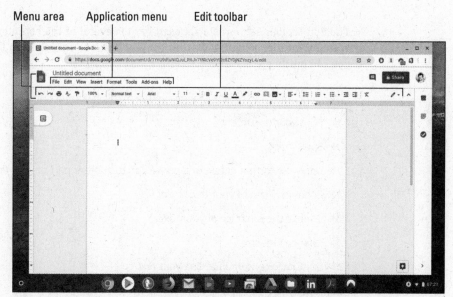

FIGURE 8-2:
The Docs
Applications
menu and Edit
toolbars.

The Applications menu contains a standard set of application-specific control options, including

>> **File:** File-specific options and controls for creating, saving, exporting, printing, setting up your page, and otherwise managing your documents at the file level.

>> **Edit:** Copy, paste, delete, and otherwise move and manipulate text. Also used to find specific text in your document.

>> **View:** Modify your Docs view by adding and removing toolbars, or change the layout of the main document area.

>> **Insert:** Add files, images, symbols, charts, headers, footers, links, and more.

>> **Format:** Manipulate the appearance of your text, including font, size, and features like underline, bold, and strikethrough, as well as the format of paragraphs (indent, spacing, and so on).

>> **Tools:** Spell check, translate text, determine word count, or define specific text.

>> **Add-Ons:** Add software plug-ins to change your Docs experience.

>> **Help:** Get help with Docs, search for menu options, and more.

The Edit toolbar serves as a shortcut bar to several of the common Edit, File, and Format features contained within the Applications menu. With the Edit toolbar, you can quickly

>> Undo and redo recent changes you've made in your document

>> Print your document

>> Spell check

>> Apply the format of text or a paragraph to another part of your document

>> Zoom in or out of your document

>> Change the font face of your text

>> Change font size

>> Bold, italicize, and underline your text

>> Add hyperlinks

>> Insert images into your document

>> Align text

>> Change line spacing

>> Add and edit bullets and numbering

>> Set indentations

>> Adjust paragraph styles

>> Change basic edit modes (edit, suggesting changes, or read only)

Changing your view

Before you begin to type your document, you might find changing your view in Google Docs helpful. One way you can change your view is to hide the Applications menu. Just click the little up arrow at the far right side of the toolbar. (When you hover over that arrow, it reads "Hide the menus".) When you click the up arrow, the Applications menu disappears from sight, as shown in Figure 8-3.

To restore the Applications menu, click the icon that looks like a *V*, located on the far right side of the Edit toolbar.

TIP

You can also use the keyboard shortcut Shift+Ctrl+F to hide and reveal the Applications menu.

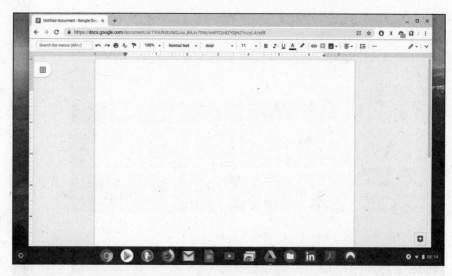

FIGURE 8-3:
Hide the
Applications
menu to make
more room for
your content.

If you're the type of person who likes to remove clutter from sight before you begin working, you might like to hide the ruler, and maybe even put Docs into Full–Screen mode. Full–Screen mode hides everything but the main document area. You can turn on Full–Screen mode by following these steps:

1. **Click View in the Applications menu.**

2. **In the View menu that appears, click Show Ruler.**

   The check mark next to Show Ruler disappears, and the View menu closes.

3. **Again, click View to open the View menu.**

4. **Choose Full Screen.**

   Docs goes into Full-Screen mode. A message appears to remind you that pressing the Esc key leaves Full-Screen mode.

5. **Exit Full-Screen mode by pressing Esc.**

TIP

If you want to eliminate all distractions, put your browser into Full–Screen mode by pressing the Full–Screen shortcut key located four keys to the right of Esc. (See Figure 8-4.) This key also maximizes the size of the Docs window if it wasn't already maximized.

Full-Screen Key

Working with Text

By default, when you open Docs, your cursor is placed in the main document area. This placement is helpful if you want to begin typing text immediately because you don't have to click in the workspace to begin. The blinking cursor (the small vertical line flashing off and on) indicates that you are ready to type. If you do not have a blinking cursor in the main document area, move your pointer anywhere over the main document area and click.

Begin typing a couple sentences or a paragraph of text. As you type, the cursor moves to the right, leaving characters to the left of the cursor. Google Docs is by default *left-justified,* meaning that all text is aligned to the left. As you approach the end of a line, the cursor automatically moves to the next line. If you are typing a word that does not fit on the line, Docs automatically moves the word to the next line.

When you are finished typing a paragraph, press Enter to start a new paragraph. If you are following any sort of paragraph style, you may need to hit Enter twice to space out your paragraphs.

Moving around your document

As you write your document, you may find that you want to make edits to your text. You can move around your document in a number of different ways. To start, take a look at the arrow keys on your keyboard. (See Figure 8-5.)

You can move your cursor by using the arrow keys to navigate to different places in your document. Press and hold the left arrow key to move the cursor leftward until it reaches the left end (left margin) of your line. After you've hit the beginning of the line on the left side, keep pressing the left arrow key, and you will notice your cursor go to the right side of the line above. Conversely, pressing the right arrow key moves the cursor rightward along the line. As you approach the right margin of the line, keep pressing the arrow key to go to the left margin of the next line down. You can also move around the document by using the up and down arrow keys to quickly move to lines above or below the current line, respectively.

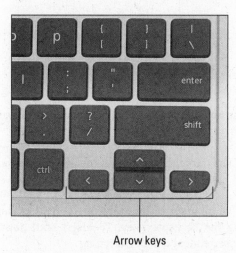

FIGURE 8-5:
The Arrow keys
on your
keyboard.

Arrow keys

You can also navigate your document by using your touchpad or mouse to move the cursor directly to the desired location. Click once to move the cursor and then begin editing using your keyboard. In the event that you have several pages of text, you can quickly navigate to various pages by following these steps:

1. **Place two fingers on your touchpad and swipe up or down.**

   If your touchpad is configured to traditionally scroll, swiping up scrolls the document up so that you can see previous pages. Swiping down scrolls you down in the document to later pages.

   If your touchpad is configured to Australian scroll, swiping up scrolls your document down to later pages. Conversely, swiping down scrolls your document up to earlier pages.

   Using your touchpad with a two-finger swipe scrolls you to the page that contains the text you would like to edit.

2. **Using one finger on your touchpad, relocate the pointer to the location of the word or words you would like to edit.**

3. **Click your touchpad.**

   Your cursor appears at the location of your pointer.

If you have a touchscreen Chromebook, move around by following these steps:

1. **Place your finger on the screen on the middle of the page and then scroll up and down by holding your finger on the screen and moving it up and down.**

2. **Tap your finger any place in the text in your document.**

   Tapping moves the cursor to this location. If you begin typing, your text will appear here.

3. **Hold two fingers on the screen on the document and slowly spread your fingers apart.**

   Spreading your fingers apart "zooms in," magnifying the text on the screen. Try it and see how far you can zoom in.

4. **To zoom back out, hold two fingers on the screen on the document and slowly bring them together.**

You can alternatively use the touchscreen and the arrow keys to move around in the document.

TIP

To delete text, move your cursor to the right of the text so that you can easily remove it by pressing the Backspace key. To insert text, position your cursor where you want the inserted text and begin typing.

You can also use a feature called Find and Replace to find a specific piece of text within your document. To find text using the Find and Replace feature, follow these steps:

1. **Click Edit in the Applications menu.**

2. **In the Edit menu that appears, choose Find and Replace.**

   The Find and replace window appears, containing multiple inputs:

   - **Find:** Enter the text you want to find.

   - **Replace:** If you want to replace the text for which you are searching, simply enter the replacement text in this text box.

   - **Match Case:** Select this check box to search for text that has the same capitalization as you typed in the Find box.

3. **Enter the text you want to locate in the Find text box.**

   As you type text in the Find text box, Docs highlights words in your document that match your search entry.

You can also quickly find text in your document by typing Ctrl+F. Doing so opens the search bar, where you can search for text in your document.

Google Docs treats blank spaces as characters. If you're looking for a particular word that's not immediately followed by punctuation, place a space after your search term to reduce the number of unneeded results. For example, if you want to find the word *pass* and your search shows you other words like *password,* type **pass** followed by a space.

4. **Sort through search results by clicking the Next or Previous buttons located in the bottom right of the Find and Replace window.**

As you navigate to the matched words in your document, Docs changes the color of the highlighted word to indicate where you are in the document.

5. **When you successfully locate the word or words in your document, close the Find and Replace window by clicking the X in the top-right corner (not the main browser window!).**

The Find and Replace window disappears, leaving your desired word highlighted and ready to be deleted or otherwise edited.

Copying and pasting text

As you create documents, you can avoid typing repetitive text by using the Copy and Paste functions. You can do copying and pasting in several ways — on the keyboard, with the touchpad, and with menu commands.

Larger documents that contain several thousand words over numerous pages may be too large to effectively navigate with just your keyboard. Your touchpad will come in handy with these documents because you can quickly locate, select, copy, and paste text.

To copy and paste text, follow these steps:

1. **Using your touchpad, move your cursor to the text you want to copy.**

You may need to scroll to a different page. To do so, you can

- Place two fingers on your touchpad and swipe up or down to scroll to a different page within your document.

- Place one finger on the scroll bar and move your pointer to the vertical scroll bar located on the right side of the screen. Click anywhere on the bar to quickly scroll to a different page. Or, on the bar itself, click and drag your cursor up or down to scroll to different pages.

2. **Click and drag your cursor over the section of text you want to copy. When all the desired text is selected, release the click.**

A highlighter follows your pointer as you drag it across the text.

You can select text using the keyboard by using the arrow keys while holding the Shift key. Go character by character by using the left or right arrow keys. Select entire lines by using the up and right arrow keys at the same time.

3. **In the Docs menu, click Edit and then click Copy.**

Alternatively, press and hold the Alt key and click the highlighted text. A menu appears in which you can choose Copy, as shown in Figure 8-6.

The selected text is copied to your Clipboard.

The Clipboard is a temporary place where text you copy resides. When you copy or cut, that text resides in the clipboard. When you paste, text in the Clipboard is inserted into your document. The Clipboard works across all applications: You can copy text on a web page you are viewing with the Chrome browser, and paste it into a document.

✂ Cut	Ctrl+X
🗗 Copy	Ctrl+C
📋 Paste	Ctrl+V
📋 Paste without formatting	Ctrl+Shift+V
Delete	
Explore 'navigating'	Ctrl+Alt+Shift+I
Define 'navigating'	Ctrl+Shift+Y
💬 Comment	Ctrl+Alt+M
📝 Suggest edits	
💡 Save to Keep	
🔗 Link...	Ctrl+K
Select all matching text	~
✗ Clear formatting	Ctrl+\

FIGURE 8-6:
Open an editing menu by Alt-clicking selected text.

4. **Using your touchpad, scroll to the location where you want to place your text and click to place your cursor there.**

5. **Open the Edit menu again and select Paste.**

The copied text is pasted into the document at the location of your cursor.

You can paste the contents of your Clipboard as many times as you like. If you need to place the text in numerous locations, simply move to each location and paste the text by following Steps 4 and 5 in the preceding list.

You can also use handy keyboard shortcuts to copy and paste text. After you select the desired text, pressing Ctrl+C copies the text to your Clipboard. After you move the cursor to the place in your document where you want the text to appear, press Ctrl+V to copy the text from your Clipboard into the document.

TIP

You can paste text over and over; pasting text from the Clipboard does not empty the Clipboard; instead, the Clipboard will contain your selected text until you perform the next copy. At that point, you replace the prior contents of the Clipboard with the new content.

Moving text by cutting and pasting

When you want to replicate text, copying and pasting is the mode of operation you should use. When you want to *move* text but *not* replicate it, however, instead of using Copy, you would use Cut. To move text in your document using the cut-and-paste method, follow these steps:

1. **Using your touchpad, click and drag your pointer across the text you want to copy; then release your click.**

The selected text is highlighted.

2. **Alt+click the highlighted text.**

A menu appears, revealing several options.

3. **Select Cut from the menu.**

The selected text disappears from the screen. Don't worry; it's sitting in your Clipboard waiting to be pasted.

WARNING

When you cut text from your document, the text vanishes, perhaps giving you the impression that you have deleted it. You haven't deleted the text, though — it has just been moved to your Clipboard. However, that text *will* be deleted if you cut or copy additional text prior to pasting the already-cut text. The Clipboard always and only holds one copied item.

4. **Using the touchpad, navigate to the location where you want to paste your text.**

5. **Alt-click in the location where you want to paste your text. In the menu, select Paste.**

The copied text is pasted in the location of your cursor.

REMEMBER

You can paste text as many times as you like. However, when you copy or cut a new selection of text, the previously cut text is replaced with the newly cut text.

TIP

Instead of using Alt+Click menus for cutting and pasting, you can instead press Ctrl+X to cut text (copy to the Clipboard), and Ctrl+V to paste text.

Formatting Text

Before you can start formatting text, you need to become familiar with a few terms that describe the different characteristics of your text:

>> **Font:** Also known in some circles as *font face,* the *font* is the style of typeface. By default, the name of the font used in Docs is Arial.

>> **Font size:** The size of your text is often used to indicate hierarchical structure or writing format or style. By default, the size of your text is 11 points. This size is about the normal size of text on an ordinary printed page.

>> **Font weight:** *Weight* refers to the thickness or boldness of the letters in a font. A *heavy* font weight means the text is bold, or very thick and dark.

>> **Font slope:** *Slope* indicates how much your text leans, and in what direction. For example, *italicizing* letters means adding a left-to-right slope.

Here are some examples:

>> This is Times New Roman font in 10 points.

>> This is 16 points.

>> **This is bold.**

>> *This is italics.*

The formatting of your text is important not only for style but also to adequately communicate your message. Font weight, slope, and size are all used to communicate meaning, emphasis, and more. Font face can also be useful for establishing a personality, tone, and brand. Google Docs gives you the ability to modify all these characteristics of your text so that your documents look great and say what you want them to say.

Changing fonts

With Docs, you can change the font of any text contained in your document. Creatively speaking, having many different fonts from different font families in a single document isn't recommended, but Docs does make it possible to change every letter in your document to a different font. Google Docs comes preloaded with eight fonts:

>> Arial

>> Comic Sans MS

>> Courier New

>> Georgia

>> **Impact**

>> Times New Roman

>> Trebuchet MS

>> Verdana

To change your font, follow these steps:

1. Using your touchpad, click and drag your cursor across the text you want to select.

Docs highlights the selected text.

2. Using the Edit toolbar, click to open the Font menu.

The Font menu is located directly to the left of the Font Size menu. The Font menu shows the name of the font currently in use. (See Figure 8-7.)

In the Edit toolbar, the Font menu appears with the name of the font for the selected body of text. By default, all text uses the Arial font.

TIP

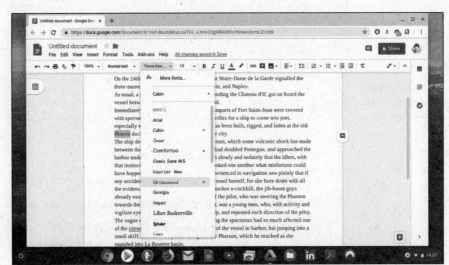

FIGURE 8-7:
Selecting a font in
Google Docs.

3. Select one of the fonts listed.

Your highlighted text is changed to the selected font.

If no text was highlighted when you changed the font, the new font will apply only to new text. Any text typed from the current location of the cursor will appear with the font face of the selected font.

Adding new fonts

The Google Docs default list of fonts is a brief list of eight. Other word processors, such as Microsoft Word, Adobe Acrobat, or Apple Pages, have extensive lists of fonts by default. Google provides users with an initial list of the most globally popular fonts to keep things simple at first. You can, however, add fonts to your Docs. Follow these steps:

1. Click the Font menu in the Edit toolbar.

2. Select More Fonts to add fonts.

The Font selection window, shown in Figure 8-8, gives you a robust list of new fonts from which to choose. Scroll down through the list to reveal more fonts.

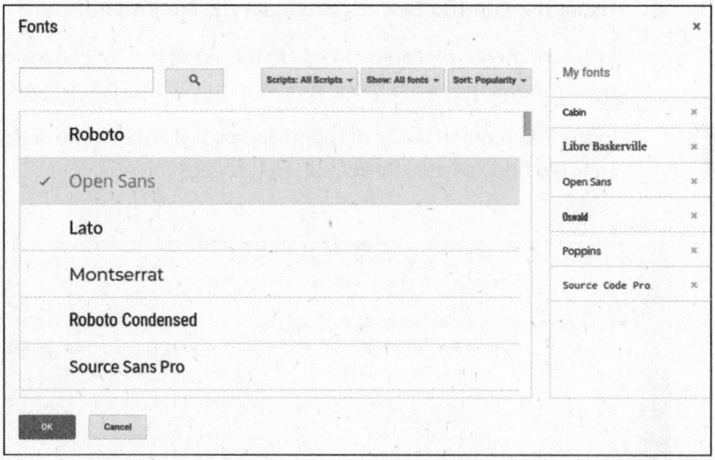

FIGURE 8-8:
Adding new fonts
to Google Docs.

3. Select the desired fonts by clicking each.

Each selected font is highlighted in blue and given a check mark.

4. Click OK to finish adding the fonts to your Font menu and exit.

When you are ready to change the font of your text, you can choose from a list containing your original fonts, plus your newly selected fonts from the Font menu.

Removing fonts from the Font menu

The more fonts you add, the more fonts you will have to rifle through when trying to make a decision on changing the font of your text. The time may come when you want to remove fonts that you added to your list. Think of it as decluttering or spring cleaning. To remove fonts from Docs, take these steps:

1. **Open the Font menu in the Edit toolbar.**

2. **Select More Fonts.**

    The Font window appears. On the left of the window, a list of new fonts appears; on the right, a list of fonts currently in use by your Docs account.

3. **Scroll through the list of fonts on the right side of the window under My Fonts and locate the font or fonts you want to remove. Then, to remove a font, click the *X* located to the right of that font's name.**

    The font vanishes from the list of available fonts.

4. **Click OK.**

TIP

Removing a font from your list of fonts doesn't affect your documents, even if they contain a font you removed from the menu. Further, after you use a font in your document, you can change more text to use that font even if you removed it from your Font menu. (However, a removed font won't be available in any *new* documents, or existing documents that don't contain the font.)

TIP

Adding fonts to Google Docs makes these fonts available for Google Sheets and Google Slides as well. They aren't, however, available in other Chromebook apps, such as Text.

Styling fonts

You can easily confuse the *style* of your font with the *face* of your font. Font face is simply the font itself. Think of a font as a designer pair of jeans. A fashion designer made the jeans to look a particular way. However, no matter how the jeans were made, you can still style the jeans by cuffing the bottoms, cutting the jeans off at the knees, and so on.

You can accentuate a font by applying various styles to the font itself. Those styles include

» **Size:** Makes your text bigger or smaller, depending on where it fits in a hierarchy.

» **Bold:** When you make text **bold**, the text becomes visibly thicker. This is why a bold font is said to have a *heavy font weight.*

>> **Italics:** A slanted font is often referred to as *italic.*

>> **Underline:** Places a line under your text (for example, to indicate <u>importance</u>).

>> **Strikethrough:** Places a line through the middle of your text. Useful in communicating a change in your text or simply to ~~make~~ illustrate a point.

>> **Superscript:** Lifts the text above the line and reduces its size. You may remember this from high school algebra, like the 2 in X^2.

>> **Subscript:** Moves the text slightly lower and reduces its size. This is like the 2 in the chemical formula for water, H_2O.

>> **Color:** Track changes, distinguish individual users in collaboration, or simply add style to your text by changing the color of the text itself or by adding a permanent color highlight.

Text size

You can change the size of your text by following these steps:

1. **Using your touchpad, click and drag your cursor across the text you want to change; then, when you've selected the desired text, release your click.**

   The selected text is highlighted.

2. **Open the Font Size menu in the Edit toolbar.**

   It's the number found between the Font menu and the Bold button. (See Figure 8-9.)

   The size of a font is called the *point size.* The *point* is the smallest whole unit of measure in typography. In the industrial era, *typesetting* was the process of manually setting letters into a printing press to print whole sheets of text. The original point varied in actual size between 0.18mm and 0.4mm. In the modern era, the point (abbreviated *pt.*) size doesn't necessarily correspond directly to an actual size on the printed page. Today, a *desktop publishing point* is defined as 1/72 of an *international inch*, or about 0.353mm.

3. **Select the desired font size.**

   Your selected text becomes the chosen size.

You can quickly make selected text bold by clicking the Bold button (which displays a capital B) located in the middle of the Edit toolbar. You can also bold your selected text by pressing Ctrl+B.

Font size selector

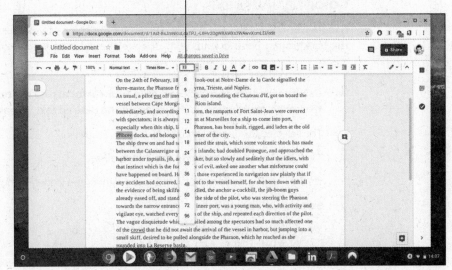

FIGURE 8-9:
Selecting
different
text sizes in
Google Docs.

Applying bold, italics, underline, or strikethrough

To style a specific selection of text with bold, italics, underline, or strikethrough, follow these steps:

1. **Using your touchpad, click and drag your cursor across the text you want to change; then, when you've selected the desired text, release your click.**

   The selected text is highlighted.

2. **Open the Format menu in the edit toolbar.**

3. **Select Bold, Italic, Underline, or Strikethrough.**

   Your selected text changes accordingly.

TIP

As a quick alternative, you can style selected text just by clicking the appropriate button in the middle of the Edit toolbar. Click the B button for bold, the I button for italic, or the U button for underline. (No button exists for strikethrough on the standard Edit toolbar.) Similarly, you can apply styles by pressing Ctrl+B (bold), Ctrl+I (italic), Ctrl+U (underline), or Alt+Shift+5 (strikethrough). Pressing again undoes the same style.

Coloring your text

Google Docs gives you the ability to change the color of your text or the color of the background behind your text. Change the color of your text by using these steps:

1. **Using your touchpad, click and drag your cursor across the text you want to change; then, when you've selected the desired text, release your click.**

The selected text is highlighted.

2. **Click the Text Color menu in the Edit toolbar.**

It's the heavily underlined A found to the right of the Underline button.

3. **Select your desired color.**

Your selected text now appears in the selected color.

To apply a highlight to your text, you can do so by following these steps:

1. **Using your touchpad, click and drag your cursor across the text you want to change; then, when you've selected everything, release your click.**

The selected text is highlighted.

2. **Open the Highlight Color menu in the Edit toolbar.**

It's to the right of the Text Color button and looks like a tiny, slanted highlighter.

3. **Select your desired color.**

Your selected text now appears highlighted in the selected color.

Aligning your text

The *alignment* of your text determines the orientation of the edges of lines, paragraphs, or pages in your document. Google Docs gives you several options for changing the alignment, including:

» **Left alignment:** This is the default alignment for new documents in Docs. The text is flush with the left margin of your document.

» **Right alignment:** The text is flush with the right margin of your document.

» **Center:** The middle of your document is the half-way point between the left and the right margins. With centered alignment, all text is centered on this midway point, regardless of the relation between document margins and document dimensions.

» **Justified:** *Justifying* your text aligns the text evenly along both the left and right margins. To ensure that the left and right side of your text are flush with the left and right margins, Docs introduces additional spaces between each word. This paragraph is published in Justified alignment; see how the left and right edges line up neatly?

You can change the alignment of text in your document by the line, paragraph, or page by following these steps:

1. **Using your touchpad, select the text you want to realign.**

The selected text is highlighted.

2. **Click the align button in the Edit toolbar.**

The alignment buttons appear.

3. **Click the desired alignment button.**

The selected text is realigned. Alignment buttons are shown in Figure 8-10.

Justify toolbar

Justify button

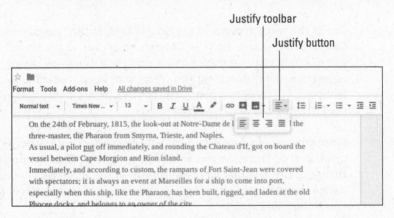

FIGURE 8-10: Left, Right, Center, and Justified alignment buttons in Google Docs.

TIP

You don't have to select the entire paragraph to change its alignment. You need only to place the cursor anyplace in the paragraph before changing its alignment.

Clearing formatting

Sometimes you need to start with a blank slate. You might be given a document that requires editing, or maybe you got a little too enthusiastic with the formatting tools that Google Docs provides you. Regardless of the reason, Docs makes it incredibly easy to wipe out all formatting in a section of text or a complete document. To clear your formatting, follow these steps:

1. **Select the formatted text.**

   The selected text is highlighted.

   TIP

   To clear the formatting of an entire document, press Ctrl+A instead of selecting a section of text. Pressing Ctrl+A selects the entire document.

2. **Open the Format menu in the Applications menu.**

3. **Select Clear Formatting.**

   The selected text is reset to defaults: left-aligned text with all style elements — including color, underline, strikethrough, italics, bold, and so on — removed. Font sizes are not affected by Clear Formatting.

Saving Documents

One of the many reasons to use Google Docs is the symbiosis between Docs and Google Drive. Google Drive is Google's cloud-based storage solution that allows you to safely store your files and access them from any device with an Internet connection. Every document you create with Docs is saved to your Drive folder so that you can access it at home, on the road, at work, or anywhere else you might need it, using any device with a browser.

When you create a new document with Docs, Docs automatically saves the document to your Drive. As you edit your document, Docs continuously saves each change to Drive so that you have almost no risk of losing your information. Docs has no manual Save feature for this very reason: You may forget to save your document, but Docs won't.

Rest assured, your work is safe with Google.

Naming your document

When you open a new document with Docs, the default name for the document is Untitled Document. However, you won't want to leave your document named this way. Drive doesn't have a problem with storing multiple files with the same name, but such naming may easily confuse you. It's best, then, to immediately give your document a more intuitive name. To name your document, follow these steps:

1. **Open a new document.**

The easiest way to do this is simply to launch Docs from the Launcher.

A Chrome web browser opens and loads Docs.

2. **If Docs shows you a list of documents that you have previously edited, click the colorful + (plus sign) button in the lower-left corner of the Google Docs page to start a new document.**

3. **Click File from the menu at the top of the Google Docs window.**

4. **Click Rename.**

The cursor moves to the document name at the top of the Google Docs window, as shown in Figure 8-11.

Renaming a document

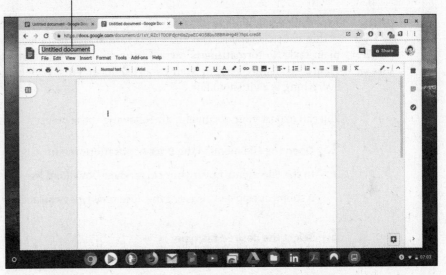

FIGURE 8-11:
Changing the
name of a Google
Docs document.

5. **Type the new name for your document in the Name field and press Enter.**

The name Untitled Document in the top-left corner has been replaced with the new name you entered.

Your document now appears in Google Drive with the new name. As you continue to make edits to the document, those changes will be updated and saved in real time.

Exporting documents

Unfortunately for you, the entire world does not use the Google platform exclusively. Therefore, you may need to export your documents to formats that others may be comfortable with. Docs presently allows you to export documents to a few standard formats, including

>> Microsoft Word (.docx)

>> OpenDocument (.odt)

>> Rich Text (.rtf)

>> PDF (.pdf)

>> Plain Text (.txt)

>> Web Page (.html, Zipped)

WARNING

Exporting documents to different file types may change or remove the formatting within your document. The Plain Text format, for instance, is as the name says: plain text. No formatting is carried through when you export your document to Plain Text. Before sending your exported documents, review them to ensure that everything is as it should be.

You can export your documents by following these steps:

1. Open the File menu in the Docs Applications menu.

2. In the File menu, hover your cursor over Download As.

A submenu appears, revealing the document types available for export. (See Figure 8-12.)

3. Select the desired file type.

Your Docs file is exported in the desired file type and is automatically downloaded to your Chromebook's Downloads folder.

4. To view the downloaded file on your computer, click the arrow next to the filename in the bottom of your browser window.

A menu revealing several options appears.

5. Select Show in Folder.

The Files app launches, showing you the file in your folder.

If you want your newly exported document to be saved in Google Drive, you can move the document from the Downloads folder on your Chromebook to your Google Drive. To do so, open the Files app, find your Downloads folder and the new exported document, and copy it to Google Drive. I cover this procedure in Chapter 7.

Download as button

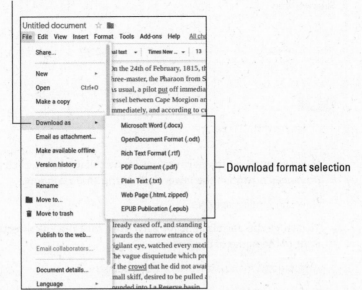

FIGURE 8-12:
Exporting your
document to a
new format with
the Download As
submenu.

— Download format selection

TIP

Your original document is unaffected when you export your document to a new format. Your original document is still there, and you can continue making changes to it.

Collaborating in Docs

By default, Docs and Drive make your files inaccessible to anyone other than yourself. You can, however, change the visibility settings on your files and invite specific people, or even the entire world, to comment, view, or edit your documents. To share a document with specific people, follow these steps:

1. **Open your document with Docs.**

2. **Click the blue Share button in the top-right corner of your Docs window.**

   A window appears, giving you several options for sharing your document. (See Figure 8-13.)

REMEMBER

3. **In the Invite People text box in the pop-up window, enter the email address of each person with whom you want to share your file.**

   Be sure to separate multiple email addresses with commas.

   If the email address is in your address book, Docs will try to auto-fill their information.

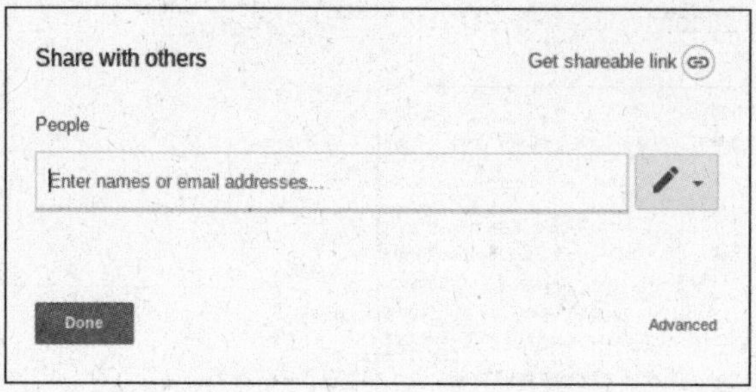

FIGURE 8-13:
The Share
window lets you
share documents
with others.

> **Share with others**   Get shareable link ⊝
>
> People
>
> [Enter names or email addresses...]   ✏ ▾
>
> [Done]   Advanced

4. **If you want to set the permissions of the collaborators, click the Advanced button in the lower right of the Share window.**

   A second window appears.

5. **To change the permissions for each user, click the link directly to the right of the name of the invitee.**

   A drop-down menu with three options appears:

   - **Can View:** Allows users only to view the document.

   - **Can Comment:** Allows users to view the document and comment on the document but not to change any content or security settings.

   - **Can Edit:** Allows users to view, comment, and edit the document and change permissions.

   This is shown in Figure 8-14.

6. **Select from the menu the permission setting you want to apply to this collaborator.**

7. **Select the Notify People via Email box directly above the Send button to notify the specified collaborators, by email, that you have shared a document with them.**

8. **Click Send.**

   Your document is made available to the collaborators immediately.

> **TIP**
>
> The collaborators who are invited to view, edit, or comment on your document will have to log into Google Docs using the email address with which you shared the document. If a collaborator doesn't have a Google Account under the email address that you used, you have to invite her by using her Google Account address. She also has the option to create a Google Account using the email address to which you sent the invitation.

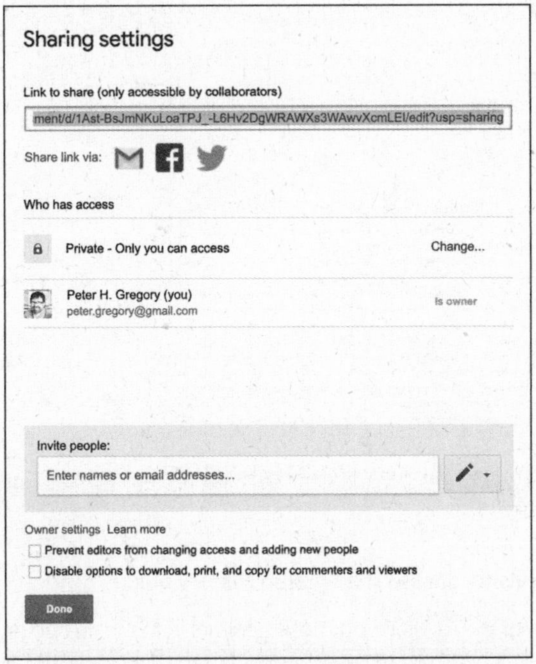

FIGURE 8-14:
Advanced Share settings let you specify editing rights for each person.

Tracking Document Revisions

Keeping track of revisions is very important when creating and working with documents, especially when multiple collaborators are working with them. Luckily, Google Docs handles version control masterfully. As you and your collaborators make changes to your documents, Docs will time-and-date stamp those changes so that you can view previous versions of your document and even revert to an earlier version if you need to.

Revision tracking is a default feature of Docs. To view your revision history, follow these steps:

1. **Open a document with Docs.**

2. **Open the File menu in the Docs Applications menu.**

3. **Select Version History and then See Version History.**

   A Version History box appears in the right portion of your screen. (See Figure 8-15.) The box contains the various versions of your document, in order from most recent to oldest.

FIGURE 8-15:
The Version
History box.

4. **Click a revision date in the Version History box.**

A preview of the revision you chose appears in the main document area. Changes that occurred between versions appear in green. When you hover over each change, the name of the person who made the change is shown.

5. **To make a copy of a previous version of the document, click the menu button to the right of the revision and then click Make a Copy.**

You now have a new document with the original name that includes the date that version was saved. Your current document remains unchanged.

6. **To restore your document to an older version, click the Restore This Version button at the top of the Google Docs window.**

The restored version becomes the current version.

Using Docs Offline

Google Docs is a web-based word processor, which means that you must have an Internet connection to access all its features. However, an offline version of Docs is available in the event that you find yourself without a connection to the Internet.

To use Google Docs offline, follow these steps:

1. **To use Google Docs offline, you must first enable Google Drive for offline use. To ensure that Google Drive is properly enabled, open the Launcher and click the Google Drive icon.**

   A Chrome web browser appears and takes you to your Drive.

2. **On the right side of the screen, click the Settings icon (it looks like a little gear).**

   A menu appears, revealing several options.

3. **Click Settings.**

   A window appears, giving several general settings options.

4. **Locate the Offline check box and select it.**

5. **Click Done.**

   The window disappears, indicating that the changes have been made. Your Docs files will now be synced and available for offline editing.

6. **To test whether you have properly enabled offline access, turn off your Wi-Fi by opening the Settings panel in the bottom-right of your screen and clicking the blue Wi-Fi button.**

   This turns off Wi-Fi off, and the button changes from blue to gray. You are now offline.

7. **With your Wi-Fi turned off, switch back to Google Drive, locate your synced documents, and click to open one.**

   If your document opens and you are able to edit it, you know that you have successfully engaged offline use and synced your documents. As you edit your document, a little message appears to the right of the menu that reads, "All changes saved offline."

While offline, you won't be able to access some of the features available to Docs users that are connected to the Internet. You will, however, be able to create documents and save them. Later, when you connect to the Internet, Drive uploads the saved documents and enables all Internet-only features.

» **Entering and formatting numbers**

» **Using Sheets to calculate**

» **Saving, exporting, and collaborating with Sheets**

Chapter **9**

Summarizing Sheets

B efore the era of computers, accounting and other business finance–related mathematical computations were performed with good old paper and pencil. Accounting worksheets provided on-sheet organization with *rows* and *columns* that intersected to create *cells*. Each printed page held one *spreadsheet*, with all the pages bound into a *workbook*. Each cell in a spreadsheet contained some sort of value, and calculations could be performed and written into corresponding cells in other rows and columns. The same terms are used for electronic spreadsheets and workbooks, but the calculating power goes far beyond what was possible in even the most sophisticated hard-copy workbooks.

When personal computers came on the scene, they revolutionized the way that businesses and finance professionals conducted business. Digital spreadsheets made it easier to enter data and automatically calculate results. And, of course, editing without needing a pencil eraser or white-out was a miracle!

Spreadsheets have evolved quite substantially over the years. It all started with Visicalc, and then Lotus 1-2-3, and Microsoft Multiplan. Today, although Microsoft Excel and Apple's Numbers have quite a bit of market share, Google Sheets is fast on the rise and has some extremely powerful features just by nature of being a part of the Google online ecosystem. In this chapter, you take an introductory look at Sheets: You can explore the Sheets interface and learn how to enter data into a cell, edit data, and perform basic calculations. Collaboration is also important with Sheets, so you learn how to save and export your data and share it with others for collaboration; and when you don't have an Internet connection, you will be able to use Sheets offline.

This chapter describes the steps used to create worksheets in which you can create lists of things like budget items, business records, expenses, and the like.

Navigating Google Sheets

Google Sheets is Google's functional equivalent to Microsoft Excel and Apple Numbers. If you've had any experience working with Excel or Numbers, you'll find the Sheets interface to be quite similar. If this is your first time using a spreadsheet tool, you'll find that Sheets is extremely intuitive.

 To get started, launch Google Sheets by opening the Launcher and clicking the Sheets icon. The Sheets application opens in a Chrome browser window and creates a new, untitled spreadsheet, shown in Figure 9-1. If you have used any worksheets in the past in your Google account, you see a list of those spreadsheets. Click the + (plus sign) button at the lower-right corner of the window to create a new, blank spreadsheet.

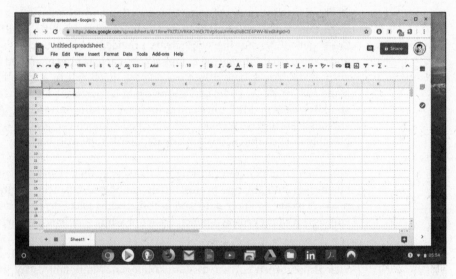

FIGURE 9-1:
Google Sheets.

Surveying the Sheets menu area

The Sheets work area is broken into a couple of key areas: the menu area and the main document area, which is the actual spreadsheet. The menu area, by default, is composed of the Applications menu, Edit toolbar, and Formula bar, as shown in Figure 9-2.

Menu area   Application menu   Edit toolbar

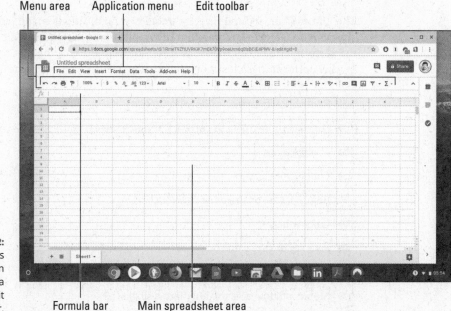

FIGURE 9-2:
The Sheets
Application
menu, Formula
bar, and Edit
toolbar.

Formula bar   Main spreadsheet area

The Applications menu in Google Sheets is located at the top of the menu area and is home to several application–specific controls and options, including

>> **File:** File-specific options and controls for creating, saving, exporting, printing, and otherwise managing your document on the file level.

>> **Edit:** Copy, paste, delete, and otherwise move and manipulate data.

>> **View:** Modify your view by adding and removing toolbars or change the layout of the spreadsheet by adding or removing gridlines, freezing columns and rows, and more.

>> **Insert:** Insert rows, columns, cells, worksheets, charts, images, and more.

>> **Format:** Manipulate the appearance of your data, auto-format number data, align cell contents, and otherwise edit the appearance of your cells.

>> **Data:** Sort and filter your data.

>> **Tools:** Spell check, protect the sheet to ensure that data isn't overwritten, or create a form to gather data.

>> **Add-ons:** A gateway to adding features and functions to Google Sheets. This is a more advanced feature that I don't discuss further in this book.

>> **Help:** Get help with Sheets, search for menu options, and more.

The Edit toolbar, located directly under the Applications menu, contains several shortcuts to features contained in the Applications menu. The Edit toolbar makes the performance of routine tasks faster and easier. With the Edit toolbar, you can quickly perform these tasks on one or more cells in your worksheet:

» Print your worksheet, undo, or redo edits

» Format number data as currency or percentages

» Change fonts

» Change font size

» Bold, italicize, or strikethrough your text

» Color your text

» Fill a cell or cells with color

» Add, edit, or remove cell borders

» Merge multiple cells together into a single cell

» Edit the horizontal alignment of the contents of a cell

» Edit the vertical alignment of the contents of a cell.

» Allow text in a cell to wrap to multiple lines

» Add comments or charts, and perform common calculations

The Formula bar is located directly under the Edit toolbar. You use the Formula bar to insert data into cells and to type formulas for performing calculations.

Working with the spreadsheet area

The spreadsheet area of your Sheets workspace is located directly under the Formula bar. The spreadsheet is made up of a grid of columns and rows. The top of the columns is the column header, and the left side of the rows is the row header. Columns are referenced by letters (A, B, C, and so on), and rows are referenced by numbers (1, 2, 3, and so on). Permanent scroll bars are located at the right and bottom of your spreadsheet so that you can quickly scroll left and right, and up and down, through your spreadsheet.

At the bottom of the spreadsheet area, a *tab* labeled Sheet1 appears. The name of your current worksheet is Sheet1. You can, however, have multiple worksheets — represented by tabs — in one Sheets workbook.

Row numbers and column letters are imperative for precisely communicating locations within a spreadsheet. A cell's coordinates are always communicated first with the column letter and then with the row number. For example, A8 means column A, row 8.

In Sheets, you refer to a range of cells in a single row or column by specifying the starting cell coordinates and the ending cell coordinates separated by a colon. For example:

```
A8:A20
```

This example references a range of cells starting in the A column at row 8 and ending at row 24. Figure 9-3 illustrates what this range looks like.

To reference a *matrix* of cells (meaning a range of cells, spanning multiple rows and columns), you specify the coordinates of the top-left corner and the bottom-right corner of the matrix separated by a colon. For example:

```
A8:C20
```

Figure 9-4 illustrates what this range looks like in the spreadsheet when selected.

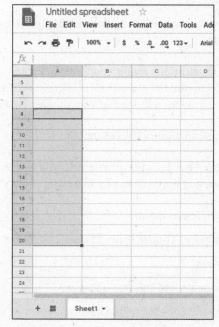

FIGURE 9-3:
Cells A8 through A20.

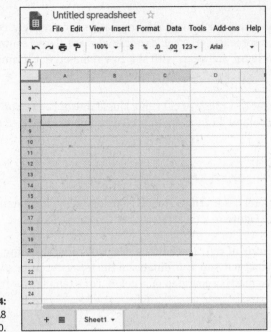

Customizing your view

Before you dive into your first spreadsheet, you might find it helpful to change your view in Google Sheets.

If you prefer to hide the Applications menu, along with the Edit toolbar, you can do so by opening the View menu and choosing Full Screen. When you select Full Screen, the Applications menu and Edit toolbar vanish. (See Figure 9-5.)

To exit Full Screen mode, simply press the Esc key.

REMEMBER

If you prefer to have nothing but cells on your screen, you can remove the Applications menu, Edit toolbar, and Formula bar by following these steps:

1. **Click View in the Applications menu.**

2. **In the resulting View menu, choose Formula Bar.**

   The Formula bar vanishes.

3. **Open the View menu again and choose Full Screen.**

   The Applications menu and Edit toolbar disappear, as shown in Figure 9-6.

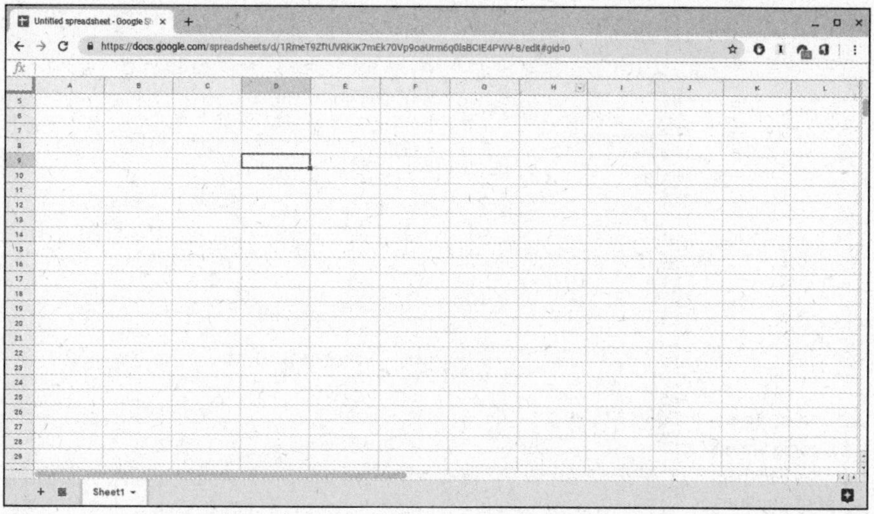

FIGURE 9-5:
Google Sheets in
Full Screen mode.

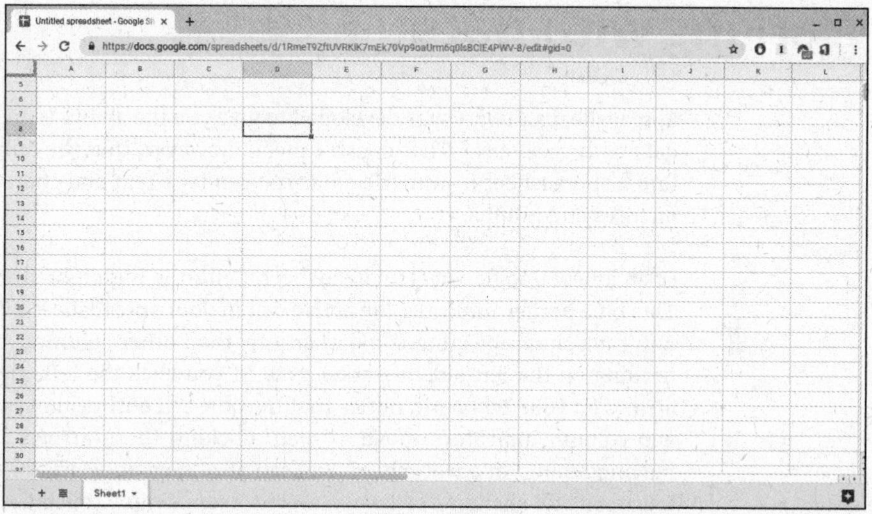

FIGURE 9-6:
Google Sheets
in Full Screen
mode with no
Formula bar.

In your spreadsheet, each cell is outlined with very thin gray lines called *gridlines*. Gridlines are not borders; they are imaginary boundaries, for reference only, and they won't appear when you print your worksheet. If you would like to work without gridlines, you can hide them by opening the View menu and clicking Gridlines. Figure 9-7 shows a spreadsheet without gridlines.

To turn gridlines back on, just open the View menu and choose Gridlines.

REMEMBER

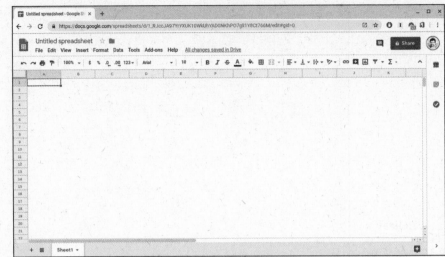

FIGURE 9-7:
A Google Sheets
spreadsheet
without gridlines.

Working with Data

Spreadsheet software was developed to give you the ability to manipulate numeric data with great ease. That doesn't mean, however, that the only data that can go into a spreadsheet is numeric data. You can type text and characters, or even add pictures and graphs.

Open a new Google Sheets spreadsheet. Cell A1 is highlighted with a blue border. This blue border indicates the active cell in your spreadsheet. Also notice that the A in the column heading is a darker gray than other columns, and that the 1 row heading on the left side is darker gray. If you click the left, right, up, and down arrows on your keyboard, notice that the blue cell outline moves, and the gray row and column indicators move as well. Clicking these arrows is the method for moving around in a worksheet. You can also move the cursor with your mouse or touchpad and click in a cell. On a touchscreen, simply touch the cell.

To enter data into a cell, make sure that the blue border is around a cell and begin typing. As you type, your entries appear in the highlighted cell, as well as in the Formula bar, as shown in Figure 9-8.

When you finish typing, press Enter to save what you've typed in the cell. Pressing Enter also moves the highlight bar to the next cell down. If the text you entered is larger than the cell, your text will hang over into adjacent cells until you resize the column width or row height. (I tell you about resizing cells in the section "Resizing columns and rows," later in this chapter.)

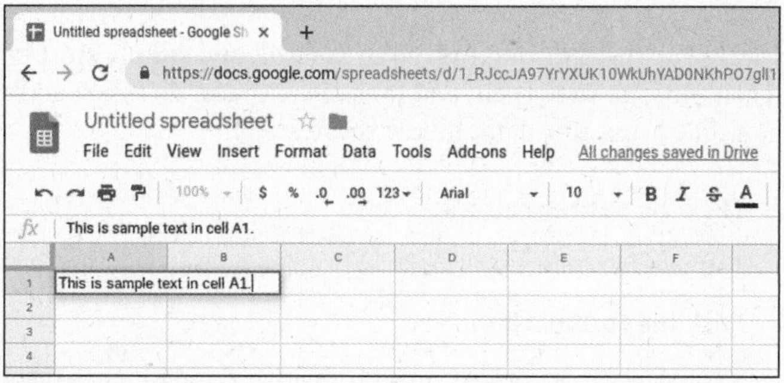

FIGURE 9-8:
Data entered appears in the selected cell and the Formula bar.

Moving around in a spreadsheet

As you enter more and more data into your spreadsheet, you may need to hop around to different cells to update your entries. You can move to different cells in a number of ways with Sheets. To start, take a look at the arrow keys on your keyboard.

Google Sheets can contain as many as 400,000 cells with a maximum of 256 columns. You don't have to create the cells to be able to use them; you can simply navigate to them by using your directional arrows. Move one cell up, down, left, or right by pressing the corresponding directional arrow key once. If you want to quickly move several cells in any particular direction, press and hold the corresponding directional arrow.

You can also navigate your spreadsheet by using your touchpad or mouse. Click the desired cell once to move the cursor and then begin typing using your keyboard. If you need to get to a section of your sheet that is several rows down or columns over, you can quickly navigate there by following these steps:

1. **Place two fingers on your touchpad and move them in the direction you desire.**

    If your touchpad is configured to traditionally scroll, swiping up scrolls up, and swiping down scrolls down. On the other hand, if your touchpad is configured to Australian scroll, swiping up scrolls down, and swiping down scrolls up. Using your touchpad with a two-finger swipe scrolls you to the general area of the cell or cells that you want to edit.

2. **Using one finger on your touchpad, move the pointer to the cell you desire.**

3. **Click your touchpad.**

    The desired cell is now active, enabling you to insert new text or change text that's already there.

TIP

To overwrite the cell contents, go to the cell, and simply start typing. To delete the cell contents, go to the cell, and press Backspace. To insert additional data in a cell that already contains data, follow these steps:

1. **Click the desired cell once.**

The selected cell is highlighted with a blue border.

2. **Click the Formula bar.**

A blinking cursor appears in the Formula bar, indicating that you can add, edit, or delete text using your keyboard.

3. **Add, edit, change, and remove text as you like; then press Enter.**

You can also use a feature called Find and Replace to find a specific piece of data within your spreadsheet, as shown in Figure 9-9. To find data using the Find and Replace feature, follow these steps:

1. **Open the Edit menu and choose Find and Replace.**

The Find and Replace window appears. In this window, you can specify what you want to search for and what you want the search string replaced with, among other options.

You can move the window around on the screen in case it's covering cells you're working with.

2. **Fill in the information you want to use for your search.**

You can specify any of the following options:

- **Find:** The text or data you want to find.

- **Replace:** To replace the data for which you're searching, simply enter new data here.

- **Search:** In this section, you can specify the scope of the search in a drop-down menu, including every sheet in your document, the current sheet, or a specific range of cells. You can also select boxes to match case or entire contents of a cell, or to search formulas and formula expressions.

- **Match Case:** Select this box to search for text exactly as you type it (regarding any use of upper- or lowercase, or any combination) in the Find box.

- **Match Entire Cell Contents:** The complete cell must match your search query.

- **Search Using Regular Expressions:** Search for a particular character pattern.

- **Also Search within Formulas:** Search formulas, in addition to the contents of cells.

TIP

Use the provided check boxes to fine-tune your search and reduce potentially inaccurate search results.

3. **Click Find.**

4. **Sort through search results by clicking the Find button at the bottom-right of the Find and Replace pop-up window.**

   As you navigate through the search results in your document, Sheets changes the highlight color on the cell to indicate where you are in the spreadsheet.

5. **When you successfully locate and replace the word or words in your spreadsheet, click the *X* in the top-right corner of the Find and Replace window to close that window.**

   The window disappears, but the text you searched for remains highlighted and ready to be deleted or otherwise edited.

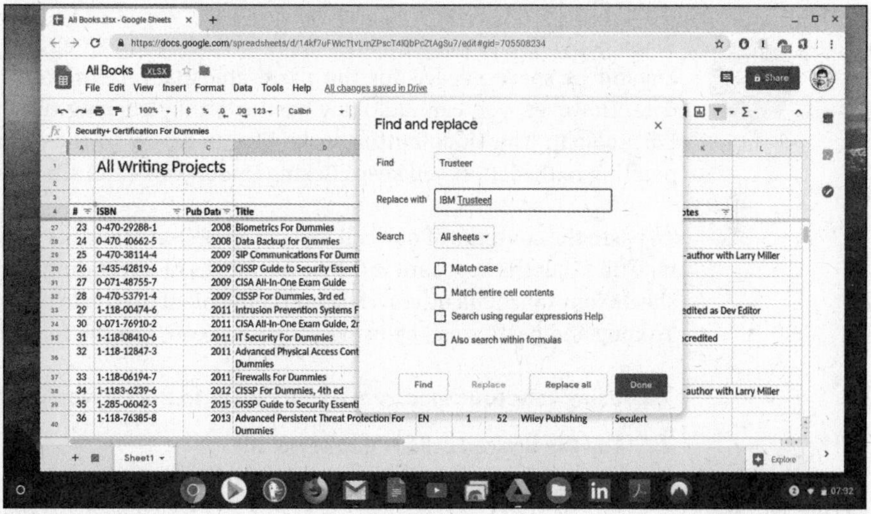

FIGURE 9-9:
Find and Replace content in Google Sheets.

Copying and pasting data

As you enter data into your spreadsheet, you can avoid typing repetitive text by using the Copy and Paste functions. Copying and pasting can be done in a couple of ways — on the keyboard, with the touchpad, or a combination of both. To copy and paste a single cell, follow these steps:

1. Select the cell that you want to copy.

TIP

To copy and paste a range of cells, select the first cell in the range, hold the Shift key, and then select the last cell in the range.

The selection area is highlighted in blue.

2. Open the Edit menu and choose Copy.

The selected cell's contents are copied and stored in memory, also referred to as the Clipboard.

WARNING

The Clipboard can remember *only one thing* at a time. If you copy a selection of text and then copy another selection of text without pasting the first selection of text, Sheets forgets the first selection.

3. Navigate to the cell where you want to paste the copied data.

4. Once again, open the Edit menu. This time, choose Paste.

The data copied to the Clipboard is now pasted into the selected cell.

TIP

When copying and pasting large areas of data, you can easily underestimate the amount of space needed for the paste and inadvertently overwrite meaningful data. However, you can undo any past action by clicking the Undo button in the Edit toolbar. The Undo button looks like an arrow in the shape of a half-circle pointing to the left. If you keep clicking Undo, your edits are undone, one at a time.

To paste the contents of one cell in a cell that's several rows or columns away, you may find that the keyboard is too slow a means of navigating through your spreadsheet. Your touchpad offers a fast and convenient option to quickly copy and paste. To copy and paste a cell by using your touchpad, use the following steps:

1. Using your touchpad, move your cursor to the cell you want to copy.

2. Tap the desired cell once to select it.

TIP

To select a range of cells, tap the first cell in the range and, without releasing your finger, move to the other end of the range you want to copy, and then release.

3. Open the Edit menu and select Copy.

The selected cell is copied to the Clipboard.

4. Using your touchpad, scroll to the desired location, and tap the desired cell.

To paste a range of cells, select the cell you want to be the top-left corner of your pasted range.

5. Open the Edit menu and choose Paste.

The copied selection is pasted in.

TIP

To save time, you can use shortcut keys to copy and paste cells. Press Ctrl+C to copy a cell or cells, and press Ctrl+V to paste the copied cells. You can also quickly undo a paste (or many other actions) by pressing Ctrl+Z.

TIP

Alt-click your selection to reveal a menu of actions, including Copy and Paste. (See Figure 9-10.)

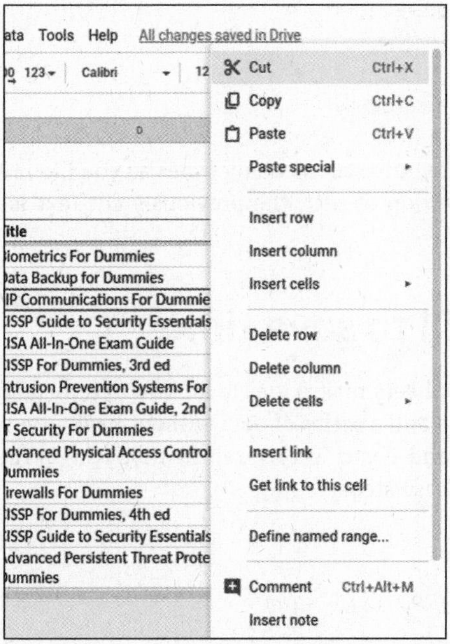

FIGURE 9-10:
Actions that you can carry out on a cell or selection of cells in Google Sheets.

Moving data with Cut and Paste

When you want to replicate data, Copy and Paste is the mode of operation you should use. When you want to *move* data but not replicate it, however, use Cut. To move data in your sheet using the Cut and Paste method, follow these steps:

1. Using your touchpad, click to select the cell whose contents you want to move (or click and drag your cursor across all the cells whose contents you want to move) and then release.

The cell(s) are highlighted.

2. **Alt-click the highlighted cell(s).**

A pop-up menu appears, revealing several options.

3. **Select Cut from the menu.**

A dashed border surrounds your selection, indicating that the enclosed data has been cut.

4. **Using the touchpad, navigate to the location where you want to paste your data.**

5. **Alt-click the cell where you want to paste your data.**

A pop-up menu appears.

6. **Select Paste.**

The data is moved accordingly.

You can paste data that you've cut as many times as you like. However, when you copy or cut a new selection of text, the previously cut text is replaced with the newly cut text.

Using Autofill to save time

The Autofill feature in Sheets makes it easy for you to copy and paste a particular pattern of data or to expand a series of data without having to manually enter the data or use the Copy and Paste feature repeatedly. To use Autofill to expand a series of data, follow these steps:

1. **In cell A1, type** July 28.

2. **In cell A2, type** July 29.

3. **In cell A3, type** July 30.

4. **Click cell A1 and select these cells by dragging your cursor down to cell A3.**

Notice that a tiny blue square appears in the bottom-right corner of your selection, as pictured in Figure 9-11. This blue square is called the Autofill square, and it has magical power.

5. **Click the blue Autofill square and drag your selection down to Cell A10.**

6. **Release your click.**

Sheets automatically fills your selection with the identified date sequence, as shown in Figure 9-12.

You can use Autofill to complete most sequences as long as you give Autofill enough information to guess what your sequence is. If Autofill can't identify your sequence, it simply replicates your data as a pattern.

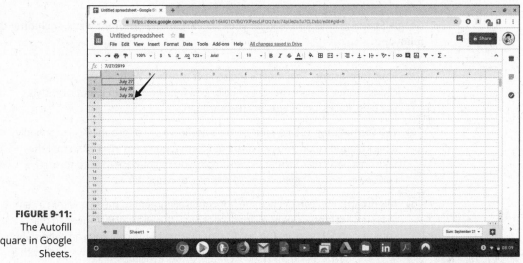

FIGURE 9-11:
The Autofill square in Google Sheets.

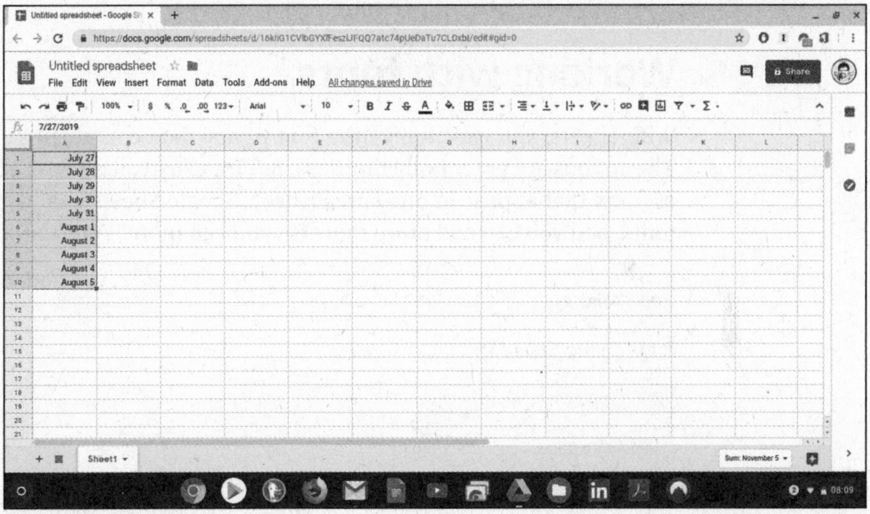

FIGURE 9-12:
Sheets completes the sequence of dates.

Formatting Data

Google Sheets gives you great control over the appearance of the content in your spreadsheet. You can change the formatting of a complete spreadsheet, rows, columns, or single cells. You can, in some instances, apply multiple style changes to the contents within a cell. For instance, you can apply different types of formatting, such as bold or italics, within one cell. On the other hand, you can't mix font sizes within a single cell.

Google Sheets allows you to style your sheet in many different ways, including the following:

>> **Font formatting:** *Font* means the style of typeface. With Sheets, you can change fonts, change the size or color of a font, or apply to a font new styles like bold, italics, underline, or strikethrough.

>> **Cell formatting:** You can put borders around a cell or group of cells, or apply a background color. You can also auto-format numbers in a cell so that they take on a particular format. For example, you might want to auto-format currencies, percentages, dates, and times, to name a few.

>> **Alignment:** You can change the horizontal alignment of the text within a cell to be left-, center- or right-aligned, or change the vertical alignment so that your text appears at the top, middle, or bottom of the cell. You can even style text so that it wraps to another line in your cell; this feature allows a cell with a lot of content to occupy multiple lines of text.

Working with fonts

With Sheets, you can change the font of any data contained in your spreadsheet. The options are potentially limitless, but for clarity, it's better to limit the number of fonts that appear in one spreadsheet. Google Sheets comes preloaded with six fonts, and you can add more fonts if you need more. Your initial font options are

>> Arial

>> Comic Sans MS

>> Courier New

>> Georgia

>> **Impact**

>> Times New Roman

>> Trebuchet MS

>> Verdana

To change your font, follow these steps:

1. **Using your touchpad, select the cells you want to change by clicking and dragging your cursor.**

Sheets highlights the selected cells.

2. **Open the Format menu; then open the Font submenu.**

The Font submenu reveals available font choices.

TIP

The Font submenu is titled with the name of the font for the selected body of text. By default, all text appears in the Arial font.

3. **Select any one of the fonts listed.**

The contents of the highlighted cells are changed to the selected font.

If the selected cells contain no data, the new font will apply to new text you add later.

Adding new fonts

The Google Sheets default list of fonts is a brief list of eight. Other spreadsheet programs such as Microsoft Excel or Apple Numbers have extensive lists of fonts by default. Google provides users with an initial list of the most globally popular fonts to keep things simple at first. You can, however, add fonts to your spreadsheets. To do so, follow these steps:

1. **Click the Font menu in the Edit toolbar.**

2. **Select More Fonts to add fonts.**

The Font selection window, shown in Figure 9-13, gives you a robust list of new fonts from which to choose. Scroll down through the list to reveal more fonts.

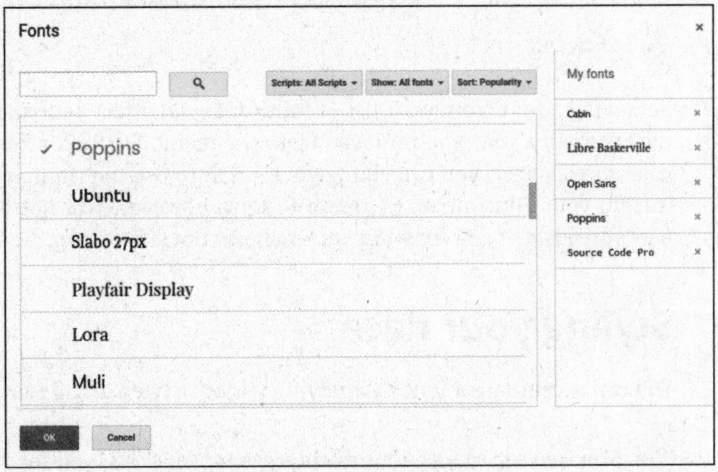

FIGURE 9-13:
Adding new fonts to Google Sheets.

3. **Select the desired fonts by clicking each one you want.**

Each selected font is highlighted in blue and given a check mark.

4. **Click OK to finish adding the fonts to your Font menu and exit.**

When you are ready to change the font of your text, you will be able to choose from a list containing your original fonts, plus your newly selected fonts from the Font menu.

TIP

Adding fonts to Google Sheets makes these fonts available for Google Docs and Google Slides as well.

Removing fonts from the Font menu

The more fonts you add, the more fonts you will have to rifle through when trying to make a decision on changing the font of your text. Sometime in the future, you might decide that you have too many fonts and it's time for some decluttering. To remove fonts from Sheets, take these steps:

1. **Open the Font menu in the Edit toolbar.**

2. **Select More Fonts.**

The Font window appears. On the left of the window, a list of new fonts appears; on the right, a list of fonts currently in use by your Sheets account appears.

3. **Scroll through the list of fonts on the right side of the window under My Fonts and locate the font or fonts you want to remove. Then, to remove a font, click the X located to the right of that font's name.**

The font disappears from the list of available fonts.

4. **Click OK.**

TIP

Removing a font from your list of fonts does not affect your spreadsheets, even if they contain a font you removed from the menu. Further, after you use a font in your spreadsheet, you can change more text to use that font even if you removed it from your Font menu. (A removed font, however, will not be available in any new spreadsheets, or existing spreadsheets not containing the font.)

Styling your data

You can accentuate a font by applying various styles to the font itself, including

>> **Size:** You can make your content bigger or smaller as you see fit.

>> **Bold:** You can make content bold, which makes the text visibly thicker. Bold font is sometimes referred to as having a *heavy weight.*

>> **Italics:** A slanted font is often referred to as italicized.

>> **Underline:** Place a line under your content to indicate importance.

>> **Strikethrough:** Place a line through the middle of your content. This is useful in communicating a change in your text or to illustrate a point.

>> **Color:** Track changes, distinguish individual users in collaboration, or simply add style to your content by changing the color.

Changing font size

You can change the size of your content by following these steps:

1. **Using your touchpad, select the cells you want to change by clicking and dragging your cursor.**

The selected text is highlighted.

2. **Open the Font Size menu in the Edit toolbar.**

It's the number found to the left of the Bold button in the Edit toolbar. When you click it, a menu appears, revealing several font sizes (in points) to choose from, as shown in Figure 9-14.

3. **Select the desired font size.**

Your selected data is now the chosen size.

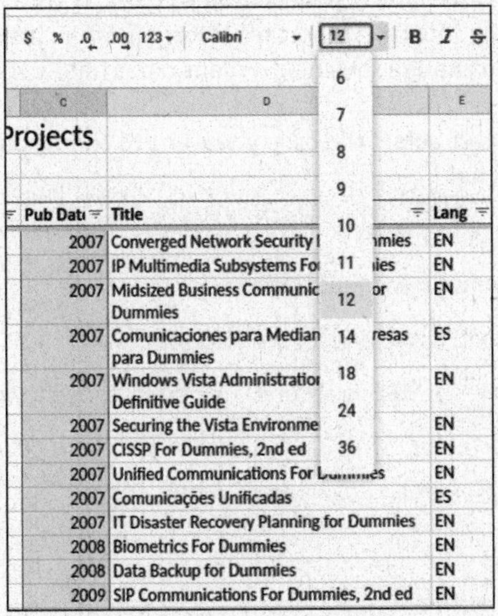

FIGURE 9-14:
Selecting font sizes in Google Sheets.

Applying bold, italics, underline, or strikethrough to your content

To apply formatting to a specific selection of cells, follow these steps:

1. **Using your touchpad, select the cells you want to change by clicking and dragging your cursor.**

   The selected cells are highlighted.

2. **Apply bold, italics, underline, or strikethrough, as needed.**

   You can use either of the following methods:

   - **To add bold, italics, or strikethrough:** Click the appropriate button in the middle of the Edit toolbar — the **B** button for bold, the *I* button for italic, or the **S** button for strikethrough. (No button exists for the underline on the standard Edit toolbar.)

   - **To add an underline:** Open the Format menu in the application menu and select Underline.

   Your selection changes appropriately.

TIP

You can quickly apply styles to your data by using hotkeys. Just press Ctrl+B (for bold), Ctrl+I (italic), Ctrl+U (underline), or Alt+Shift+5 (strikethrough).

Coloring your content

Google Sheets gives you the ability to change the color of your data so that you can visually group your data, indicate important information, or just give your spreadsheet a little pizazz! To change the color of your data, follow these steps:

1. **Using your touchpad, select the cells you want to change by clicking and dragging your cursor.**

   The selected cells are highlighted.

2. **Open the Color menu in the Edit toolbar.**

   It's the **A** button found to the right of the **S** button.

   A Color menu appears, revealing several color options, as shown in Figure 9-15.

3. **Select your desired color.**

   The data in the selected cells now appears in the selected color.

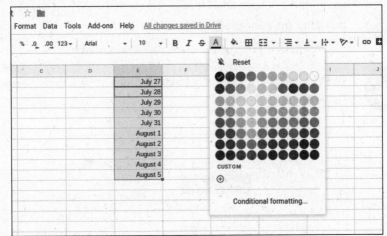

FIGURE 9-15:
Selecting colors
for text in
Google Sheets.

Changing alignment

Google Sheets gives you several options for changing the horizontal and vertical alignment of your data. Horizontal alignment options include

>> Left

>> Right

>> Center

Vertical alignment options include

>> Top

>> Middle

>> Bottom

To adjust the alignment of your data, follow these steps:

1. **Using your touchpad, select the cells you want to realign by clicking and dragging your cursor.**

The selected cells are highlighted.

2. **In the Edit toolbar, find and click the appropriate Alignment button.**

The Horizontal Alignment button is located a few buttons to the right of the text color button. The Vertical Alignment button is located to the right of the Horizontal Alignment button.

A menu with the alignment options appears.

3. **Click the desired alignment.**

The selected cells of data are realigned accordingly.

REMEMBER

You can hover over the alignment buttons to see their function, as shown in Figure 9-16.

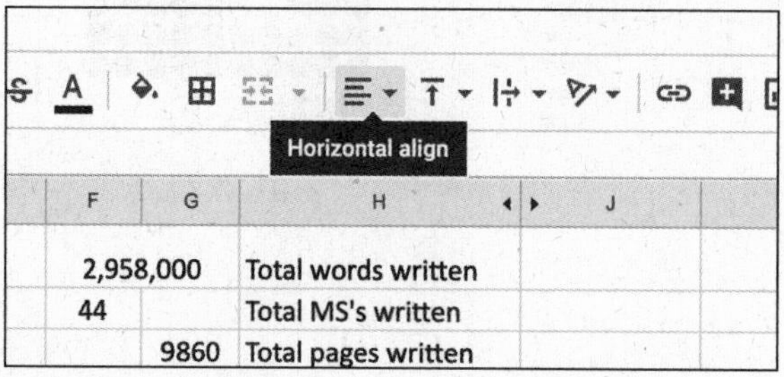

FIGURE 9-16:
Hovering over alignment buttons reveal their purpose.

	F	G	H	◀ ▶	J	
	2,958,000		Total words written			
	44		Total MS's written			
		9860	Total pages written			

(Horizontal align tooltip shown)

Wrapping text in a cell

By default, when you enter text into a cell, the text appears on a single line, so in order to show all the entered text, you may have to adjust the width of your cell. However, Sheets has a feature called *wrap text* that causes text to go to the next line after it reaches the maximum width of your cell. With this feature, you can set text to wrap in one cell or in every cell in a sheet. To activate wrap text, follow these steps:

1. **Using your touchpad, select the desired cells by clicking and dragging your cursor.**

The selected cells are highlighted.

2. **Open the Format menu.**

3. **Choose Wrap Text.**

Text that extends beyond the boundaries of your cell walls will be wrapped to another line, as shown in Figure 9-17. In this figure, the text in cell B4 is too long for the cell, and it spills over the cells to the right. The text in cell B5 is set for wrap text, so all the text stays in the cell, which takes multiple lines.

Clearing formatting

Sometimes you just need to start over. The good news is that Sheets makes it incredibly easy to wipe out all formatting in a section of cells or your complete spreadsheet. To clear your formatting, follow these steps:

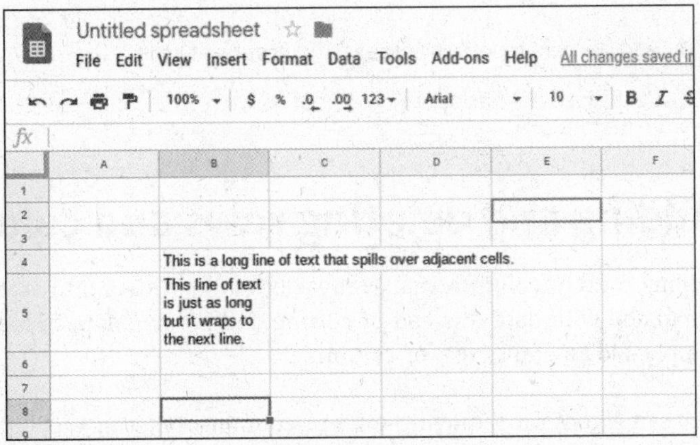
Untitled spreadsheet
File Edit View Insert Format Data Tools Add-ons Help All changes saved i
100% $ % .0 .00 123 Arial 10 B I
A B C D E F
This is a long line of text that spills over adjacent cells.
This line of text is just as long but it wraps to the next line.

FIGURE 9-17: The wrap text feature in action.

1. **Select the formatted cells you want to clear.**

   The selected cells are highlighted.

2. **Open the Format menu in the Applications menu.**
3. **Select Clear Formatting.**

   The selected data is reset to defaults: left-aligned, with all style elements — including color, underline, strikethrough, italics, bold, and so on — removed.

TIP

To clear the formatting of an entire document, press Ctrl+A instead of selecting cells. Pressing Ctrl+A selects the entire worksheet. (If your workbook has multiple worksheets or tabs, pressing Ctrl+A clears formatting only in the worksheet you are viewing.)

Customizing Your Spreadsheet

When you open Sheets for the first time (and when you click the + (plus sign) button to create a new spreadsheet), you're presented with a blank canvas of empty, uniform cells organized in a neat grid pattern. Sheets allows you to customize this grid of information so that it looks and works exactly how you like. In addition to all the text formatting discussed earlier, you can

- » Change the height of rows and the width of individual (or all) columns
- » Add and remove columns and rows
- » Merge multiple cells together into one cell
- » Hide rows and columns

>> Add borders to individual cells and groups of cells

>> Customize the background color of cells

Adding and deleting rows and columns

Adding rows or columns makes it easier to insert data into areas that are already populated with data. Instead of cutting and pasting data to make room, you can simply add an empty row or column.

The same goes for removing rows or columns. Deleting a column or row is a fast way to remove extraneous cells from your spreadsheet. When you get into formulas (see the section "Making Calculations with Formulas," later in this chapter), you will also find that adding and deleting rows and columns keeps your formulas and formatting intact.

Adding a new row or column

You can add a new row or column by following these steps:

1. **Using your touchpad, move your cursor to the row or column header of the row or column next to which you want to insert a new row or column and Alt-click the row or column header.**

Column headers are indicated by a letter. Row headers are indicated by a number.

A menu appears, revealing several options. The menu for rows is shown in Figure 9-18.

2. **Insert a new row by choosing Insert 1 Above or Insert 1 Below, or insert a new column by choosing Insert 1 Left or Insert 1 Right.**

A new row or column is inserted accordingly.

You can see from the menu that you can do other things with a row or column, including:

>> Delete a row or column

>> Clear a row or column

>> Hide a row or column

>> Resize a row or column (meaning, its width or height)

>> Group all cells in a row or column into a single cell

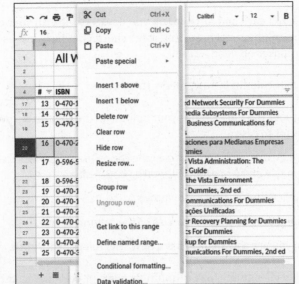

FIGURE 9-18:
The Alt-click menu for rows in Google Sheets.

TIP

Don't worry about making your spreadsheet too big. Size is never a problem. The largest spreadsheet you can make with Sheets can have up to 400,000 cells and as many as 256 columns.

Deleting a row or column

You can delete a row or column by following these steps:

1. Using your touchpad, move your cursor to the header of the row or column you want to delete.

2. Alt-click the row number or column letter.

A menu appears, revealing several options.

3. Click Delete Row or Delete Column.

The row or column is deleted. The remaining rows or columns move together to fill the gap.

Resizing columns and rows

The row and column sizes in Google Sheets are set by default to an arbitrary size. You can build a perfectly functional spreadsheet and never resize any columns or rows. However, resizing is a great way to ensure that your data is viewable and useful. If a string of text is too big for the current column width or row height, Sheets lets you quickly change the width or height to accommodate your needs. Also, if your columns are too wide or your rows too high, which may result in your having to scroll back and forth (or up and down) to view all your content, you can make some columns narrower (or rows shorter), which makes room for more content to appear on your screen.

To resize your column or row, follow these steps:

1. **Using your touchpad, move your pointer to the column or row header you want to resize.**

   Make sure that your pointer is over the line on the right side of the column or bottom side of the row that you would like to resize.

   Your pointer turns into a set of arrows.

2. **Click and drag to change the size of the column or row.**

3. **When you are satisfied with the new size, release your click.**

TIP

You can also change the size of multiple rows or columns at the same time. To do so, the columns or rows must be sequential. For example, you can resize columns 1, 2, and 3 at the same time, but you can't resize columns 1, 2, and 5 at the same time. To resize multiple columns or rows, follow these steps:

1. **Using your touchpad, click the header for the first column or row in the series you want to resize.**

   The selected row or column is highlighted.

2. **Shift-click the header for the last of the columns or rows in the series you want to resize.**

   Every row or column in the series is selected.

3. **Relocate your pointer so that it rests over the line dividing two rows or columns in your selection.**

   The pointer turns into a set of arrows.

4. **Click and drag the column or row to resize.**

5. **When you're satisfied, release your click.**

   Each row or column in the series is resized.

Hiding columns and rows

Hiding rows and columns is handy when you're presenting a spreadsheet and want to hide a row or column of notes, or when some of your data is necessary for calculations but not relevant enough to be shown. Hiding is a great way to keep data in its place but out of sight. To hide a row or column, follow these steps:

1. **Using your touchpad, move your pointer over the header of the row or column you want to hide.**

2. **Alt-click the row or column header.**

   A menu appears, revealing several options.

3. **Select Hide Column or Hide Row, whichever is appropriate.**

   The associated row or column vanishes, leaving only a set of arrows over the column or row dividing line.

   To restore your hidden column or row, click these arrows.

Merging cells

Sometimes you will want or even need to have a heading over several columns or rows. To do this, you need to merge multiple cells together so that they form a single cell spanning multiple columns or rows. To merge cells together, follow these steps:

1. **Shift-click the contiguous cells you want to merge.**

   The selected cells become highlighted.

2. **Click the Merge Cells button in the Edit toolbar, located nine buttons from the right.**

   The highlighted cells merge.

WARNING

   Any data in merged cells may be lost. Be sure to have a copy of the cell's contents prior to merging.

3. **To unmerge the cells, select the newly merged cell and click the Merge Cells button again.**

   The cells that you merged are restored to being individual cells. If you placed content in the merged cell, that content will appear in the first row or column of the previously merged set.

Formatting numbers

People use spreadsheets primarily to organize and calculate numeric data. With Google Sheets, you can auto-format your cells to accommodate several numeric data types, including

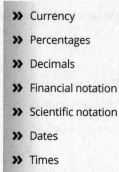

>> Currency

>> Percentages

>> Decimals

>> Financial notation

>> Scientific notation

>> Dates

>> Times

Formatting cells for these numeric types can be done by following these steps:

1. **Using your touchpad, select the cell or cells you want to format.**

2. **Open the Format menu.**

3. **Move your pointer over Number in the menu.**

    A submenu appears, revealing several formatting options.

4. **Select the desired formatting style, as shown in Figure 9-19.**

    The selected cells now auto-format numeric entries to match the selected style.

FIGURE 9-19:
Applying
auto-formatting
to selected cells
in Google Sheets.

Grouping cells with colors and borders

When working with spreadsheets containing large amounts of data, the numbers and letters can begin to blend together. You can distinguish groups of cells with borders or colors to make navigating your spreadsheet easier. Borders and cell shading can also add a nice touch of style to your spreadsheets. You can add borders to your spreadsheet by following these steps:

1. **Using your touchpad, select the cells you want to style by clicking and dragging your cursor.**

The selected cells are highlighted.

2. **Click the Border button in the Edit toolbar.**

The Border button, which looks like a little square with four squares inside, is a few buttons to the right of the Bold, Italic, and Strikethrough formatting buttons.

A menu appears, giving you several options.

3. **To simply place a border around your cells, locate the image that shows a border outline and click it.**

The images in the Border menu, as shown in Figure 9-20, illustrate precisely where the border will go if selected. You can also change the border style to dotted or dashed by selecting the Line option in the Border Style menu, or change the color of your border by using the Border Color option.

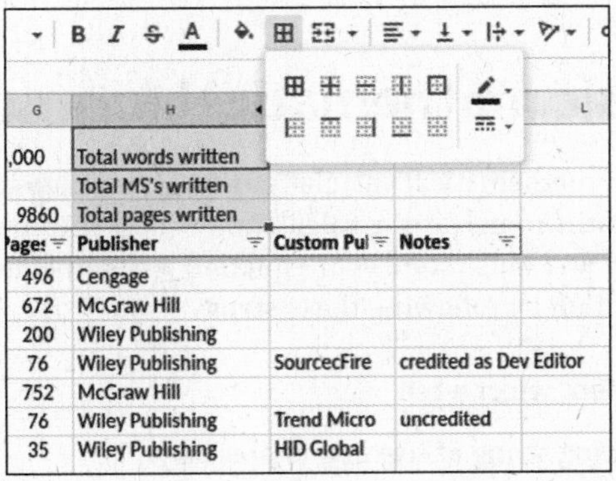

TIP

FIGURE 9-20: Adding a border to cells in Google Sheets.

You can also create visual separation in your spreadsheet by incorporating color into your cells. To apply a color background to a cell or group of cells, follow these steps:

1. **Using your touchpad, select the cells you want to color by clicking and dragging your cursor.**

   The selected cells are highlighted.

2. **Click the Background Color button in the Edit toolbar.**

   This button is located just to the right of the Bold, Italic, and Strikethrough buttons and looks like a paint can being poured out. When you hover over the button, the words *Fill Color* appear.

   A menu appears, giving you several options.

3. **Select a color from the menu.**

   The background of the selected cells is changed to the chosen color.

Making Calculations with Formulas

Google Sheets is a powerful spreadsheet tool. With Sheets, you can perform analysis on text and numeric values alike, and incorporate financial, mathematical, and statistical analysis. The following sections serve as an intro to Sheets' basic functions and formulas.

Adding basic mathematical formulas

Sheets can perform mathematical calculations for you. All you have to do is tell Sheets that you want it to perform a calculation on the information you enter in the cell. To do this, you must start your equation with an equals sign (=). Make sheets do basic addition by following these steps:

1. **With Sheets open, select a cell.**

2. **Type the following string of characters precisely:**

   ```
   =50+50
   ```

3. **Press Enter.**

   Sheets solves the equation and displays the answer, 100.

TIP

Although the cell itself displays 100, if you look on the Formula bar, you see the formula that still reads what you typed in: =50+50.

You can use several mathematical operators to perform calculations with Sheets. They include

>> **Addition:** +

>> **Subtraction:** –

>> **Division:** /

>> **Multiplication:** *

Sheets interprets the order of operations according to simple rules: It performs calculations within parentheses first, followed by multiplication or division (from left to right), and finally, addition or subtraction (from left to right).

To ensure that Sheets always follows the mathematical order of operations you intended, use parentheses to group operations together. For example, in a cell, enter the following equation:

```
=((5+5)*8)/2
```

You get the answer 40. When more than one set of parentheses exists, Sheets performs the instructions within the innermost set first and then works its way outward. Without parentheses, the equation becomes

```
=5+5*8/2
```

This returns the answer 25. Use parentheses to ensure that your operations are performed in the order you intended.

WARNING

Building formulas can become complex very quickly. To edit a formula, select the cell that contains the formula and then click in the Formula bar at the top of your Sheets window to edit the formula. Typing in the cell itself overwrites the contents, leaving you to start again!

Adding formulas to calculate values in cells

Google Sheets was designed for use beyond just standard calculator functions. You can also use Sheets to perform calculations using data in multiple cells within your spreadsheet. Instead of entering numbers into your equations, you can enter cell coordinates. To see how this works, you first have to have numbers in some cells, so this example walks you through adding some data and then entering the formula for Sheets to calculate:

1. **With Sheets open, enter the number** 25 **into cell A2.**

2. **Enter the number** 50 **into cell A3.**

3. **Enter the number** 75 **into cell A4.**

4. **In cell B5, enter the following equation:**

   ```
   =A2+A3+A4
   ```

5. **Press Enter.**

   Sheets adds cells A2, A3, and A4 together and then displays the answer — 150 — in cell B5.

   Next, try changing the data in any of the cells A2, A3, or A4, and see how the value in cell B5 changes immediately.

TIP

Don't forget to put the equals sign (=) before a formula, otherwise the contents of the cell will contain the characters in the formula, instead of the result that Sheets would get by performing the calculation.

You can also use Google Sheets to perform a calculation using values in cells along with other values in the formula. Try it yourself with these steps:

1. **With Sheets open, enter the number** 25 **into cell A2.**

2. **Enter the number** 50 **into cell A3.**

3. **Enter the number** 75 **into cell A4.**

4. **In cell A5, enter the following equation:**

   ```
   =(A2+A3+A4)*10
   ```

5. **Press Enter.**

   Sheets adds cells A2, A3, and A4 together and then multiplies the total by 10. The resulting answer is 1500, which it displays in cell A5, as shown in Figure 9-21.

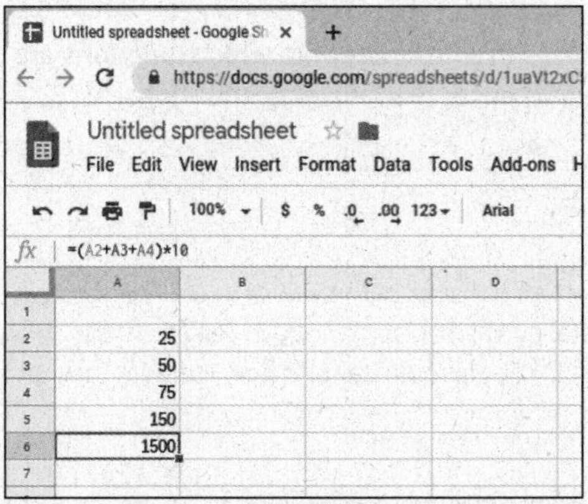

FIGURE 9-21:
Using formulas in
Google Sheets to
add the values of
cells together.

Working with spreadsheet functions

Sheets has an extensive library of functions that perform a vast array of computations. However, the most widely used functions in Sheets are

>> **SUM:** Adds all the numbers in a range of cells.

>> **AVERAGE:** Outputs the average of the values in a specific set of cells or in a range.

>> **COUNT:** Count how many numbers are in a list of cells. You can specify cells or enter a range.

>> **MAX:** Outputs the largest number in a specific set of cells or a range.

>> **MIN:** Outputs the smallest number in a specific set of cells or a range.

Functions simplify the process of writing complex formulas and reduce the amount of typing needed to get the desired result. To try using the SUM function, follow these steps:

1. **With Sheets open, enter the number** 25 **into cell A2.**

2. **Enter the number** 50 **into cell A3.**

3. **Enter the number** 75 **into cell A4.**

4. **In cell A6, enter the following equation:**

   ```
   =SUM(A2:A4)
   ```

5. **Press Enter.**

   The formula tells Sheets that you want to add the values in cells A2 through A4. The output value is 150, which Sheets displays in cell A6.

6. **To use parentheses to set the order in which functions are used in the equation, in cell A6, enter the following equation:**

```
=(SUM(A2:A4)*10)
```

7. **Press Enter.**

   Sheets first calculates the sum of the values in cells A2 through A4 and then multiplies the total by 10, displaying 1500 in cell A6. This is shown in Figure 9-22. Note the content in the Formula bar and how it differs from the Formula bar in Figure 9-21.

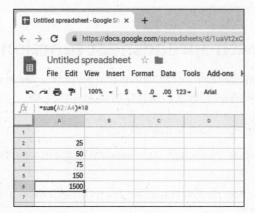

FIGURE 9-22: Using functions to add the contents of cells together.

Saving Documents

As you work in Google Sheets, Google will save almost every change in real-time to your Google Drive account (remember that Google Drive is your cloud-based storage that allows you to safely store your files and access them from any device with an Internet connection). Every file you create with Google Sheets is saved to your Drive folder so that you can access it at home, on the road, at work, or anywhere else you might need to, and from any device you happen to be using at the time. As is the case with Docs, Sheets has no manual Save feature.

Naming your document

When you open a new spreadsheet with Sheets, the default name for the spreadsheet is Untitled Spreadsheet. You don't, however, want to leave your spreadsheet untitled. Drive doesn't have a problem with storing multiple files with the same name, but it's best if you name your spreadsheet immediately so that you save yourself a little confusion. To name your spreadsheet, follow these steps:

1. **Open a new spreadsheet.**

   The easiest way to open a new spreadsheet is by launching Sheets from the Launcher.

   A Chrome web browser opens and loads Sheets.

2. **Click the "+" to start a new worksheet.**

   After Sheets is open, the name of your new document, Untitled Spreadsheet, appears in the top-left corner, as shown in Figure 9-23.

3. **Click Untitled Spreadsheet in the top-left corner of your spreadsheet.**

   The cursor is positioned preceding the words Untitled Spreadsheet.

4. **Type the new name for your spreadsheet and press Enter.**

   The name Untitled Spreadsheet is now replaced with your new name.

   The next time you look at Google Drive, you'll see the new filename, which is your renamed spreadsheet. As you continue to make edits, the spreadsheet document will be updated and saved in real time.

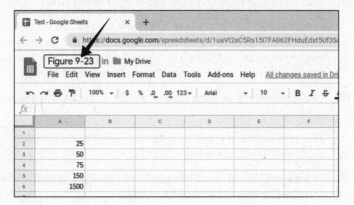

FIGURE 9-23:
You can change the spreadsheet's name.

Exporting documents

From time to time, you may need to export your spreadsheets to formats that others may be comfortable with. Sheets allows you to export spreadsheets to a few standard formats, including

» Microsoft Excel (.xlsx)

» OpenDocument (.ods)

» PDF (.pdf)

» Comma-separated values (.csv)

» Tab-separated values (.tsv)

» Web page (.html)

WARNING

Exporting documents to different file types may change the formatting within your document. For example, exporting to the CSV and TSV formats strips out all formatting, such as borders, fonts, and colors. Before sending along your spread-sheets after an export, you should review them to ensure that everything is as it should be!

You can export your documents by following these steps:

1. **Click File and hover your cursor over Download As.**

   A submenu appears, revealing the file types that are available for export.

2. **Select the desired file type.**

   You see a preview of your exported spreadsheet.

3. **Click the Export button in the upper right of the Sheets window.**

   Google Sheets now asks you to specify the name of the file to create, as well as the location. By default, your file will be located in the Downloads folder. You can, however, click a different folder on the left side of the Save File As window, including Google Drive or even a folder within Google Drive.

4. **Click the folder you want to save the file in, click the filename, and then click Save.**

   Your spreadsheet is exported in the desired file type to the location you specified. (Take a look at Figure 9-24.)

5. **To view the downloaded file, open the Files app, go to the folder you specified in Step 4, and look for the file.**

TIP

When you export a spreadsheet, there are several options in the Export window, including whether you want to export just the tab displayed or all tabs, page orientation (portrait or landscape), formatting, margins, and more. Try these to see how your exported spreadsheet appears. (You can always delete these files later using the Files app.)

TIP

Exporting a spreadsheet doesn't change the original spreadsheet; instead, it makes a copy of it in the specified format. The original Google Sheets file is still there, and you can continue to edit it as much as you like.

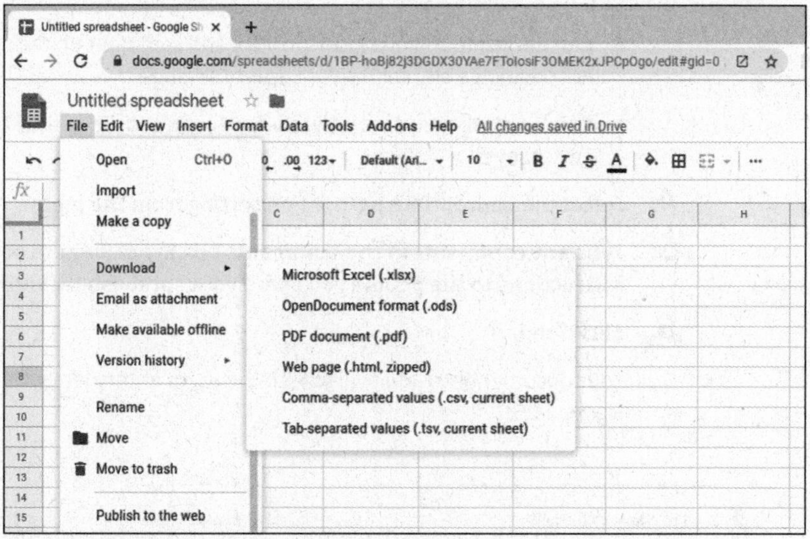

FIGURE 9-24:
Exporting a
spreadsheet
to a folder in
Google Drive.

Collaboration with Sheets

By default, Google Sheets and Google Drive make your files inaccessible to everyone other than you. You can, however, change the visibility settings on your files
and invite specific people, or even the entire world, to comment, view, or edit your
document! To share your Spreadsheet with specific people, follow these steps:

1. **Click the blue Share button in the top-right corner of your Sheets window.**

   A window appears, giving you several options for sharing your spreadsheet.

2. **Enter the email address of each person with whom you want to share
   your file in the Invite People field at the bottom of the window.**

   Be sure to separate the addresses with commas.

   If the email address is in your address book, Sheets tries to autofill the
   information.

3. **To set the permissions of the collaborators, first click the link directly to
   the right of the Invite People field.**

   A menu with three options appears:

   • **Can Edit:** Allows users to edit the spreadsheet, comment, view, and change
     permissions

- **Can Comment:** Allows users to view and comment on the spreadsheet but not to change any content or security settings

- **Can View:** Allows users only to view the spreadsheet; they cannot make any changes

4. **Select the appropriate permission setting from the menu.**

5. **Type any comments in the Comments box if you want to send any instructions to the people you share your spreadsheet with.**

6. **Click Send.**

    Your document is made available to the users immediately, as shown in Figure 9-25.

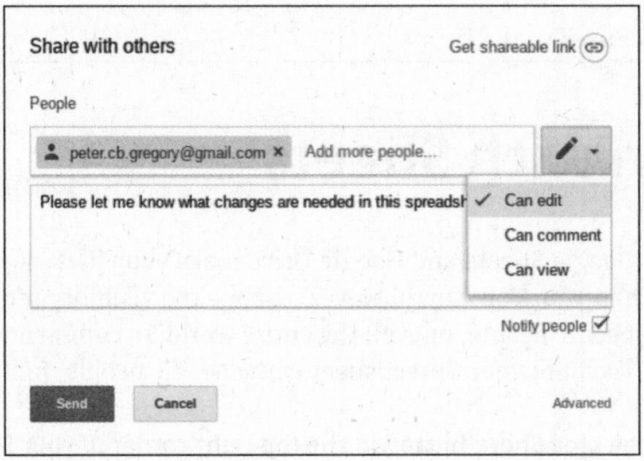

FIGURE 9-25: Sharing a spreadsheet with other people.

TIP

The users who are invited to view, edit, or comment on your spreadsheet have to log in to Google Docs using the email addresses with which you shared the spreadsheet. If a user doesn't have a Google Account under the email address you used, you have to invite her with the address she uses for her Google Account. She also has the option to create a Google Account using the same email address.

Tracking Versions of Your Spreadsheet

Keeping track of revisions is very important when creating documents with multiple collaborators. Fortunately, Google Sheets handles version control masterfully. As you and your collaborators make changes to your spreadsheets, Sheets stamps those changes with the time and date so that you can view previous versions of your spreadsheet and even revert to an earlier version if you need to.

Version tracking is a default feature of Google Sheets, so you don't need to do anything to take advantage of it. To view your version history, follow these steps:

1. **Open the File menu, hover over Version History, and tap See Version History.**

A Version History box appears in the right portion of your screen. The box contains the various versions of your spreadsheet in order from the most recent to the oldest. If you made multiple changes on any given day, a tiny black arrow appears to the left of the date; click the arrow to see the details for that date. The names of the people who saved the spreadsheet are also shown. (If you are not sharing your spreadsheet, it will always be your name.) See Figure 9-26.

2. **Click a version date in the Version History box.**

A preview of the version you chose appears in the main document area. Changes that occurred between versions appear in green.

3. **To change versions, click Restore This Version.**

Google Sheets will ask you to name this version.

The restored version becomes the current version, and the previous version of the application is saved in the Version History, so you can revert back to it if needed.

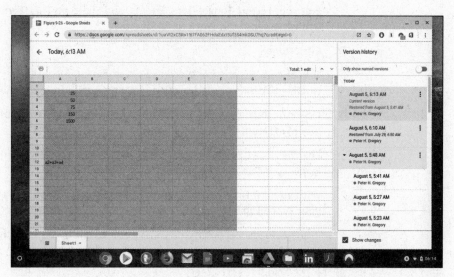

FIGURE 9-26:
Viewing versions of a spreadsheet in Google Sheets.

Using Sheets Offline

Google Sheets is a web-based spreadsheet tool, which means that you must have an Internet connection to access all its features. However, an offline version of Sheets is available in the event that you find yourself without a connection to the Internet.

While offline, you can't access some of the features available to Sheets users who are connected to the Internet (such as downloading new fonts). You can, however, create spreadsheets and save them. Later, when you connect to the Internet, Drive uploads the saved spreadsheets and enables all Internet-only features.

To use Google Sheets offline, you must first enable Google Drive for offline use. Follow these steps to make sure that you're set up for offline use:

1. **Open the Launcher and click the Google Drive icon.**

   A Chrome web browser appears and takes you to your drive.

2. **On the right side of the screen, click the Settings icon (it looks like a gear).**

3. **In the resulting menu, click Settings.**

   The Settings window appears.

4. **In the Offline section, select the check box that reads, Create, Open and Edit your recent Google Docs, Sheets, and Slides on This Device While Offline to sync your work for offline use.**

5. **Click Done.**

   Your Sheets files are now synced and available for offline editing. You can test whether you have properly enabled offline access by turning off your Wi-Fi.

6. **Open the Settings panel in the bottom-right of your screen and click the blue Wi-Fi icon.**

   The Wi-Fi icon turns from blue to gray, indicating that your Chromebook is no longer connected to the Internet.

7. **With your Wi-Fi turned off, switch back to Google Drive and open one of your synced spreadsheets.**

   If your spreadsheet opens and you are able to edit it, you know that you have successfully engaged offline use and synced your documents.

Chapter **10**

Preparing Presentations

Presentations have come a long way in the past 40 years. You might recall that family picture night used to involve a slide projector with 50+ pictures loaded into a circular carousel that Mom or Dad would click through while the kids and neighbors sat in misery. Then there was the overhead projector with transparencies. Now people use interactive presentations that involve text, images, audio, and video. There are several presentation creation applications available today, and you can probably guess the gold standard in corporate America: Microsoft PowerPoint.

PowerPoint has become so entrenched in business and education that the name is almost used interchangeably to mean *presentation*, the way people refer to tissues as Kleenex and lip balm as ChapStick. But the cultural penetration of PowerPoint didn't keep Google from creating a free presentation software that could rival it.

Google Slides is a free, web-based, presentation software that gives you the ability to make high-powered, engaging presentations that you can access anywhere in the world thanks to the vast nature of the Google platform. This isn't an either/or proposition, however. Slides created with Google Slides can be viewed and edited with PowerPoint, and vice versa.

In this chapter, you learn how to create beautiful presentations with Google Slides. Use existing templates or create your own; add, edit, and style images and text; collaborate with teams around the globe; and export your presentations to multiple formats so that you can share your presentations with colleagues, coworkers, classmates, and more. Google Slides is a powerful tool for communication in any setting.

Navigating Google Slides

Slides is Google's presentation software and works well for those looking for an alternative to Microsoft's PowerPoint, which is arguably the industry leader in presentation software. Like the rest of the Google office suite, Slides is easy to use for beginners and experienced presentation makers alike. If you have any experience with PowerPoint, the transition will feel very easy to you. As with other Google tools, Slides can easily read and also create presentations in PowerPoint format that another person using PowerPoint can also use.

To launch Google Slides from your Chromebook, open the Launcher and click the Slides icon. The Slides application opens in a Chrome browser window and creates a new untitled document resembling what you see in Figure 10-1.

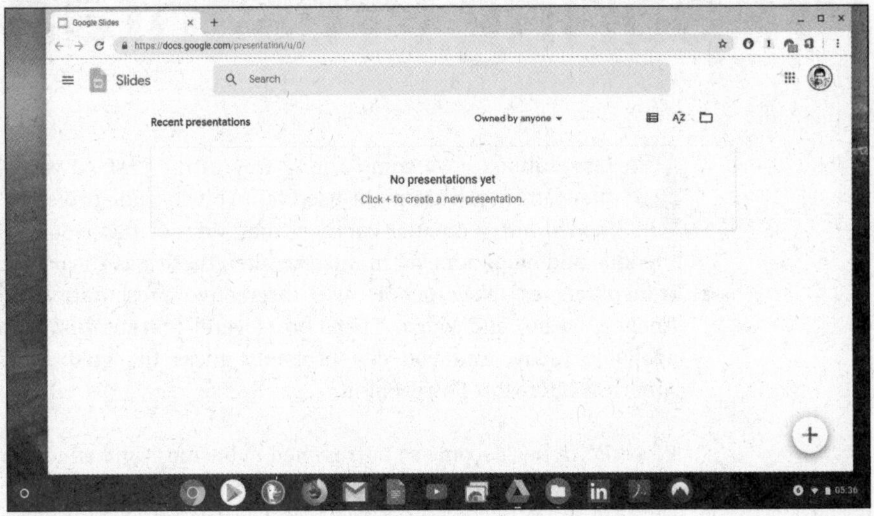

FIGURE 10-1:
The Google Slides startup screen.

Creating your presentation

To begin creating your presentation, click the colorful + (plus sign) icon near the lower-right corner of the Slides window. Slides creates the first slide for you — a blank title slide. To the right, Slides shows a list of themes that you can select from if you like. (See Figure 10-2.) You can scroll through the many different color and style themes. When you see one that you like, just click it, and all the slides you create in your presentation styled according to the theme you selected.

Note that themes have names. The name of the default theme is Simple Light.

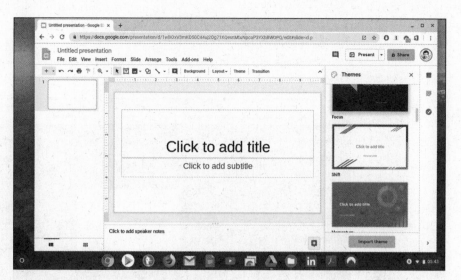

FIGURE 10-2:
Your new
Google Slides
presentation
with the Themes
selector.

TIP

After you select a theme or to dismiss the list of themes, just click the X at the top of the Themes selector. To bring the Themes selector back, click the Theme button on the Slides toolbar.

After selecting a theme, the next order of business is to select the shape of the slides in your presentation. Slides gives you three standard options for screen shapes with respect to the aspect ratio of your screen (or the projector that you might plan to use to present your slides):

>> **Standard 4:3:** This was the standard shape of all video captured from the early days of motion pictures. It's often referred to as the video format of the 20th century.

>> **Widescreen 16:9:** This is the shape of video shown in cinemas and the standard for widescreen HD televisions and most laptop and computer monitor screens.

>> **Widescreen 16:10:** Also referred to as 8:5, this format is the format of tablet computers, as well as some computer and monitor screens.

If you don't pick the desired aspect ratio for your presentation at this point, Slides defaults to 16:9.

To select your aspect ratio, follow these steps:

1. Click File in the Slides menu and then, in the window that appears, scroll down and select Page Setup.

A page setup window appears, revealing the three aspect ratio options in the drop-down list, shown in Figure 10-3.

2. **Choose an option and click Apply.**

   The shape and size of your presentation is set as selected.

FIGURE 10-3:
Selecting an
aspect ratio
for your
Google Slides
presentation.

Surveying the Slides menu area

Google Slides is divided into four main areas: the menu area, the slide navigator, the slide editor, and the speaker notes editor. The menu area itself can be broken up into two parts: the Applications menu and the Edit toolbar. These areas are all shown in Figure 10-4.

The Applications menu

The Applications menu features several options:

>> **File:** File-specific options and controls for creating, saving, exporting, printing, and otherwise managing your presentation overall.

>> **Edit:** Copy, paste, delete, and otherwise move and manipulate the contents of your presentation. Also, you can look for content and undo or redo previous changes.

>> **View:** Modify your view by adding and removing toolbars, zooming in, showing the ruler or speaker notes, and going into Presentation mode.

>> **Insert:** Add images, text boxes, video, lines, shapes, tables, word art, animation, comments, and other objects.

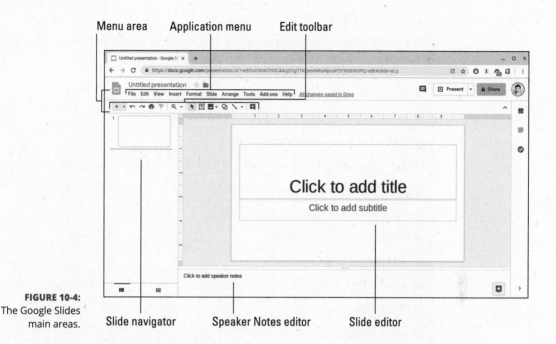

Menu area   Application menu   Edit toolbar

FIGURE 10-4:
The Google Slides
main areas.

Slide navigator   Speaker Notes editor   Slide editor

>> **Format:** Manipulate the appearance of your text, apply styles, edit paragraph formats, crop images, and so on.

>> **Slide:** Add, edit, duplicate, or delete slides, layouts, themes, or transitions — basically, perform any function that pertains to the slide.

>> **Arrange:** Arrange objects like text boxes, images, videos, and so on so that they align neatly.

>> **Tools:** Spell check, research information, or define words.

>> **Table:** Insert tables and add, edit, or delete rows and columns. This feature is visible only when you have a table that is already in your slide.

>> **Add-ons:** Find and obtain additional capabilities for Google Slides to make your presentation even better.

>> **Help:** Get help with slides or search for menu options.

The Edit toolbar

The Edit toolbar, located directly beneath the Applications menu, contains several shortcuts to commonly used features contained in the Applications menu. The

Edit toolbar makes the performance of routine tasks faster and easier. With the Edit toolbar, you can quickly perform these tasks:

>> Add slides to your presentation

>> Undo/redo changes you've made to your presentation

>> Print all or a part of your presentation

>> Apply formatting found in one part of your slide to another part of your slide

>> Zoom into and out of your presentation

>> Set your pointer to select objects

>> Add text boxes to your slide

>> Add images to your slide

>> Add or draw shapes

>> Add or draw lines

>> Add comments

>> Change slide backgrounds

>> Select a different layout for your slide

>> Change themes

>> Change slide transitions

The slide navigator

The slide navigator is located directly under the Applications menu and to the left of the slide editor. Slides you add to your presentation appear in the slide navigator in miniature. Use the slide navigator to rearrange slides, delete slides, hide slides from presentations, and copy and paste slides within the navigator.

Any selected slide has a yellow border. When selected, a slide appears in the slide editor to the right of the slide navigator. When you create a new presentation, you have one slide in your presentation, and therefore just one slide in the slide navigator. You can add more slides to your presentation by following these steps:

1. **Click the arrow beside the Add Slide button in the Edit toolbar.**

It's the first button on the left side of the toolbar.

A menu appears with six layout options for your new slide, shown in Figure 10-5.

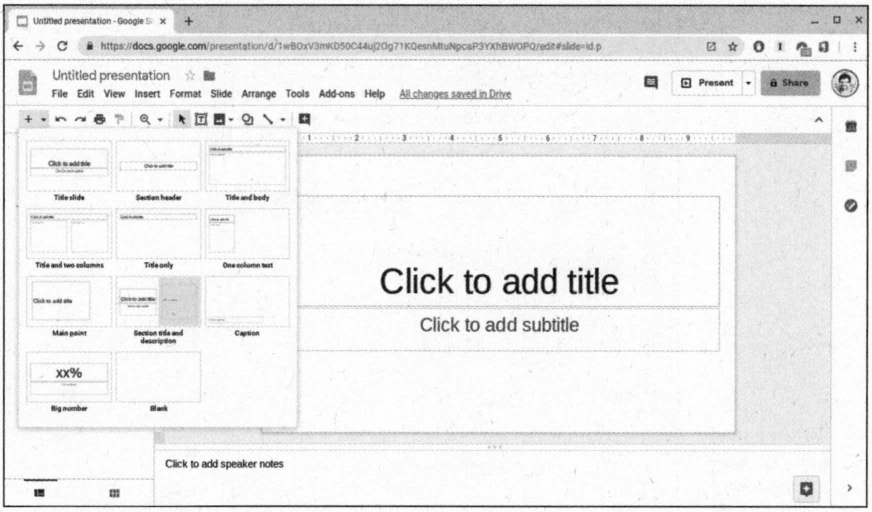

FIGURE 10-5:
Adding a slide
and choosing a
layout.

FIGURE 10-5:
Adding a slide
and choosing a
layout.

2. **Click any slide layout in the menu to select it.**

Your new slide appears in the slide navigator directly following the active slide.

If you click the + (plus sign) part of the Add Slide button, Slides puts a new, blank slide after the slide you are viewing, with the same layout of the slide you are viewing. You can also quickly add slides by pressing Ctrl+M.

If you add a slide in the wrong place in your presentation, you can rearrange your slides by following these steps:

1. **In the slide navigator, locate the slide you want to move.**

2. **Click and drag the slide up or down your slide navigator to the desired location.**

A location indicator, like the one pictured in Figure 10-6, moves with your selection as you scroll through the slide navigator.

3. **Place the location indicator between the two slides where you would like to relocate your select slide, and then release the click.**

The slide is moved to the new location.

To delete a slide from your presentation, use the following steps:

1. **Click the slide you want to delete in the slide navigator.**

The selected slide is highlighted with a blue border.

You can select multiple slides by Ctrl-clicking each slide.

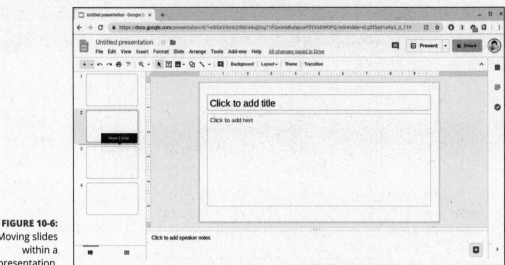

FIGURE 10-6:
Moving slides
within a
presentation.

2. **Alt-click the selected slide.**

   A menu with several options appears.

3. **Select Delete Slide.**

   The selected slide is deleted immediately.

TIP

You can also delete a slide by selecting the slide in the slide navigator and pressing the Backspace or Delete key.

The slide editor

The slide editor (see Figure 10-7) is the large work area located directly below the menu area and directly to the right of the slide navigator. In the slide editor, you can add text, images, video, and other elements to your slide. The selected slide in the slide navigator will appear in the slide editor area, thus making it available to be edited.

Below the slide editor is a speaker notes editor, in which you can add notes about the current slide. The notes aren't visible to the audience when you show your presentation, but they can serve as memory cues and talking points for you so that you aren't simply reading the contents of your slides.

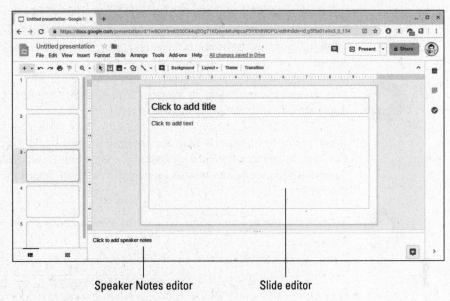

FIGURE 10-7:
The slide editor is
where you add
and edit content
in a single slide.

Speaker Notes editor   Slide editor

Customizing your view

Before you dive into your first presentation, you might find it helpful to change
your view in Google Slides. You can compact the Applications menu area by clicking the Hide the Menus button, which appears as a tiny up arrow to the far right
of the toolbar, beneath the Share button. When you click this button, the Applications menu compacts and disappears from sight, as shown in Figure 10-8.

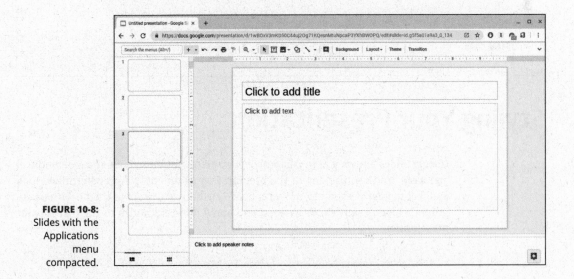

FIGURE 10-8:
Slides with the
Applications
menu
compacted.

To restore the menu, click the Show Menus button at the far-right of the Edit toolbar. When the Applications menu is hidden, this button appears as a tiny down arrow.

TIP

You can also use the keyboard shortcut Shift+Ctrl+F to toggle between having the Applications menu displayed or compacted.

If you prefer to completely hide the Applications menu and the Edit toolbar, you can do so by opening the View menu and choosing Full Screen. (Figure 10-9 shows Slides with the menu and toolbar hidden.) To exit Full Screen mode, simply press the Esc key.

TIP

To hide the speaker notes editor, open the View menu and choose Show Speaker Notes.

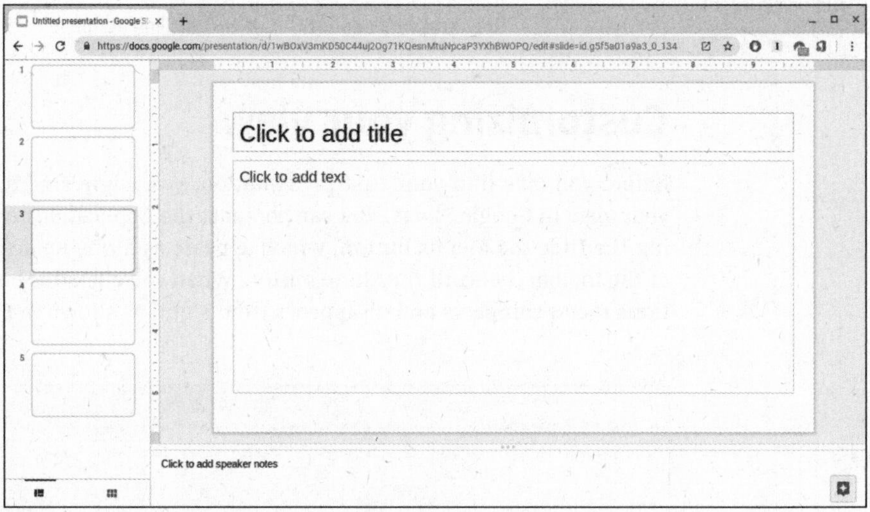

FIGURE 10-9:
Google Slides in Full-Screen mode.

Styling Your Presentation

Google Slides allows you to customize your presentation to have the look and feel you want. You can use any of the prebuilt themes to apply a predetermined look and feel to your presentation. You can also customize your own theme with background colors, textures, or images, and apply different styles to the text in your presentation.

Changing background color or background image

Each slide in your presentation will have a default background specific to the theme you selected for your presentation. If you selected the Light theme, for example, your background will simply be a solid white. You can, however, change the color of the background of your slide by following these steps:

1. **Using the slide navigator, select the slide that will receive the new background.**

   The selected slide appears in the slide editor.

2. **Click the Background button in the Edit toolbar (or select Change Background in the Slide menu).**

   The Background window appears, as shown in Figure 10-10.

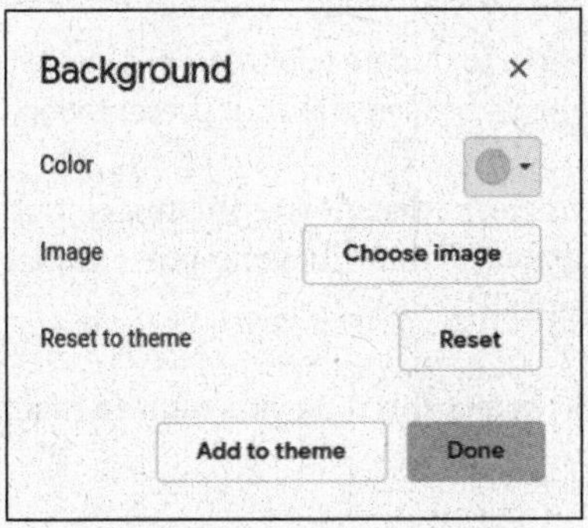

FIGURE 10-10: The Background window in Google Slides.

3. **Open the Color drop-down list and choose the new color for the background of your slide.**

   The color is applied to the background of the current slide.

4. **Click Done to apply the changes to the current slide.**

   Alternatively, you can click Add to Theme to update the current theme, which will also apply the changes to every slide with the same layout in your presentation.

To add a background texture or an image to the background of your slide or slides, follow these steps:

1. **Select an image and click Select, shown in Figure 10-11.**

   The image is applied as a background to the current slide.

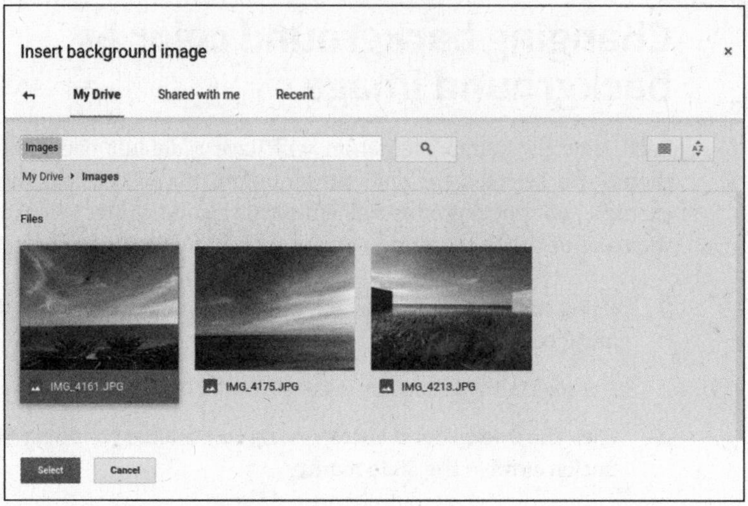

FIGURE 10-11:
Browsing for a slide background image.

2. **Click Done to apply the changes to the current slide.**

   Or you can click Add to Theme to update your theme, which will apply the changes to every slide of the same layout in your presentation.

If you decide that you want to clear the color or the image out of a slide, you can easily reset a single slide or every slide in your presentation to your theme's default by following these steps:

1. **Using the slide navigator, select the slide you want to reset.**

   The slide appears in the slide editor.

2. **Click the Background button in the Edit toolbar.**

   The Background window appears.

3. **Click Reset.**

   The background for the selected slide is reset to the theme's default.

4. **Click Done to apply the changes to the current slide.**

   Alternatively, click Add to Theme to update your theme, which will apply the changes to every slide with the same layout in your presentation.

Applying a different theme

The good news is that if you change your mind about a theme, you can change it, even long after you've begun building your presentation. To change your theme, follow these steps:

1. **Click the Theme button in the Edit toolbar.**

   The Theme Gallery appears to the right of the slide editor.

2. **Scroll through the list of available themes to view available options.**

3. **Click a theme's thumbnail to select it.**

   The theme is highlighted, indicating your selection.

4. **Click OK.**

   The selected theme is applied to your presentation.

Importing a presentation theme

Google Slides provides you with a small assortment of themes to get you going with your Slides presentations. However, endless numbers of themes are available for you online that can be imported into your theme gallery. To import a new theme, follow these steps:

1. **Obtain a theme from a friend, colleague, or trusted Internet site and download the theme to your Chromebook or your Google Drive.**

2. **Click the Theme button in the Edit toolbar.**

   The Theme Gallery window appears.

3. **Click Import Theme.**

   The Import Theme pop-up window appears.

4. **Choose a theme that's already available in your Drive account — these are shown under Presentations — or choose one from your Chromebook by clicking Upload.**

5. **After you select a theme, click Select.**

   The theme is uploaded and applied to your presentation.

Working with Text

In Google Slides, each piece of content that you add to a slide is treated as an object, including images, tables, charts, videos, and even text blocks. You can then arrange and organize objects on the slides to fit the desired look and feel of each slide.

To simplify things and provide some continuity within your presentation, your theme comes with several predefined slide layouts. These are particularly useful in ensuring that text boxes such as those for titles appear in the same location from slide to slide. You don't have to use layouts, however; you can make every slide appear as you want by adding and deleting objects at will. The benefit to this approach is that it gives you a blank canvas on which to create the exact look you like. Using default slide layouts ensures that your text is in the same place from slide to slide, however, so avoiding layouts can produce slides that appear sloppy or out of sync.

To apply a defined layout to a slide, follow these steps:

1. **Create a new slide by pressing Ctrl+M or by clicking the New Slide button on the left end of the toolbar.**

   A new slide appears in the slide navigator with a default layout applied.

2. **Using the slide navigator, select the newly created slide.**

   A yellow highlight appears on the selected slide.

3. **Click the Layout button on the Edit toolbar.**

   A menu appears, revealing multiple options.

4. **Select the layout you want to apply to your selected slide.**

   The layout is applied to the slide.

TIP

You can explore the different layouts available in your current theme by changing the layout of your slide and then looking at the new layout on your slide. You may see one or more text boxes, and possibly other graphics features such as colors, patterns, or images, depending on the theme you have selected.

Adding and deleting text boxes

New layouts primarily involve the placement of *text boxes*, which are containers for the text on your slides. When you want to add text to a slide, you must first add a text box, and then you can begin adding text within the text box.

You can add a text box to any slide, regardless of that slide's layout. The following steps show you how. (To minimize confusion, in this example, you add a text box to a blank slide.) Follow these steps to add a text box:

1. **Create a new slide by pressing Ctrl+M.**

   A new slide appears in the slide navigator with a default layout applied.

2. **Using the slide navigator, select the newly created slide.**

   A yellow highlight appears on the selected slide.

3. **Click the Layout button in the Edit toolbar.**

   A menu appears, revealing multiple options.

4. **Select the Blank layout.**

   Nearly every theme has a layout called Blank that has no text boxes at all, and very little else, in most cases.

5. **Click the Text Box button in the Edit toolbar.**

   The Text Box button is on the menu bar and shows a capital T with a box around it.

   After you click the Text Box button, your pointer turns into crosshairs.

6. **In the slide editor, move your pointer to where you would like to draw your text box.**

7. **Click and drag your pointer across the slide.**

   A rectangular box appears that can be resized depending on the movement of your pointer.

8. **When you're satisfied with the shape and size of your text box, release the click.**

   Your text box is created and made active, like that shown in Figure 10-12.

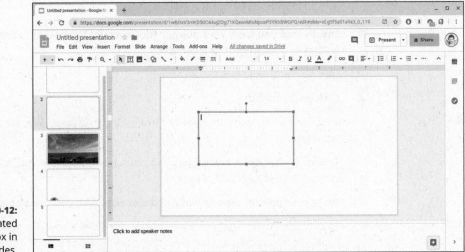

FIGURE 10-12:
A newly created text box in Google Slides.

You can delete a text box almost as easily as you created it by following these steps:

1. **Ensure that you have your pointer tool selected by clicking the Select button located in your Edit toolbar or by pressing Esc.**

   Your pointer should look like an arrow.

2. **Click the edge of the text box that you want to delete.**

   The text box becomes highlighted with a blue border. The cursor no longer appears in the text box.

3. **Using your keyboard, press the Backspace or Delete key to delete your text box.**

   Alternatively, click Edit on the menu bar and then click Delete.

   The text box vanishes.

Resizing, moving, and rotating a text box

After you create a text box, you may need to adjust its placement on your slide by moving the text box, resizing the box to adjust its shape and size, or rotating the text box, which rotates the contents accordingly. This section shows you how to make these adjustments.

Resizing

To resize a text box, follow these steps:

1. **Ensure that you have your pointer tool selected by clicking the arrow button located in your Edit toolbar.**

   Your pointer should look like an arrow.

2. **Click your text box.**

   If your text box doesn't have any text in it, click within the general area of the text box.

   The text box becomes highlighted, and resize points appear in the corners and in the middle of each side of the box.

3. **Move your pointer over one of the resize points on your text box.**

   Your mouse pointer changes shape to a double-sided arrow. See how the double arrow changes as you hover over different resize points? The arrow changes orientation. This change is a clue that shows you how you can use each resize point to change the shape of the text box.

4. **Click and drag the resizing point to shrink or enlarge the text box.**

The box resizes with the movement of your pointer.

5. **Release the click when you are satisfied with the new shape of your text box.**

Moving

You can move your text box by following these steps:

1. **Ensure that you have your pointer tool selected by clicking the arrow button located in your Edit toolbar.**

Your pointer should look like an arrow.

2. **Click your text box.**

If your text box doesn't have any text in it, click in the general area of the text box.

The text box becomes highlighted.

3. **Move your pointer over the text box.**

Your mouse pointer changes into four arrows, one pointing in each cardinal direction.

4. **Click and drag the text box to a new location on the slide.**

The box moves with the movement of your pointer.

5. **Release the click when you are satisfied with the new location of your text box.**

Rotating

Google Slides also gives you the ability to rotate your text box at will. This feature comes in handy when you want to create a vertical text label or add styling to your slide. To rotate your text box, follow these steps:

1. **Ensure that you have your pointer tool selected by clicking the arrow button located in your Edit toolbar.**

Your pointer should look like an arrow.

2. **Click your text box.**

If your text box doesn't have any text in it, click in the general area of the text box.

The text box becomes highlighted, indicating your selection.

3. **Move your pointer over the alignment handle (the tiny circular dot that extends above the top center of your text box).**

   Your mouse pointer changes into crosshairs.

4. **Click and drag the crosshairs left to rotate the box counterclockwise, or to the right to rotate the box clockwise.**

   The box rotates in the direction and angle of your pointer movement. Your pointer indicates the degree of the angle as you rotate.

5. **Release the click when you're satisfied with the new angle of your text box.**

   Figure 10-13 shows a slide with a text box rotated to the right.

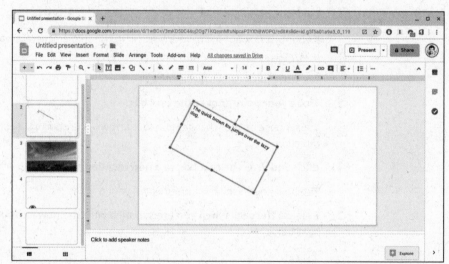

FIGURE 10-13:
A text box has been rotated in Google Slides.

Copying and pasting text boxes

As you create presentations, you can easily add text boxes by using the Copy and Paste functions. To do so, just follow these steps:

1. **Ensure that you have your pointer tool selected by clicking the Select button located in your Edit toolbar.**

   Your pointer should look like an arrow.

2. **Click the text box you want to copy.**

   If your text box doesn't have any text in it, click in the general area of the text box.

   The text box becomes highlighted, indicating your selection.

3. **Press Ctrl+C.**

The text box and its contents are copied into memory.

4. **Use the slide navigator to set the slide where you want to paste your text box.**

5. **Press Ctrl+V.**

The text box is pasted to the new slide. Move and adjust it as needed.

Copying text boxes from one slide to others is a handy way to make a block of text appear on several slides without having to manually retype the text on every slide.

When you paste a text box onto another slide, it's placed in the exact same position it occupied on the slide containing the text box you copied.

Formatting text

With Slides, you can change the font and text size of any text contained in your presentation. The options are potentially limitless, but for clarity, it's better to limit the number of fonts that appear in one presentation. Google Slides comes preloaded with only a handful of fonts.

To change your font, follow these steps:

1. **Using your touchpad, click the text box containing the text that you want to format.**

The text box is highlighted in yellow.

To change only a section of the text in a text box, make your selection by double-clicking the text box and then dragging your pointer over the text you want to change. See Figure 10-14 for an example.

2. **Open the Font menu on the Edit toolbar.**

The Font menu is located directly to the left of the Font Size menu.

The Font menu displays the name of the font for the selected body of text. By default, all text is written with the Arial font.

3. **Select one of the fonts listed.**

All the selected text is formatted with your newly selected font.

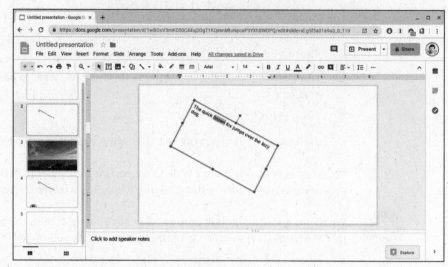

Adding and removing new fonts

The Google Slides default list of fonts is short. Google provides users with an initial list of the most globally popular fonts to keep things simple at first. You can, however, add fonts to your Slides font list. Follow these steps:

1. **Select some text in a text box on a slide in your presentation.**

2. **Open the Font menu in the toolbar.**

    The text on the Font button is the name of the font currently used for your selected text.

3. **Choose More Fonts.**

    The Fonts window appears (see Figure 10-15), giving you a robust list of new fonts. Scroll down through the list to reveal more fonts.

4. **Select the desired fonts by clicking them.**

    Each selected font is highlighted in blue and given a check mark.

5. **Click OK to finish adding the fonts to your Font menu and close the Fonts pop-up window.**

When you're ready to change the font of your text, you can choose one of your newly selected fonts from the Font menu.

The more fonts you add, the more fonts you have to rifle through when trying to make a decision on changing. To remove fonts that you added to your list, take these steps:

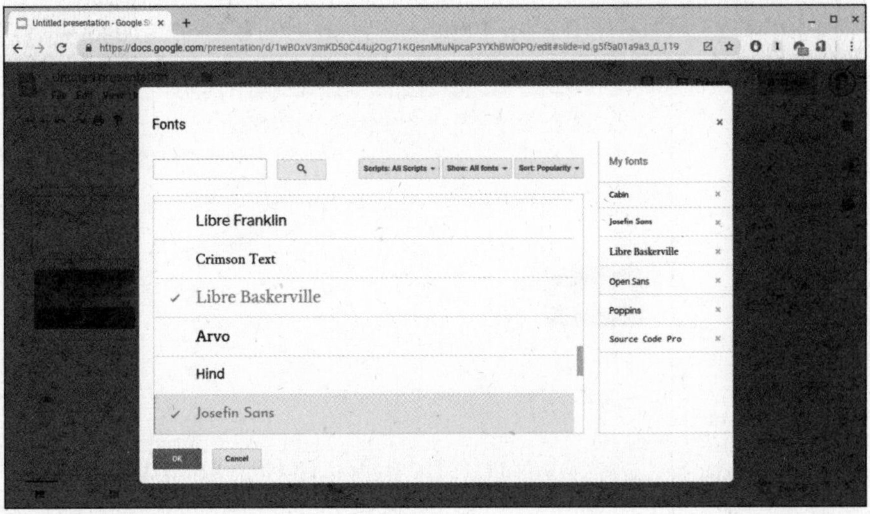

FIGURE 10-15:
Adding fonts to
Google Slides.

1. **Open the Font menu in the toolbar.**

2. **Click More Fonts.**

   The Fonts pop-up window appears, displaying a list of fonts. On the right, the My Fonts list displays the fonts currently in use by your Slides account.

3. **Scroll through the My Fonts list to locate the font or fonts you want to remove. To remove fonts, click the X located to the right of each font.**

   The selected fonts vanish from the list of accessible fonts.

4. **Click OK.**

Changing text size

You can change the size of your text by following these steps:

1. **Using your touchpad, double-click the text box that contains the text you want to format.**

   The text box is highlighted in blue. A blinking cursor appears.

2. **Click and drag your pointer to select the text whose size you want to change.**

   The selected text is highlighted.

3. **Click the Font Size menu.**

   It's the number located to the left of the B (Bold) button in the Edit toolbar.

4. **Select any desired font size.**

   Your selected text becomes the chosen size, as shown in Figure 10-16.

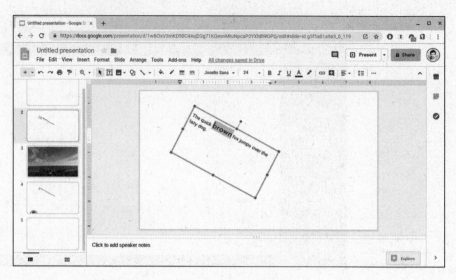

FIGURE 10-16:
Changing the size
of selected text in
Google Slides.

Applying boldface, italics, underline, or strikethrough

To make a specific selection of text bold, italic, underlined, or strikethrough, follow these steps:

1. **Using your touchpad, double-click the text box that contains the text you want to format.**

The text box is highlighted in yellow. A blinking cursor appears in the text box.

2. **Select the text you want to change by clicking and dragging.**

The selected text is highlighted.

3. **Apply boldface, italics, underline, or strikethrough as needed.**

To apply a formatting, use one of the following methods:

- **To add boldface, italics, or strikethrough:** Click the appropriate button in the middle of the Edit toolbar — the B button for bold, the I button for italic, or the U button for underline. (No button exists for strikethrough on the standard Edit toolbar.)

- **To add strikethrough:** Open the Format menu, click Text, and select Strikethrough.

Your selection changes appropriately.

TIP

You can quickly apply styles to your data by using hotkeys. Just press Ctrl+B (for bold), Ctrl+I (italic), Ctrl+U (underline), or Alt+Shift+5 (strikethrough).

Coloring your text

Slides gives you the ability to change the color of your text or the color of the background behind your text (that is, to add a highlight). You change the color of your text by following these steps:

1. **Using your touchpad, double-click the text box that contains the text you want to color.**

2. **Select text by clicking and dragging.**

The selected text is highlighted.

3. **Click the Text Color button in the toolbar.**

It's the underlined *A* found to the right of the Underline button.

The color palette appears, as shown in Figure 10-17.

4. **Select the desired color.**

Your selected text now appears in the selected color.

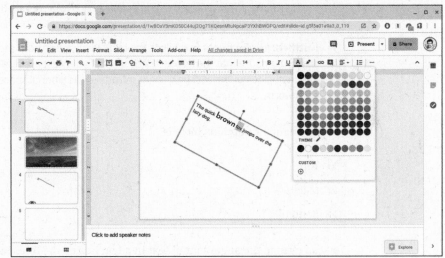

FIGURE 10-17:
Changing the color of selected text in Google Slides.

To apply a highlight to your text, follow these steps:

1. **Using your touchpad, double-click the text box that contains the text you want to format.**

2. **Select text by clicking and dragging.**

The selected text is highlighted.

3. **Click the Highlight Color button in the toolbar.**

   This button looks like a highlighter pen and appears at the right of the Text Color button. The Highlight Color palette appears.

4. **Select your desired color.**

   Your selected text now appears highlighted in the selected color.

Aligning your text

The *alignment* of your text determines the orientation of the edges of lines or paragraphs in a text box. Slides gives you several options for changing the alignment. Horizontal alignment choices include

>> **Left:** This is the default alignment for new text boxes in Slides. The text is flush with the left side of the text box.

>> **Right:** The text is flush with the right side of the text box.

>> **Center:** The middle of your text box is the halfway point between the left and the right sides. With centered alignment, all text is centered on this midway point.

>> **Justified:** *Justifying* your text aligns the text evenly along both the left and right sides. To ensure that the left and right sides of your text are flush with the left and right sides of the text box, Slides introduces additional spaces between each word.

Vertical alignment options include

>> Top

>> Middle

>> Bottom

You can change the alignment of text in a text box by the line, paragraph, or page by following these steps:

1. **Using your touchpad, double-click the text box that contains the text you want to realign.**

2. **Select the text you want to realign by clicking and dragging.**

   The selected text is highlighted.

3. **Click the Align button in the Edit toolbar.**

   The Alignment tool opens, as shown in Figure 10-18. You can select left, center, right, and justified alignment, as well as top, middle, and bottom alignment.

4. **Click the desired alignment.**

   The selected text is realigned.

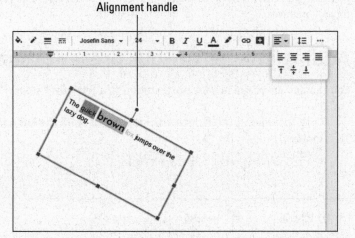

Alignment handle

FIGURE 10-18: Changing the alignment of text in Google Slides.

Clearing formatting

Google Slides offers a feature that makes it incredibly easy to clear out the formatting that you applied to a body of text. This feature can save you quite a bit of time if you intend to clear the formatting from several text boxes. To clear formatting, follow these steps:

1. **Using your touchpad, click once on the text box you want to select.**

   The selected text box is highlighted.

2. **Click Format and then click Clear Formatting in the menu bar.**

   The alignment of the selected text is reset to left alignment, and all style elements are removed, including color, underline, strikethrough, italics, bold, and so on.

Working with Images

Presentations need more than just some text boxes and a colored background to make them interesting. Images can help tell your story. The good news is that you can add images of all types to your presentation. Slides also gives you the ability to apply basic tweaks to your images so that you can make them look just right. With Slides, you can add images from files or use your device's camera to take pictures. You can then rotate, resize, relocate, add borders, and even apply shapes to your pictures.

Adding images to your presentation

You can add an image to your presentation in a few quick steps:

1. **Click the Image button, located nine buttons from the left on the Edit toolbar.**

   A small menu appears, as shown in Figure 10-19.

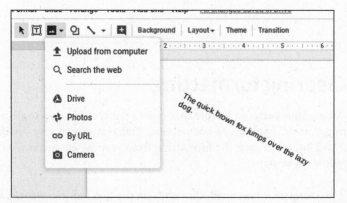

FIGURE 10-19:
The Image
selector menu.

2. **Select the source for the image you want to insert into your slide.**

   The options for the source for your image are as follows:

   - **Upload from Computer:** Any image you previously created or downloaded that is stored in your Chromebook

   - **Search the Web:** A Google Images search to find an image on the Internet

   - **Google Drive:** An image you previously stored in your Google Drive

- **Google Photos:** An image you uploaded to Google Photos
- **By URL:** An image whose URL you happen to know
- **Camera:** A picture you take using the camera on your Chromebook

3. **Choose the desired option for obtaining an image for your presentation.**

   The image is added to your slide.

You can also add an image from the Internet by following these steps:

1. **Click the Image button on the toolbar.**

   The Insert Image window appears.

2. **Click By URL.**

   A text box appears in which you can paste the URL to the image you want to add from the Internet.

3. **Type or paste the URL for the image you want to add to your slide.**

   If the URL works, Slides shows you a preview of the image, as shown in Figure 10-20.

4. **Click Select.**

   The image appears on your slide.

FIGURE 10-20:
Adding an image
from the Internet
using a URL.

Resizing, rotating, and relocating images

After you add an image, you may need to adjust its placement on your slide. You can do so by moving the image, resizing the image, or rotating the image. This section shows you how to perform each of these actions.

Resizing

To resize an image, follow these steps:

1. **Ensure that you have your pointer tool selected by clicking the Select button located in the toolbar.**

   Your pointer should look like an arrow.

2. **Click your image to select it.**

   The selected image is highlighted. Resize points appear in the corners and in the middle of each side of the image.

3. **Move your pointer over one of the corners of the image.**

   Your mouse pointer changes shape to a double-sided arrow.

4. **Click and drag the corner to shrink or enlarge the image.**

   The image resizes proportionately.

   Resizing your image using the points located in the middle of the sides of your image stretches the image without respect for the image's original proportion.

5. **When you're satisfied with the new size, release the click.**

Moving

You can also move your image to a different place on your slide by following these steps:

1. **Ensure that you have your pointer tool selected by clicking the Select button located in the toolbar.**

   Your pointer should look like an arrow.

2. **Click your image to select it.**

   The selected image is highlighted.

3. **Move your pointer over the middle of the image.**

   Your mouse pointer changes into four arrows, one pointing in each cardinal direction.

4. **Click and drag the image to a new location on the slide.**

   The image moves with the movement of your pointer.

5. **When you're satisfied with the new location of your image, release the click.**

Rotating

Google Slides also gives you the ability to rotate your images. This feature comes in handy if you need to reorient an image to be in line with your slide. To rotate your image, follow these steps:

1. **Ensure that you have your pointer tool selected by clicking the Select button located in the toolbar.**

   Your pointer should look like an arrow.

2. **Click your image to select it.**

   The selected image is highlighted.

3. **Move the pointer over the circular dot that extends above the top center of the image.**

   Your mouse pointer changes into crosshairs.

4. **Click and drag the image left or right toward the angle you desire.**

   The image rotates in the direction and angle of your pointer movement. Your pointer indicates the degree of the angle as you rotate, as shown in Figure 10-21.

5. **When you're satisfied with the new angle of your image, release the click.**

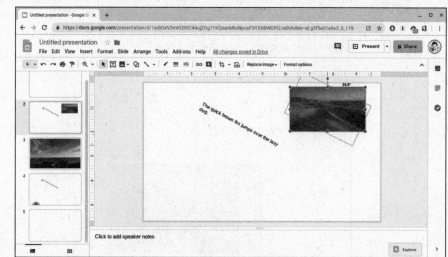

FIGURE 10-21:
Rotating an image in Google Slides.

Cropping images

In Google Slides, you can crop your images. *Cropping* means cutting off portions of an image to retain only the desired area. You may be familiar with cropping images if you have a smartphone and have taken pictures using fun applications like Instagram. Figure 10-22 illustrates what the Slides Crop tool looks like.

To crop an image, follow these steps:

1. Select the image you want to crop.

The selected image is highlighted.

2. Click the Crop Image button at the far right of the Edit toolbar.

Alternatively, you can Alt-click the image and select Crop.

Crop marks appear on the corners and sides of the image, indicating that you've enabled cropping.

3. Using the touchpad, move the pointer over one of the black crop marks.

The pointer changes to arrows pointing in two directions, indicating where to drag the crop mark.

4. Click and drag the crop marks to the desired size.

The portion of your image that falls outside of the crop margins appears grayed out.

5. Click the Crop Image button in the Edit toolbar once again.

Your crop settings are applied to the image.

TIP

After you have cropped your image, if you decide that you removed too much from your image, just click the Crop Image button again. You'll be shown your original image and the current cropping. You can readjust cropping as needed. Click the Crop Image button when you're done.

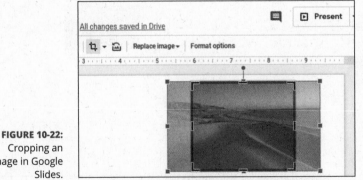

FIGURE 10-22: Cropping an image in Google Slides.

TIP

While in cropping mode, you can still resize and move an image.

Google Slides also comes with an image-masking option. *Masking* essentially places your image into a shaped container. The only parts of the image that are shown are the portions not *masked* by the mask filter. Figure 10-23 shows an image with a shape mask applied.

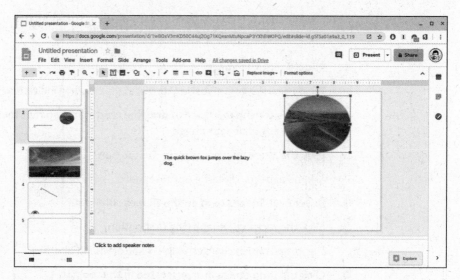

FIGURE 10-23:
Masking an image in Google Slides.

To mask an image, follow these steps:

1. **Select the image you want to mask.**

The selected image is highlighted.

2. **Click the Mask Image button on the toolbar.**

The Mask Image button is the down-pointing arrow located on the right portion of the Crop Image button.

A menu appears, revealing several shapes.

3. **Using the touchpad, navigate through the menu and select the shape you would like to apply to the image.**

The mask appears on your image. To change the placement and size of the mask, click the Crop Image button. Doing so reveals crop marks on the sides and corners of the mask.

4. **Using the touchpad, move the pointer over one of the black crop marks on the image.**

Your pointer changes to arrows pointing in two directions, indicating where to drag the crop marks.

5. **Click and drag the crop marks to the desired size.**

   The portion of the image that falls outside of the crop margins appears grayed out.

6. **Click the Crop Image button in the Edit toolbar.**

   The mask settings are applied to the image.

If you decide that you do not like the crop or image mask that you applied to your image, you can remove it by following these steps:

1. **Double-click the image.**

   The original image is revealed, along with the cropping indicators.

2. **Using the touchpad, click and drag the crop marks so that they are flush with the edges of your image.**

3. **Click the Mask Image button in the toolbar.**

   A menu appears, revealing several options.

4. **Hover over Shapes to open the Shapes submenu.**

5. **Click the rectangle shape (the first option).**

   The image mask is changed to the shape of your image.

6. **Click the Crop Image button located in the toolbar.**

   The crop marks are removed from the image and it is restored to its uncropped state.

TIP

Sometimes you have to try cropping or masking a few times until you get it just right. You can also undo your masking or cropping by clicking the Undo button that is near the left end of the toolbar.

Viewing Presentations in Presentation Mode

When you're ready to make a presentation with Google Slides, you can launch Presentation mode. Presentation mode shows nothing but your finished slides so that you can navigate through them while you present. To launch Presentation mode, follow these steps:

1. **Using your slide navigator, click the first slide in your presentation.**

   Slide 1 becomes highlighted. When you launch Presentation mode, the presentation commences at the active slide in your navigator. If you want to start from the beginning, ensure that you've selected your first slide.

2. **Click the Present button in the top-right portion of your screen.**

   The Present button is three buttons from the right.

   Your presentation launches into full-screen Presentation mode, as shown in Figure 10-24.

   Near the top of the screen, the message "Press Esc to exit full screen" appears for a few moments.

   A presentation menu appears near the bottom of the screen; after several seconds, the menu disappears. You can make it reappear by moving the pointer near the bottom of the screen.

3. **To exit Presentation mode, press the Esc key.**

   Your presentation closes, and the slide editor reappears.

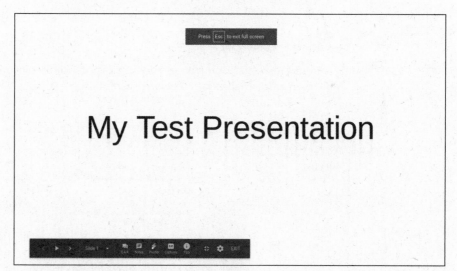

FIGURE 10-24: Viewing a presentation in Presentation mode.

While in Presentation mode, you can navigate between slides a number of different ways. To move forward in your presentation, press the down- or right-arrow key, or the spacebar. To move backward in your presentation, press the left- or up-arrow keys.

Presenting on additional displays

Running Presentation mode on your Chromebook is a great way to test your presentation before you actually present it to an audience. When you're ready to present, you'll likely be presenting by using a projector or flat-screen television. To launch your presentations using an additional display device, you first need to connect the projector or TV to your Chromebook. (If you don't know how to connect an additional display to your Chromebook, flip to Chapter 17.) After your additional display is connected to and recognized by your Chromebook, launch your presentation using these steps:

1. **Using your slide navigator, click the first slide in your presentation.**

   Slide 1 is highlighted.

2. **Click the arrow on the right side of the Present button in the top-right portion of your screen.**

   A menu with three options appears:

   - Presenter View

   - Present from the Beginning

   - Present on Another Screen

3. **Select Presenter View.**

   Presentation mode commences without going into Full Screen mode, and the Presenter View appears, as shown in Figure 10-25.

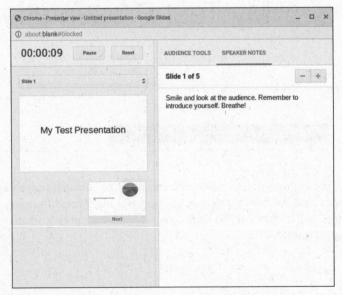

FIGURE 10-25: Showing a slide presentation in Presenter View.

4. Click and drag the presentation window to the display you're using to present and leave the Speaker Notes window on the display your audience won't see.

5. In your presentation window, click the Full Screen Mode button in the Presenter toolbar in the bottom-left corner of the window, as shown in Figure 10-26.

Your presentation goes into Full Screen mode, ready for you to present.

FIGURE 10-26:
The Presenter
toolbar.

Using Presenter View

When you launch a presentation in Presenter View, a window launches that contains all your slide notes, as well as some navigation tools and a timer so that you can keep track of how much time you're using in your presentation. (The Speaker Notes window appears in Figure 10-25, shown previously.)

The window is broken into two main areas. The left side of the window contains your presentation controls. The right side of the window contains any and all notes written for the current slide. Navigate through your presentation by clicking the slide subtitled Next. Navigate backward by clicking the slide subtitled Previous. You can also skip to slides by clicking Slide # and selecting a slide from the drop-down list that appears. You can also pause the timer by clicking Pause, and resume by clicking Resume. If you click Reset, the timer starts back at zero.

TIP

Don't read your notes aloud; instead, use them as talking points or cues for presenting. Present to your audience and let the slides merely be props that support your presentation.

Saving Presentations

As you work in Google Slides, Google saves almost every change in real time to your Google Drive account. Drive is Google's cloud-based storage solution that allows you to safely store your files and access them from any device with an Internet connection. Every file you create with Presentation is saved to your Drive folder so that you can access it at home, on the road, at work, or anywhere else you might need to. You can access it from anywhere even if you never name your presentation, in which case it will be called "Untitled Presentation." As is the case with Docs and Sheets, Slides has no manual Save feature.

Naming your presentation

When you open a new presentation with Slides, the default name for the presentation is Untitled Presentation. You don't, however, want to leave your presentation untitled forever. Drive doesn't have a problem with storing multiple files with the same name, so it's best if you name your presentation so that you save yourself a little confusion later. To name your presentation, follow these steps:

1. **Open a new or existing presentation.**

   The easiest way to open a presentation is simply to launch Slides from the Launcher.

   A Chrome web browser opens and loads Slides — and automatically opens a new presentation.

   After Slides is open, the top-left corner of the screen displays your presentation's name: Untitled Presentation, as shown in Figure 10-27.

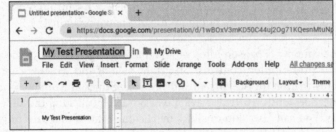

FIGURE 10-27:
Renaming a slide
presentation.

2. **Click Untitled Presentation.**

   The appearance of the name Untitled Presentation changes so that you can type in a new name.

3. **Type a new name for your presentation and press Enter.**

   The new name that you chose to replace Untitled Presentation appears.

Your newly named presentation now appears in Google Drive. As you continue to make edits to the presentation, the file is updated and saved in real time.

Exporting your presentation

From time to time, you may need to export your presentation to formats that others may be comfortable with. Google Slides presently allows you to export to a few standard formats:

- » Microsoft PowerPoint (.pptx)

- » ODP Document (.odp)

- » PDF Document (.pdf)

- » Plain Text (.txt)

- » JPEG image (.jpg)

- » PNG image (.png)

- » Scalable Vector Graphics (.svg)

WARNING

Exporting documents to different file types may change the formatting within your document or possibly strip out formatting completely. Before sending along your presentation after an export, you should review it to ensure that everything is as it should be!

You can export your presentation by following these steps:

1. **Open the Files menu in the Applications menu within Slides.**

2. **Hover over Download As to reveal a submenu containing file types available for export.**

3. **Select the desired file type.**

Your Slides file is exported to the desired file type and automatically downloaded to your Chromebook.

4. **Choose a name for the exported file and then click Save.**

5. **To view the file on your Chromebook, open the Files app and navigate to the folder in which you saved the exported file.**

6. **Double-click the filename to launch an app to display the presentation.**

Collaborating in Slides

By default, Slides and Drive make your files inaccessible to everyone other than you. You can, however, change the visibility settings on your files and invite specific people, or even the entire world, to comment on, view, or edit your presentation. To share your presentation with specific people, follow these steps:

1. **With Slides open, click the Share button in the top-right corner of the screen.**

The Sharing window appears, giving you several options for sharing your presentation.

2. **In the People text box, enter the email address of each person you want to invite to access your file.**

Be sure to separate the addresses with commas.

If the email address is in your address book, Slides tries to auto-fill the contact's information.

3. **Set the permissions for each collaborator by clicking the pencil icon to the right of the person's email address.**

A list with three options appears:

- **Can Edit:** Allows users to edit the presentation and change permissions

- **Can Comment:** Allows users to comment on the presentation but not to change any content or security settings

- **Can View:** Allows users only to view the presentation

  Figure 10-28 shows these options.

4. **Select the appropriate permission setting from the list.**

5. **Select the Notify People via Email check box to notify the specified users, by email, that you have shared a presentation with them.**

6. **Click Send.**

Your Slides presentation is immediately made available to the users you invited.

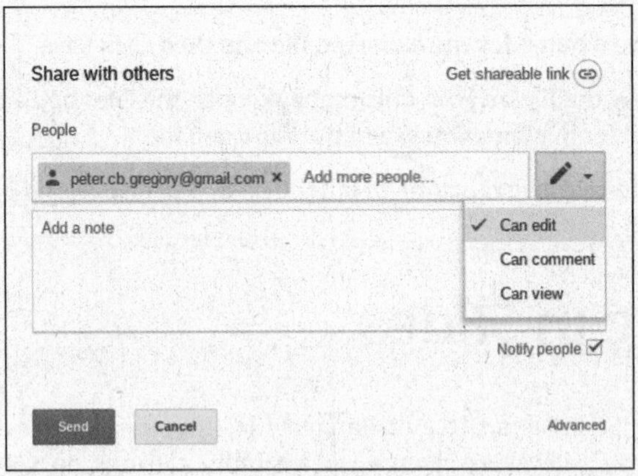

FIGURE 10-28:
Sharing a slide presentation and setting access permissions for each invitee.

Share with others   Get shareable link ⊖

People

👤 peter.cb.gregory@gmail.com ✕   Add more people...   ✏ ▾

Add a note   ✓ Can edit
                                                   Can comment
                                                   Can view

                                                Notify people ☑

Send   Cancel   Advanced

TIP

A user who is invited to view, edit, or comment on your presentation has to log into Google using the email address with which you shared the presentation. If she doesn't have a Google Account under that email address, you have to invite her with the address she uses for her Google Account. She also has the option to create a Google Account using the email address with which you invited her.

Tracking Revisions

Keeping track of revisions is very important when creating documents with multiple collaborators. Luckily, Google Slides handles version control masterfully. The Version History tool, however, is not intended to be used as a Track Changes tool that is used in Google Docs. As you and your collaborators create changes to your presentation, Slides will time-and-date stamp those changes so that you can view previous versions of your presentation and even revert to an earlier version if you need to.

Version tracking is a default feature of Slides, so to view your version history, follow these steps:

1. **Open the File menu in the Applications menu within Slides.**

2. **Choose Version history and then choose See Version History.**

   A Version History box appears in the right portion of your screen. The box contains the various versions of your presentation in order of most recent to oldest.

3. **Click a revision date in the Revision History box.**

   A preview of the revision appears in the presentation area. Changes appear in green. Figure 10-29 shows a presentation with two available versions.

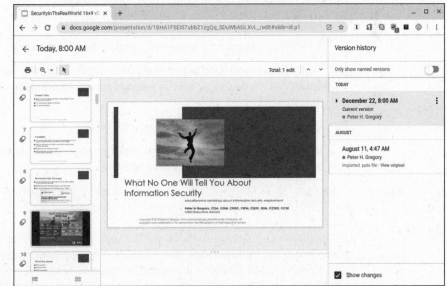

FIGURE 10-29: Viewing available versions of a Google Slides presentation.

4. **To change the current version to the version you're viewing, click Restore This Revision.**

   The restored version becomes the current version, and the previous version of the application is saved in the revision history so that you can revert to it at any point, if needed.

Using Slides Offline

Google Slides is a web-based presentation tool, which means that you must have an Internet connection to access it and all its features. However, an offline version of Slides is available in the event that you find yourself without a connection to the Internet.

To use Google Slides to work on your presentations offline, you must first enable Google Drive for offline use by following these steps:

1. **Open the Launcher and click the Google Drive icon.**

   A Chrome web browser appears and takes you to your Drive.

2. **On the right side of the screen, click the settings icon (it looks like a gear) and in the resulting menu, click Settings.**

3. **Select the check box to sync your work for offline use.**

4. **Click Done.**

   Your Slides files are now synced and available for offline editing.

5. **Test whether you have properly enabled offline access by turning off your Wi-Fi. To do this, open the settings panel in the bottom-right of your screen.**

6. **Click the blue Wi-Fi logo to turn off your Wi-Fi.**

7. **With your Wi-Fi turned off, switch back to Google Drive, locate your synced spreadsheets, and click to open one.**

   If your Slides file opens and you are able to edit it, you know you have successfully engaged offline use and synced your documents.

Offline, you can't access some of the features available to Slides users that are connected to the Internet, such as downloading new fonts or searching the Internet for images to insert into your presentation. You can, however, create presentations and save them. When you connect to the Internet, Drive uploads the presentations and enables all Internet-accessible features.

Chapter **11**

Using Other Office Tools

G oogle has made tremendous headway with its suite of office products: Gmail for email, Docs for word processing, Sheets for spreadsheets, and Slides for presentations. These are popular both in business as well as with home users. And, as previous chapters note, they all work great on Chromebooks. That said, you may have your reasons for considering and using alternatives.

The undisputed leader in office software around the world in business, schools, and homes is Microsoft Office, whose powerhouse programs include Outlook for email, calendar, and contacts, Word for word processing, Excel for spreadsheets, PowerPoint for slide presentations, OneNote for note-taking, Skype for collaboration, and OneDrive for storing data in the cloud. These tools are all available in the Office suite. They are also available for Chromebooks, and they work great on Chromebooks as well as Windows PCs and even Macs.

For the average user, it's fair to say that Microsoft Office and Google's suite of tools are roughly equivalent in terms of features and functions. *How* you get things done varies a bit between the two. But if you are reasonably good at Google Docs, for instance, you'll require no time at all to be productive with Microsoft Word. The same can be said of Sheets versus Excel and Slides versus PowerPoint. Only a professional user will spot the differences, but for everyone else, Google versus Microsoft is a little bit like Coke versus Pepsi, Ford versus Chevy, or the Yankees versus the Mets. They're all good and they get the job done.

In this chapter, you dive into the Microsoft Office Online world, including installing and using all the tools. I don't go into as much detail on the Microsoft Office tools as I do the Google tools (Gmail, Docs, Sheets, Slides, and Drive) in other chapters, but I show you enough to get started. If you are using Office tools on your Chromebook, I recommend you pick up a copy of *Office 2019 All-in-One For Dummies,* by Peter Weverka as well as *Office 365 All-In-One For Dummies,* by Peter Weverka and Timothy L. Warner.

But wait! No, I'm not about to try to sell you Ginzu knives, but you do have even more choices to consider. This chapter looks at Apple's iCloud suite of office tools as well. Yes, Virginia, you can run Apple iCloud apps on a Chromebook. Oh, and the chapter covers about using Adobe Reader for reading, inserting comments, and signing PDFs.

Getting Started with Office Online

 To get started with Office Online, make sure that you're logged into your Chromebook. Open your Chrome browser and go to https://www.office.com/.

As with Google's suite of tools, you can use the basic version of Office Online for free. Office Online includes 5GB of free storage in OneDrive and versions of Word, Excel, and PowerPoint. The information offered in this chapter deals mainly with the use of a free account.

If you don't have a Microsoft Office account, this is a good time to create one. You need to use the free or the paid versions of Office. To create a Microsoft account, go to https://www.office.com/ and click the Sign In link. Then, find the link to create an account. Your email address will be your user ID (even if it's a Gmail address), and you need to create a password and answer some other questions. After your account is set up, go back to www.office.com and sign in. After signing in with your new account, you see the Office Online home page, shown in Figure 11-1.

TIP

As any good for-profit company would, Microsoft will try to convince you to go with one of the paid versions of Office 365 instead of Office Online. It is unnecessary to get a paid account unless you know for certain that you require features that are available *only* with the paid versions.

If you use Office Online, you want to bookmark the landing page because this page is where you begin. On the landing page, you can access all the free Office Online tools, which I briefly explore in this section.

FIGURE 11-1:
The Microsoft
Office main page.

Verifying your Office account

As soon as you begin some operation in Office Online (sending your first email, for example), you are asked to verify your account. Office Online asks for your mobile number so that it can send you a code to enter. This safeguard helps to prove that you are logging in to your Office account rather than some hacker who luckily guessed your user ID and password (or obtained them in some other way). Figure 11-2 shows an example of a verification screen.

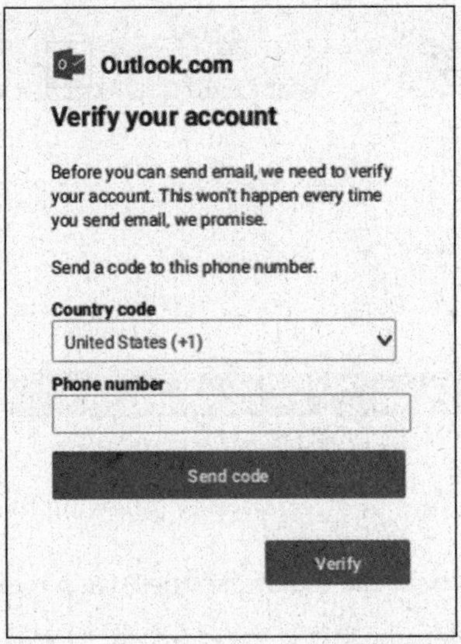

Outlook.com

Verify your account

Before you can send email, we need to verify your account. This won't happen every time you send email, we promise.

Send a code to this phone number.

Country code

United States (+1)

Phone number

Send code

Verify

FIGURE 11-2:
Office Online
uses text
messages to
verify your
identity.

OneDrive

OneDrive is the app you use to store your data in the cloud. If you know the basics about Google Drive, you already understand OneDrive: You have folders and files that you can upload and download; you can also create and edit them using word processing, spreadsheet, and presentation tools.

From the Office Online main page, click OneDrive. Your list of files and folders appears. The first time you use OneDrive, you see a Welcome page with an offer to show you around. I suggest that you take a minute for the nickel tour.

TIP

One nice thing about Office Online is that apps open in new browser tabs, which means that your Office Online main page is still there on another tab. Sure, you can get back to it with your browser bookmark, but it's even easier to click the tab to get back to the main page.

The main OneDrive window shows two default folders, Documents and Pictures, and a file called Getting Started With OneDrive. Until you are familiar with One-Drive, I suggest you keep that Getting Started file as a handy reference. Your initial OneDrive page should resemble Figure 11-3.

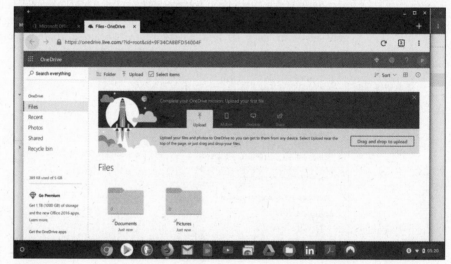

FIGURE 11-3:
The OneDrive main page.

In OneDrive, you can upload files or directories by following these steps:

1. **Click the Upload button near the top of the OneDrive screen.**

   A small File Upload window appears.

2. **Click Files.**

   The file selector window appears.

3. **On the far left, click the Menu button (three horizontal lines).**

   You can access only the Downloads folder here. If the file you want to upload to OneDrive is in the Downloads folder on your Chromebook, you can select it.

4. **After you have selected files, click Open on the far right side of the window.**

   The selector window closes and your selected files are uploaded to OneDrive.

If you want to upload files from other folders, such as any in your Google Drive, you can do that, but you need to use a drag-and-drop method (which, by the way, works for any files on your Chromebook). First, make sure your that browser is not in Full-Screen mode. Reduce the size of the window a little bit until you see a part of the desktop. Then follow these steps to upload files from other folders:

1. **Navigate to your main OneDrive page, which shows your folders and files.**

2. **Open the Files app and position it so that you can see both the Files app and your browser.**

3. **Click the Files app and then Navigate to the folders or files that you want to upload to OneDrive.**

4. **Click and drag the files you want from the Files window to the middle of the OneDrive window in your browser. (See Figure 11-4.)**

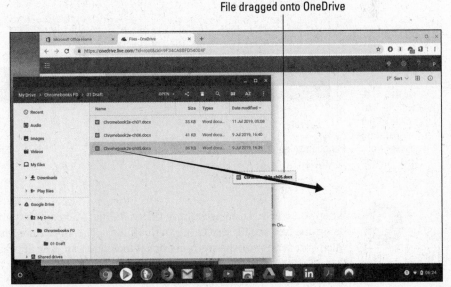

File dragged onto OneDrive

FIGURE 11-4: Dragging and dropping files from your Chromebook or Google Drive to OneDrive.

Outlook Email

Outlook is the Microsoft Office Online app used for email, as well as for managing calendars and contacts.

To launch Outlook, log in to Office Online, which gets you to the Office main page (refer to Figure 11-1). Click Outlook, which opens that app in a new tab in your browser. The first time you log in, you might be asked some questions, including your preferred language and your time zone. After you get through any of those one-time formalities, you see the Outlook main page, which includes the display of an initial message welcoming you to your new Outlook.com account. Figure 11-5 should pretty closely resemble what you see.

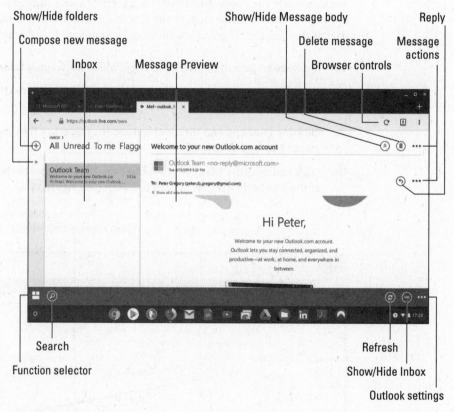

FIGURE 11-5:
The Outlook main page with a welcome message from the Outlook Team.

When you create a user account in Office Online, Microsoft assumes that you'll be using its free email service at Outlook.com. The first time you start Outlook, Microsoft sends you the welcome email message that now appears.

Outlook is functionally equivalent to the combination of Gmail, Google Calendar, and Google Contacts — all in one app. Along with Figure 11-5, which shows all the different parts of the Outlook main window, here's a brief tour of Outlook so that you can find your way around:

>> **Inbox:** Contains a list of your incoming email messages. By default, it displays the sender's name, subject line, and the first few words of the body of the message. At the top of the Inbox area, you see the words All, Unread, To Me, and Flagged. These are buttons that permit you to view all or some of your messages according to these categories.

>> **Message Preview:** The body of the message selected in the Inbox. The subject line is at the top; beneath that is the sender's name and email address, followed by the body of the message.

>> **Compose New Message:** Click this big, circled + (plus sign) button to compose a new message.

>> **Show/Hide Folders:** Click this button to view all your email folders. If you have a lot of them, you can scroll up and down through them all.

>> **Function Selector:** Enables you to select the email, calendar, and contacts functions.

>> **Search:** Lets you search through your email for a specific message by name, subject line, or contents.

>> **Refresh:** Instructs Outlook to check for new, incoming email.

>> **Show/Hide Inbox List:** Toggles the display of your Inbox. Clicking this button displays the selected email message in your Inbox at nearly full screen.

>> **Settings:** Triggers a little window in which you can view and change Outlook options, get help, or sign out of Outlook.

>> **Reply:** Compose a reply to the sender of the message being displayed.

>> **Message Actions:** Brings up a little menu in which you can mark a message as read, flag the message, mark the message as junk, mark the message as a phishing scam, or delete the message.

>> **Show/Hide Message Body:** Determines whether you can view an entire message or just a part of it.

>> **Trash:** Delete the message being displayed.

>> **Message Actions:** Yes, for some reason, there are two of these Message Actions buttons. This one lets you mark the message as read, flag it, move it to another folder, or ignore it.

Before you can begin sending and receiving email with Outlook, you need to connect your Gmail account to Outlook. To do so, follow this procedure:

1. **In the main Outlook window, click the Settings icon in the lower-right corner (the three little dots).**

2. **Click Options.**

   The Mail Options window opens.

3. **Click Mail, then Accounts, then Connected Accounts.**

   The Connected Accounts window opens.

4. **Under Add a Connected Account, click Gmail.**

   The Connect Your Google Account window opens, as shown in Figure 11-6.

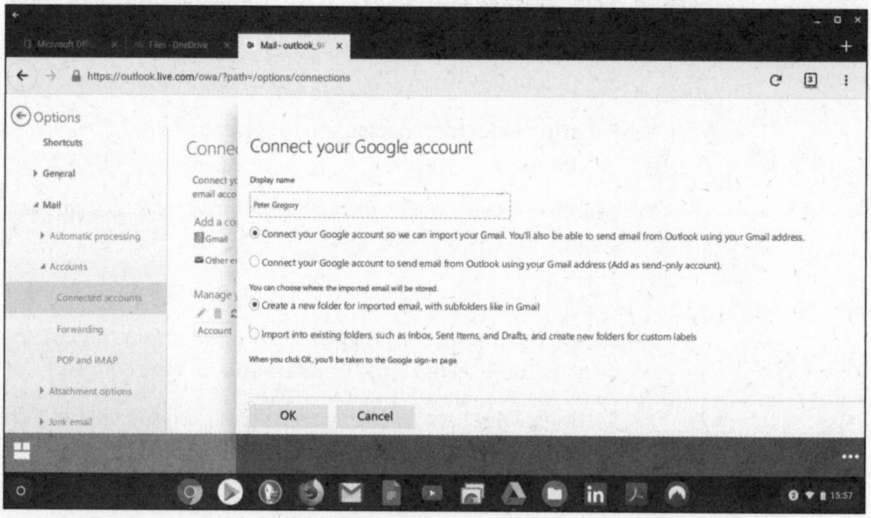

FIGURE 11-6:
Adding your
Gmail account to
Outlook.

5. **Be sure your Display Name is shown correctly. Change it if you want.**

6. **Read the options below the Display Name field carefully and select the one you want.**

   Your selection will determine how you use Outlook. In this example, I selected the second option so that I can send and receive Gmail using Outlook.

7. **Read the option about where you want your Gmail content to be stored in Outlook and make a selection.**

   I selected the "Create a New Folder for Imported Email" option.

8. **Click Okay.**

   The Google login page appears.

9. Fill in your Google user ID and password.

On the next page, Microsoft Outlook informs you of its intention to move email in your Gmail account over to Outlook.

10. Read the actions carefully and then click Allow if you agree.

After clicking Allow, you can use Outlook to send and receive email using your Gmail account.

11. Click the left arrow to the left of Options to return to the main Outlook window.

REMEMBER

After you log in to your Gmail account with Outlook, Google sends you an email with the subject "Security alert" informing you that Microsoft was granted access to your Google account. Whenever you receive Security Alert emails from Google, read it carefully to make sure that the activity that Google describes is legitimately yours.

Follow these steps to compose a new email message:

1. Click the blue, circled + (plus sign) near the upper-left corner.

The Compose Message window appears, as shown in Figure 11-7.

2. Fill in the recipient's email address(es), as well as any additional people you want to CC.

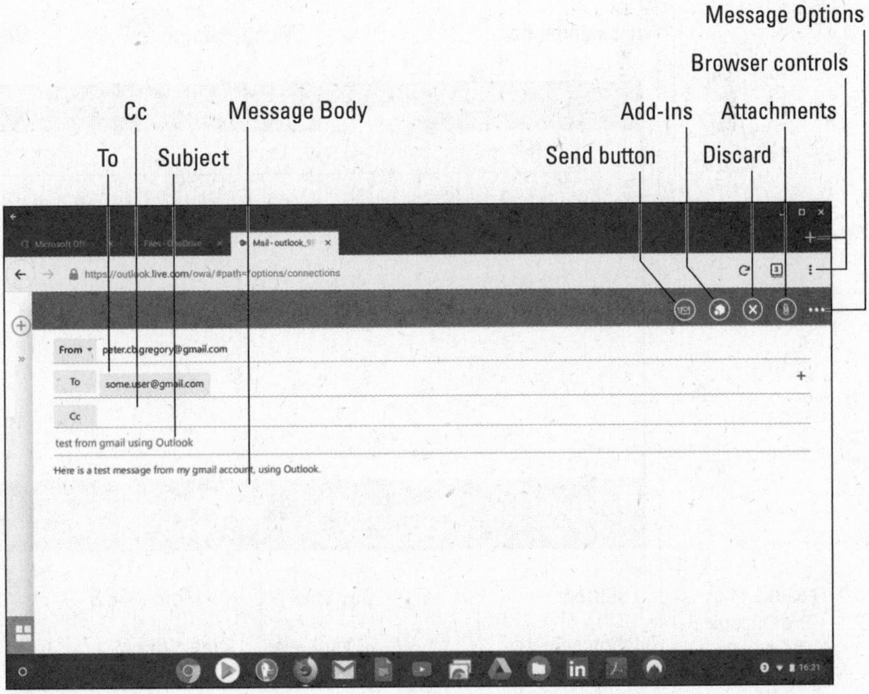

FIGURE 11-7:
Composing a new message with Outlook.

3. **Enter the subject in the subject line and your message in the message body.**

4. **When you're ready to send your message, click Send.**

Outlook Calendar

Similar to Google Calendar, Outlook has a built-in calendar system that lets you make appointments, set reminders, and invite others to events. To access Outlook Calendar, click the function selector at the lower-left corner of the Outlook window; it looks like three little white boxes. Next, click Calendar. The main calendar is displayed (see Figure 11-8) and contains the following controls:

» **Month selector:** This is the range of months (and adjacent years) across the top of the calendar. Click one to view that month.

» **View/Hide Day sidebar:** You can show or hide a view of "today" and any appointments, reminders, or events that are scheduled for today.

» **Settings:** Change elements of your calendar like the days of the week and hours of the day you work, reminders, display colors, and shared calendars.

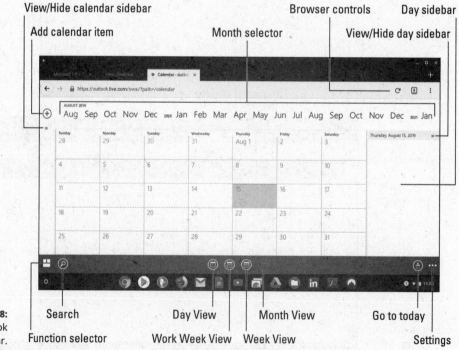

FIGURE 11-8:
The Outlook
Calendar.

>> **Go to Today:** Click option to instantly view the current day on your calendar. If you are viewing one day at a time, your screen shows you the current day. If you're showing any of the week or month views, the calendar goes to the week or month that includes today.

>> **Day/Week/Month view:** Choose whether you want to view one day at a time, a work week, a full week, or an entire month.

>> **Search:** Look for an event in your calendar.

>> **Function selector:** Go to Outlook mail or contacts.

>> **View/Hide Month sidebar:** Toggle a view of the current month, which appears as tiny.

>> **Add Calendar Item:** Add a new appointment, reminder, or event.

To add an item to your calendar, click the Add Calendar Item button (refer to Figure 11-8). The window shown in Figure 11-9 opens and allows you to fill in some details:

>> **Event:** Describe the event or reminder.

>> **Location:** Enter an address, a city name, the name of a business, friend, or anything else. Outlook helps you with place names by trying to guess what you are typing (which is sometimes helpful, but also annoying at times).

>> **Start Date and Time:** Enter whatever you want.

>> **Duration:** With a default of 30 minutes, you can select any appropriate value, even All Day.

If you click More Details, the window expands in size and shows several more fields.

>> **Show As:** Select Free, Working Elsewhere, Tentative, Busy, or Away.

>> **Reminder**. Outlook will send you a reminder before the beginning of the event. You may also select None to tell Outlook not to remind you.

>> **Save to Calendar:** If you have more than one calendar, Outlook wants to know which one to save to.

>> **Repeat:** Outlook asks whether this is a repeating event, such as an anniversary, a weekly chore, or a monthly appointment. If you select this, you have more details to specify, including the frequency of the event and number of times it should occur (or on what date it should end).

When you have filled everything out, click the Save button (a disk-like icon near the upper right side of the calendar window. The event or item appears on your calendar.

This section barely scratches the surface of the Office Online Calendar. It offers so much more, like the ability to invite others to appointments and events, manage multiple calendars, and more. Pick up a copy of *Office 365 All-In-One For Dummies*, by Peter Weverka and Timothy L. Warner, if you want to dive into Outlook and all that it offers.

FIGURE 11-9:
Adding an event to the Outlook Calendar.

Outlook Contacts

Outlook contacts keeps track of the people in your life, or work, or both! Like an address book or a Rolodex, Outlook Contacts helps you remember all those details. Google Contacts does this, too, so Outlook Contacts doesn't have any particular advantage here.

To view your contacts, click the function selector (the icon with little squares at the bottom-left corner of the Outlook window) and then click People. The People window appears.

If you've just opened a new Outlook account, you probably have no contacts there. To add a contact, follow these steps:

1. **Click the familiar blue, circled + (plus sign) button.**

   The Add Contact window appears.

2. **Enter the contact's name, email, and phone in the appropriate fields, shown in Figure 11-10.**

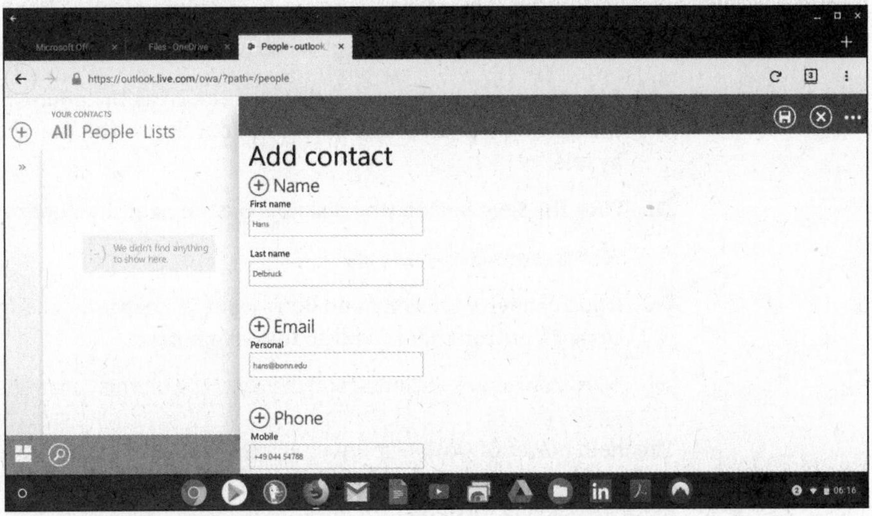

FIGURE 11-10:
Adding a contact to Outlook.

3. **Scroll down to also enter other items like the name of the contact's company, home and work addresses, multiple phone numbers, nickname, birthday, anniversary, web page, and any notes you might want to include in a free-form notes field.**

4. **When you're done, click the Save button.**

   If you change your mind and don't want to add the contact now, click the circled *X* button that is next to the Save button.

That's all there is to it!

TIP

Anywhere you see a + (plus sign) button when you're adding a contact, clicking it expands to include several other fields that you can fill in if you want.

After you have added a contact, you see the entry in the list to the left. On the right side, several links to other tasks appear, such as for setting up a calendar event (which invites the contact), or sending an email. If you sync the contact to your phone (covered later in this book), you can call the person if you filled in a phone number.

You can edit a contact later on by following these steps:

1. **Select the contact from the list of contacts on the left side of the Contacts window.**

2. **Click the pencil icon at the lower-right corner of the window.**

3. **Scroll to the fields you want to add or change and enter the information.**

4. **To remove one of the contact's details (such as the phone number), go to the that item and use the Delete key to remove the characters one by one.**

5. **Click the Save button (the disk-like button near the upper-right corner).**

   Your changes are saved.

6. **If you change your mind and don't want to keep your changes, click the circled *X* button that is next to the Save button.**

   Your changes are discarded and the contact's information is unchanged.

The main power of Outlook Contacts is the ability to send email to people without having to remember their email address. In Outlook email, when you are composing a message, a nifty feature in Outlook email called Autocomplete helps you by filling in the rest of a recipient's email address after you've typed the first few letters of their email address or their name.

Word

 Microsoft Word is one of Microsoft's flagship software products, going back to 1983. Today, Microsoft Word is the gold standard for business word processing, and it's available on Chromebooks.

Okay, a bit of a disclaimer: The version of Word in Office Online and on Chromebooks is not quite as full-featured as the versions available for Windows and Macs. But for many users, Word has more capabilities than they will ever need. In fact, I'm writing this part of the chapter on my Chromebook using Word, and a part of it using Word Online on my Mac.

To open Word, go to your Office Online main page (https://www.office.com) and click Word. Figure 11-11 shows the Word Online main page.

On the Word main page, you have a lot of options. You can open a new blank document, open a document from one of many templates provided by Word, or upload a file from your Chromebook and edit it with Word. Word employs toolbars called the Ribbon. If you look again at Figure 11-11, you can see that the Home tab is open. On this tab, you can format your text in many different ways, including your choice of font, font size, bold, underline, text color, highlight color. You can format paragraphs to be left- or right-justified, centered, or full, and you can add bullets and numbering. If you click the Layout tab on the Ribbon, you see you find ways to control page size and orientation, margins, and more. On the Review tab, you can run the spelling and grammar checker, insert comments, and count the number of words in your document.

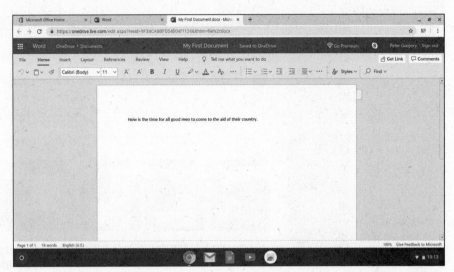

FIGURE 11-11:
Using Word from
Office Online on a
Chromebook.

TIP

If you are expect to use Word a *lot* on your Chromebook, you might consider using the Word app instead of using Word through your browser. However, to do so, you need a paid subscription to Office 365. However, given that Google Docs is already fully functional and free, you would probably base a decision to pay for Word on the need for one or more advanced features in Word that aren't in Google Docs.

Word and Google Docs are compatible. In other words, you can create and work on a document in Word and then send it to someone else who can work on it using Google Docs. Until you get into some of the very advanced features of Word, such as the use of Word template ".dot" files, you'll never run into a problem.

To download the Word app, follow these instructions:

1. **Open the Google Play store app.**

2. **Search for *Microsoft Word.***

   You should see the app that resembles what you see in Figure 11-12. Be sure that it says Microsoft Corporation under the app name; otherwise, you're not viewing the right app!

3. **Click the Install button at the right.**

4. **When installation is complete, click Open. Or, click the Launcher and then click Word.**

5. **The first time you start Word, it may ask for permission to access photos, media, and files on your device; if so, click Allow.**

6. **Sign in to your Office Online account and enter your user ID and password as directed.**

FIGURE 11-12:
The Word app
in the Google
Play Store.

Word works great on Chromebooks, whether you use the web app or download the local app. Entire books have been writing about Word, so you can find far more information than I have time and space to show you here; to learn more, pick up a copy of *Office 365 All-In-One For Dummies,* by Peter Weverka and Timothy L. Warner.

Excel

Microsoft Excel is the undisputed king of spreadsheets in the business world. And as you can with Outlook and Word, you can use Excel on your Chromebook. In this section, you dive right in.

To start Excel, log in to Office.com and click the Excel button. When Excel starts, you see a screen similar to what appears in Figure 11-13. You have several choices: You can start a new, blank spreadsheet by clicking any of the several templates shown; you can upload a spreadsheet (called a *workbook*) that is stored on your Chromebook; or you can open a spreadsheet that is stored in your OneDrive. Figure 11-14 shows Excel with the New Blank Workbook template chosen.

As with Google Sheets, a spreadsheet in Excel consists of cells arranged in rows and columns. You can put numbers or other text such as dates (or just words, phrases, and sentences) in a cell. You can adjust the height of rows and the width of columns. You can put in formulas to calculate things, like the total or average of cells in a column of cells.

Microsoft Excel and Google Sheets are compatible, which means that, for the most part, you can create a spreadsheet in one program and use it in the other.

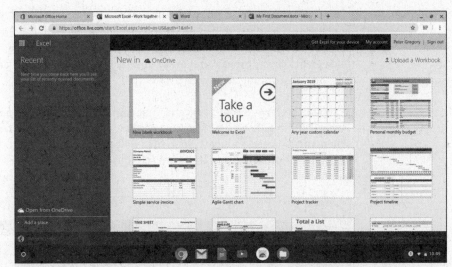

FIGURE 11-13:
Microsoft Excel's starting page.

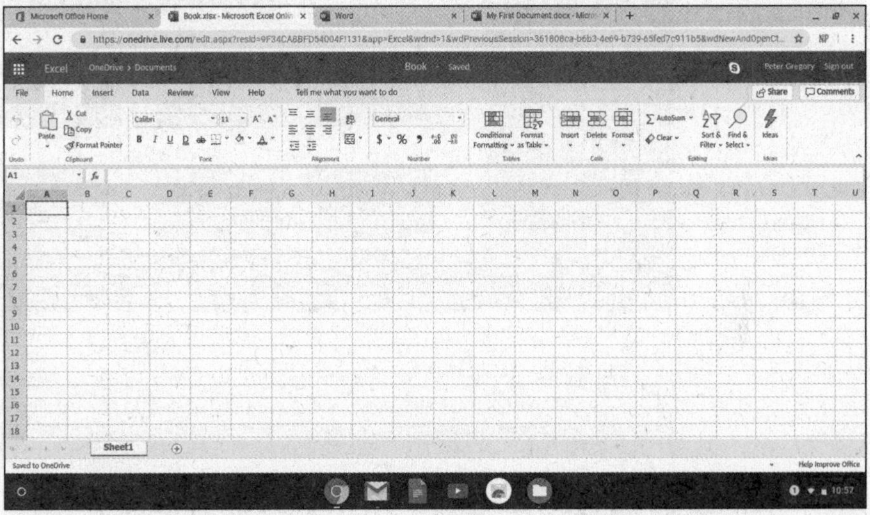

FIGURE 11-14:
A new, blank spreadsheet in Microsoft Excel.

TIP

If you need some of the more advanced features in Microsoft Excel, you might consider downloading the Excel app to your Chromebook. However, as is true of the downloadable Word app, you must have a paid subscription to Office 365 if you want to use the Excel app locally on your Chromebook.

PowerPoint

PowerPoint is Microsoft's presentation app, and it's very much like Google Slides. More accurately, Google Slides is a lot like Microsoft PowerPoint. As is true of other Microsoft Office applications, PowerPoint is the ruler of presentation applications. Just as you can do with Word and Excel, you can create a presentation in PowerPoint that someone else can view and make changes to using Google Slides. This doesn't mean that every minute feature is available and exactly alike, but they do work together pretty well.

To open the PowerPoint program, first log in to www.office.com and click the PowerPoint link. PowerPoint starts and shows a screen like the one in Figure 11-15. When you proceed to create your first PowerPoint slide presentation, you start with a blank presentation, as shown in Figure 11-16.

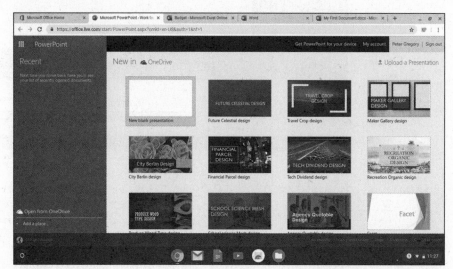

FIGURE 11-15:
The Microsoft PowerPoint starting page.

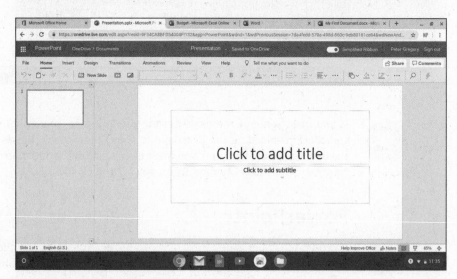

FIGURE 11-16:
A new, blank presentation in Microsoft PowerPoint.

The paradigm for PowerPoint is just the same as that for Google Slides. Each page is called a slide; slides have different layouts; and you can add and arrange text boxes, shapes, and images on each slide. The place for speaker's notes is the same as in Google Slides, and you can view your presentation in a presentation mode that allows others see your big, beautiful slides on a big screen or projector while you sit back and view it in Presenter's view, which lets you read your notes and not forget what you want to say.

TIP

You can download the PowerPoint app onto your Chromebook if you need more advanced features. Doing so requires you to purchase an Office365 subscription. By the way, this is the case not only on Chromebooks but also on Windows and Mac computers.

OneNote

The OneNote app is made for general note-taking and organizing notes according to categories that the user sets up. OneNote is quite popular for busy people who need to organize random bits of information on many different topics.

To start OneNote, log in to Office at www.office.com and click the OneNote icon. If you haven't used OneNote before, a window opens that offers to give you a short tour of OneNote's features. I suggest you take the time to view this — it takes only a minute. The tour asks you a couple of questions about how you might use the program, and it sets up a set of initial categories for storing your notes. I chose the "personal" categories and accepted the defaults. The result was some pre-made categories that you can see in Figure 11-17.

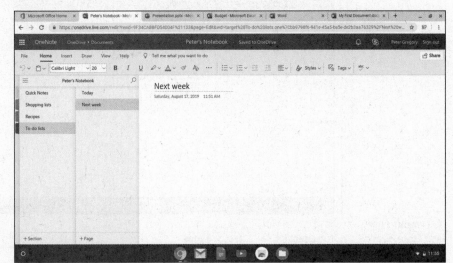

FIGURE 11-17:
OneNote's initial screen with categories chosen in the tour.

In this section, I describe the areas and controls in OneNote, which I identify in Figure 11-18.

» **Sections:** The main categories in which your notes will appear.

» **Pages:** The individual notes that appear in each category.

» **Page title:** The name of a note.

» **Page body:** Where you enter the details of your note, whether it's a shopping list, a recipe, a list of invitees for an event, or notes from an important telephone call.

» **New Section:** Click this to create a new section for notes.

» **New Page:** Click this to create a new note.

» **Toolbar:** Lets you change the appearance of text and paragraphs in your notes.

» **Menu bar:** Leads you to additional toolbars that give you more options and features in your notes.

As with other Google and Microsoft Office tools, you can share a note by clicking the Share button near the upper-right corner.

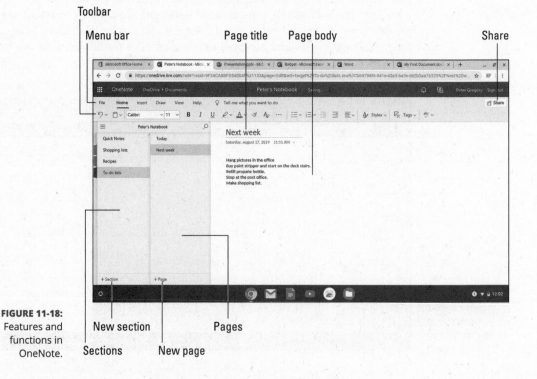

FIGURE 11-18: Features and functions in OneNote.

Collaborating in OneDrive

Just as Google Drive gives two or more persons the ability to edit a Docs document, Sheets spreadsheet, or Slides presentation at the same time, Microsoft's OneDrive allows multiple people to edit a document, spreadsheet, or presentation at the same time.

For two or more people to edit a document at the same time, the document owner must share the document with others. To share in Excel, you click the Share button; in Word, you click the Share or Get Link button. Figure 11-19 shows a user in Excel sharing a spreadsheet with another user. When you fill in a user's email address and then click Share, the recipient(s) receives an email that contains a URL that users can click to open the document and view or edit it.

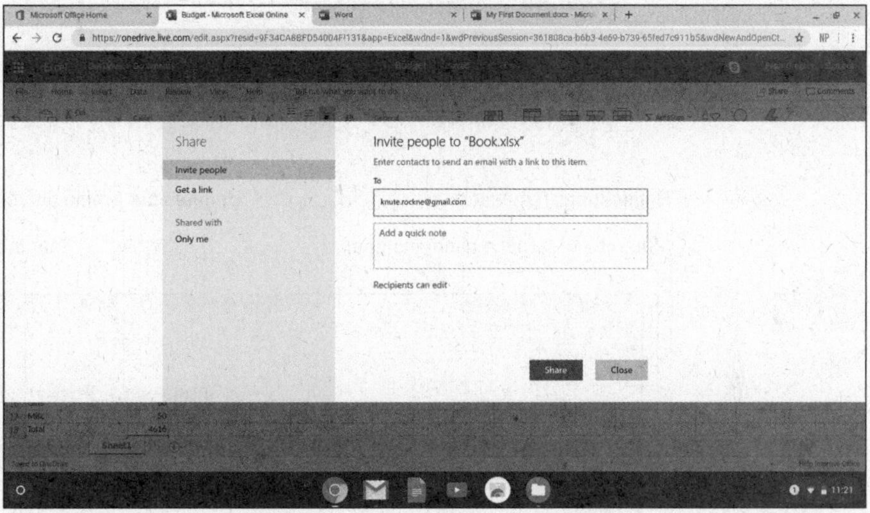

FIGURE 11-19: Sharing a spreadsheet with another user in Microsoft Excel.

Skype

Skype gained a reputation around the world as an Internet-based instant messaging tool. This popularity got the attention of Microsoft, which bought the company in 2011. Skype is now a part of Microsoft's Office suite.

You can use Skype for instant messaging between people. Because Skype works on not only Chromebooks but also Windows and Mac computers, as well as iPads, iPhones, and Android tablets and smartphones, you and your friends and associates are able to stay in touch and reach each other almost any time. Further, you can send not only text messages but also images, and you can even have live video and audio conversations.

TIP

For a nominal fee, you can also use Skype to place actual telephone calls to any phone number in the world. To do so, you need to register a credit card. You may, however, be able to try a free trial to see what this service is like.

Skype is available in other forms, too. You can add Skype to your Chrome browser as an add-on, and you can download and use the Skype app.

Follow these directions to start and use Skype:

1. Go to the Office.com home page and click the Skype icon.

The main Skype window appears, as shown in Figure 11-20.

Note the Enable Notifications window at the left. Skype asks permission to send you notifications, which will appear in the Notifications area on your Chromebook. Receiving notifications can be useful because it lets you know when someone has sent you a message on Skype.

2. To view your Skype contacts, click the Contacts icon near the left side of the Skype window.

Notifications requested   Update your profile photo

Search   Dial a phone number   Your mood message

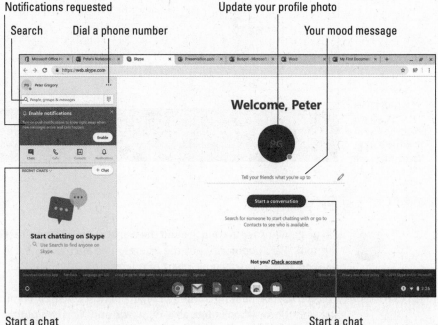

FIGURE 11-20:
The Skype main window on a Chromebook.

Start a chat   Start a chat

3. **Add contacts by clicking the Add Contact link and searching by a contact's name, email, phone, or Skype ID.**

If you know someone's Skype ID but you can't find that contact in a search, you need to send an invite to that person, who can then accept you as a contact.

4. **To start a Skype conversation, click Contacts and then select a contact by clicking it in the list of contacts.**

A new conversation window opens on the right side of the Skype menu.

5. **Start typing where you see the words "Type a message here" and then click the Send Message icon to send your message.**

Clicking Enter when typing a message in Skype starts a new paragraph. Send a message by clicking the Send Message icon.

If the person you're contacting can receive Skype notifications on an available device, that person immediately sees your message. Figure 11-21 shows a sample conversation.

TIP

On a Chromebook, the Skype web app works only with the Google Chrome browser. If your preferred browser is, say, Firefox, you'll have to go back to Chrome to use Skype.

You can explore much more in Skype. One of the best resources is the Skype Help guide, found at `https://support.skype.com`.

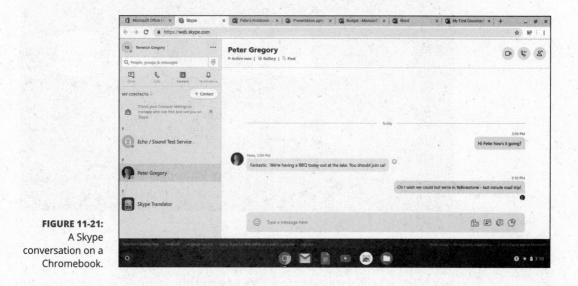

FIGURE 11-21:
A Skype conversation on a Chromebook.

Checking Out Apple's iCloud Suite

As if the Google and Microsoft office suites weren't enough, you can also considers Apple's offering, iCloud, which is as complete as the others. iCloud provides an email app and apps for a calendar, contacts, notes, and reminders. iCloud also offers the Pages word processing app, the Numbers spreadsheet app, Keynote for presentations, and more.

iCloud will be relevant for you if you're an Apple household (or business) and want to get your Chromebook in on the action. But in contrast to Microsoft Office, iCloud offers no downloadable apps for your Chromebook; instead, all apps are in the cloud that access through your browser, just as you do Google Docs, Sheets, Slides, and so on.

 To get started in iCloud, go to www.icloud.com If you don't have an account, you can sign up for one at no cost. After you set up an account and log in, you see the iCloud main page (see Figure 11-22).

 iCloud on a Chromebook works only on the Chrome browser. Sorry, Firefox and DuckDuckGo fans!

TIP

FIGURE 11-22:
The iCloud main
page.

iCloud file storage

In Apple's iCloud suite, you store files (documents, pictures, and anything else you would save in Google Drive or on your Chromebook) in the iCloud storage service, called iCloud Drive. iCloud Drive makes all your files available from all your devices anytime you're online.

Using the iCloud file storage site is so similar to using Google Drive and Microsoft OneDrive that you can refer to those sections, earlier in the chapter, if you need help getting to it. The main page of iCloud looks like what you see Figure 11-23. By the way, you get here by clicking the iCloud logo after you log in to iCloud at www.icloud.com.

FIGURE 11-23:
The iCloud Drive
main page.

In the iCloud service, Apple creates folders for Pages, Numbers, and Keynote. Some of the other folders shown in Figure 11-23 are folders I have added.

Pages

Pages is Apple's iCloud word processing program, and guess what? Pages is similar to Google Docs and Microsoft Word. As with Docs and Word, you can create documents in one of these programs and later open and edit documents in either of the other two — that is, they're all basically compatible with one another.

Pages, however, is not as fully functional in a web browser as are the Pages apps for Macs, iPads, and iPhones. But for basic editing, you may be fine. When you open a document with Pages, you see a little warning that tells you that Chrome on a Chromebook does not *fully* support Pages (see Figure 11-24). With Firefox or DuckDuckGo, Pages doesn't work at all. Still, you can get away with using Pages for basic editing while using the Chrome browser on a Chromebook. Figure 11-25 shows the Pages app, where I'm editing the text in this very paragraph.

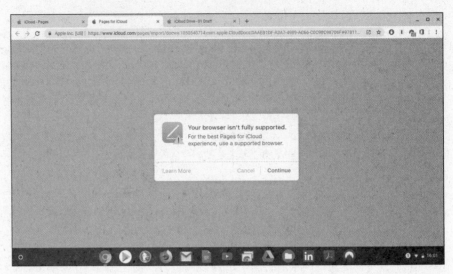

FIGURE 11-24:
Pages is not fully
supported on
Chromebook
browsers.

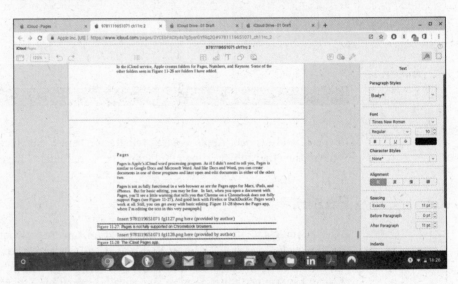

FIGURE 11-25:
The iCloud
Pages word
processing app.

To edit a document with Pages, go to the iCloud main page and open the Pages app. Then, navigate to the file you want to edit (or click Add a Document to create a new one). Click the paintbrush icon on the right side of the toolbar to open a toolbox that provides tools for performing all the usual kinds of character and paragraph formatting that you may need to do.

Numbers

Numbers is the spreadsheet program in Apple's iCloud suite. I know I'm beginning to sound like a broken record if you've read all the way through this chapter, but Numbers is similar to Google Sheets and Microsoft Excel — so much so that you can interchange worksheets with all three programs.

To open a spreadsheet with Numbers, go to the main iCloud pages and click Numbers. Then browse the spreadsheet you want to open, or create a new one. Figure 11-26 shows a spreadsheet that has been opened with iCloud Numbers. Click the paintbrush icon near the upper-right corner to open a formatting window so that you can format the cells, rows, and columns in your spreadsheets.

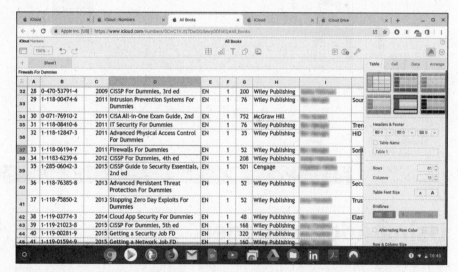

FIGURE 11-26:
The iCloud Numbers spreadsheet app.

With Numbers, you can input numbers, dates, and text in individual cells. You can also input formulas that show the result of calculations on the values of one or more cells. Numbers lets you work with fonts, colors, shading, and borders so that you can spruce up your spreadsheets for the appearance you need to make them more readable and useful.

When you open a spreadsheet with Numbers, you see a little warning that tells you that Chrome on a Chromebook does not fully support Numbers. Basic features will still function in Numbers on a Chromebook.

TIP

Keynote

Keynote is Apple's iCloud presentation program, and it's compatible with Google Slides and Microsoft PowerPoint. All the same basic functions found in Slides and PowerPoint are in Keynote as well. Like Pages and Numbers, Keynote is not fully supported in the Chrome browser on your Chromebook. Still, you can get the basics done. Figure 11-27 shows a presentation open with Keynote.

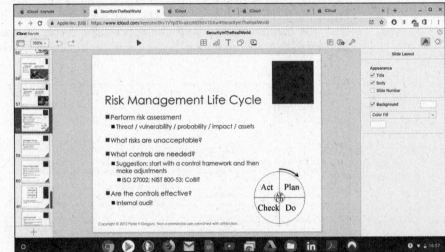

FIGURE 11-27:
The iCloud Keynote presentation app.

Using Adobe Reader

PDF, or Portable Document Format, is a widely recognized standard for documents the world over. Although your Chrome browser can read and display PDF documents right in the browser window, you may want — or need — to display PDF documents using the Adobe Reader app.

One reason you may need to use Adobe Reader is if you've been asked to sign a PDF document, or you want to add comments to a PDF document. If this applies to you, and you want to do this on your Chromebook, you're in luck.

To get the Adobe Reader application, follow these steps:

1. **Open the Google Play Store app.**
2. **Search for Adobe Reader.**

3. **Make sure the app you select is from Adobe.**

4. **Click the Install button and then click the Open button to open Adobe Reader.**

To open a file with Adobe Reader:

1. **Open the Adobe Reader app.**

2. **Click the Files button at the bottom center of the Adobe Reader window.**

3. **Navigate to the file you want to open.**

4. **Click the filename.**

    The document opens, as shown in Figure 11-28.

TIP

You can also open a PDF document with Adobe Reader by opening the Files app, Alt-clicking the file you want to open, and clicking Select Open With and then Adobe Acrobat.

5. **To create a comment in the PDF files you are viewing, click the blue circled pencil icon at the lower-right corner of the page.**

    A toolbar appears that allows you to insert comments or make suggested changes to the text.

6. **To save a PDF file into which you have inserted comments or suggested changes:**

    a. **Click the Share button near the upper-right corner of the Adobe window.**

    b. **Select Save to Files.**

    c. **Navigate to the desired folder in Files.**

    d. **Type the name for the file.**

    e. **Click Save.**

7. **To print your PDF file:**

    a. **Click the Share button.**

    b. **Select Print.**

    c. **Select a printer and any desired print options.**

TIP

Adobe Reader does not look in Google Drive for your PDF files, but only on your Chromebook or in OneDrive, DropBox, or the Adobe Document Cloud (Adobe's file storage service that is similar to Drive, OneDrive, and iCloud).

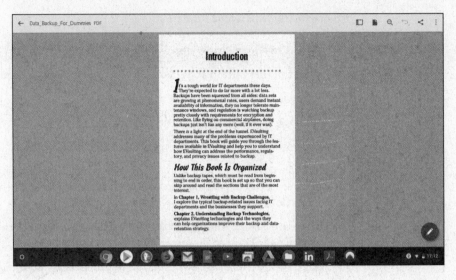

FIGURE 11-28:
The Adobe
Reader app.

3

The Chromebook Recreational Vehicle

Streaming albums, songs, or customized radio stations with Google Play

Capturing only your best angles with your Chromebook camera

Watching videos on your Chromebook or streaming them over the Internet with Google Play Video and YouTube

Sharing photos and videos using Google Photos

Watching photos and videos taken on your smartphone on your big Chromebook screen

Staying in touch with family and friends or conducting a business meeting from around the globe with Google Hangouts and Skype

Purchasing, renting, and reading books on your Chromebook with Google Books and Kindle

Chapter **12**

Mustering Your Music

B efore the Internet, the primary delivery mechanism for broadcast music was radio and television. Broadcast media effectively dictated what was popular simply because you had no other way to get exposed to new music unless you scoured the record (or CD) bins at the local music store. Or maybe you had friends with cool older siblings who gave out mixtapes to broaden your musical horizons. The Internet turned the entire media industry on its head by providing access to anything (everything!), anywhere, anytime.

These days, purchasing physical music media is primarily done by collectors and super-fans. Broadcast radio is shrinking and consolidating, and satellite radio is still hanging on. The expansion of the Internet, broadband access, and wireless technology have revolutionized the way the world consumes music. It's a buyer's market in the music industry.

In this chapter, you explore the ins and outs of Google's digital music platform, Google Play Music. Upload your digital music library to Google Play and have it sync to your Chromebook and other wireless devices. Search the Google Play catalog of more than 20 million songs and stream them to your Chromebook. Learn how to create playlists that you can share with other Google Play users, or simply search for radio stations that play an endless stream of tunes to get you through the day. It's never a dull moment with Google Play.

If you are a Pandora, Spotify, Apple Music, or Amazon Music user, you can fully enjoy those services on your Chromebook. Even the high-end TIDAL Music service is available. This chapter explores them as well.

Getting Started with Google Play

Google Play is Google's online marketplace, very similar to Apple's iTunes Store. Google Play sells videos, televisions shows, books, music, and applications for Android, Chromebook, the Chrome browser, and more.

 As is the case with all the applications on the Google platform, access to apps is linked to your Google Account. If you have multiple Google Accounts, make sure that you're logged in to your Chromebook with the account that you want to be associated with Google Play. Launch Google Play by opening the Launcher and clicking the Google Play Music icon.

If you're logging into Google Play for the first time, a Welcome screen appears. You need to decide what level of service you want. Google Play Music offers two levels of service. The free version is free indefinitely, but it has limited functionality.

With the free version, you can

>> Upload your music collection (up to 20,000 songs) and stream it to any Chromebook, Android, iOS, laptop, or other web-enabled, Internet-connected device.

>> Purchase new music through Google Play, and download it or stream it to your Chromebook, Android, iOS or other device.

With the paid version, you get everything the free version offers, but you also can

>> Listen to custom radio stations with personalized recommendations.

>> Access the Google Play catalog of 20 million songs, completely advertisement-free.

 There's no such thing as a free lunch. The free Google Play Music service is great, but you are going to hear advertising now and then. But if you upgrade to the paid service, the ads vanish!

TIP

Creating a Standard Account

To begin using the standard (free) version of Google Play, follow these steps:

1. **Open the Launcher menu and click the Google Play Music icon.**

The Google Play Music app opens in a Chrome browser, and asks whether you want to select the Individual or the Family paid service.

2. **To proceed with standard access, scroll down and click the No Thanks link.**

Also, deselect the Email Me . . . link if you don't want to get news and offers about Google Play in your email.

The main Google Play Music window opens. If this is the first time you've started Google Play Music, it will ask for permission to access photos, media, and files on your device.

3. **Click Allow.**

You're taken to your Google Play Music account, as shown in Figure 12-1.

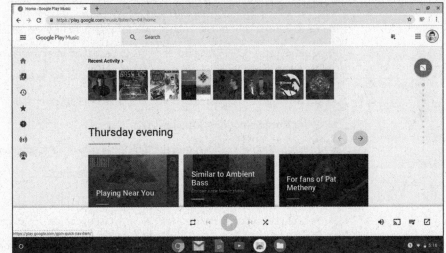

FIGURE 12-1:
Google Play Music.

The Google Play Music site has a lot of controls:

>> **Menu:** Opens a menu with more actions that you can perform, shown in Figure 12-2, and explained shortly.

>> **Home:** Click to take you back to your Google Play Music main page.

>> **Music Library:** Click to view your music library. When you first start using Google Play Music, your library is empty.

>> **Recents:** Click to show recent items you have listened to, including albums, artists, stations, podcasts, and so on.

>> **Top Charts:** Click to show currently popular music.

>> **New Releases:** Click to show new music.

>> **Browse Stations:** Click to show available radio stations.

>> **Podcasts:** Click to show any available podcasts.

>> **Play Controls:** These are

- **Repeat mode:** Repeat songs or albums.

- **Back:** Plays previous track.

- **Play:** Plays music.

- **Forward:** Plays next track.

- **Shuffle songs:** Plays songs in random order.

>> **Volume:** Adjusts music volume.

>> **Cast:** Causes your music to be played through a TV or external speaker.

>> **Queue:** Lets you view the list of songs to be played after the current selection.

>> **Mini Player:** Reduces the size of the Google Play Music window.

>> **Streaming Selections:** Shows you available selections for streaming music.

>> **View More Selections:** Just like it says.

>> **Music Selections:** Shows more stations and other music you can play.

>> **I'm Feeling Lucky:** Lets Google select what to play next.

>> **Playlist Drawer:** Shows your playlists.

>> **Search:** Lets you search for music by artist, song, album, or station.

>> **Recent Selections:** Shows albums or stations you played recently.

Okay, as promised, here are the choices available in the Google Play Music menu shown in Figure 12-2:

>> **Music Library:** Shows your purchased music. (Your library is empty until you start purchasing songs and albums.)

>> **Recents:** Shows recently played songs and albums.

» **Top Charts:** Shows the most popular music.

» **New Releases:** Shows newly released music songs and albums.

» **Browse Stations:** Shows "radio" stations that are available.

TIP

Radio stations in streaming music services are similar to "over the air" radio stations in that they often have a theme. Over-the-air radio stations are transmitted using AM or FM radio signals and are available in a small geographic area. Streaming radio stations are available over the entire world.

» **Podcasts:** Shows any available podcasts.

» **Upgrade to Family Plan:** Depending on what plan you are on, this shows the individual plan or family plan, or it may not appear at all.

» **Upload Music:** Transfer music you already own into your library.

» **Settings:** Change how Google Play Music works.

» **Trash:** Shows music you have discarded.

» **Help & Feedback:** Get help on using Google Play Music.

FIGURE 12-2:
The Google Play
Music menu.

Upgrading to a Premium Account

If you want to upgrade from the free version of Google Play Music to the paid service, follow these steps:

1. **In the Google Play Music main window, click the Menu button (refer to Figure 12-1).**

   The menu appears.

2. **Click Subscribe Now.**

   Your subscription choices appear. You might be as lucky as I was, and Google will have an offer like what you can see in Figure 12-3. Select Individual or Family and click your choice.

   If you already have one or more credit cards registered with Google, it asks you to select which one to use. If you don't, you're asked to enter a credit card number. (Google will probably ask for your credit card even if you have a free trial, because it hopes that you will think their music service so fine that you'll agree to the paid subscription.)

   A page loads, asking you to select the genres you like, as shown in Figure 12-4.

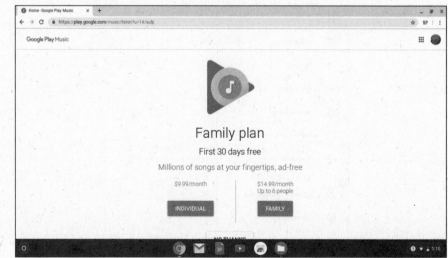

FIGURE 12-3: Selecting your Google Play Music subscription.

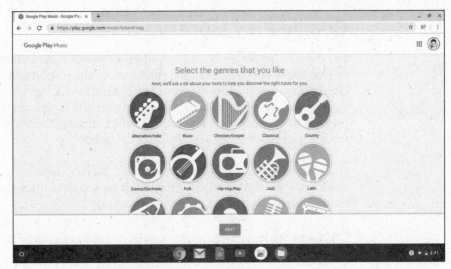

FIGURE 12-4:
Selecting your
favorite genres.

3. **Select the genres you like.**

   As you click each one, the icon shows a checkmark. If you select one by mistake, just click it again to deselect it. Be sure to scroll down because more choices may exist than are visible on the screen.

4. **When you have made your genre choices, click Next.**

   A new page loads, asking you to select the artists you like. As with the genre selection above, click each one you like. If you scroll down far enough, you might see a Show More Artists icon. Click that to show more, and keep selecting. If you selected several genres in Step 3, you might see quite a list of artists to choose from!

   If you find that you're viewing artists you don't care for, you can also click Back to change your genre selections.

5. **When you have completed your artist choices, click Done.**

   Google Play loads your account, signaling the completion of the account creation process.

Accessing Music in Google Play

With Google Play Music, the world is your oyster. After you've selected your favorite genre(s) and artists, Google Play Music displays popular radio stations that play the music you like, as well as other music selections such as Local Favorites, Recommended New Releases, and Top Albums.

Google Play Library

The Google Play library is where all of your favorite radio stations reside, as well as your music uploads and music purchases. In the standard (free) account, your Google Play view defaults to your music library. If you aren't in your library, you can get there by locating and clicking the Music Library link on the left side of the page, or by clicking the Menu icon and then clicking Home. Your library loads, revealing all your music that's available to stream.

If you opted for the standard account and haven't uploaded or purchased any music, your library is initially empty. Even so, you have three options for playing music (or four, if you have a premium account):

>> **Radio Stations:** Stream music from Google Play's universe of radio stations organized by genre and artist.

>> **Add Your Music:** Upload your own music.

>> **Shop:** Search the Google Play store for songs that you want to purchase and add to your Google Play library.

>> **Listen:** If you are a paid subscriber to Google Play Music, simply search for any music you want to listen to. You can make selections by genre, artist, album, and song.

REMEMBER

With the standard free account, Google Play allows you to upload up to 50,000 songs. If your collection is bigger than that, just upload the music you listen to most and leave the back catalog on a jump drive.

Google Play Radio

On Google Play Music, a "radio station" is simply a music stream in a particular genre. It's not the same as AM or FM stations, but is more like the stations on Sirius or XX, but without DJs. Google Play Music "radio" stations play only music, all day and all night.

TIP

If you don't purchase songs or albums in Google Play Music, your main option is to find and select radio stations to stream for as long as you want. If you have the free version, you hear advertisements from time to time.

Google Play Radio has dozens (maybe hundreds) of radio stations. From the main page, click any of the little dots beneath the big orange I'm Feeling Lucky icon on the right side of the screen (refer to Figure 12-1). Each one takes you to a different selection of stations to listen to.

Click one of those dots to try it. Doing so takes you to a station page, or a page with a selection of stations. Hover over them to see the white-and-gray Play button, and click one to start listening.

When a station starts playing, the name of the song that is playing appears at the bottom-right corner of the window. Album art might appear as well. In the middle of the window at the bottom, the Play button is now a Pause button. To the right of that is the Skip button. If you have a free account, you can skip up to six times an hour; if you have a paid subscription, you can skip all you like (but if you are skipping *that* much, maybe you want to choose another station). To the right of Skip is the volume control. The next icon is the Cast button, which you use to cause your music to play through a Bluetooth speaker, a TV or monitor with a Google Chromecast device, or some other device that you can cast to.

TIP

If you like a radio station, you can add it to your music library. Just click the Add to Library link, and the station will be listed in your music library.

Mini Player

After you have your music streaming the way you like, you can switch to the mini player if you have other things to do on your Chromebook and want to keep an eye on your music player. See Figure 12-5, which shows the mini player in front of a browser window.

TIP

The first time you click the Mini Player icon, you're asked to install it. Click the Install button to proceed. After that, whenever you click the Mini Player icon, it will appear as shown in Figure 12-5.

FIGURE 12-5:
The Google Play
Music mini
player.

The Mini Player has a limited set of controls, from left to right across the bottom of the mini player window:

>> **Thumbs Up:** Click this if you like the song that is playing.

>> **Skip Back:** Play the previous song. This control is relevant only if you are listening to an album. On a radio station, this control is grayed out.

>> **Pause:** Stop the music momentarily. When you have paused it, the icon changes to Play. Click Play to continue playing.

>> **I'm Feeling Lucky Radio:** This control is just above the Pause/Play button and switches you to I'm Feeling Lucky radio, where Google chooses the music to play.

>> **Skip:** In an album, clicking this control makes the next song play. On a radio station, it skips to the next song to be played (in the free version of Google Play Music, you can skip up to six times per hour).

>> **Thumbs Down:** Click if you don't like a given song. This control also skips to the next song.

TIP

The upper-right corner of the Mini Player has a settings button (3 little dots). The main function of that button is to cause the Mini Player to always be on top — that is, always be visible by being on top of your browser or other windows. If the Mini Player is in the way of something, you can just move it, minimize it, or deselect the always-on-top setting.

Searching for an artist's station

Even with the free version of Google Play Music, you have an almost infinite number of stations available to play. If you search for a favorite artist in the search bar, many different stations appear, including one named for the artist. Not every song will be by that artist, but the songs will all be of the same genre — and many of the songs played *will* be by the artist so named.

Purchasing music you hear on a radio station

While listening to music on a Google Play Music station, you might hear a song that you just have to own. Google Play Music makes doing so easy, but to see how to do it, take another look at the radio controls, shown in Figure 12-6.

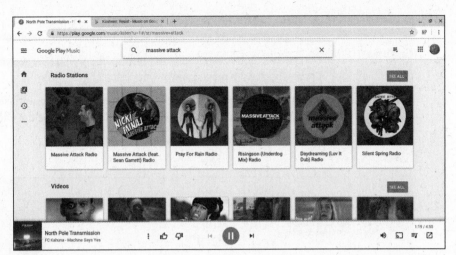

FIGURE 12-6:
The Google Play
Music radio
controls.

To the left of the Pause, Thumbs Up and Thumbs Down buttons is an Options menu button (three vertical dots). Click the Options button to gain access to the following actions:

>> **Start Radio:** Starts a radio station associated with the artist now playing. You can always find your way back to the previous station by clicking the Home button, clicking Recents, and selecting the station you were playing before.

>> **Share:** Lets you tell your friends about the song you are listening to.

>> **Buy:** Opens a new browser tab, where you can purchase this album and add it to your library.

To purchase music that you are listening to on Google Play Music, follow these steps:

1. **To purchase music playing on the radio, click the small menu button to the left of the Play/Pause button and click Buy; to purchase music you see in a search for music, click Buy.**

    A screen appears that looks similar to what is shown in Figure 12-7. In many cases, you will have the option to purchase an individual song or an entire album. The example in Figure 12-7 includes both options.

2. **Click the button showing the price, whether for a song or an album.**

3. **A new window appears that shows your selection and the payment method. Review these items carefully and then click Buy to purchase the selected music.**

4. **If Google asks you to verify your account, input your password.**

Google asks for this verification to prevent others who may see your unlocked Chromebook from purchasing on your behalf.

5. **When Google offers you the chance to listen to your purchased music right away, click Listen to play it or click Close to close the window.**

The music you purchased is now in your library.

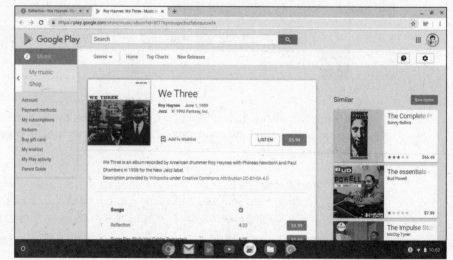

FIGURE 12-7:
Purchasing music on Google Play Music.

Uploading music

If you have music from another source in digital form, you can add it to your Google Play Music library. You might have your music files on an SD card, a thumb drive, an external hard drive, or online in Google Drive or even iCloud or OneDrive. Whatever your music's source, follow these steps to upload it to your Google Play Music library:

1. **Click the Upload Music button from the Google Play menu (refer to Figure 12-2).**

The Add Music window appears.

You now have two methods available for adding your music files. You can click Select from Your Computer, or you can drag and drop from the Files app. I describe the Select from Your Computer option here.

2. **Click Select from Your Computer.**

3. Navigate to the folders on your Chromebook that contain the music you want to upload.

4. Select the file(s) or folder(s) that you want to upload.

5. Click Open.

You might see a window that says, "To add your music, install Google Play Music for Chrome." If so, click Continue to add the Google Play Music extension to the Chrome browser. You need to install this only once on your Chromebook.

When you're done, the added music appears in your library.

Google Play queues the files and uploads them in the background.

You can monitor the progress of your file upload by clicking the Processing Music button (which displays the flashing upload indicator icon) in the bottom-left of the Google Play window.

If you have a large music collection on your Chromebook, you can upload the entire collection by following these steps:

1. Click the Google Play Music menu button (refer to Figure 12-2) and then click Settings.

2. Scroll down in the Settings window until you see the Music from This Computer section.

3. Click the Add Your Music button.

In the window that opens, you can opt to add all current music as well as any new music that you add later.

Creating Playlists

Playlists are the modern version of mixtapes. Back in the day, I made mixtapes on reel-to-reel and cassette tapes. Today, creating playlists in Google Play Music is easier than recording mixtapes. A *playlist* is a collection of songs that you want to play in a specific or randomized order. You can have a playlist for working out, another one for relaxing, another for working on your motorcycle, and another for romance. Google Play gives you the ability to build playlists composed of songs that you've uploaded to your library or, if you have a paid account, with songs available from the entire Google Play catalog. Google allows you to have up to 1,000 songs in a playlist!

All your playlists appear in the Playlists part of your library. Even when you run Google Play Music for the first time, you may have some auto playlists that are already present in your library.

To create a playlist, follow these steps:

1. **Navigate to Artists, Albums, or Songs in your music library. Continue until you are viewing songs you want to add to a playlist.**

2. **When viewing a song, hover to the right of the song title until the More Options menu appears.**

3. **Click the menu and then click Add to Playlist.**

   If you don't have any playlists, select New Playlist. If you do have one or more playlists, they appear. Figure 12-8 shows the New Playlist window.

4. **Enter the name of your playlist in the Name text box and give it a nice description in the Description text box.**

5. **For now, keep the playlist private by keeping the Make Public selector off.**

6. **Click Create Playlist.**

   Your new playlist appears in the Playlist area of your library.

To add more songs, simply repeat the preceding procedure by selecting songs and adding them to existing or new playlists.

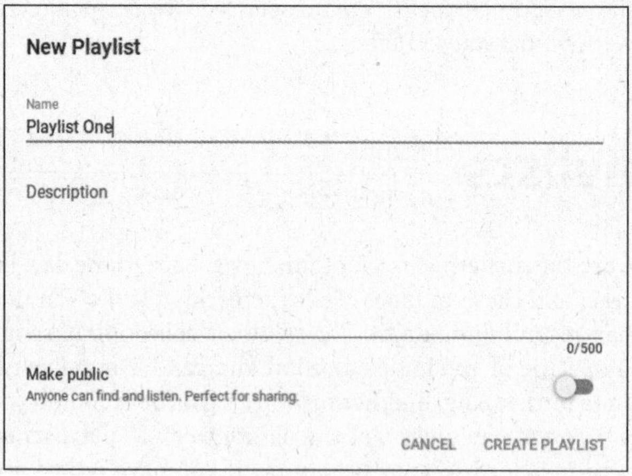

FIGURE 12-8:
Creating a new playlist in Google Play Music.

Sharing playlists

Chances are good that you'll create an epic playlist that will be remembered for all the ages. It would be nearly criminal to keep such a playlist to yourself. You need to share it! To share a playlist, follow these steps:

1. **Click Music Library in the Play Music window.**

2. **Click Playlists.**

Your playlists appear.

3. **Click the playlist you want to share from your list of playlists.**

Your playlist is displayed.

4. **Click Share.**

The Share Playlist window appears, revealing sharing details and options, as shown in Figure 12-9.

5. **At the bottom of the window, click the Make Public selector.**

6. **Click Done.**

Your playlist is now searchable in Google Play and available to all users.

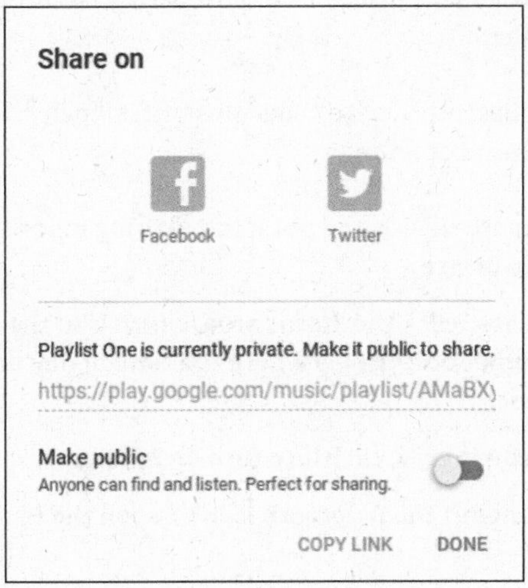

Share on

Facebook   Twitter

Playlist One is currently private. Make it public to share.

https://play.google.com/music/playlist/AMaBX

Make public
Anyone can find and listen. Perfect for sharing.

COPY LINK   DONE

FIGURE 12-9:
The Playlist share window.

If you want to share your playlist with friends through email or on social media, you can generate a link to your playlist and send it out to every deserving soul in your network. Locate your playlist link by following these steps:

1. **Open the Options menu for the playlist.**

   The Playlist Options menu appears.

2. **Click the Share button.**

3. **Choose Copy Link.**

   The URL is copied onto the Clipboard. You may then send the link to others through email or social media.

   You also see two links for Facebook and Twitter. Clicking one or the other opens a new window in which you can create a social media posting that includes the link for your playlist.

Playing music on external devices

In addition to playing music on your Chromebook, you can connect headphones or external speakers by plugging them in to the headphone jack, if it exists. But you have more options as well: You can play music on Bluetooth speakers or "cast" your music to an external device such as a Chromecast connected to a TV, or to a monitor that has speakers.

To play music to a Bluetooth device, you must first "pair" the device to your Chromebook. Follow this procedure:

1. **Turn on the Bluetooth device and put it into pairing mode using the procedures for the device.**

2. **On your Chromebook, click the Status area, which is in the lower-right corner of the Chromebook display where the time of day and battery status icons appear.**

3. **If the Bluetooth icon is gray, click it to turn on Bluetooth.**

4. **Click the menu beneath the Bluetooth icon to open the Bluetooth settings.**

5. **Wait for the device name to appear and then click it.**

   The device should successfully pair with your Chromebook. Now, if you play music with Google Play Music, the audio should play from the Bluetooth speaker.

To cast music to an external device such as a Google Chromecast or a TV with built-in cast capability, follow these instructions (assuming that your Chromecast or other device is already set up):

1. **Start the Google Play Music app and select music to play.**

2. **Find and click the Cast button, which is near the lower-right corner of the Google Play Music window.**

   The Cast play.google.com window opens. (See Figure 12-10.)

3. **In the window, look for the name of the device you want to cast to and click that name.**

   Music should now be playing through the device.

4. **When you want to stop playing music through the device, click the device again in the Cast play.google.com window (click the Cast button to get the window to appear if you don't see it). Then click the device to disconnect it.**

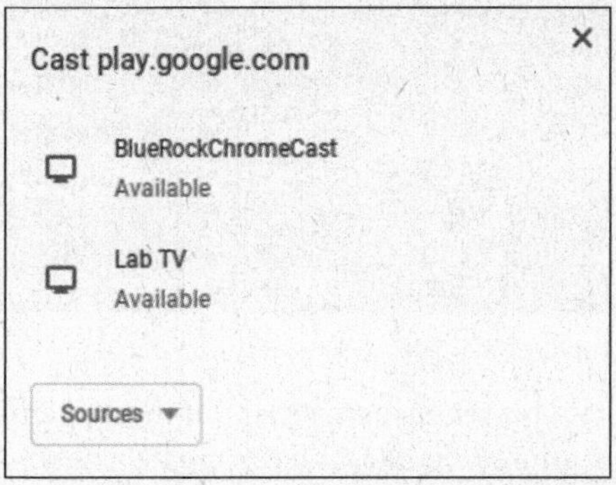

FIGURE 12-10: Casting music to an external device.

Enjoying Streaming Music with Pandora

If you are a fan of the Pandora music streaming service, you're in luck: It works just great on Chromebooks. Pandora is a bit different from Google Play Music. With Pandora, you merely select and listen to streaming music channels. You don't have a music library, and you don't purchase songs or albums. In truth, Pandora closely resembles the radio stations of Google Play Music.

Like Google Play Music, Pandora has free and paid subscription options. And, you guessed it: The free service includes occasional advertising, whereas the paid service is ad-free.

To listen to Pandora, follow these steps:

1. **Open a new tab in your Chrome browser.**

2. **Navigate to** `https://www.pandora.com/`.

3. **Log in or sign up.**

    You're now on Pandora. You see the initial screen, which looks like
    Figure 12-11.

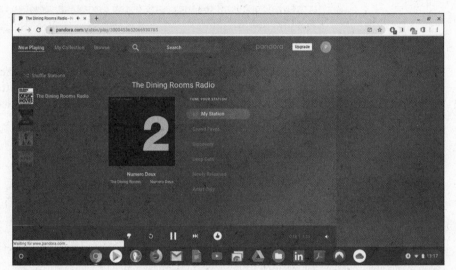

FIGURE 12-11:
The Pandora
music streaming
service.

If you're new to Pandora, you see an assortment of music genres. Browse around
and choose genres and stations you like. You can create a new station by searching
a genre or artist in the search window. Pandora shows you stations as well as
albums. When you see one you like, click the Option button (three little dots) and
then click Collect to add to your collection. You can't add playlists to your collection, but you can listen to them.

You can share any station or playlist by clicking Share from the Option menu. Like
Google Play Music, Pandora provides Facebook and Twitter Share buttons, as well
as the ability to copy a link that you can post in social media, email to a friend, or
even save as a browser bookmark.

When you tire of the advertising on your stations, click the Upgrade button near
the upper-right corner of the Pandora window (Pandora generously makes this
available no matter where you are in Pandora).

If you want more capabilities, such as casting Pandora to a Google Chromecast, you need to download the Pandora app. Just go to the Google Play Store, search for Pandora, and click Install. Then click Open to start. If you plan to use the Pandora app often, you can pin it to the Launcher.

The Pandora app, shown in Figure 12-12, is similar to the Pandora website, with a different arrangement. All the concepts are the same, however. You browse stations and playlists, add those you like, and listen to them.

FIGURE 12-12:
The Pandora app for Chromebooks.

Streaming with Spotify

If Spotify is the music service that floats your boat, you're in luck; it is fully supported on the Chromebook. Spotify is a bit like the streaming radio part of Google Play Music: You browse and search for genres and artists you like and build a collection of music to stream for every mood.

If you're new to Spotify and want to try it, just click the Sign Up link and fill in the form. Doing so takes you to a Download Spotify page, as shown in Figure 12-13. Click the Chromebook link that should appear near the bottom of the window (you may need to scroll down).

Clicking this link doesn't actually download anything, but it takes you to the browser version of Spotify where, as with Google Play Music and Pandora, you browse and search for the kinds of music you like.

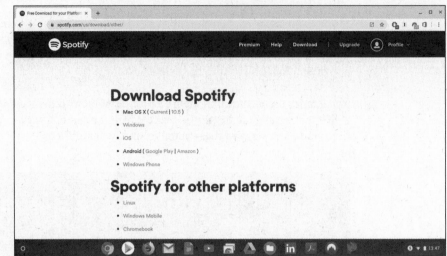

FIGURE 12-13:
The Spotify
download page.

You may notice, near the bottom-left corner of the Spotify window, a Download App link, shown in Figure 12-14. Clicking this indeed downloads the Spotify app, which you can pin to the Launcher if you plan to use it a lot. Again as with Pandora and Google Play Music, you can take your pick: Use the app or the web player to enjoy Spotify music and curate your own playlists. You can also opt to download and install Spotify from the Google Play Store.

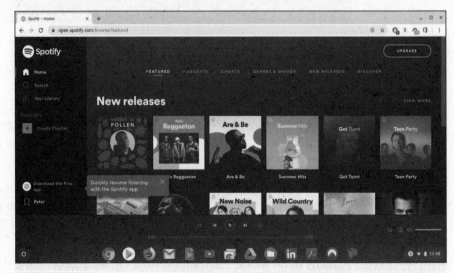

FIGURE 12-14:
The Spotify
streaming music
service web
player.

Amping Up Amazon Music

 If you're an avid fan of the Amazon Music service, you're in luck because it works great on a Chromebook. It's so simple that I could practically skip this section altogether.

Amazon Music offers two levels of membership:

>> **Prime Music:** Two million curated songs that are included with the popular Amazon Prime membership

>> **Amazon Music Unlimited:** Fifty million songs available in student, individual, family, and single-device (Amazon Echo or Fire TV) plans

To use Amazon Music in either plan, follow these steps:

1. **Start your Chrome browser and go to** `https://music.amazon.com/`.

2. **Sign in using your existing Amazon credentials, or create a new Amazon account.**

3. **Select Prime Music or Amazon Music Unlimited if you aren't already a subscriber.**

4. **Select Albums, Artists, Songs, Genres, or music you have purchased from Amazon in the past. (See Figure 12-15.)**

5. **Enjoy your music!**

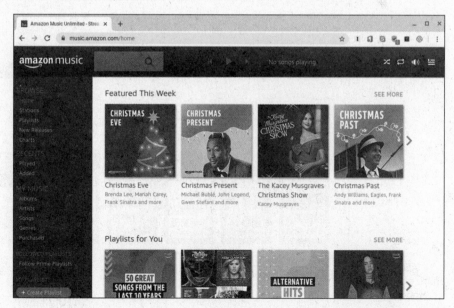

FIGURE 12-15: The Amazon Music stream service.

The Amazon Music service plays through your Chrome browser. No separate app is needed.

Rocking with Apple Music

You might think that Apple Music would not be available on a Chromebook. Think again. Apple Music, the paid subscription service from Apple that launched in 2017, is available on virtually all devices: Windows PCs, Macs, Android phones and tablets, iPhones and iPads, and Chromebooks. It's fully functional as well.

The Apple Music service works through an app that you download from Apple. To get started with Apple Music on your Chromebook, follow these easy steps:

1. **Launch the Google Play Store app.**

2. **Search for Apple Music and then click Install.**

Apple Music is now installed on your Chromebook, as shown in Figure 12-16.

3. **Click Open.**

4. **Follow the prompts to sign in with your Apple account.**

5. **Start playing music.**

Your player fills the screen, as shown in Figure 12-17.

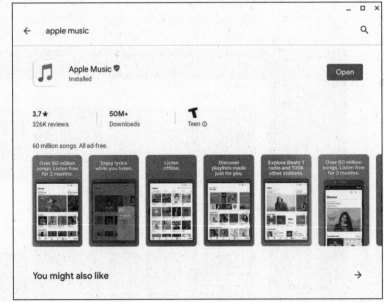

FIGURE 12-16:
Installing the Apple Music music player on a Chromebook.

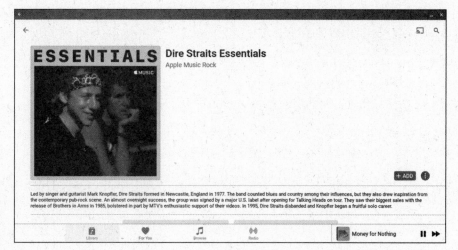

FIGURE 12-17:
The Apple Music music player spinning classic rock hits.

IN THIS CHAPTER

» **Using your Chromebook to take photos**

» **Editing photos**

» **Sharing photos with others**

» **Viewing photos taken with a smartphone on your Chromebook**

» **Viewing photos on external media**

Chapter **13**

Having Fun with Photos

The Chromebook is an excellent multimedia device. With it, you can take photos, listen to music, watch videos, share media files, surf the web, and more. Every Chromebook currently on the market comes with a built-in camera that gives you the ability to video chat and to capture photos for sharing on the web. Further, you can load photos from your smartphone and external media, edit the pictures, view them on a big screen, and share them across the web. The Chromebook is no slouch when it comes to multimedia.

In this chapter, you learn how to access the built-in camera to take pictures. You also find out how to edit your pictures by resizing, rotating, adding color filters, and more. I show you how to access and manipulate photos on removable storage like SD cards. You also see how to get photos from your smartphone to your Chromebook and share them with others.

Navigating the Chromebook Camera

The Camera application that runs on your Chromebook is a native application, meaning that you don't need Internet access to connect to it because it resides on your Chromebook itself. You can take pictures while offline, which is handy if you ever want to take pictures while you're in an Internet desert.

To launch your Chromebook Camera app, open the Launcher and click the Camera icon.

When the Camera app is open, your Chromebook camera is activated. Two things indicate that your Chromebook camera is on:

>> In the Camera app, a video appears of yourself sitting in front of your Chromebook. Smile!

>> The tiny light next to your Chromebook camera turns on, indicating that the camera is on. This light is typically above the screen in the middle.

The Camera app window has a few distinct areas that you should be aware of. In the top-right corner, you have the window controls. You can make the camera application fill the screen by clicking the square in the top-right corner. Click it again to restore the application to its default size. If you want to close the application altogether, click the X in the top-right corner.

On the bottom of the application window, a large white button and several smaller icons appear. (See Figure 13-1.) These icons are your *camera control area*. In this area, you can take photos, access recent photos, and turn features on and off.

FIGURE 13-1: The Camera app.

Taking a Picture

To take a picture, launch the Camera app and follow these steps:

1. **Hover your mouse pointer over the white Picture button in the camera control bar. (Don't click it yet.)**

2. **Look at the tiny light next to your Chromebook camera.**

   This ensures you're looking straight into the camera in your photo.

3. **Click the white Picture button.**

   Your Chromebook makes a camera noise and takes your picture.

TIP

Picture quality depends largely on the quality of the camera and the skill of the operator. Chromebook cameras are pretty good, given the size and application, but they struggle to deliver the goods in certain settings. Here are some suggestions to take a good photo with your Chromebook camera:

» If you're taking a photo of yourself, make sure you're as bright as or brighter than what's behind you. Avoid backlighting: Try to not take photos in front of windows or with the sun or any bright lights behind you (unless you want a silhouette shot to look like you're in the witness protection program!).

» Make sure that you're well lit (no, not intoxicated). Your background may be dim, but if you don't have light shining on you, the camera will struggle to capture a nice photo. (Can you tell that light is a big deal?)

» Most of the time, your Chromebook will be positioned lower than you, and therefore, the majority of photos appear as though someone shorter than you took them. Try to take a photo with your Chromebook angled straight-on with you.

Using the camera timer

The camera timer is the family vacation's best friend. Remember your mom or dad positioning the camera, hitting the timer button, and then running back into frame for the awkward family photo in front of *every* monument in Washington, D.C.? Well, some things never change. The camera timer is here to stay, at least for the time being, and it's as functional as it ever was.

To take pictures using a timer, follow these steps:

1. **In the Camera app, locate the Timer. If the Timer button (near the lower-left corner of the camera app display) has a slash through it, click it.**

   It now has a 3 in it.

   After you click the Picture button, the countdown appears on the screen, as shown in Figure 13-2, and indicates the status of the countdown Timer.

2. **If you're ready to take a picture, click the white Picture button.**

   Your Chromebook beeps three (or ten) times before taking the picture. You'll know that the picture was taken when you hear a camera sound.

   You can configure the timer to wait three seconds or ten seconds. To view and change this setting, click the Settings button and then click Timer Duration. Select the desired option, as shown in Figure 13-3.

REMEMBER

Whenever you take a photo with the camera, with or without the timer, always look at the tiny light to ensure that you're looking directly into the camera. Unless you go for an arty pose, looking into the camera delivers the best results. Say "Cheese!"

FIGURE 13-3:
Changing the
Timer setting.

Viewing Photos Taken with a Smartphone on Your Chromebook

Face it: When you're out and about, whether hiking, biking, at a sporting event, or spending time with friends, you're not lugging your Chromebook about, taking photos. You're using your smartphone. With cameras that take incredible pictures, our smartphones are always with us, and with a moment's notice, we can snap pictures and take high-quality video, too.

Google has made it incredibly easy to view and transfer photos from your smartphone to other devices. The Google Photos app makes all this both possible and automatic, as well. Follow these steps to ensure that photos you take on your smartphone are copied to Google Photos:

1. **Install Google Photos on your smartphone.**

    It's probably already installed on your Android phone. On an iPhone, go to the App Store, search for Google Photos, install, and log in to your Google account.

2. **Give Google Photos permission to access photos on your smartphone.**

3. **Open Google Photos, go to Settings, and ensure that the Back Up & Sync setting is turned on (see Figure 13-4).**

   With this setting, you find that every photo you take on your smartphone soon appears in the Google Photos app on your Chromebook and any other devices running the Google Photos app.

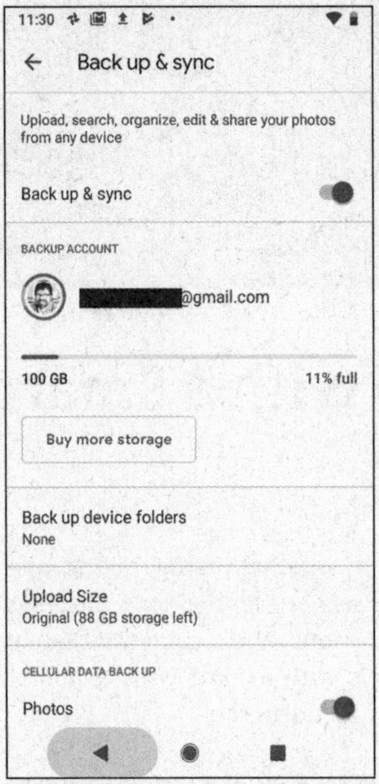

FIGURE 13-4:
Configuring Google Photos to back up photos on an Android phone.

Similarly, you can upload photos taken with your Chromebook to Google Photos. Follow these steps:

1. **Open the Files app on your Chromebook.**

2. **Navigate to Images.**

3. **Click a photo to upload.**

4. **Click the Share button, as shown in Figure 13-5.**

5. **Click Upload to Photos.**

A new window opens, showing the photos you selected.

6. **Click the Upload button at the lower-right corner of the window.**

Your photo soon appears in Google Photos.

Viewing Photos on Your Chromebook

After you take photos on your Chromebook, the photos are stored in the Images folder in the Files app. If you want to view your photos, follow these steps:

1. **Launch the Files app.**

2. **Click the Images button on the left side of the Files app to navigate to your Chromebook photos.**

3. **Click the Switch to Thumbnail View button, if needed. (See Figure 13-6.)**

Switching to thumbnail view allows you to view more photos at one time, although they're smaller.

4. **To view a particular photo, double-click the image thumbnail.**

The photo loads, as shown in Figure 13-7.

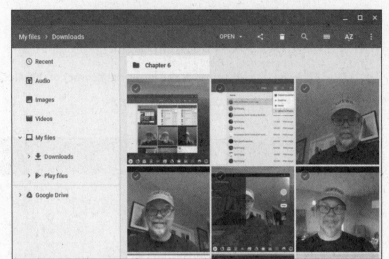

FIGURE 13-6:
Viewing images
on your
Chromebook.

FIGURE 13-7:
Reviewing your
Picasso.

Sharing Photos

Why keep all your brilliant photos to yourself? To have them be truly appreciated, you should share them with others.

Earlier in this chapter, I show you how to get your photos into Google Photos. From there, you can share them in many ways. Follow these steps to share photos:

1. **Open the Google Photos app on your Chromebook.**

2. **Select the photo(s) you want to share.**

3. **Click the Share button at the lower-right corner of the Google Photos window. (See Figure 13-8.)**

A variety of sharing options appears, including email recipients. You can also create a shared album, print, or save photos online to other services such as OneDrive.

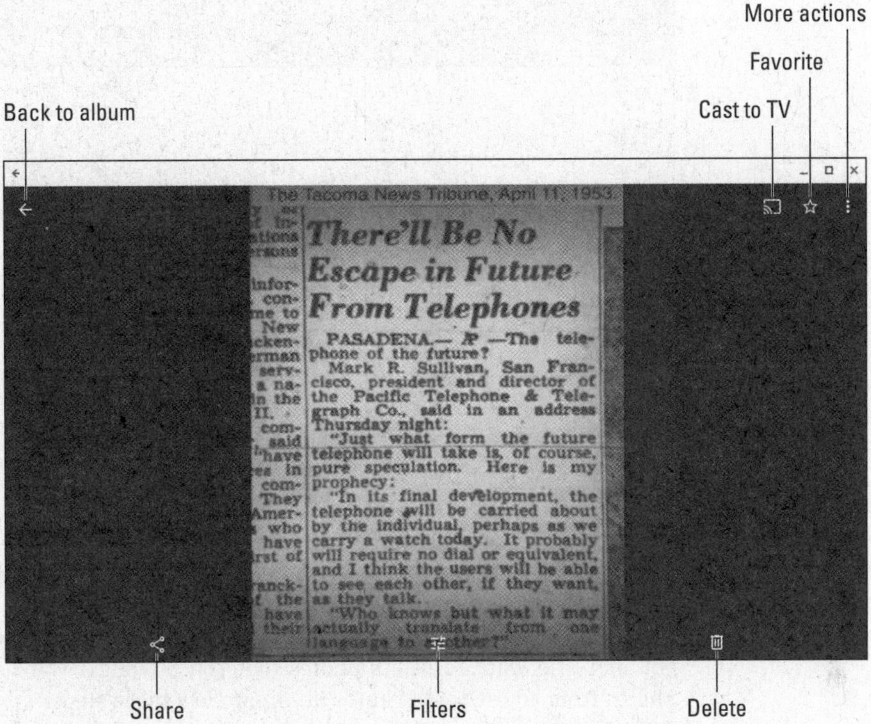

FIGURE 13-8: Sharing photos with others.

Deleting Photos

Not every photo that people take is beautiful and worth keeping forever. This section discusses how to delete photos from your Chromebook and from Google Photos.

Deleting photos stored locally on a Chromebook

Photos taken with the Chromebook camera are stored locally. To delete a photo, follow these steps:

1. **Launch the Files app.**

2. **In the Files app, navigate to Images to view the photos on your Chromebook.**

3. **Click the photo you want to delete.**

4. **Click the Trashcan icon, shown in Figure 13-9.**

    The photo is deleted.

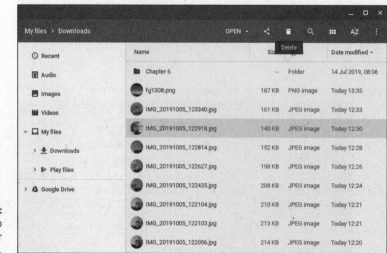

FIGURE 13-9:
Deleting a photo from your Chromebook.

Deleting photos from Google Photos

Although you may feel that the storage in Google Photos is practically unlimited, you may still want to delete photos that you no longer want to keep. To delete photos from your Google Photos library, follow these steps:

1. **Open the Google Photos app.**

2. **Find and click a photo you want to delete.**

3. **Click the trashcan icon near the upper-right corner of the window.**

    A small window appears that reads, "Remove from Google account, synced devices, and shares within Google Photos?"

4. **Click Move to Trash.**

    The photo is deleted.

Transferring Photos from a Digital Camera to Your Chromebook

You don't have to capture photos with the Chromebook Camera to be able to work with and otherwise edit, manipulate, or distribute your photos. Most major digital cameras today store your photos on removable storage devices called *SD cards.* (See Figure 13-10.) The majority of Chromebooks on the market today have an SD-card slot for quickly accessing your data, such as photos, among other things.

FIGURE 13-10: A standard SD card.

Some devices use a Micro SD card, a tiny version of an SD card. Most Chromebooks that have an SD card slot have the full-size slot, necessitating the use of an adaptor. Figure 13-11 shows a Micro SD card being inserted into an adaptor.

To access photos on an SD card, follow these steps:

1. **Place your SD card into the SD card slot on your Chromebook.**

Chromebook may automatically offer to import all the photos on the SD card to Google Drive. It's entirely up to you whether you opt to do this. If you proceed, the photos on your SD card are copied to Google Photos.

2. **Click the SD card in Files to begin browsing its contents.**

See Chapter 7 for more information about using the Files app.

FIGURE 13-11:
A Micro SD card
being inserted
into an SD card
adaptor.

Viewing and Editing Photos

Whether you're accessing photos on an SD card or your Chromebook hard drive, you can edit the photos by following these steps:

1. **In the Files window, browse to the photo you want to edit and double-click the photo file.**

   Chromebook opens the photo in a photo viewer. To the right and left of the image are left and right arrows, which you can use to browse through your photos. Across the bottom, you see tiny thumbnails of all the photos in the current directory. You can click a photo to view it full size.

2. **Move your mouse to the upper-right portion of the photo viewer.**

   A control bar containing several options is revealed.

3. **Click the Edit icon, which looks like a pencil.**

   Several editing controls are revealed beneath the photo.

   The Chromebook Picture Editor gives you the ability to make minor modifications to your photos, as shown in Figure 13-12. These edit features include:

   - **Auto-fix:** Adjusts color balance and contrast if needed.

   - **Crop:** Isolates a portion of the photo that you want to keep and discards the rest.

- **Re-size:** Reduces the "granularity" of a photo and stores the image in a smaller image file.

- **Brightness:** Makes your picture darker or lighter. You can make colors in your picture pop by adjusting the contrast, as well.

- **Rotation:** If your picture is in the wrong orientation, rotate it to the left or the right using this feature.

- **Undo and Redo:** Lets you undo and redo recent edits.

4. **When you're satisfied with your edits, press Exit to save your changes.**

WARNING

Your original file is overwritten with the changes that you make using the Photo Editor. If you want to save your modified photo to a different file and preserve the original, you must deselect the Overwrite Original box, located in the bottom-left of the control bar in the Photo Editor.

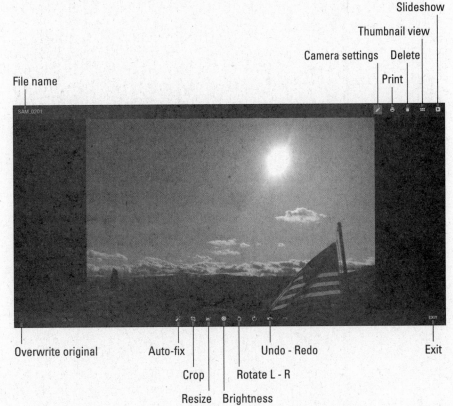

Slideshow

Thumbnail view

Camera settings   Delete

Print

File name

SAM_0201

Overwrite original   Auto-fix   Undo - Redo   Exit

Crop   Rotate L - R

Resize   Brightness

FIGURE 13-12:
The Chromebook photo editor.

Chapter **14**

Playing Video on the Chromebook

Watching video used to be relegated to televisions and video playback devices like VHS players, DVD, and Blu-ray. However, thanks to the prevalence of high-speed Internet access, increasingly powerful computers, and wireless broadband, the Internet has become a primary delivery mechanism for video content of all kinds, from "television" series to how-to videos and videos of cats.

Streaming video has become one of the major uses of Internet bandwidth in the 21st century. According to a report from Cisco (one of the largest manufacturers of commercial networking equipment), 80 percent of all Internet traffic is video (in the United States, it's a staggering 85 percent). Recent statistics show that more than 1.9 billion unique users visit YouTube each month. People watch more than 1 billion hours of video each day and upload more than 500,000 hours of video to YouTube every day. You'll never catch up, and you'll never reach the end of the Internet!

In this chapter, you learn how to play videos on your Chromebook with the internal video player, as well as how to browse for and stream videos through Google

Play Video. You also learn how to navigate Google's YouTube network and how to create, edit, and share videos using YouTube.

Creating a Video with Your Chromebook

The built-in Camera app on your Chromebook can take still pictures as well as create video. To record a video on your Chromebook, follow these steps:

1. **Start the Camera app using the Launcher.**

2. **In the Camera app, click the Video button just below the Take Photo button.**

Your Chromebook is now ready to start recording a video. See how the Take Photo button has changed; it is now the Start Recording button, and it has a red dot on it.

3. **Click the Start Recording button. Smile!**

You hear a musical clicking sound when you click the button, and the button changes to all red with a white square in the middle, indicating that video is now being recorded.

As the video is being recorded, you also see a counter on the upper center of the screen that shows how many minutes and seconds you've been recording.

4. **When you are ready to stop recording, click the Stop Recording button.**

Watching Video on Chromebook

Video files are simply a series of still images, much like a flipbook. Hence, they tend to be much larger than pictures and audio files, largely because of the length of the videos, the quality of the video, and even the quality of the embedded audio. Although the Chromebook allows you to download video from the Internet, doing so can fill up the available storage rather quickly (because a Chromebook comes with dramatically less internal storage than traditional PCs and Macs do). So rather than download video files on your Chromebook, store them (along with other media files) on external storage devices like USB memory sticks or SD cards, or keep them on Google Drive and Google Photos for instant playback on any of your Internet-connected devices.

 Chromebook has a video player that plays most video files. To access video files already on your Chromebook, follow these steps:

1. **Open the Files app and navigate to the Videos folder.**

   Or, if your video is on a USB memory stick or SD card, insert the USB stick or SD card into the appropriate plug and find it with the Files app. Figure 14-1 shows an example.

2. **Double-click the video file you want to play.**

   The Video Player app automatically starts and plays your selected video from the beginning, as shown in Figure 14-2.

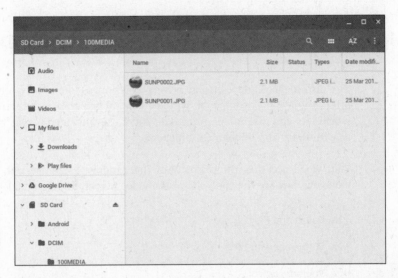

FIGURE 14-1: The Files app showing an external storage device.

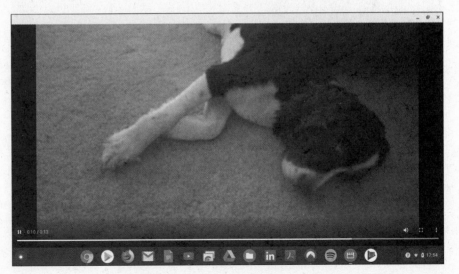

FIGURE 14-2: Playing a video in the Chromebook video player.

Before you remove an SD card from your Chromebook, you need to tell the Chromebook that you want to remove it. Click the Eject button and then remove the card when its name disappears from the Files window. This ensures the integrity of your data on the SD card. Figure 14-3 shows the Eject button for my SD card.

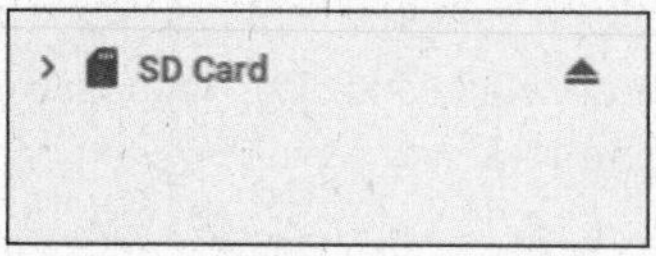

FIGURE 14-3:
Click the Eject button before removing an SD card.

> 📇 SD Card ⏏

Navigating the Chromebook Video Player

The Chromebook video player is very barebones, like a very old school VCR. It offers the usual Chromebook window control bar across the top of the window, which lets you minimize, maximize, and close the video player window — same as with every app on your Chromebook.

Your video occupies the majority of the window space. Near the bottom of the video window are the controls for the video player, which include

» Pause and Play buttons

» Status bar with time indicator

» Volume control

» Full Screen mode control

By default, the Chromebook video player starts your video as soon as that video loads. If you want to pause your video, click the Pause button near the lower-left corner of the window. While the video is stopped, the Pause button turns into a play button. To resume playing, click the Play button.

You can also use the spacebar to pause and resume videos.

Skipping around a video

If you want to skip ahead to your favorite part of a video — or maybe resume where you left off — you can do so with the Chromebook video player. To skip around in a video, follow these steps:

1. **While your video is open and playing, locate the position indicator in the status bar.**

   The position indicator is a little white ball that moves left to right on a white line across the bottom of the player window as the video plays.

   The video control overlay also appears at the bottom of the window, revealing several video control options, including Pause, Full Screen, and Volume Control.

   If you don't see these controls, give the pointer a nudge with your touchpad, and they should appear. Also make sure that the window playing video is on top!

2. **Click and drag the position indicator forward or backward to the place in your video where you would like to start watching.**

   The video skips to the selected location in the timeline.

TIP

You don't have to pause your video to skip around in the video. However, you can pause the video to ensure that the video doesn't keep playing when you skip to different locations in the video.

Activating Full Screen mode

By default, the Chromebook video player plays the video at the optimal viewing size. You can, however, make the video occupy the entire screen by using Full Screen mode. To engage Full Screen mode, follow these steps:

1. **While your video is open and playing, move your pointer over the bottom of the video player.**

   The video control overlay appears at the bottom of the window, revealing several video control options, including Pause, Full Screen, and Volume Control.

2. **Click the Full Screen button on the right side of the overlay.**

   The video player enlarges to fill the screen, as shown in Figure 14-4.

3. To exit Full Screen mode, press the Esc key.

FIGURE 14-4:
Chromebook's
video player in
Full Screen mode.

Adjusting the volume

To control the volume in the Chromebook video player, follow these steps:

1. **Locate the volume control slider on the right side of the overlay.**

   The video control overlay appears at the bottom of the window, revealing several video control options, including Pause, Full Screen, and Volume Control.

2. **To mute the volume, click the Speaker icon. To mute it, click it again.**

   When muted, the icon appears with a slash through it, indicating that the volume has been reduced to zero.

3. **Increase or decrease the volume by moving the slider — to the right to increase and to the left to decrease.**

   The volume changes per the direction you move the volume slider.

Using Other Video Players on a Chromebook

Although the Chromebook's built-in video player is nice, it doesn't always play every video format around. If you have a device that you're pretty sure is recording video, but you see a black screen, you can choose among several other video player apps to try. Or, perhaps you yearn for a video player with more controls. The best one out there is the VLC video player. I've used it for more than a decade on PCs, Macs, and now on my Chromebooks. To get the VLC app, go to the Google Web store (not the Play Store!), search for VLC for Android, and install it.

To watch videos with VLC, open the app, click the menu in the upper-left corner, click Open, and then browse to the movie you want to view (see Figure 14-5).

FIGURE 14-5:
Selecting a video to play with the VLC video player.

Transferring a Video from an Android Phone to a Chromebook

You probably have your smartphone with you practically all the time, and sometimes you want to shoot some pics or video. Playing it back on that tiny smartphone screen is not so great, though. If you want to view it on your big Chromebook screen, follow these steps:

1. **Open the video on your Android phone that you want to transfer to your Chromebook.**

2. **Tap the Share button.**

3. **Tap Save to Drive (the Google Drive logo is just above these words).**

4. **In the Document Title field, enter a name for the video if you like.**

   Or you can keep the default name, which consists of the date and time you shot the video.

5. **Tap Save.**

   The video is saved to Google Photos.

TIP

   Your Android phone might also be configured to save photos to Google Drive or Google Photos automatically.

6. **Open the Google Photos app on your Chromebook.**

   The videos you recorded appear there, as do photos you've taken on your Android phone and any other device with the Google Photos app.

7. **To play the video directly from Google Photos, double-click the video you want to play.**

   To play in Full Screen mode, click the Full Screen button at the lower-right corner of the video.

8. **To save the video to your Chromebook, click More Options at the upper-right corner of the video and click Save To Device.**

   The default filename is the date and time the video was created.

TIP

After you copy the video from your smartphone to Google Photos, you can safely remove it from your smartphone if you are low on available space. You can always play it again directly from the Google Photos app.

Transferring a Video from a Dashcam or Another Source to a Chromebook

If you have a dashcam, digital camera, or security camera that uses an SD or Micro SD card to store videos, you can play these videos on your Chromebook. Follow this procedure:

1. **Insert the SD card into your Chromebook.**

   Your Chromebook opens a new Files app window.

2. **Using the Files app, navigate to the directory where videos are stored.**

   The name of the directory will vary based on the make and model of the device that records video.

3. **When you have found the video you want to view, double-click it.**

   The built-in video player plays the video. If you hear sound but see a black screen, you need to download the VLC app, as discussed in the section "Using Other Video Players on a Chromebook," earlier in this chapter.

Getting Started with Google's Play Movies

Google Play is Google's online marketplace and is similar to Apple's iTunes store. Google Play sells videos, televisions shows, books, music, and applications for Android, Chromebook, the Chrome browser, and more. Play Movies is the part of Google Play you use to view movies and TV shows.

As is the case with all the applications on the Google platform, access to video content in Google Play Movies is linked to your Google account. If you have multiple Google accounts, make sure to be logged in to your Chromebook with the account that you want to be associated with Google Play Movies.

 You can launch Google Play Movies & TV by opening the Launcher and clicking the Play Movies & TV icon. When you do, the Play Movies & TV app launches.

Navigating Google Play Movies & TV

Google Play Movies & TV gives you the ability to purchase movies and television shows for download, as well as for streaming. Any purchases you make are tracked in the My Movies & TV section of Google Play.

The first time you launch Google Play Movies & TV, you're told that you can join your other subscription movie apps such as Amazon Prime, Hulu, and HBO Now.

Before you can purchase movies or TV shows, you need to first know how to navigate through Google Play Movie's vast database. You can search for movies and TV shows using the Search bar at the top of the window or by browsing the Google Play Movies & TV charts. For example, to browse for a movie, click Movies near the top middle of the Google Play Movies & TV window to open the Movies page, as shown in Figure 14-6, and then click Shop.

On the Movies page, you can browse movies by category. Categories might include

>> Genres including Action, Comedy, Family, Sci-Fi, Romance, Drama, and Documentaries

>> Time periods including Recent, the 2000s, 1990s, 1980s, and Classic

>> Award Winning

>> Highly Rated

Browsing videos by category is a great way to discover outstanding, thought-provoking cinema and mindless entertainment alike.

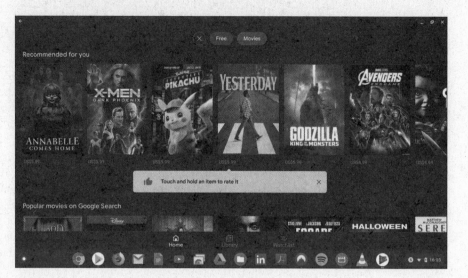

FIGURE 14-6:
Browsing movies
in Google Play
Movies & TV.

Purchasing movies and TV shows

Google Play Movies & TV gives you several options to view movies and television shows. You can either purchase content and access that content for an indefinite amount of time, or you can rent content that's available for viewing for a specified amount of time. Renting is a cheaper option, but if you like to watch certain movies over and over again, or if you want to build a database of flicks you can dial up whenever you want, purchasing may be the way to go.

To purchase or rent a movie on Google Play Movies, follow these steps:

1. **With Google Play Movies & TV open, click the Search icon near the upper-right corner of the window. Enter the name of the movie or TV show (for example, *Beetlejuice*), and then click the Search button.**

   Google Play loads the search results.

2. **Click the video you want to watch (see Figure 14-7).**

   The Movie Profile page loads.

3. **Click the Buy button at the bottom of the screen. (To rent the movie, click Rent.)**

   A payment window appears, presenting you with the option to buy your movie.

REMEMBER

Newer movies and televisions shows are typically available for purchase or rent in 4K (highest definition) or high definition (HD)). 4K has a much greater picture quality than HD. For this reason, Google asks you to pay more for 4K during the checkout process.

TIP

If you don't have a 4K TV or monitor, you're better off buying or renting your movie in HD, if you are offered a choice. If you do have a 4K TV or monitor, you can view the movie in much higher quality by selecting 4K.

4. **Click the Rent or Buy button.**

A Google Wallet window appears, as shown in Figure 14-8, asking you to select your payment method and review your purchase before confirming.

TIP

If you haven't set up your Google Wallet, you need to do so at this point. Follow the prompts to add the desired payment method to your Google account. After you've set up your account, you can quickly conduct purchases on the Google network.

5. **If you're satisfied with your purchase decision, click Buy.**

Google asks you to enter your Google password to prove that it's you and not another person using your Chromebook who wants to watch a free movie!

The movie or TV show you purchased appears in My Movies & TV and is available to play. If you rented the content, it's available in My Movies & TV for only a limited time before it's removed.

FIGURE 14-8:
The Google
Wallet window.

Playing movies and TV shows

After you purchase movies or TV shows in Google Play Music & TV, they appear in your Library and are available for playing. To play your movies and TV shows, follow these steps:

1. **With Google Play Movies & TV open, click Library on the bottom center of the page.**

Your movies and TV shows are loaded.

2. **Move your pointer over the desired content and click Play.**

Your video content begins playing in a new window.

By default, the video plays in Full Screen mode on your Chromebook. You can pause the video by following these steps:

1. **While the video content is playing, move your cursor anywhere on the window.**

The video control overlay, containing several video controls, appears.

2. **Click the Pause button in the middle of the screen.**

The Pause button looks like two vertical bars.

The video playback pauses.

3. **To resume playing your video, move your pointer back over the video control overlay and click the Play button.**

The Play button displays a sideways triangle.

TIP

You can also pause playback by pressing the spacebar briefly. To resume playing, press the spacebar again.

Adjusting the volume

To control the volume in the Google Play Movies & TV, follow these steps:

1. **Move your pointer over the bottom of the Google Play Movies & TV window.**

The video control overlay appears, revealing several video control options.

2. **Locate the Volume icon on the left side of the overlay.**

3. **To mute the volume, click the Speaker icon.**

When muted, the icon appears with a slash through it, indicating that volume has been reduced to zero.

4. **Increase or decrease the volume by moving the slider — to the right to increase and to the left to decrease.**

The volume changes per the direction you move the volume slider.

Casting to a TV

Casting means playing back audio or video content from one device to another device, such as a smart TV. If you have a TV set up for casting, you can cast a movie that you're playing on a Chromebook to a TV. To cast a movie to a TV, follow these steps:

1. **Start playing the movie on your Chromebook.**

2. **Pause playback by clicking Pause or tapping the spacebar.**

3. **Find and click the Cast icon, which is near the upper-right corner of the window.**

If devices are available to cast to, you see a menu from which you can select a device. (See Figure 14-9.)

4. **Select the device you want to cast to.**

Movie playback now continues on your smart TV. You use the Play and Pause controls on your Chromebook to pause and resume the movie.

TIP

You need to read the instructions for your smart TV to understand how to cast to it. You'll find that it takes a bit of experimenting to get it working.

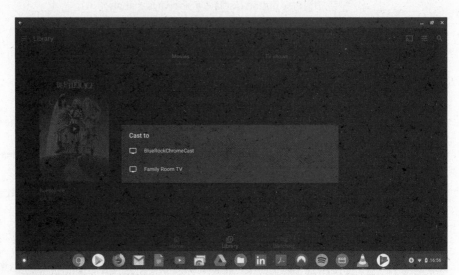

FIGURE 14-9:
Casting a movie
to a Smart TV.

Exploring YouTube

YouTube is a free video-sharing website that has grown into one of the most trafficked sites on the Internet. YouTube's video database is largely user generated.

YouTube has become a go-to source for all kinds of video: unfiltered field reporting, documentation of conflict, music videos, self-help and how-to, thought-provoking documentaries, family archives, humorous interpretations, chance happenings, TV commercials from long ago, and more. Users can create channels to store and categorize endless minutes of video. With YouTube, you can upload and edit videos, share video content around the web, keep track of video views, and so much more.

YouTube is a great tool for Chromebook users because it can serve as a bottomless repository for captured video footage. To access YouTube, open the Launcher and click the YouTube icon. When you do so, YouTube loads in the Chrome web browser.

YouTube asks you to log in to your Google account. You want to do this so that you can view your subscriptions and so that YouTube can suggest videos that are consistent with your interests.

Navigating YouTube

When YouTube has loaded, all the available options can cause sensory overload. Covering all the intricacies of YouTube would take an entire book, but this section gives you a few tips to get you started.

The main page of YouTube contains several video options for suggested viewing. Much of what YouTube suggests is driven by your viewing habits and subscriptions. If you like videos of smiling kittens, for instance, YouTube suggests videos of kittens to capture your attention. YouTube also sells advertising placements to businesses, so you may see an advertisement or two at the beginning of a video and occasionally during a longer video. Along the left side of the screen are options for finding videos you've seen and videos you haven't seen yet.

The most useful way to find new videos is by using the Search bar at the top of the screen. YouTube has more than 2 billion unique visitors every month, and those visitors typically search for video content just as they would search for a web page by using Google's search engine. This search functionality has made YouTube one of the largest search engines in the world.

Enter a term in the Search bar, click the Search button (which looks like a magnifying glass), and then scroll through the pages of search results to find the video you're searching for. To aid in your search, YouTube ranks the results by relevance to your search query. If you haven't found the video you're looking for by the third or fourth page of search results, you may want to refine your search.

Playing and pausing video

Playing a video on YouTube is as straightforward as searching for it. Just find the video you want to play in YouTube's search results and click the image or title. YouTube loads the Video Profile page and begins playing your selection automatically.

The bottom bar of the video, pictured in Figure 14-10, contains all your play controls, status bar audio controls, and viewing settings.

To pause the video, click the Pause button on the left side of the control bar. (The Pause button looks like two vertical bars.) When video is paused, pressing Pause again (or the Play button) resumes playback. You can also pause and play by tapping the spacebar.

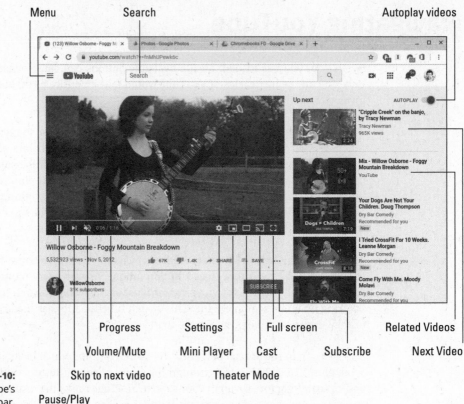

Menu   Search   Autoplay videos

Progress   Settings   Full screen   Related Videos

Volume/Mute   Mini Player   Cast   Subscribe   Next Video

Skip to next video   Theater Mode

FIGURE 14-10:
YouTube's
control bar.   Pause/Play

Activating Full Screen mode

By default, YouTube plays the video at the optimal viewing size. You can, however, make the video occupy the entire screen by using Full Screen mode. To engage Full Screen mode, click the Full Screen button on the right side of the video's control bar. To exit Full Screen mode, press the Esc key.

Adjusting the volume

To control the volume in the YouTube player, follow these steps:

1. **Locate the Volume icon on the left side of the control bar.**

2. **To mute the volume, click the Speaker icon.**

    When muted, the icon appears with a slash through it, indicating that the volume has been reduced to zero.

3. **Increase or decrease the volume by moving your pointer over the volume icon and clicking and dragging the volume slider that appears.**

Move the slider left to decrease volume, right to increase it.

Casting to a smart TV

As with Google Play Movies, you can cast the playing of a YouTube video to a smart TV. Follow these instructions:

1. **Start playing the video.**

2. **Pause playback by clicking the Pause button or tapping the spacebar.**

3. **Find and click the Cast icon, which is near the lower-right corner of the video playback window.**

You need to read the instructions for your smart TV to understand how to cast to it. You might have to experiment with it a bit to get it working.

TIP

4. **If you have devices you can cast to, you see a menu from which you can select the device you want to cast to.**

Video playback continues on your Smart TV. You use the Play and Pause buttons on your Chromebook to pause and resume the movie.

Chapter **15**

Chatting with Friends and Family

A stand-up comic mused about the paradigm shift from landline phones to mobile phones, remarking on how calling a phone number used to mean calling a *place*, but today it means calling a *person*, no matter where that person is. Fast forward to today. People can now communicate with typed words, audio, and even video, no matter where they are. What a time to be alive.

Google is in transition with its video and text chat apps. Google Hangouts, which has been Google's video chat service for many years, is being transitioned into two new products, Hangouts Chat and Hangouts Meet. Then there's Google Duo, a new video chat service that lets you talk with friends and family live, as well as record video messages that recipients can listen to later. Google also offers Google Voice, with text, phone calling, and voice-mail capabilities. This chapter spends time with each of these services.

But Google Hangouts, Duo, and Voice are not the only games in town. Skype is also wildly popular and is available on Chromebooks. With Skype, you can text, have audio and video calls, and even call real phone numbers (as opposed to only Skype connections). You'll learn how to do texting and video chats with your Skype friends.

All these services run on Chromebooks as well as on Windows computers, Macs, Android phones, and iPhones. You can stay in touch with people no matter where they are.

One more thing: If you want to chat with your friends and family through Hangouts, Duo, and Voice, you need to add them to your contacts. You find out how to do that at the end of the chapter.

Hanging Out with Hangouts

Hangouts is the future of voice calls in the Google world, but it's so much more than that, too. With Hangouts, you can send messages and make audio and video calls. You can organize group text messaging chats with up to 150 people at one time and organize free video calls for up to ten people.

 Hangouts might already be installed on your Chromebook. Here's how to find out:

1. **Open the Google Play Store.**

2. **Search for Google Hangouts.**

   If Google Hangouts is already installed, you see the Uninstall and Open buttons.

   If Google Hangouts is *not* already installed, you see the Install button, as shown in Figure 15-1. Go ahead and click Install to install Duo on your Chromebook.

3. **Click the Install button to install Hangouts.**

   The Hangouts app is installed on your Chromebook.

4. **Click Open to launch Hangouts.**

   Hangouts asks whether you want to associate your phone number in your Google profile with the Hangouts app. Doing so permits others to reach you on Hangouts if they know your phone number.

   Hangouts next asks whether it can have access to your contacts. Granting it access permits you to easily reach people on Hangouts.

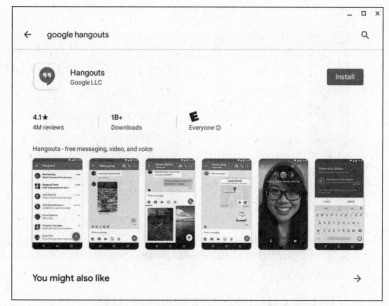

FIGURE 15-1:
Installing
Hangouts on a
Chromebook.

Texting with Hangouts

You can easily send text messages to other Hangouts users. After opening the Hangouts app, follow these steps:

1. **Click the + (plus sign) symbol near the lower-right corner of the Hangouts window.**

2. **Scroll through and select a contact to send a message to.**

   Hangouts switches to a text conversation mode, as shown in Figure 15-2.

3. **Type your message where it says Write a Message.**

4. **Click the Send button at the lower-right corner of the window.**

   In this same texting window, you can also initiate an audio call or a video call, as described in the following sections.

Audio calls on Hangouts

You can start an audio call on Hangouts with anyone in your contacts list. To start an audio call, open a texting session as described in the previous section and then click the Call icon near the upper-right corner of the window (refer to Figure 15-2). If your contact has Hangouts on a device, that contact is alerted to your call and can accept it to start your conversation.

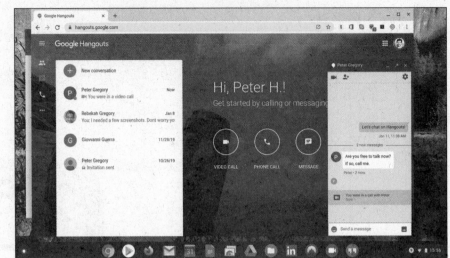

FIGURE 15-2:
Sending text
messages with
Hangouts.

Video calling on Hangouts

Video calling is a natural with Hangouts. As with texting and audio calls, you just open a new conversation window and then click the Video Call icon near the upper-right corner of the Hangouts window, shown in Figure 15-3. Figure 15-4 shows a video call on Hangouts. Each party needs to click the green Click to Join the Video Call button; after they do, they are connected with video and audio.

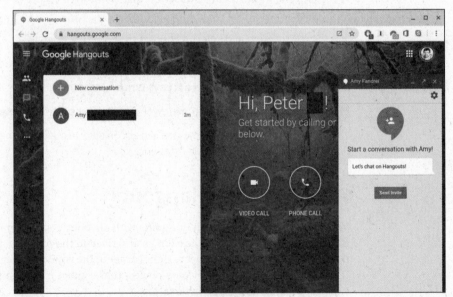

FIGURE 15-3:
Selecting a user
to chat with on
Google Hangouts.

FIGURE 15-4:
A video call on
Google Hangouts.

To end the call, both parties need to click the red Hangup icon that's at the bottom center of the window.

Sending photos on Hangouts

While you have the Hangouts conversation window open with a contact, you can tap the Attach Photo or the Take Photo button at the bottom of the conversation window.

When you click Attach Photo, you're prompted to select the photo (or other type of file, such as a PDF) from your Chromebook. You can also select a file in your Google Drive.

When you click Take Photo, the Camera window opens, and you can take a picture. Hangouts then shows you the photo and sends it to the recipient if you click the blue check box.

Making a phone call with Hangouts

If you don't want to make a video call, or if you simply want to give someone a ring and don't have your phone handy, you can call that person by following these steps:

1. **Launch Hangouts.**

2. **Click the Add Telephone link that appears above the Invite button.**

    The Call a Phone Number dialog box appears.

3. **Enter the phone number you want to call and click Call.**

   Hangouts calls the number entered.

REMEMBER

   If you're in the United States or Canada, calls to these countries are free. Calls outside the United States or Canada may incur long-distance charges, which are charged to the credit card you have on file with Google Wallet.

4. **Click the icon in the control menu that looks like a video camera with a slash through it.**

TIP

   The video camera turns off. If you're making a phone call, you can avoid burning extra battery by having your video camera off.

5. **Enjoy your call!**

6. **When you're ready to disconnect, click the Leave Call button at the top of the Hangouts window.**

Sharing your screen with Hangouts

Sharing your screen on a hangout is a great way to demonstrate an activity on your Chromebook remotely. Or maybe you just want to show someone a bunch of photos or videos without having to package and email them. Sharing your screen is great for a number of scenarios. You can share your screen by following these steps:

1. **While you're in an active hangout, click the green Screenshare arrow on the left side of the Hangouts window.**

   A dialog box appears, asking you to confirm that you want to present your entire screen to everyone participating in your hangout.

2. **Click Share.**

   In place of your video stream at the bottom-right corner of the Hangouts window, an image of your desktop appears. Anyone who joins your hangout can see your computer screen.

3. **Exit Screensharing mode by clicking the Screenshare icon on the left side of the Hangouts window once again.**

   The main Hangouts window reappears.

Getting Started with Duo

Like the majority of applications on the Google platform, Duo is a web-based application that makes it easy for you to connect with people all over the world. Duo enables you to video chat or send video messages to other users through

Gmail or a slew of Chrome browser plug-ins. With your Chromebook, however, Google has upped the ante by creating an application that resides on your Chromebook and taps into the Duo system, giving you a better experience all around.

Depending on when you purchased your Chromebook, Duo might already be installed, but perhaps not. Here's how to find out whether you have Duo or to install it if not:

1. **Open the Google Play Store.**

2. **Search for Google Duo.**

   If Google Duo is already installed, you see the Uninstall and Open buttons.

   If Google Duo is not already installed, you see the Install button, similar to Figure 15-1. Go ahead and click Install to install Duo on your Chromebook.

3. **Enter a mobile device number when prompted.**

   Duo asks you for a mobile number to associate with your Duo account. This association enables people to reach you on Duo if they know your mobile number.

 You can launch Duo by opening the Launcher, searching for Duo, and clicking the Duo icon. Duo then displays, as shown in Figure 15-5.

FIGURE 15-5:
The Duo home screen.

Recording a video message with Duo

You can record a video message with Duo and send it to one or more recipients. Family members can record video birthday greetings that they send to Uncle Ned, who can then watch the video when he's online. And, Uncle Ned can watch it more than once. To send a video message, follow these simple steps:

1. **Open the Duo app on your Chromebook.**

2. **Click Send a Video Message.**

   Duo enters recording mode, but it's not recording yet. You should see your own live image looking back at you (which may feel a bit creepy if you haven't done this before).

3. **When you're ready to start, tap the red-and-white Record button in the lower center of the window, as shown in Figure 15-6.**

FIGURE 15-6: Preparing to record a video message in Duo.

4. **Start speaking your message, and when you're done, click the Stop Recording button (which is in the same place as the Record button).**

   Duo plays back the video you recorded, over, and over, and over, until you proceed to the next step.

5. **Click Next.**

   Duo shows your contacts.

6. **Select one or more recipients on the left by clicking each of them, one at a time.**

7. **Click the blue Send button at the bottom center of the window.**

   Duo sends your video message to your recipients.

TIP

When searching your contacts to send a video message, if you see their name and number beneath Connect on Duo, you can proceed and send them a message. If, however, the word *Invite* appears next to their name, this means that they are not yet using Duo. You can click Invite, which sends them a message and invites them to install and set up Google Duo. After they have done so, you and your contact can send video messages or chat on live video.

REMEMBER

Video messages sent by Duo expire in 24 hours. You can watch it as much as you like, but after 24 hours, it will be gone.

TIP

The procedure for sending an audio message is the same as for a video message. Before you start recording your message, click Voice just below the Record button. Then, just like a video message, click Record, speak your message, click Stop, and then select your recipients.

Voice and video chatting with Duo

With Duo, you can place live video calls to anyone in the world who also has the Duo app and reasonably good Internet access. Best of all, it's free! To start a live video call, follow these steps:

1. **Start the Duo app.**

2. **Scroll through your contacts (or search, if you have a lot of them).**

3. When you find the desired contact, click him or her. The contact information appears, as shown in Figure 15-7.

4. **Click Video Call.**

   The recipient's computer (whether a Chromebook, Android phone, iPhone, Mac, or PC) notifies the recipient of the incoming call.

   If the recipient accepts your incoming call, you are connected via video and audio, and your call can begin, as shown in Figure 15-8.

5. **When you've finished your call, you or the other party clicks the End Call button at the bottom center of the window.**

   If you don't see the End Call button, just give your touchpad a nudge and the calling controls, including End Call, appear.

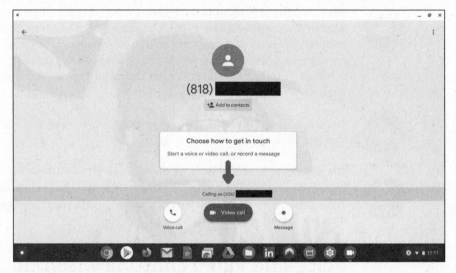

FIGURE 15-7:
Displaying a
contact in Duo
in preparation
for a video or
voice call.

FIGURE 15-8:
Video chatting
with Duo.

Calling and Texting with Google Voice

Google provides a lot of choices when it comes to communicating with others. Another nifty service is Google Voice, which lets you make phone calls and send and receive text messages using a new "virtual" phone number.

Setting up Google Voice

Follow these steps to get started with Google Voice:

1. **Go to** `https://voice.google.com` **with your browser.**

    The main Google Voice website launches. You can scroll down to read all about Google Voice to see if this is something you're interested in trying out.

2. **Click the For Personal Use button to proceed.**

3. **A menu appears in which you select Android, iOS, or Web. If you're on your Chromebook, select Web.**

    You can use Google Voice on any of these devices.

    The Welcome page appears.

4. **Click Continue.**

    The Choose a Google Voice Number screen appears. In the search field, type in a city name or area code.

    A list of available numbers appears.

5. **Click Select on a number you want to use.**

    The verification process begins.

6. **Click Verify and follow the instructions.**

    You need to provide a real phone number (landline or mobile). Google then sends a code (via text or a phone call), which you type in to the Verify field to complete the process.

After you set up your Google Voice account, it's available on all your devices, including Windows laptops, Macs, Android phones and tablets, iPhones, iPads, and, oh yeah, Chromebooks. You can send and receive phone calls, receive voice mail, and text and receive text messages, all via the web or Google Voice apps.

On your Chromebook, after your Google Voice account is set up (and after you've been using it for a while), your main window will resemble Figure 15-9.

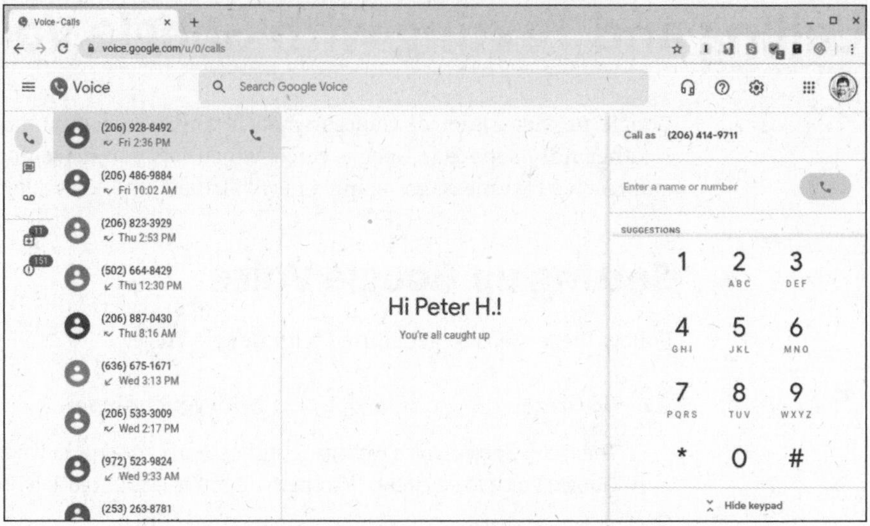

FIGURE 15-9:
The Google Voice
main screen.

Sending text messages with Google Voice

Sending text messages with Google Voice is easy; just follow these steps:

1. **From the Google Voice main window, click the Messages button near the upper-left corner.**

   Your history of recent messaging appears in the left side of the window.

2. **Click Send New Message.**

   The cursor moves to the To field in which you can begin typing in a person's name. A list of suggestions will appear that you can scroll through and select.

3. **Select a recipient from the list or enter a new phone number.**

   If you've exchanged messages with this person before, the message history appears.

4. **Type a new message in the Type a Message field at the bottom of the window.**

5. **Click the Send icon to send the message.**

   The Send icon is to the right. Messages you send, and messages sent to you, appear in the main window.

REMEMBER You can send and receive messages in Google Voice with other Google Voice users, as well as any mobile phone numbers.

Making a call with Google Voice

Although making phone calls with Google Voice simple, here are the steps:

1. **From the Google Voice main window, click the Call button near the upper-left corner of the window.**

   A list of recent calls appears on the left side of the window. A dial pad appears on the far right.

2. **Select a recipient from your contacts by typing a name or number in the Enter a Name or Number field. Or tap the numbers on the keypad to call a number that is (or is not) in your contacts list.**

   The recipient's phone rings. If the recipient accepts the call, you can begin talking.

3. **Tap the hangup icon to end the call.**

Other Google Voice features

All the features of Google Voice could easily fill an entire chapter, but in this section, I just give you a few pointers to other features that I enjoy with my Google Voice account:

» **Voice mail:** People can call you and leave voice mail if you don't pick up. Google Voice can send you an email (or text) transcript of the voice-mail message.

» **Call screening and pick-up:** When someone calls your Google Voice number, you can have that incoming call ring on one or more of your phones simultaneously. You can pick up the call, and Google Voice will tell you who is calling. You can accept the call or send it to voice mail. If you send the call to voice mail, you can listen to the caller's message while the caller is still talking, and you can even pick up the call in progress and talk live if you want.

» **Calls on any device:** You can send and receive calls with your Google Voice number on any device on which you have the Google Voice app installed. This includes mobile phones, tablets, laptop computers, and desktop computers.

» **Call schedules:** People can call your Google Voice number 24 hours a day, but you can set a schedule so that your mobile and landline phones don't ring during certain hours.

You can explore many other features and settings by clicking the Settings button near the upper-right corner of the Google Voice window.

Communicating with Skype

Skype was the first highly popular worldwide chat and video chat services in the world. Founded in 2003, Skype catapulted to fame through its ease of use and the fact that you could make free Skype voice calls to anyone in the world who also had Skype and a decent Internet connection. By 2010, Skype had hundreds of millions of users.

Skype is now part of the Microsoft ecosystem. It is available on Chromebooks, as well as practically every other kind of device out there: Windows PCs, Macs, Linux, Android phones and tablets, iPhones, iPads, and more.

TIP

Although Hangouts and Duo are a part of the Google family of apps, Skype is clearly the world's leader in chat and video chat. Chances are, you have more friends using Skype than anything else.

Getting started with Skype

To get started with Skype, head on over to the Web Store and search for Skype. You'll find that Skype is offered as a Chrome browser extension, as shown in Figure 15-10. Click Add to Chrome to install it.

FIGURE 15-10:
The Skype icon appears within the Chrome browser.

To launch Skype, click the Skype logo in the Chrome browser. A little window appears, asking whether you want to launch Skype or share on Skype. Click Launch Skype. After you launch Skype, the main Skype window appears, as shown in Figure 15-11.

If you are using Skype for the first time, you're taken through the new account process in which you provide some information such as your name, email address, and phone number. You're prompted to create a Skype ID, which is a set of characters without spaces. After you enter what you want for your Skype ID, Skype tells you whether it is available; if so, you can proceed; if not, you can try other names until you find one that hasn't been used.

Text chats   Manage contacts

Video calls   Call a landline

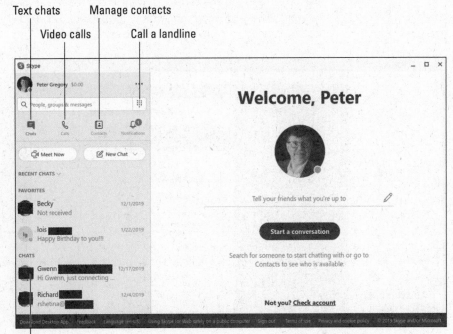

FIGURE 15-11: The main Skype window.

Contacts

TIP

SkypeIDs are like personalized license plates. You need to keep trying until you find a name that hasn't already been taken. All the good names are gone until you come up with something new and clever.

Adding Skype contacts

Before you can send messages or have video chats on Skype, you need to add people to your Skype contacts by sending a contact request. Follow these steps to add Skype contacts:

1. **In the main Skype window, click Contacts (near the upper-left corner).**

2. **In the Skype Contacts window, click + Contact.**

The Add a New Contact window opens, as shown in Figure 15-12.

3. **Enter the Skype contact name in the Find People field.**

   After the contact approves your request, you have a new contact in Skype!

   It works the other way around as well. If you send someone your Skype ID, that person can add you as a contact, and you then receive a Skype message asking whether you would like to connect with the person. Click Block if you do not want to connect, or click Accept if you do want to connect.

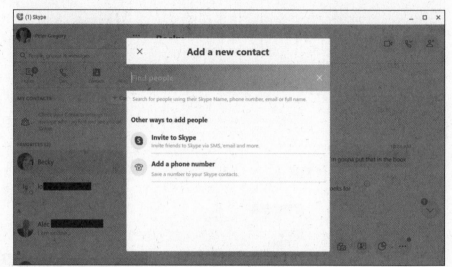

FIGURE 15-12:
Adding a contact
to Skype.

Sending text messages with Skype

To send a message to a Skype user, follow these steps:

1. **In the main Skype window, click Chats to go to the Chat window.**

   (There's no harm in clicking Chats if you're already there.)

2. **Click a contact you want to chat with.**

   The Chat window occupies the right two-thirds of the Skype window.

3. **Start typing messages near the bottom of the Chat window where it says "Type a message."**

   Your messages appear on the right side of the window, and your contact's messages appear on the left side. As you continue chatting, your conversation rolls off the top of the Chat window. You can scroll through the message history to see older messages. Figure 15-13 shows a Skype texting conversation.

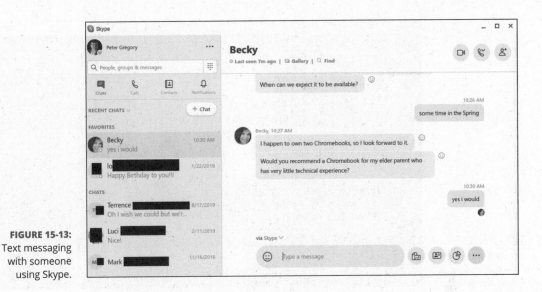

FIGURE 15-13:
Text messaging
with someone
using Skype.

Chatting on Skype video

Skype is great for live video chats as well. Skype is so easy to use that you probably don't even need me to tell you how to proceed, but here goes anyway:

1. **In the main Skype window, click Chats.**

2. **Click the contact with whom you want to have a live video chat.**

3. **Click the Video Call button near the upper-right corner of the window.**

   If your contact's Skype app is running, it plays a little tune that's distinctive to Skype, signaling your incoming call.

4. **After the contact accepts the call, you can see and hear each other. (See Figure 15-14.)**

5. **When you're done with the call, hang up by clicking the red button with the phone icon.**

   If the other party disconnects first, you need not take any action; the call automatically disconnects.

   You can also chat on Skype using audio only by clicking the Audio Call button to the right of the Video Call button. (It looks like an old-fashioned telephone handset.)

FIGURE 15-14:
A live video chat using Skype.

Working with Google Contacts

Google Contacts is just that: a list of the people you communicate with, via email, video, text, and even good old-fashioned snail mail. Google Contacts is your online address book, accessible from all your devices and from any other device (such as a hotel kiosk computer) when you log in to Google services.

 Google provides no separate app for your contacts; instead, you just point your browser to `https://contacts.google.com/`. You see the Contacts main window, as shown in Figure 15-15.

Adding contacts

You can easily add a contact to Google Contacts by clicking the Create Contact button found near the upper-left corner of the Google Contacts window. A new window appears, as shown in Figure 15-16, where you can fill in the contact's name, phone number, email address, and other details.

Viewing and editing contacts

To browse your contacts in Google Contacts to see whether you already have a certain contact there, start typing the contact's name in the Search field. As you type,

Google Contacts displays contacts just below the search bar. If any of the visible contacts is the one you are looking for, you can click it to view it.

Create contact   Search for contacts

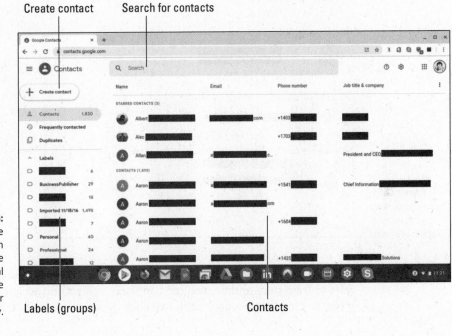

FIGURE 15-15:
The Google
Contacts main
window. The
author's personal
contacts are
redacted for
privacy.

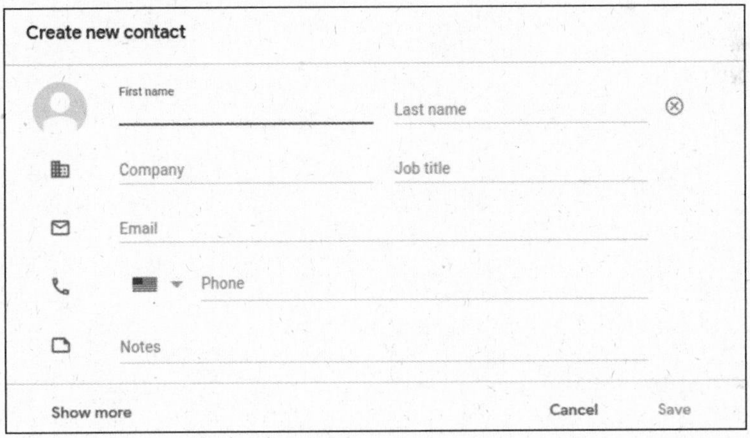

Labels (groups)   Contacts

FIGURE 15-16:
Adding a new
contact with
Google Contacts.

Create new contact

First name   Last name

Company   Job title

Email

Phone

Notes

Show more   Cancel   Save

To edit a contact, click the pencil icon in the window where the contact appears, as shown in Figure 15-17. You can now update any of the existing fields or add new information. When you're done making changes, click Save. If you think you messed up, click Cancel.

FIGURE 15-17: Updating contact details with Google Contacts.

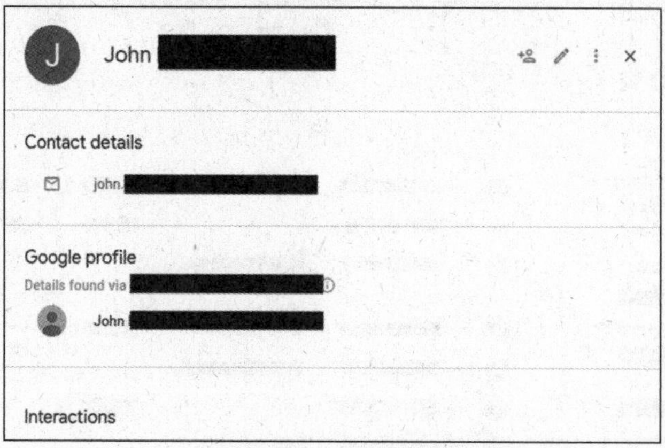

If you have contacts with whom you frequently correspond or otherwise need to refer to from time to time, you can add them as favorites, which causes them to go to the top of your contacts list. Just click the star next to the contact.

IN THIS CHAPTER

» Finding books in Google Play

» Purchasing and uploading books

» Buying and reading books with Kindle

» Reading books on your Chromebook

Chapter **16**

Reading Ebooks on the Chromebook

E *book* is short for electronic book. Starting around 2006, several consumer devices were created specifically for serving up large collections of novels in a single device. Amazon created the Kindle, Barnes & Noble created the Nook, and Apple created iBooks, which is the book platform that resides on all of their iDevices. The benefits of ebooks are numerous, but perhaps the biggest is convenience. With ebooks, you no longer have to lug around heavy paper books; now, you can store hundreds of books on a single slim device.

Although ebooks will never entirely replace the experience of turning pages, writing notes in the margins, and pressing a keepsake such as a flower from a wedding into the pages of a book, reading books on your Chromebook is an excellent way to enjoy a good novel. The Google Play store is home to more than 5 million titles, and that number continues to grow.

In this chapter, you learn how to load Google Play Books on your Chromebook and how to navigate the Play Bookstore. I show you how to add new books to your library — and some books in the Play Bookstore are available for free! Using your Chromebook, you can read your books online and offline, regardless of where you are. And in case you're one of the millions of Kindle users, you're in luck because this chapter explains how Kindle works on Chromebooks.

Navigating Google Play Books

One way to read books on the Chromebook is with Google Play Books. Google Play Books is where you search for and purchase titles and where you can find all your book purchases and uploaded books.

 To launch Google Play Books, open the Launcher and click the Google Play Books icon.

 If Google Play Books doesn't appear among the choices in your Launcher, add it by following these steps:

1. **Open the Launcher and click the Chrome Web Store icon.**

   The Chrome Web Store opens.

2. **Type the words** Google Play Books **into the Search bar and press Enter.**

   Google Play Books appears as the first or second search result.

3. **Click the Add to Chrome button next to Google Play Books and follow the prompts to add Google Play Books to your Chromebook Launcher.**

Searching and purchasing books

If this is the first time you've worked with Google Play Books, you may not have much to see when you open the app. However, you can change that situation quickly. Open Google Play Books by clicking Play Books in the Launcher and then click the Shop Books link in the top–right corner of the window. The Google Play Bookstore loads in a new window, giving you the option to search for and purchase books.

To purchase a book, follow these steps:

1. **In the search bar at the top of the Google Play Bookstore, enter the name of the book for which you're searching. Press Enter.**

   The search results populate the screen, as shown in Figure 16-1.

2. **Browse through the search results to locate the desired book and click the thumbnail of the cover.**

   If the book you're looking for doesn't appear in the search results, revise your search to use fewer words and thus expand your search results.

 You can search for books by author, title, and subject.

   After you click the image of the book cover, the book profile page loads. On this page, you can read a description of the book, read reviews, search for similar texts, and purchase the book for reading on your Chromebook.

FIGURE 16-1:
Google Play
Bookstore
search results.

3. **If you're ready to purchase the book, click the Buy button, located to the right of the book thumbnail.**

A Google Wallet window appears, as shown in Figure 16-2, asking you to confirm your purchase. If you don't have a payment method on file, you must first add one before you can purchase the book. See Chapter 12 in the section on Google Play Music for setting up payments with Google.

Google Play

	A Tale Of Two Cities: eBook Edition	$0.99
		+ tax ⓘ

G Pay   Mastercard-1203   ›

By tapping 'Buy EBOOK', you accept the following terms of service: Terms of Service - Buyer (US), Privacy Notice.

BUY EBOOK

FIGURE 16-2:
Paying for a
book with
Google Wallet.

4. **Click Buy Ebook.**

The purchase is completed, and the book is added to your Google Play Books library.

Even if you don't want to spend money, you can still add new books to your library by choosing one of the free books available in the Google Play Bookstore. The free books are mixed into Google Play, but you can get access to a list of the top free books by following these steps:

1. **Click the Top Free link at the top of the Google Play Bookstore window.**

   The complete Top Free Books chart loads.

2. **Browse through the chart and click the thumbnail of a book you're interested in.**

   The book's profile page loads.

3. **If you want to read the book, click the Ebook Free button next to the book cover thumbnail near the top of the window.**

   A Google Wallet pop-up window appears, asking you to confirm your free purchase.

4. **Click Accept and Buy to complete your free purchase.**

   A notification appears to confirm the addition of the free book to your library, as shown in Figure 16-3.

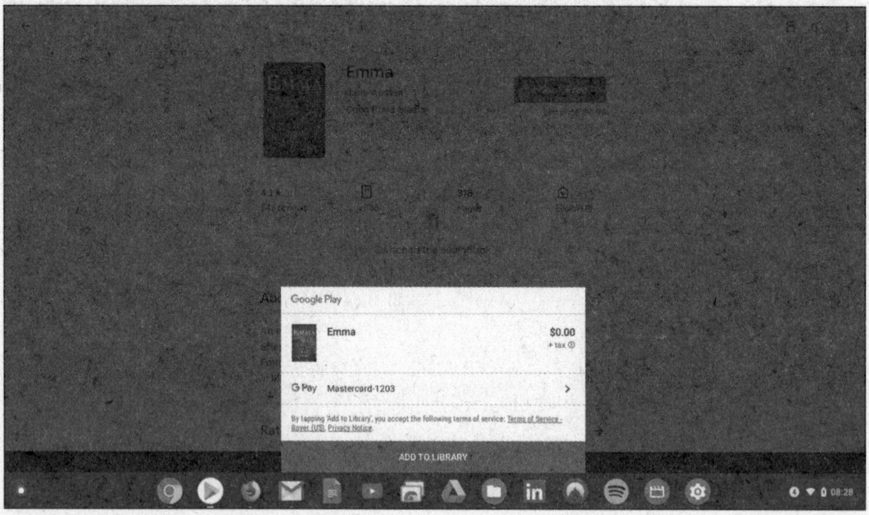

FIGURE 16-3: Adding a free book to your library.

Previewing a book

You might be interested in a book but want to take a peek before you buy it — the way you can flip through a book in a bookstore. Google Play Books lets you do this. To preview a book, follow these steps:

1. **Select a title that interests you.**

   If a preview is available, the Free Sample button appears next to the price.

2. **Click Free Sample.**

   Google Play Books opens the book using the reader (more about that later in this chapter). You can scroll through some of the pages of the book, as in Figure 16-4. The reader tells you how many pages are available in the preview, and you can use the progress bar at the bottom to quickly scroll through the content available in the preview.

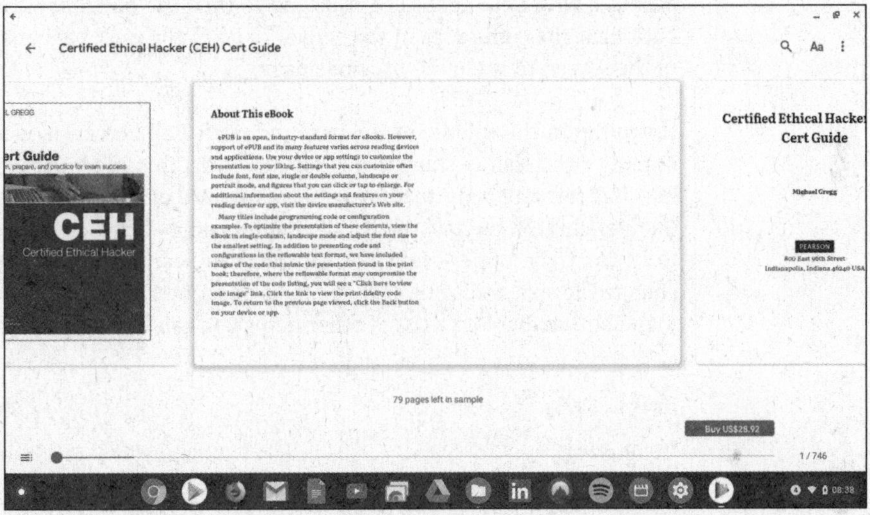

FIGURE 16-4: Scrolling through a book preview.

Reading Ebooks with Your Chromebook

Every book that you purchase or preview through Google Play Books is stored in your Google Play Books library in the cloud and is accessible from any device that has an Internet connection. This accessibility is a great feature, allowing you to access your library on any number of devices.

To start reading a book, just click that book's thumbnail image in your Google Play Books library. As you read, you can advance through pages by *scrolling* — using finger gestures on the touchpad of your Chromebook — or by clicking near the left or right edges of the screen. Scrolling is a great way to advance quickly to a spot in the book.

You can access books in your library from all your devices, and Google Play Books keeps track of your reading. If, for instance, you begin reading a book on one device, and later resume on another, Google keeps track of where you left off. It's practically magic.

Reading in Full Screen mode

When you start reading an ebook with the Google Play Books app, you start in Full Screen mode. This means that all you see on the entire Chromebook screen are the contents of the book you are reading. To advance pages, use sideways scrolling gestures with your mouse or trackpad to turn the page forward or backward. Or, click near the right edge of the screen to go to the next page, or near the left edge of the screen to go to the previous page.

If you tap in the middle of the page, you exit Full Screen mode. Now you can see reading controls, as shown in Figure 16-5. In this mode, you can slide the little blue ball left and right to quickly move forward or backward in the book. Click the Chapters button to view the list of chapters, and click a chapter to immediately go to it. Near the upper-right corner, you can search for content in the book and change the size and color of the text, as described in the next section. Clicking the Menu button displays a list of other items you can see and the actions you can take.

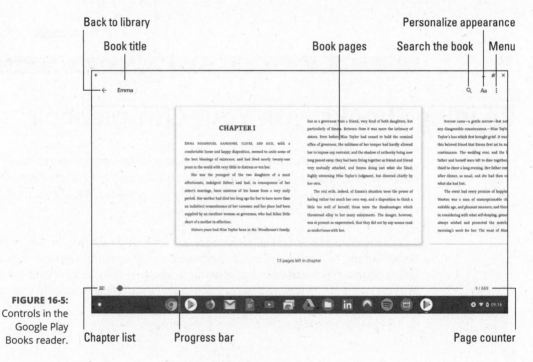

FIGURE 16-5:
Controls in the Google Play Books reader.

Personalizing your view

While you're reading your book, you can personalize the density of the lines of text, increase or decrease the size of the letters, and even change the typeface of the ebook text. To customize your view, follow these steps:

1. **In your Google Play Books library, click the book you want to read.**

The book loads into the window.

2. **Click the Aa icon in the top-right of the window. (If you don't see it, tap the image of the book in the reader to expose the controls at the top and bottom of the window.)**

The Display Options window appears, revealing several options for customizing your ebook view, as shown in Figure 16-6.

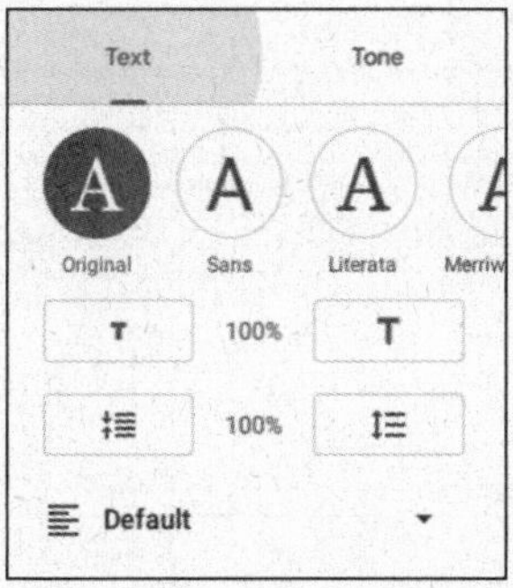

FIGURE 16-6:
Changing Display
Options when
reading an ebook.

3. **Make changes in the menu.**

Google applies those changes to the text in real time.

4. **When you're finished making changes, click outside the Display Options window.**

The window disappears.

Using bookmarks

As you read through your ebooks, you may want to place a bookmark to remember your place. With Google Play Books, you can place multiple bookmarks so that you can quickly return to sections of a book. Place a bookmark by following these steps:

1. **In your Google Play Books library, click the book you want to read.**

The book is loaded into the window.

2. **Turn to a page you want to bookmark.**

3. **Click the menu icon in the top-right corner of the window. (Refer to Figure 16-5.)**

4. **Click Bookmark This Page.**

   A bookmark appears on the page, as shown in Figure 16-7, indicating that the page has been bookmarked. When you're not in Full Screen mode, a bookmark appears above the scrollbar at the bottom of the reading window.

FIGURE 16-7: Bookmarked pages in the Google Play Books reader.

To quickly navigate to your bookmarked pages:

1. **Tap anywhere on the page to exit Full Screen mode if needed.**

2. **Click any of the bookmarks that appear just above the timeline, as shown in Figure 16-7.**

   You're taken immediately to the desired bookmarked page.

Viewing the definition of a word

As you're reading, you may come to a word that you aren't familiar with. If you're reading the book while connected to the Internet, you can quickly see the definition of the word by Alt-clicking it or tapping the word with two fingers. A window appears, shown in Figure 16-8, containing the popular definitions of the word. Click anywhere outside of the definition window to make it disappear.

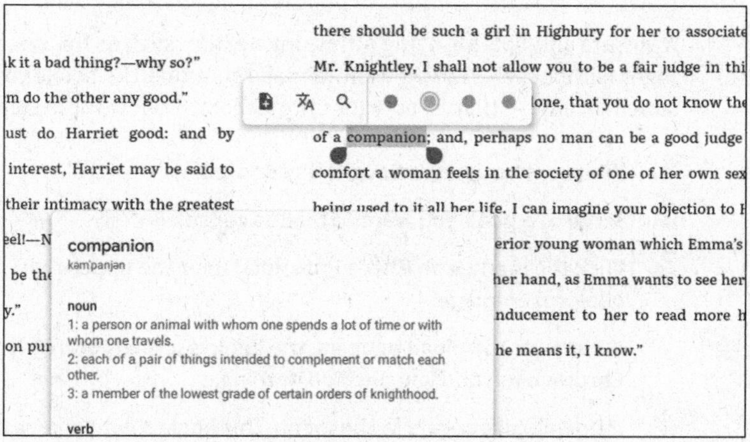

FIGURE 16-8:
Viewing the
definition of a
word.

> k it a bad thing?—why so?"
>
> m do the other any good."
>
> ust do Harriet good: and by
>
> interest, Harriet may be said to
>
> their intimacy with the greatest
>
> eel!—N
>
> be the
>
> y."
>
> on pur
>
> there should be such a girl in Highbury for her to associate
>
> Mr. Knightley, I shall not allow you to be a fair judge in thi
>
> one, that you do not know the
>
> of a companion; and, perhaps no man can be a good judge
>
> comfort a woman feels in the society of one of her own sex
>
> being used to it all her life. I can imagine your objection to l
>
> erior young woman which Emma's
>
> her hand, as Emma wants to see her
>
> nducement to her to read more l
>
> he means it, I know."
>
> **companion**
> kəmˈpanjən
>
> **noun**
> 1: a person or animal with whom one spends a lot of time or with whom one travels.
> 2: each of a pair of things intended to complement or match each other.
> 3: a member of the lowest grade of certain orders of knighthood.
>
> **verb**

TIP

Using Alt-click or a two-finger tap, you can also highlight the word in one of several colors as you can see in Figure 16-8 (in the ebook but not the print book because it's not in color).

Reading ebooks offline

As is the case with most of what you do on a Chromebook, all your books are stored in the cloud in your Google Play Books library. Further, if your Chromebook has enough space, Google Play Books also downloads your book to your Chromebook. If you want to read a newly purchased book offline, chances are that you'll be able to without having to do anything!

If you are a voracious reader and have an extensive library, eventually you'll need to make room for new ebooks. Follow these steps to remove a downloaded book from your Chromebook (note, though, that you're *not* removing it from your library; you're just no longer storing it locally on your Chromebook):

1. Open your Google Play Library.

2. Scroll to a book you want to remove from local storage on your Chromebook.

3. Click the menu icon (three little dots) near the upper-right corner of the book's cover image.

4. Click Remove Download.

You can remove a book regardless of whether you're online.

If you are anticipating being offline for a while (such as for a trans-Atlantic airline flight without Wi-Fi), you want to make sure that the books you want to read are stored locally — that is, on your Chromebook. Follow these steps:

1. **While online, launch Google Play Books.**

2. **Scroll to a book you want to make available locally.**

3. **Click the menu icon (three little dots) near the upper-right corner of the book cover image.**

   If Remove Download appears, the book is already stored locally on your Chromebook and you need do nothing.

4. **If Download appears in the menu, this book is *not* on your Chromebook, so click Download to save a copy of your book on your Chromebook. (See Figure 16-9.)**

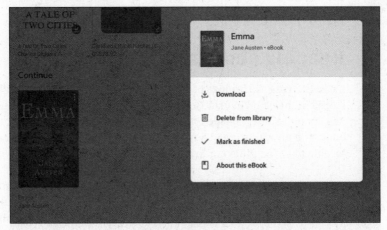

FIGURE 16-9: Making a book available for offline reading.

Reading ebooks on the Google Play Books website

You don't actually have to download the Google Play Books app to read ebooks. Instead, you can enjoy a similar experience right within the Chrome browser. To get to your library on the website, go to https://books.google.com/. Your library appears, as shown in Figure 16-10. To read an ebook, just click its image.

While reading, the display, navigation, and bookmark features are similar to how they appear in the Google Play Books app. (See Figure 16-11.)

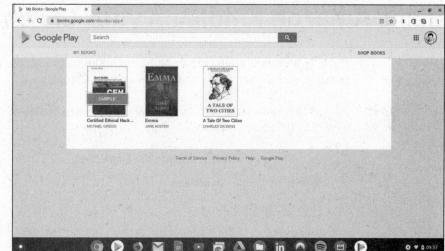

FIGURE 16-10:
Google Play Books in the Chrome browser.

Bookmark

Back to library

Personalize   Search

Book title   Book pages   Contents   Help

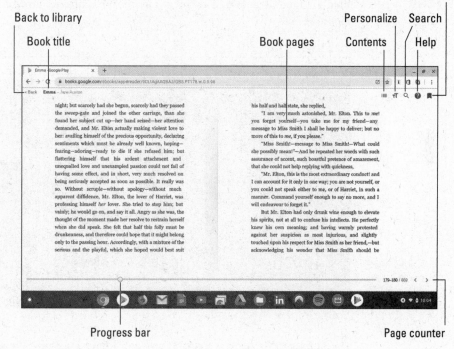

FIGURE 16-11:
Reading an ebook in Google Play Books in the Chrome browser.

Progress bar   Page counter

Using Amazon Kindle on your Chromebook

If you're already a Kindle reader and have a Kindle library, you can access your library and read your Kindle books right on your Chromebook.

 To read Kindle books in your library, you first need to download the Kindle Cloud Reader by following these steps:

1. **Go to the Google Web Store (not the Play Store).**

2. **Search for Kindle Cloud Reader.**

3. **Click Add to Chrome.**

   A window opens with the message, "Add Kindle Cloud Reader?"

4. **Click Add App.**

When you have the Kindle Cloud Reader app, you start it with the Launcher. The Kindle Cloud Reader opens in a tab in the Chrome browser, as shown in Figure 16-12.

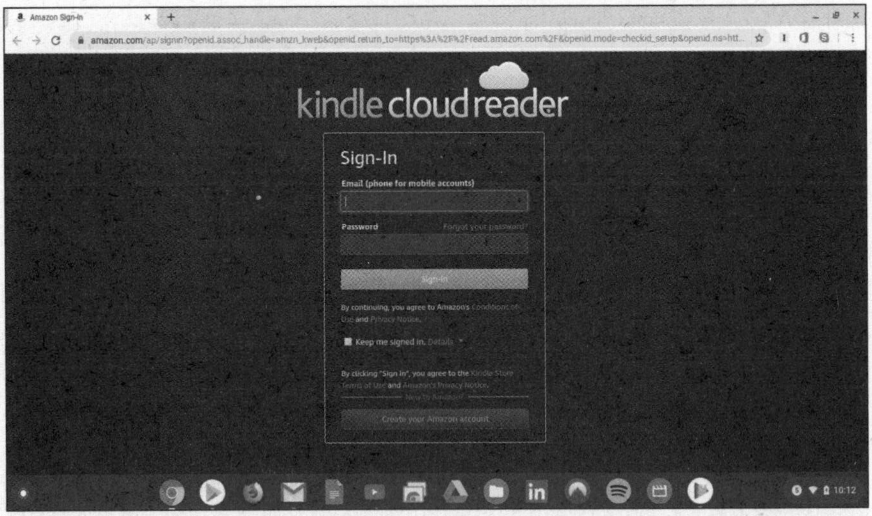

FIGURE 16-12:
The Kindle Cloud Reader app's login screen.

Log in to your Amazon account. If you don't have one, click Create Your Amazon account to make one. If you are already an Amazon customer, you have a Kindle account; use your Amazon login credentials to log in to Kindle. After you log in, your Kindle library appears, as shown in Figure 16-13.

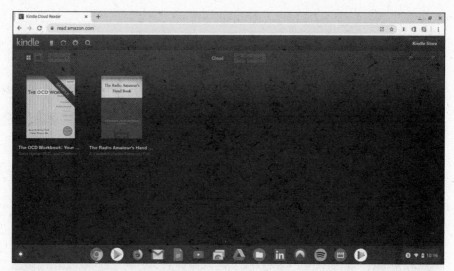

Reading Kindle books

To read a book in your Kindle library, click its book cover image. The book opens to the first page (or, possibly, the page you last read if you were reading the book on another device). (See Figure 16-14.)

When reading your Kindle book, no reading controls appear — but they are there. To view the reading controls, move the cursor near the top or bottom of the reading window to make the controls appear, as shown in Figure 16-15.

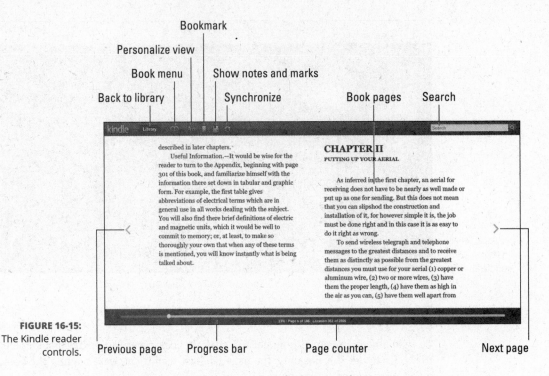

Bookmark

Personalize view

Book menu

Show notes and marks

Back to library

Synchronize

Book pages

Search

FIGURE 16-15:
The Kindle reader controls.

Previous page   Progress bar   Page counter   Next page

Purchasing Kindle books

To shop for Kindle books from your Chromebook, go to your Kindle library and click the Kindle Store button near the upper-right corner of the Kindle Cloud Reader app. Doing so takes you to the Kindle Bookstore on Amazon.com, where you can search for and select titles.

When you purchase books, they appear in your Chromebook's Kindle library.

Reading Kindle books offline

You can download Kindle books to your Chromebook to read offline. To see which books are in the cloud and which are downloaded, go to your Kindle library and click the Cloud button at the top center of the window. Your entire library of books appears. Next, click the Download button to see which ones are already on your Chromebook. To download a book that's in the cloud only, Alt-click (or two-finger click) the book title and then click Download and Pin Book, as shown in Figure 16-16.

FIGURE 16-16:
Downloading a
Kindle book.

Later on, if you are running short on local storage space on your Chromebook, you can remove downloaded books from your Kindle library. To do so:

1. **Go to your Kindle Library.**

2. **Select the book to remove from local storage.**

3. **Alt-click (or two-finger tap) the book's image.**

4. **Click Remove Book.**

   The book is not removed from your Kindle Library — just from your Chromebook.

4

Advanced Chromebook Settings

Chapter **17**

Customizing Your Chromebook

C hromebooks are made to be easy to use. Out of the box, a Chromebook user can be up and running in less than five minutes. By default, the features and functionality of a Chromebook make the user experience top-notch without much customization. However, Google recognizes that all people are different. Although Google's user-experience designers are some of the best in the world, the way people use technology isn't a one-size-fits-all proposition. For that reason, you can customize several look-and-feel aspects of your Chromebook.

In this chapter, you learn how to customize your display with your own wallpaper images, change the resolution of your display, and add a monitor to your Chromebook. You also find out how to customize the appearance and position of your shelf. Also, I explain how to manage notifications so that you can stay informed about what's happening in your Chromebook.

Customizing Your Display Settings

Out of the box, your Chromebook's default settings are what the manufacturer found to be the ideal settings for viewing, computing, and so on. Your display defaults to the best screen resolution. Your Chromebook likely also comes with some standard background images, called *wallpaper*, that you can use to change the look of your desktop area. However, if you would like to customize your display so that it better matches your taste, you can do so in several ways.

To view your settings, go to the Settings menu. Click the Settings area in the bottom-right corner of the shelf, which reveals a list of options — the Settings panel — and choose Settings — the little gear-like icon.

Changing your wallpaper

When you start your Chromebook, the image that fills your desktop background is called *wallpaper*. Your device manufacturer provides several options for wallpaper that you can try. You also have the option to change the wallpaper to almost any photo that you desire. To change your Chromebook wallpaper, follow these steps:

1. **Open the Settings panel on the shelf and choose Settings.**

   Your Chromebook Settings window appears, as shown in Figure 17-1.

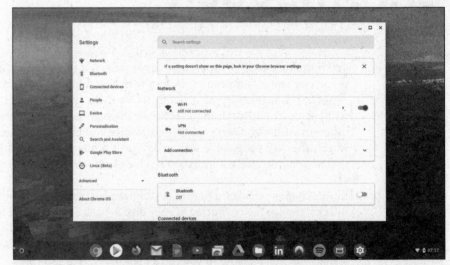

FIGURE 17-1:
The Chromebook Settings window.

2. **Click Personalization on the left side.**

3. **Click the Wallpaper button in the Personalization section.**

   The Settings window minimizes, and the Wallpaper window appears. Available images and options are displayed, as shown in Figure 17-2.

   Your Chromebook has an extensive library of images that are available in several categories, listed on the left side of the window.

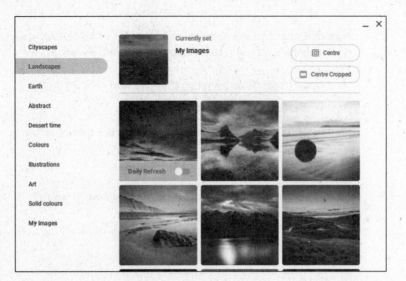

FIGURE 17-2:
Chromebook's
wallpaper
browser.

4. **If you have an image of your own that you would like to use, click My Images in the lower-left corner of the Wallpaper selection window to view your own images.**

5. **Select the desired wallpaper image by clicking the image.**

   Your Chromebook's wallpaper changes to match your selection.

TIP

   In each of the image libraries already on your Chromebook, note that in the first image, you can click the Daily Refresh selector to display a different image from that collection every day. Variety is the spice of life!

6. **Click the X in the top-right corner of the Wallpaper window.**

   The window closes and the Chromebook Settings window reappears.

Changing your screen resolution

Screen resolution, simply put, is the measure of the sharpness and clarity of the image displayed on your screen. Resolution is expressed in terms of horizontal rows and vertical columns of pixels. A *pixel* is a tiny area of illumination on a display. Think of each pixel as a dot that can vary in color and brightness; together, all these dots make up the images you see on the screen. For instance, the typical flat-screen television may have a resolution of 1920 x 1080, which means that the image is 1920 pixels wide and 1080 pixels tall. When you increase or decrease your resolution, the physical size of your screen doesn't change. What changes is the number of pixels you're packing into that physical area. High resolution equals more pixels, which equals greater clarity.

Now that you have a general idea of what screen resolution means, customize your Chromebook's screen resolution by following these steps:

1. **Open the Settings panel on the shelf and click Settings.**

   Your Chromebook Settings window opens.

2. **In your Chromebook Settings window, click Device on the left side of the window.**

3. **In the Device section, click Displays.**

   The Displays Settings window appears, as shown in Figure 17-3.

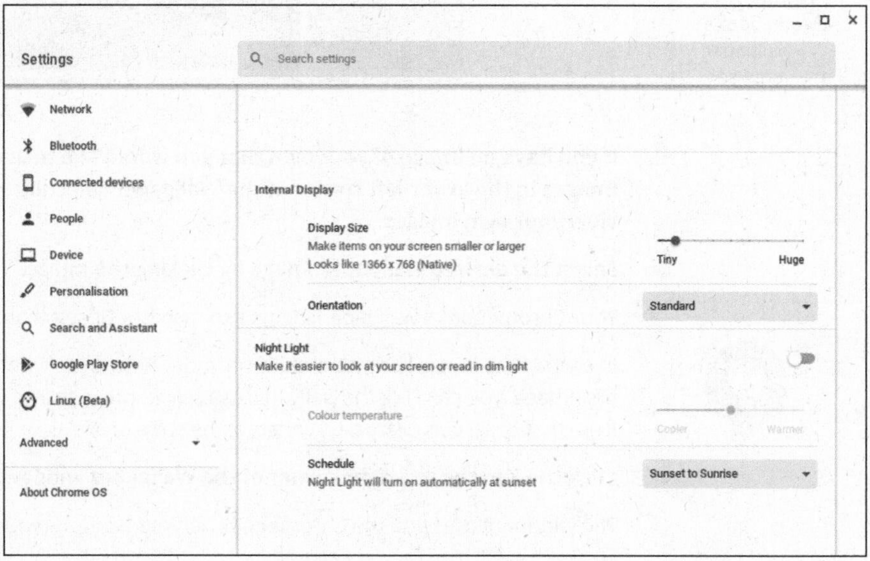

FIGURE 17-3:
The Chromebook Displays Settings window.

4. **Scroll down to the Internal Display section (refer to Figure 17-3).**

5. **Scroll the Display Size slider back and forth to choose a new resolution.**

   As you scroll, the resolution (the horizontal and vertical pixel count) is indicated.

   Your Chromebook display automatically adjusts to match your selection. Figure 17-4 shows what the screen might look like at an extremely low resolution. Such a setting makes it easier for the elders among us to read text on the screen easily.

6. **When you're satisfied with your selection, click the X located in the top-right corner of the window.**

   The Chromebook Settings window closes.

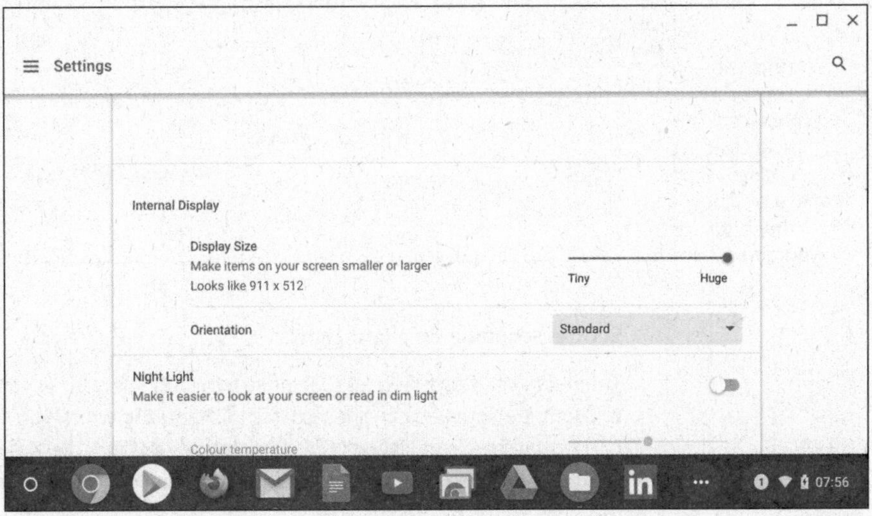

FIGURE 17-4: Chromebook's display with a low resolution.

Using the Night Light feature

Many laptop computers, tablets, and smartphones are now equipped with a "night mode" display setting. This setting lowers the color "temperature" of the display from a bright blue-white to a yellow-ish display. The science behind this feature is related to how the human brain interprets bright white light. The brain thinks it's sunlight. If you are using your device late at night, your brain might think it's daytime, and consequently, you could have trouble falling asleep. (In other words, bright smartphone and laptop displays are the new caffeine.) The night mode, called Night Light on a Chromebook, automatically adjusts your display color so that it appears more yellowish (akin to candlelight or firelight) at night.

Night Light does not adjust the actual brightness of the display, but rather its color temperature. Follow the steps below, and you'll see what I'm talking about:

1. **Click Settings on the shelf and then click Device on the left side of the Settings window that appears.**

2. **Click Displays and then scroll down until the Night Light section appears, as shown in Figure 17-5.**

3. **Click the Night Light selector.**

   The screen's color shifts into the yellow color spectrum.

4. **Use the Color Temperature slider to adjust the degree of color shift.**

   Setting the slider all the way to the Cooler setting is like having no Night Light set at all.

FIGURE 17-5:
Use the
Chromebook
Night Light
settings to
configure night
mode for
your display.

Night Light
Make it easier to look at your screen or read in dim light

Color temperature

Cooler   Warmer

Schedule
Night Light will turn off automatically at sunrise

Sunset to Sunrise

5. **Set the schedule for Night Light.**

The default setting is Sunset to Sunrise (which is adjusted to your time zone and latitude), but you can set a Custom Schedule in which you specify the time of day that the Night Light turns on and off. By default, the Custom Schedule is set to On at 6 p.m. and Off at 6 a.m. When creating a Custom Schedule, move the slider to the desired times.

Using an external display

Working with a laptop all day long can result in eyestrain for some people. Thank-fully, you have the option to use an external display device with your Chromebook. To add and customize an external display device, follow these steps:

1. **Locate the display (HDMI) port on your Chromebook.**

The majority of Chromebooks on the market come with at least one HDMI port, such as the one shown in Figure 17-6.

FIGURE 17-6:
A Chromebook
HDMI display
port.

HDMI port

2. Ensure that your external display device is powered on.

3. Connect the external display device to your Chromebook using an HDMI cable.

Your Chromebook screen may flicker briefly as it auto-configures the new display. At length, the external display device shows the image from your Chromebook.

You can now begin working from your Chromebook using both screens.

TIP

If you have a flat-screen television, you can also connect your Chromebook to your TV for an extra-large display. This capability can be great for viewing your pictures, movies, YouTube, and so on.

An external monitor can work with a Chromebook in two ways:

>> **Mirrored:** This means that everything you see on your Chromebook display is shown on the external display. The external display is a "mirror" of your Chromebook display.

>> **Extended:** This means that the external monitor represents additional ("extended") space to show apps and windows.

To switch between mirrored and extended display as well as to change other settings, follow these steps:

1. Open the Settings panel on the shelf and click Settings.

Your Chromebook settings appear.

2. Click Device in the left margin of the Settings window and then click Displays.

The Displays Settings window appears, as shown in Figure 17-7, and you see the Arrangement configuration, where your two (or more) displays are shown side-by-side in the Displays Settings window.

The Arrangement configuration allows you to choose whether your external display is mirrored or extended.

3. To change this, select or deselect the Mirror Internal Display check box.

When you change the display, a notification appears, like the one shown in Figure 17-8.

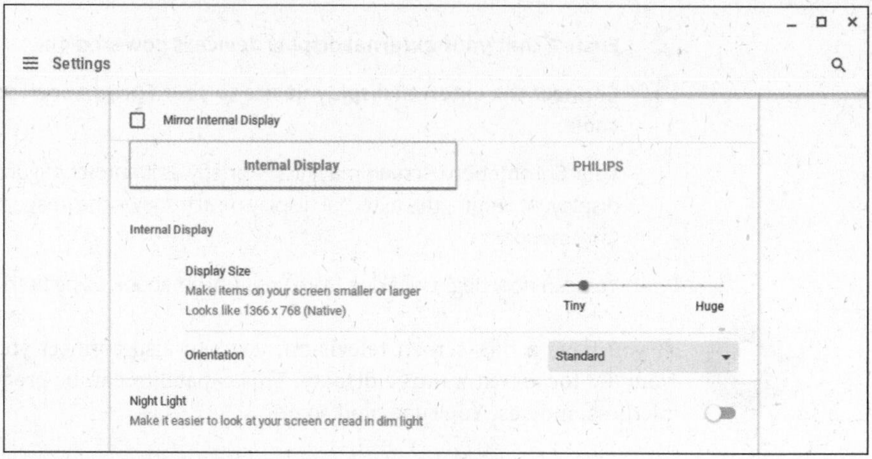

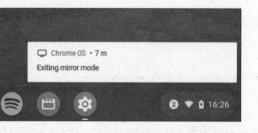

FIGURE 17-7:
Manage the
arrangement of
multiple displays.

FIGURE 17-8:
Chromebook tells
you when you've
entered or exited
Mirror mode.

4. **(Optional) If you chose not to mirror the displays, configure the arrange-ment of the two monitors by dragging the depictions of the displays to match the orientation of the actual displays.**

   Configuring the arrangement of the representative monitors allows you to logically arrange how your physical monitors work in relation to one another. For example, if your external monitor is to the left of your Chromebook, you can drag the little boxes representing the displays so that their orientation on the screen resembles their physical orientation, which comes in handy is when you move the mouse pointer between the two displays. When the displays on the Arrangement configuration screen are arranged like the actual displays, the mouse pointer can move smoothly from one display to the other.

You can also adjust the resolution of an external display. To do so, follow these steps:

1. **Open display settings, as in the previous procedures in this section.**

2. **In the Arrangement section, click the external display symbol and then scroll down past the Arrangement section.**

   The configuration settings for the external display appear, as shown in Figure 17-9. In this section, you can adjust the resolution (the number of rows and columns of pixels), the size of text that appears in windows and apps, and whether your external display is oriented in the usual way, or whether the display is rotated 90, 180, or 270 degrees.

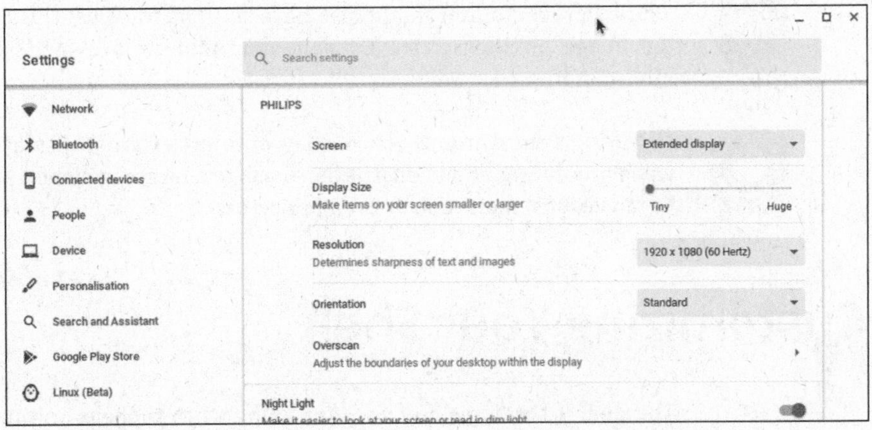

FIGURE 17-9: Configuring an external display.

3. **If the image on the external display is too big or too small, click Overscan to open the Overscan section of the display configuration settings.**

   Symbolic arrows appear on the external display to assist in this effort, as shown in Figure 17-10.

FIGURE 17-10: Configuring the Overscan setting to correct external display positioning.

Overscan adjusting indicators

4. **Press the arrow keys on your keyboard to adjust the image size and position.**

5. **To accept your changes, click OK; to ignore your changes, click Reset.**

TECHNICAL
STUFF

Your external monitor might also have settings to adjust the size and position of the image on the screen. Consult your monitor's owner's manual for more information.

TIP

Mirroring your Chromebook display onto an external display device is helpful when presenting or demonstrating a task to a larger audience. Display devices can be televisions, monitors, or even projectors.

Customizing Your Shelf

The shelf is the home base for controlling what happens on your Chromebook. By default, the shelf is located along the bottom of your screen. Your app menu (similar to the Start button on a Windows PC) appears on the left side of your shelf. Next to the Launcher icon are shortcuts to your favorite apps. You can find your notification panel and status area on the right side of your shelf. (Flip to Figure 2-1 in Chapter 2 to take a quick look at these elements.)

Hiding your shelf

By default, your shelf is always visible on the screen. You can, however, set the shelf to be hidden when you're not using it. To auto-hide your shelf, follow these steps:

1. **With the pointer somewhere on the wallpaper, Alt-click (or two-finger tap).**

2. **In the pop-up menu that appears, select Autohide Shelf.**

Whenever you launch an application, the shelf hides to give you more usable space on your screen. To reveal the shelf when you're working in a browser window, simply move your pointer so that it hovers over the shelf area at the bottom of the screen, and it will reappear.

Changing the position of your shelf

By default, your shelf is located along the bottom of your screen. To move the shelf to the left or right side of your screen, follow these steps:

1. **Alt-click (or two-finger tap) the background of your Chromebook.**

2. **In the menu that appears, hover your cursor over Shelf Position.**

   A submenu appears, as shown in Figure 17-11.

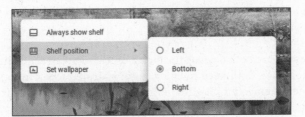

3. **Select the option that corresponds with the side of the screen to which you'd like to move your shelf.**

   The shelf relocates to the designated side, as shown in Figure 17-12.

TIP

If the shelf is located at the bottom of the screen and contains a lot of app icons (as mine does), they won't all show if you move the shelf to the left or right side of the screen. This spillover is indicated by an icon displaying three dots. Click this icon to make the remainder of your app icons appear.

Additional launcher icons here

Connecting Bluetooth devices to your Chromebook

Bluetooth, which has saved the world from the tangle of headphone and speaker wires, is a wireless protocol that you can use to connect devices together up to a distance of 30 feet apart.

You connect Bluetooth devices through a process known as "pairing." To connect devices together, both need to be put into "pairing mode," which allows them to make a new connection. It's like introducing a couple of your friends on a blind date: You introduce them to each other, and from then on, what happens is up to them.

The kinds of devices you can connect to your Chromebook include speakers, headphones, earbuds, and external pointing devices such as a mouse or trackpad. Other more specialize devices qualify as well, such as those little tags that you put on your keychain after you misplaced them — again. (In my household, we also have one of those little automotive diagnostic plugs that you plug into the diagnostic port of your car so that an app on a smartphone or Chromebook can read the codes and give us an idea of how our car is feeling today.)

To connect a Bluetooth-enabled device to your Chromebook, follow these steps:

1. **Click the Settings area on the shelf and then click the Settings gear.**

   The Chromebook settings window opens.

2. **Click Bluetooth in the Bluetooth section.**

   The Bluetooth settings window opens. Look to see whether the word *Off* or *On* appears just below the Bluetooth logo.

3. **If Bluetooth is off, turn it on by clicking the Bluetooth logo.**

4. **Read the instructions, if necessary, for the device you're using to learn how to put it into pairing mode.**

   Pairing a device often involves holding down its Power button, or another button, for some seconds.

5. **When the device's name appears under the Unpaired Devices heading, as shown in Figure 17-13, click it.**

6. **If your Chromebook and the device agree to pair, the device name and the word *Connected* appear under the Paired Devices heading, as shown in Figure 17-14.**

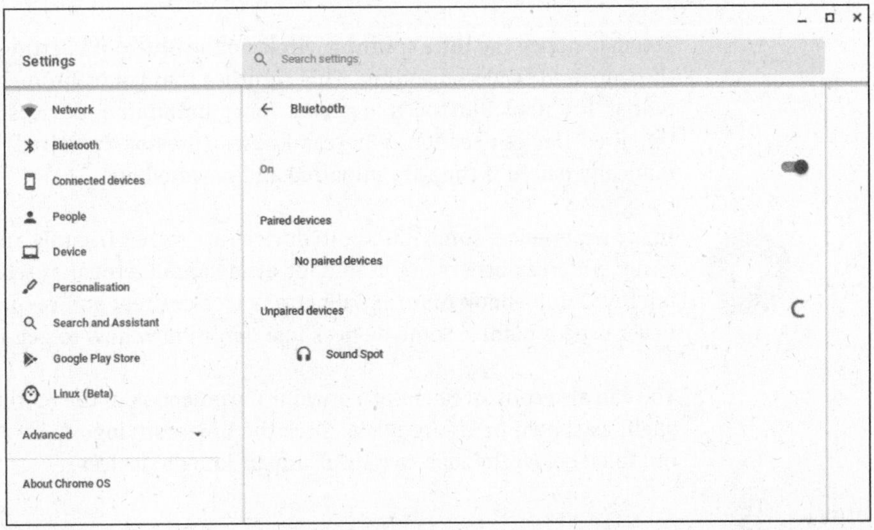

FIGURE 17-13:
Getting ready to pair a Chromebook to a Bluetooth device.

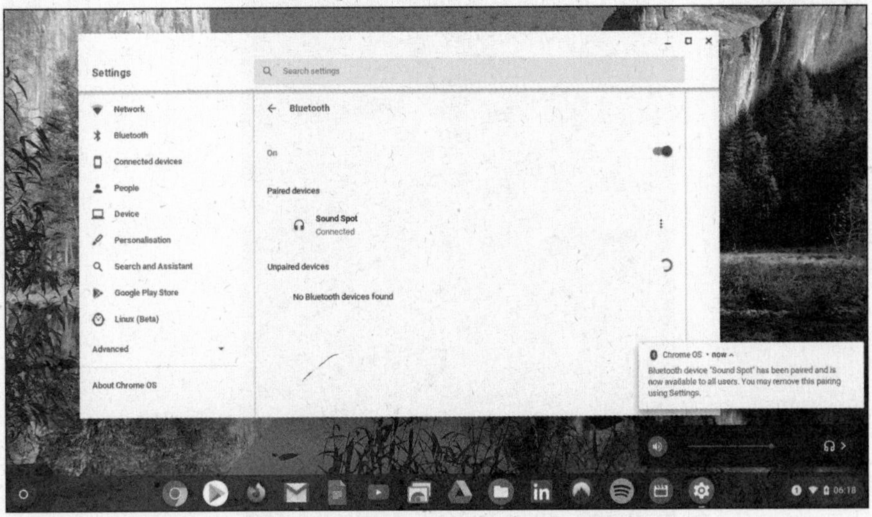

FIGURE 17-14:
Chromebook has successfully paired with a Bluetooth device.

In the future, your Chromebook should automatically pair with the same device if both are turned on and near each other, and if Bluetooth is active on your Chromebook.

Later on, to disconnect a device, you can just turn it off. Or you can turn off Bluetooth on your Chromebook. Yet another way is to go into the Bluetooth Settings window, click the device name, and click Disconnect. If you want your Chromebook to forget about your device forever, click the device in the Bluetooth Settings window and click Remove From List.

You may notice the little spinning circle on the Bluetooth Settings window beneath the Unpaired Devices heading. This signifies that your Chromebook is always listening for new Bluetooth devices. New, unfamiliar devices are listed in the Unpaired Devices section, whereas known (previously paired) devices are automatically paired if they are unpaired and powered on.

TIP

In my experience, some Bluetooth devices are rather friendly and pair and re-pair easily, whereas others are cranky or even cantankerous, at which time I have to tell my Chromebook to forget about a device entirely and re-pair it as though I'd never used it before. Some devices just don't know how to get along.

You can also control Bluetooth on your Chromebook in the Settings window on the shelf, as shown in Figure 17-15. Click the Bluetooth logo to turn Bluetooth on and off. Click below the logo to pair or unpair known devices.

FIGURE 17-15:
Configuring Bluetooth right in the Shelf Settings window.

Managing Notifications

A lot can go on "under the hood" of your Chromebook, and your Chromebook can get rather chatty in telling you about it through notifications. Some of these notifications might just be noise to you, but others are potentially useful. Sometimes the noise is so loud that you might feel like foregoing notifications altogether; however, a few are vital, such as for software updates.

Notifications are the messages that appear on the lower-right side of the Chromebook display — and sometimes they can run all the way to the top-right side of the display!

To close individual notifications, click the tiny *X* in the upper-right corner of the notification, as shown in Figure 17-16. To manage notifications settings, follow these steps:

1. **Open the Settings window on the shelf.**

2. **Click the word *Notifications* that appears beneath the Notifications logo.**

A window showing a list of apps appears, as shown in Figure 17-17. Note that the list might be longer than the display window; scroll through the list to view apps that can send notifications.

3. **To prevent an app from sending notifications, deselect the check box next to its name.**

For example, if you don't want the Chromebook's camera app to notify you every time you take a picture, deselect the box next to Camera.

4. **To temporarily suspend all notifications, click the Do Not Disturb selector.**

You can also click the Notifications logo in the Shelf Settings window. Great shortcut, right?

To turn notifications back on, click the Do Not Disturb selector again.

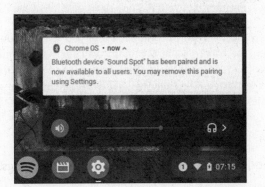

FIGURE 17-16:
A notification on the Chromebook display.

TIP

Here's a nice shortcut for Notifications: On the shelf to the left of the clock, battery, and Wi-Fi symbols, a small, white circle with a number in it appears if you have notifications waiting. (See Figure 17-18.) If you click that circle, the Shelf Settings window appears, and the notifications appear above it.

FIGURE 17-17:
Configuring
notifications
settings on a
Chromebook.

FIGURE 17-18:
See how many
notifications are
waiting for you to
view them.

Notification count

Configuring Your Touchpad

Unless you have a touchscreen Chromebook and you use the touchscreen for all your interactions, the touchpad is the main way for you to interact with your Chromebook. You use it to open apps, click buttons and selectors, and move the cursor about on a web page. The touchpad has a few settings that you may want to explore to see whether you prefer different ways of using it.

To configure the touchpad, follow these steps:

1. **Click the Settings area of the shelf and then click the Settings icon.**

The Chromebook Settings menu opens.

2. **Click Device in the left margin of the Settings window.**

3. **In the Device section, click Touchpad.**

The Touchpad window displays, as shown in Figure 17-19, with the following settings:

- **Tap-to-Click:** This is one of my favorite features. When you enable this feature and then have the pointer over a button or a link, a single tap on the touchpad works the same as clicking in the lower-left corner of the touchpad (which offers an audible and tactile click). To enable Tap-to-Click, click the selector.

- **Tap-dragging:** This is an easier way to use drag-and-drop. Enable it by clicking the selector.

- **Touchpad speed:** This feature determines how fast the pointer moves about the screen when you slide your finger across the touchpad. Click anywhere on the slider to see how this works; it takes immediate effect.

- **Scrolling:** You can set scrolling to be traditional, or "Australian," which sets scrolling to work in the opposite direction to your scrolling gesture on the touchpad.

4. **When you are done with your Touchpad settings, close the window by clicking the X.**

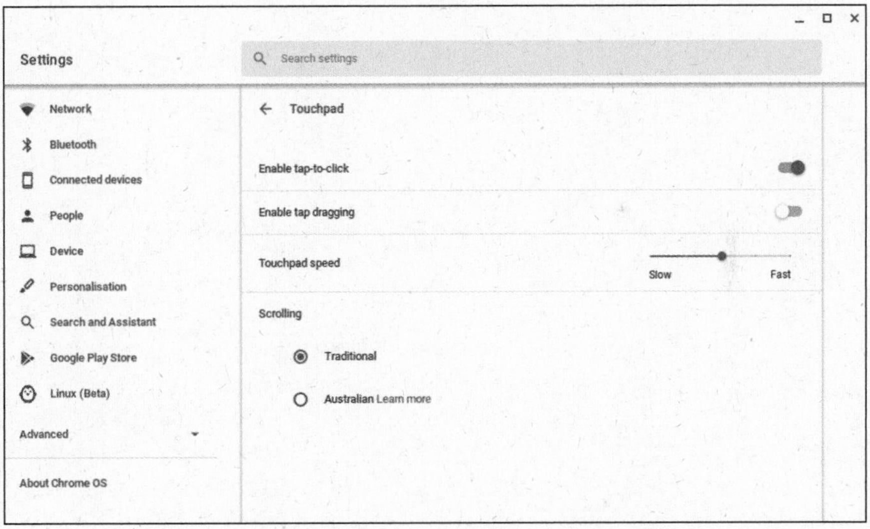

FIGURE 17-19: Configuring the Chromebook touchpad.

Chapter **18**

Securing Your Chromebook

E vil abounds in the world, and it takes many forms. In the context of computers and the Internet, countless cybercriminal organizations, gangs, and lone hackers lurk with the intention of pilfering, stealing, defacing, and destroying — for profit, for enjoyment, and because they can. Doubtlessly, you've heard about breaches, small and large, and ransomware, viruses, and other plagues and calamities.

The good news is that you have a Chromebook! Chromebooks are not targeted the way Windows, Macs, Android phones, and iPhones are. Chromebooks themselves are quite secure and are fitted with the latest safeguards. But that doesn't mean you don't have to be careful. Cybercriminals have many ways to try to trick people out of information and money.

Sometimes increased usability can mean increased security concerns. Face it: The more protection you put in place, the more hassle there is. Today's airports are a great example of this. To prevent an attack on a plane, we endure the hassle of taking off shoes, belts, jackets, and hats and removing computers, metal objects, and liquids from our luggage as we walk through x-ray machines and body-image scanners. Chromebook security is the same way. You can add or remove as much security as you want, but there are consequences both ways — and unfortunately, security isn't always convenient.

In this chapter, you learn how to protect against malicious invaders and manage your access to your Chromebook through user accounts and Guest mode. You see how to increase your peace of mind by locking your screen and managing your passwords and ensure that you aren't leaving valuable information around by managing your privacy settings. You can even get the ultimate protection through Google Advanced Protection. Concerned that something is amiss with your Chromebook? Power wash it to ensure that it's as clean as can be and start fresh! Also, this chapter tells you about webcam filters, privacy screen filters, and cable locks for keeping prying eyes and hands away.

Conducting User Management

Google takes security seriously, and thus the Chromebook is no slouch when it comes to security, as well. To access a Chromebook, you must have a Google Account. This requirement is just as much about enhancing your interaction with the Chromebook and the Google platform as it is securing your interaction. By default, when you first use your Chromebook, you have the option to log in with a Google Account, or you can use the Chromebook as a guest. Guest users don't get any of the privileges that registered users get. In fact, Guest mode is a lot like surfing the web incognito because none of your traffic is tracked, stored, or otherwise logged in the Chromebook.

When you log in to your Chromebook with a Google Account, that user account becomes the master account, or *Owner account,* of the Chromebook. With this account, you can administer and manage all other users who access the Chromebook, or you can restrict users whom you don't want to access the Chromebook.

Adding and deleting users

Account management is an essential part of securing your Chromebook. By default, anyone with a Google Account can log in and utilize your Chromebook. The good news is that Chromebook doesn't allow each user to access other users' data; however, you may not want your computer to be accessible to everyone on the planet. If you would like to limit access to your Chromebook to specific users, follow these steps:

1. **Log in to your Chromebook with the Owner account's username and password (that's probably you).**

2. **Open the settings panel on the Shelf and click Settings.**

   The Settings window opens.

3. **Click People.**

4. **Click the Manage Other People button in the People section.**

   The People window appears, as shown in Figure 18-1.

Settings		— ▢ ✕
	Q Search settings	
📶 Network	← Manage other people	
✳ Bluetooth		
🖥 Connected devices	Enable Guest browsing	⬤━
👤 People	Show usernames and photos on the sign-in screen	⬤━
🖥 Device	Restrict sign-in to the following users:	⬜◯
✏ Personalisation		
🔍 Search and Assistant		
▶ Google Play Store		
⊙ Linux (Beta)		
Advanced ▾		
About Chrome OS		

FIGURE 18-1: Managing users on a Chromebook.

5. **Select the Restrict Sign-In to the Following Users selector.**

   A form located below this selector activates, revealing all the users who have logged into your device already, as shown in Figure 18-2.

REMEMBER

   If you're the only person who has accessed the Chromebook up to this point, the only account you see in this box is yours. Notice that next to your account name is the word *Owner,* which means that your account is the owner of the Chromebook. With the Restrict Sign-In to the Following Users option enabled, the only users who can access your Chromebook are listed with your account.

6. **To add users, in the Add Person text box, enter the email addresses for the Google Accounts to which you wish to grant access. Press Enter.**

   The names are added to the list of approved accounts, as shown in Figure 18-3.

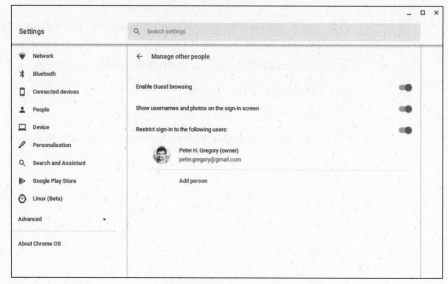

FIGURE 18-2:
Viewing active user accounts on a Chromebook.

FIGURE 18-3:
Adding names to the list of users allowed to use your Chromebook.

TIP

The Add Person form calls for either a name or an email address. To save on headaches or errors, use only the email addresses assigned to the Google Accounts that will access your Chromebook.

To delete an added user, click the *X* to the right of the user's name in the list. No *X* appears to the right of the owner's name because the owner's access can't be revoked. Users who aren't listed as the owner can't modify the user settings for your Chromebook. If they attempt to do so, a notification appears, like the one shown in Figure 18-4.

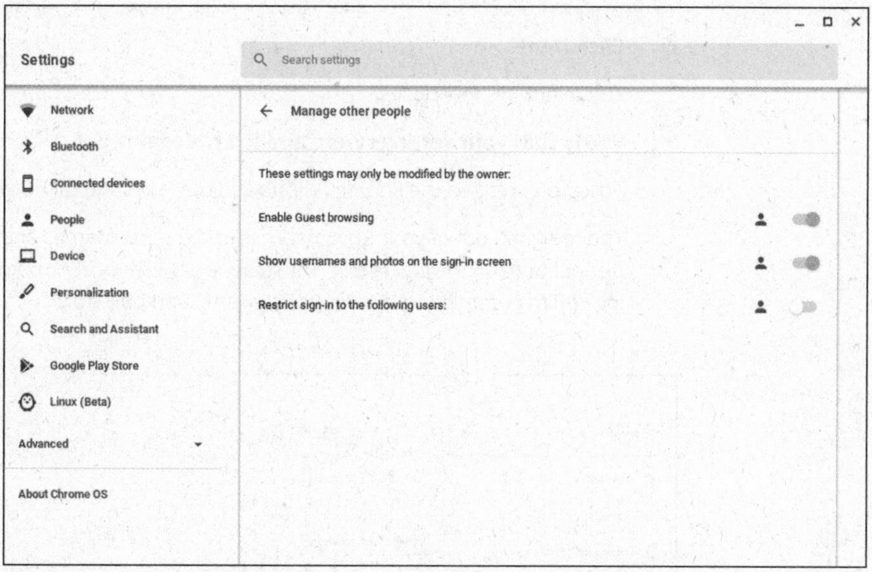

FIGURE 18-4: Changing user settings is permitted by the owner only.

Hiding users on the login screen

When you add new users to your Chromebook, their names and profile pictures are shown on the login screen. Showing these can make access for frequent users easy and convenient. However, it also reduces security: The approved user accounts are in plain sight, so potential intruders don't have to work so hard. Instead of having to guess both a username and a password, intruders need guess only a password. To hide users so that they don't appear on the login screen, follow these steps:

1. **Log in to your Chromebook with the Owner account's username and password.**

2. **Open the settings panel on the Shelf and click Settings.**

   The Settings window opens.

3. **Click People.**

4. **Click the Manage People button in the People section.**

5. **Deselect the Show Usernames and Photos on the Sign-In Screen selector, as shown in Figure 18-5.**

6. **Click Done.**

The Users window closes.

7. **Verify that your settings were applied by logging out.**

To log out, reopen the Settings window in the Shelf and click Sign Out.

You're signed out of your Chromebook, and the usernames and photos disappear from the login screen. Instead, a generic login box appears, requiring you to enter your full account username and password.

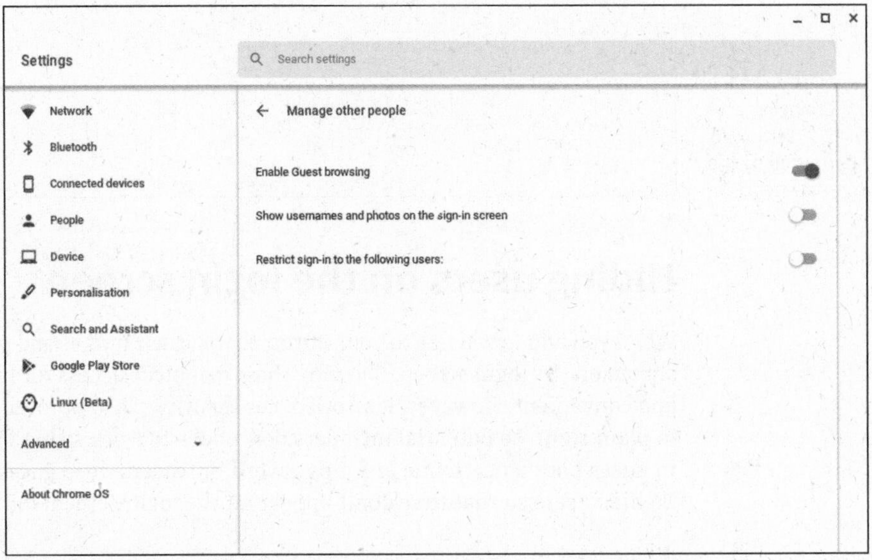

FIGURE 18-5:
Hiding user accounts on the login window.

Guest mode

Guest mode is an easy way to allow anyone to use your Chromebook without putting your personal account — or your Chromebook's settings — at risk. Key features, such as saving data to the device, changing settings, or otherwise modifying the Chromebook, are disabled. Any changes, downloads, or tweaks done to the Chromebook while in Guest mode are deleted when the Chromebook is powered off or when the guest logs out. If you ever want to give someone quick access without having to create a user account, Guest mode is the way to go!

Even so, you may find that Guest mode leaves you more vulnerable than you like. In that case, you can revoke guest browsing by following these steps:

1. **Log in to your Chromebook with the Owner account's username and password.**

2. **Open the settings panel on the Shelf and click Settings.**

3. **Click People.**

4. **Click the Manage People button in the People section.**

5. **Deselect the Enable Guest Browsing selector, as shown in Figure 18-6.**

6. **Verify that your settings were applied by logging out.**

   To log out, reopen the Settings window in the Shelf and click Sign Out.

   You're signed out of your Chromebook.

   If you successfully disabled Guest mode, the option to use the Chromebook as a guest disappears from the login screen. If you want to turn Guest mode back on, log back in and follow the steps above, enabling the selector in Step 5.

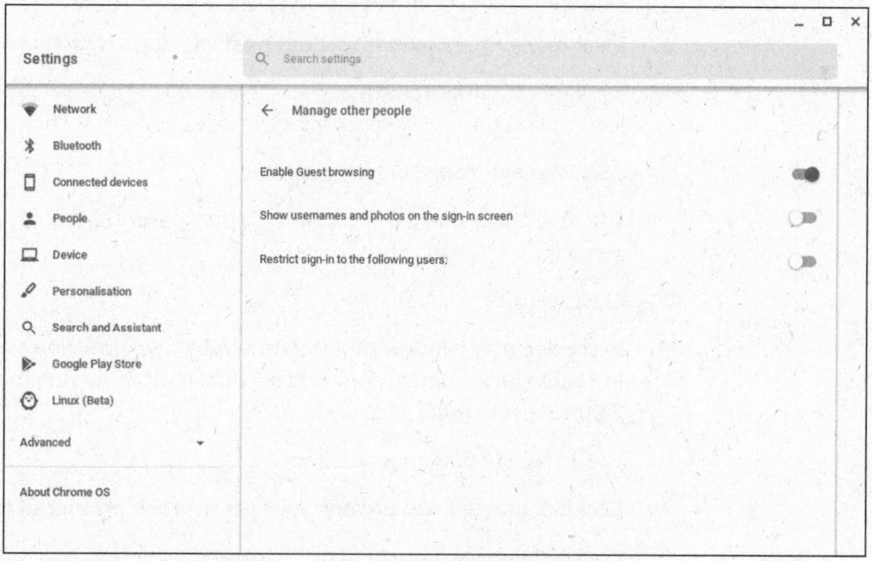

FIGURE 18-6: Disabling guest access on a Chromebook.

Using Google 2-Step Authentication

Using only user IDs and passwords isn't as safe as it once was. Criminals use malware, which is designed to steal your *login credentials,* to try to steal from you. Google comes to the rescue with Google 2-Step Authentication, a mechanism that goes further than your user ID and password and serves as an additional safeguard to ensure that, even if attackers do steal your login credentials, they still can't log in to your Google account.

With Google 2-Step Authentication, you log in to Google with your user ID and password. Then, Google pops up a window on your smartphone and asks whether you are currently trying to log in on your Chromebook. Answer Yes if you are, No if you aren't. If you are logging on your Chromebook, of course you answer Yes. Voilà — you're logged in.

REMEMBER

The security behind 2-Step Authentication is that if a hacker steals your login and password and tries to log in to Google as you, you unexpectedly receive an "Is this you?" alert on your smartphone. Answer no! Then you want to change your Google password.

To set up Google 2-Step Authentication for the first time, follow these steps on your Chromebook:

1. **Log in to your Google Account with your smartphone.**

2. **Log in to your Google Account on your Chromebook.**

   Logging on to Gmail or any other Google service is sufficient.

3. **Click the Google Account settings near the upper-right corner.**

   You click your photo or avatar if you set one up to go here. Otherwise, click the little circle in the upper-right corner of the window.

4. **Click Manage Your Google Account.**

   The page opens that lets you manage virtually every aspect of your Google account.

5. **Click Security.**

6. **In the Security window that opens, scroll down until you see the Signing In To Google section and, in that section, click the arrow to the right of 2-Step Verification.**

   The 2-Step Verification window opens.

7. **Click Get Started and provide your password, if prompted to do so.**

   Google shows your smartphone's make and model and will ask if you have it.

8. **On your smartphone, answer Yes that you are trying to change the way you sign in to Google.**

   Google may ask other questions to verify that you have your phone with you and are proceeding with 2-Step verification.

9. Click Try It Now.

On your smartphone, a window pops up, asking whether you are trying to log in from your Chromebook. Your location is shown as well.

10. Click Yes if you are indeed the user trying to log in. (See Figure 18-7.)

Google asks whether you want to set up a backup method for logging in. Google will ask you for your mobile number.

11. Enter your mobile number, select whether you want Google to call you or send you a text message, and click Send.

Google calls your phone or sends a text to your phone with a code.

12. Type in the code received in the text message and click Turn On.

This setup gives you a backup method to log in to Google in case you don't have your smartphone (back in Step 11, you can have Google call a landline phone).

When you set up 2-Step Verification, every time you log in to Google, this one little extra step gives you the peace of mind of knowing that others can't access your Google accounts easily. But if you want to get even more serious about your Google account security, read on.

Obtaining ultimate security with Google Advanced Protection

In case Google 2-Step Verification is not enough security for you, you will be glad to know that Google has developed Google Advanced Security. This service offers the ultimate protection for your Google account, making it virtually impossible for anyone but you to ever access your Google account.

Here are a few things to know about Google Advanced Protection:

>> You purchase two tiny, inexpensive security devices that you need to carry with you. (I carry mine on my key ring.) You have to purchase them only once,

>> You need to use those little security devices only the first time you log in to any Google application on each device, and on any device from which you have logged out.

>> Google Advanced Protection works not only on your Chromebook, but also on Android and Apple phones, iPads, Windows computers, and Macs.

>> On Windows, Macs, and Chromebooks, to log in to Gmail and other Google services, you must use the Chrome browser. Firefox, Edge, Safari, and other browsers won't work.

>> On Android phones and iPhones, you must use the Gmail app to access email in your Google account. Using other email apps won't work.

>> If, after using Google Advanced Protection, you decide it isn't for you, you can always turn it off and go back to using Google Authenticator or just your user ID and password.

I've been using Google Advanced Protection for more than two years, and speaking as a 20-year cybersecurity professional, I have found it to be rock solid and reliable, and have never had a bit of a problem with it.

Figure 18-8 shows me using my Google Titan key to log in to Google on my Chromebook. To learn more about Google Advanced Protection, go to https://landing.google.com/advancedprotection/.

Google Authenticator is another handy to use to improve your login security. Available for Android smartphones and Apple iPhones, Google Authenticator is used to store secure tokens used to log in to websites with sensitive information, such as financial and medical services. Although Google Authenticator is not available as an app for your Chromebook, you can still use it with your smartphone to improve the security of your most important websites. You can find out more at https://google-authenticator.com/.

FIGURE 18-8:
Using a Google
Titan USB key
to complete
logging on to a
Chromebook with
Google Advanced
Protection.

Managing and protecting Your passwords

People's use of the Internet today involves having many user accounts that require user IDs passwords, and often, but not always, an email address. Trying to remember so many passwords can be downright frustrating, but in this section, I discuss three methods for storing them that can make your use of passwords both easier and more secure. You can store them in an online password vault, in your browser, or in a hard-copy book.

TIP

There are some highly important rules about passwords that I want you to understand clearly. If you learn anything from this book, it should be these password safeguards. You can find these rules in Chapter 23, "Ten Important Security Tips."

Using an online password vault

My preferred method for storing user IDs and passwords is a password vault, which securely stores all your user IDs and passwords and will provide them to you when you need them. My favorite password vaults are LastPass (at `www.lastpass.com`), Keeper (at `www.keepersecurity.com` and shown in Figure 18-9), and Dashlane (at `www.dashlane.com`).

With an online password vault, your passwords are available on all of your devices. Here are some of the essential principles regarding the use of an online password vault:

>> The password for your password vault is the only password you need to remember (other than your Google password for logging in to your Chromebook). Thus, make sure that your password vault password is strong and not easily guessed

by others. If anyone guesses your password vault's password, they will have all your passwords!

>> Use the password-generating feature of your password vault to ensure that every password is strong and different from every other password you use. This way, if a website is hacked and the intruder obtains your password, it will work *only* for that one website and no other.

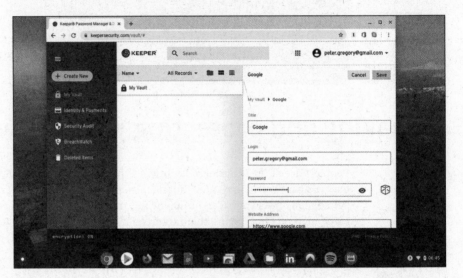

FIGURE 18-9:
Using the Keeper password vault to store a user ID and password.

TIP

The selection of a password vault solution is an important decision, because you're entrusting another party to keep your passwords safe. This is why using known, trusted brands like those mentioned in this section is essential. These companies are, after all, storing all your important login credentials. If this prospect makes you squeamish, consider using a hard-copy book, as discussed later in this chapter.

Storing passwords in the Chrome browser

In case using a password vault (see the preceding section) isn't for you, an alternative for your Internet password storage is to use your Chromebook's default feature for storing and managing your Internet passwords. This feature of the Chrome browser made it into the Chromebook, and it's great if you have several passwords for several online products.

REMEMBER

Don't worry: Chrome doesn't store your passwords without your permission. You have to approve the storage of a password the first time you enter it on a particular web page, as shown in Figure 18-10.

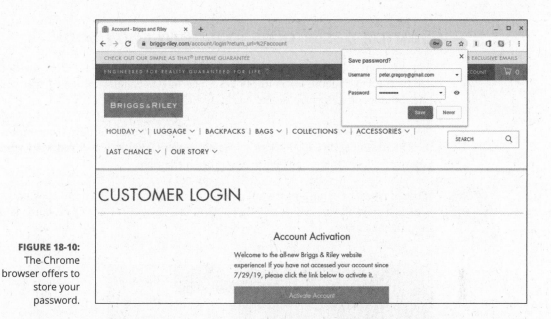

If you choose to store your password, Chrome encrypts the password and stores it in your account for later. Later on, when you go to log in to the website, the Chrome browser automatically types it in for you.

TIP

If you ever forget a password, you can go to the Password Manager and click the password you've forgotten. A Show button appears that reveals your password when clicked.

You don't *have* to save passwords in your browser; however, you may find that saving them makes your web-browsing experience better. If you opt not to save a password but change your mind later, you need to delete the website from the Never Saved section of your Password Manager. To do so, follow these steps:

1. **Ensure that you're logged in, and then open the Settings panel on your Shelf and click Settings.**

2. **Click Chrome Browser Settings.**

3. **Scroll down to Auto-fill.**

4. **Click Passwords.**

   The Password Manager window appears, revealing every stored password.

5. **In the Never Saved section, click the *X* to the right of the website you want to remove from this list.**

   Now, the next time you return to that website and enter your login credentials, you're prompted with the option to save your password, at which point you can approve saving it.

Storing passwords in a hard-copy book

You can keep your user IDs and passwords in a "little black book." This method can be the most secure of the three described in this chapter, provided that you guard that book diligently — and don't lose it!

You can purchase special-purpose, hard-copy password journals from online merchants. But seriously, you can also just get a small journal book and write your passwords down there. See Figure 18-11 for an example.

TIP

If the prospect of using a password vault is intimidating, using a hard-copy notebook is a good alternative — as long you still use unique, complex passwords and keep the book safe.

FIGURE 18-11:
Writing your passwords down in a little black book.

Keeping hackers at bay with multifactor authentication

The term *multifactor authentication* can sound a bit scary — but actually, the reverse is true: *Not* using multifactor authentication is a scary prospect. Without multifactor authentication, malware can steal user IDs and passwords and use them to log in to your user accounts in online banking sites and other places where you spend or manage money.

When you use multifactor authentication, you use something in addition to your user ID and password when logging on to web site. That "something" involves your smartphone in a simple way: When you begin to log on to a web site, you enter your user ID and password, and then you're told to enter a value displayed on your smartphone to complete your login. This technique for logging in makes it very difficult for a criminal to log in to your Internet accounts.

TIP

Earlier in this chapter, in "*Using Google 2-Step Authentication,*" I discuss multifactor authentication for getting in to Google itself.

Locking Your Screen

Walking away from your Chromebook without first logging out or shutting it off can leave you vulnerable, even for only a brief moment. Locking your screen is a great way to ensure that your device, your email, or your Google account isn't tampered with while you're away. You have three ways to lock your Chromebook screen:

>> Press and hold your Power button for a moment. A window appears onscreen that lets you power down, sign out, lock, or provide feedback, as shown in Figure 18-12. Click Lock.

>> Open the Settings menu on the Shelf and click the Lock button, as seen in Figure 18-13.

>> If your Chromebook has a Lock key on the keyboard (see Figure 18-14), press it for about a second, and your Chromebook locks and displays the password screen for your Google account.

To unlock your Chromebook, enter your Google password.

FIGURE 18-12:
Locking your
Chromebook with
the Lock menu.

⏻ Power off	➡ Sign out	🔒 Lock	▣ Feedback

FIGURE 18-13:
Locking your
Chromebook with
the Lock button
in the Settings
window.

FIGURE 18-14:
Locking your
Chromebook with
the Lock key on
the keyboard.

Setting a secure wake–from-Sleep mode

To add a little more security to your Chromebook, you can require a password to wake your Chromebook from Sleep mode. *Sleep mode* is a mode that your Chromebook uses to conserve power when not in use. Your Chromebook automatically goes into Sleep mode after eight minutes of inactivity when plugged in and six minutes of inactivity when not plugged in, but you can put the Chromebook into Sleep mode immediately by closing the lid.

By default, a sleeping Chromebook is still vulnerable. Entering Sleep mode doesn't log you out or lock your screen. So if you rarely turn off your computer, enabling a wake-from-Sleep password is probably a good idea. To set this feature, log in to your Chromebook and then follow these steps:

1. **Open the Settings panel on the Shelf and click Settings.**

2. **Enable the Show Lock Screen When Waking From Sleep selector in the People section, as shown in Figure 18-15.**

   From here on out, you need your account password to bring your computer out of Sleep mode!

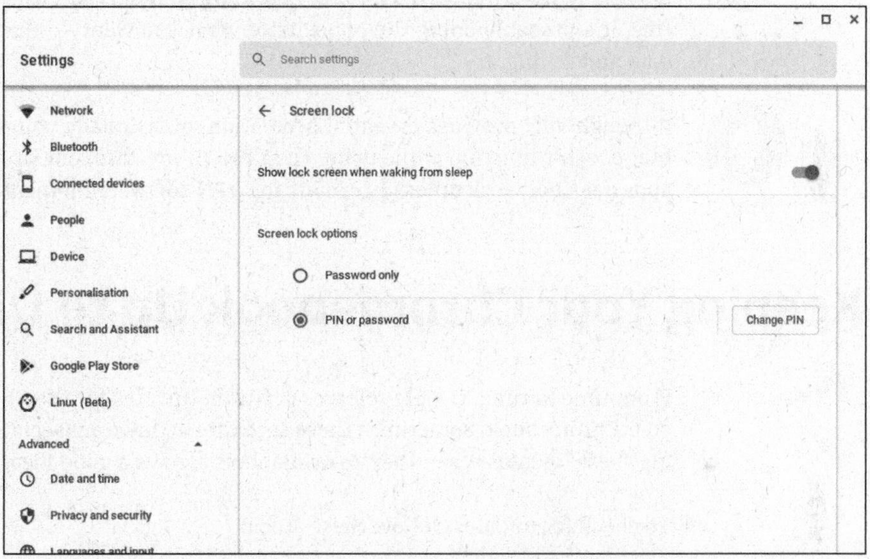

FIGURE 18-15: Enabling the wake-from-sleep password requirement.

Protecting Your Network Traffic with VPN

More often than not, public hotspots such as those found in coffee shops, airports, and hotels do not encrypt your data as it crosses the airwaves, which means that an attacker may be able to see the data you're sending and receiving. If you need to send sensitive data in public places, you might want to download a VPN app that encrypts your network traffic and keep it away from prying eyes.

VPN is short for "virtual private network," which is a fancy-pants way of saying that your network transmissions are encrypted from your Chromebook to the VPN service.

My favorite VPN software is Nord VPN (www.nordvpn.com), but some other good ones are available, including ExpressVPN (www.expressvpn.com) and CyberGhost VPN (www.cyberghostvpn.com). I use Nord VPN on my Chromebooks, MacBooks, iPhone, and Android phone.

To obtain and install a VPN program, go to the Google Web Store and search for one of mentioned here.

WARNING

I need to caution you here: There's no such thing as a free lunch. Good VPN software comes with a modest subscription fee, typically from $35 to $75 per year. Stay away from *free* VPN services. Providing VPN service costs money, and if it's free, it's probably doing the opposite of what you want — that is, usurping your data and selling it.

TIP

Although VPN provides essential protection, occasionally you may find some app that doesn't function while using the VPN. In my case, one of my online banking apps does not work unless I turn off the VPN software momentarily.

Keeping Your Chromebook Up to Date

From time to time, Google releases software updates for the Chrome OS that runs your Chromebook. Sometimes these software updates are security related, install- ing these updates when they're available is always a good idea.

To check for updates, follow these steps:

1. **Go to Settings.**

   If a software update is available for your Chromebook, you see a message like the one shown in Figure 18-16.

2. **Click Restart to Update.**

   Your Chromebook downloads the update and restarts.

When you click Settings, you might also see a message like the one shown in Figure 18-17 that tells you that apps you downloaded from the Google Play Store have updates available. When you see this message, click Update All.

TIP

In checking for Chrome OS updates, you're just looking at your notifications. It's a good idea to get into the habit of glancing down at the lower-right corner of the screen at the notifications area to see whether Chrome OS wants to tell you things, such as about updates and other issues.

FIGURE 18-16:
Checking your
Chromebook for
updates.

FIGURE 18-17:
Updating
software from the
Google Play
Store.

Protection from Viruses and Other Malware

Microsoft products MS-DOS and Windows have been plagued with computer viruses and other malware since practically the beginning of time. Android phones are now the biggest target of malware, and even the Apple Mac and iPhone are attacked. What about Chromebooks? Well, because Chrome OS is functionally similar to Android, it's safe to say that hackers are working on attacks on Chromebooks.

Even if few or no viruses target Chromebooks specifically, two potent threats exist that are highly relevant: attacks on the Chrome browser and malicious Chrome browser extensions. Because Chrome is the world's most popular browser, attacks against Chrome definitely occur.

Attacks against Chrome can, for instance, steal the login credentials you use to log in to websites (including online banking and others). These password-stealing attacks are one of the most significant threats, but not the only one.

Anti-malware programs for Chromebooks stop such attacks. I highly recommend that you select one of the following browser extensions and install it to protect you from these invisible but very potent threats:

>> AVG Online Security (see Figure 18-18)

>> Malwarebytes

>> McAfee Endpoint Security

Go to the Google Web Store to search for and install any of these.

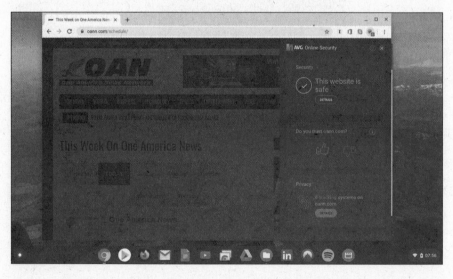

FIGURE 18-18:
AVG Online Security helps to protect you from Internet threats.

TIP

Although you may be protected from Internet hazards by one of the aforementioned tools or something similar, you should not throw caution to the wind and assume that these programs will bail you out of every kind of trouble. The nature of cybercrime makes it better for you to remain diligent even if you are protected by one of these programs.

Power Washing

Sometimes it's nice to have a clean start. Your Chromebook makes it easy for you to wipe the slate clean and start over. You may find doing so useful when you have too much junk on your device. Or maybe you want to reset your Chromebook to its default settings because you're giving your Chromebook to another person. You can wipe your device quickly, easily, and securely by using Chromebook's built-in Powerwash feature.

To power wash your Chromebook, log in to your Chromebook and follow these steps:

1. Open the Settings panel on the Shelf and click Settings.

2. Scroll to the bottom of the screen and click Show Advanced Settings.

3. Click the Powerwash button in the Powerwash section at the bottom of the screen, as shown in Figure 18-19.

A dialog box appears, telling you that a restart is required.

Settings		
🔍 Search settings		
Network		
Bluetooth	Printing	
Connected devices	Printers	▸
People		
Device	Accessibility	
Personalisation	Always show accessibility options in the system menu	⚪
Search and Assistant	Manage accessibility features	▸
Google Play Store	Enable accessibility features	
Linux (Beta)		
Advanced	Reset settings	
Date and time	Powerwash	▸
Privacy and security	Remove all user accounts and reset your Google Chrome device to be just like new.	
Languages and input		

FIGURE 18-19:
The Powerwash feature.

4. **If you're positive that you want to wipe your Chromebook clean, click the Restart button, shown in Figure 18-20.**

You can't undo power washing any more than you can unbreak an egg. After you click Restart, your Chromebook turns into a secure, power-cleaning machine. Nothing on the device will be left. The good news is that it won't touch anything on your Google Drive or other web services. But anything stored locally on your Chromebook will be gone forever.

Your Chromebook restarts, as clean as can be — just like new.

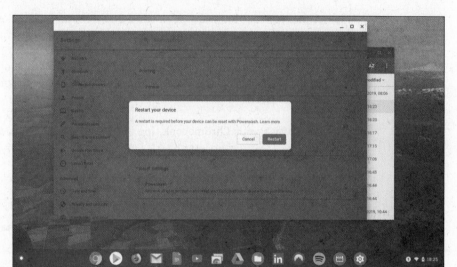

FIGURE 18-20: Are you sure?

Protecting Your Chromebook from Prying Eyes and Thieves

In this brief section, I describe protection that's more physical: covering your webcam so that no one can view whatever's happening in the room where your open Chromebook might be; using a screen privacy filter to limit what others can view on your Chromebook screen; and using a cable lock to make it more difficult for someone to steal your Chromebook.

Cover your webcam

Your Chromebook most likely has a built-in camera that faces you so that you can do live video chats, as I discuss in Chapter 14. As a security precaution, I recommend that you employ some sort of a cover for your webcam when you're not using it. You might forget to end a video call, or an attacker could figure out how to access Chromebook webcams. (However, this advice doesn't apply only to Chromebooks but also to some smart TVs – but good luck locating a secret camera on a TV!) You're better safe than sorry, particularly if your Chromebook is in private areas of your home, such as your bedroom.

Several methods are available for covering your webcam. You can use a purpose-made webcam cover (search "webcam cover" online to see what they look like). These are available at online retailers for minimal cost, and they're often given away at computer and electronics trade shows. Or you can take the budget route and use a small piece of electrical tape or a part of a sticky note.

Use a privacy screen filter

If you spend much time working with sensitive content on your Chromebook, and if you find that you're doing this in public places like coffee shops and airports, you might want to consider getting a privacy filter for your Chromebook. A privacy filter makes it easy for you to view the content on your screen, but more difficult (and nearly impossible) for others to view what's on your screen. In case you're not sure what I'm talking about, Figure 18-21 shows a typical privacy filter on a Chromebook.

FIGURE 18-21:
A privacy filter makes it more difficult for others to view the data on your screen.

Image courtesy of 3M

A screen privacy filter is a thin, semitransparent piece of plastic that goes over the top of your laptop screen. Often it's affixed with an adhesive that lets you remove the filter when you want to. The filter permits anyone directly in front of the laptop (you, and anyone right behind you) to view the screen, but anyone to the left or right of you would not be able to view what is on your screen.

Preventing the theft of your Chromebook

In case you are concerned about the actual theft of your Chromebook (and who wouldn't be!), you'll be glad to know that most Chromebooks come with a Kensington lock slot that allows you to attach a specially made security lock to your Chromebook to deter theft. In Figure 18-22, you can see how I lock my Chromebook with one of my security cable locks.

FIGURE 18-22:
Locking your Chromebook with a security cable lock.

Chapter **19**

Troubleshooting and Disaster Preparation

Technology is great until something breaks. I know, right? That saying probably goes back to the cavemen who discovered fire. The reality is, we live in an imperfect world, and nothing works perfectly all the time, even well-designed technology. For that reason, it's always good to consider those areas in which life with your Chromebook could go sideways.

You can't use your Chromebook to the fullest without Internet access. For that reason, this chapter shows you how to troubleshoot network connectivity issues. You also learn how to troubleshoot and possibly remedy issues with your battery. In case the sky starts falling and your Chromebook operating system becomes corrupt, you want to be sure that you have a restore disk so that you can reinstall Chrome OS and get back to work as fast as possible. If all else fails, Google has a vast database of helpful resources online to provide solutions for any Chromebook problem. This chapter tells you where to go and how to search through these resources to get answers fast!

Resolving Internet-Connectivity Problems

Chromebooks require a connection to the Internet to be able to serve their purpose in the portable-computing ecosystem. For that reason, every Chromebook comes equipped with high-speed Wi-Fi. Some Chromebooks even come with cellular connectivity, allowing them to get online wherever a cell signal is present. If you're having trouble connecting to a wireless network, check these possible solutions before calling tech support:

>> **Ensure that the Chromebook's Wi-Fi controller is turned on.** Check the Wi-Fi indicator in the settings panel of the shelf. If the Wi-Fi indicator is gray and the words Not Connected appear beneath it, as shown in Figure 19-1, the wireless adapter has been shut off. Turn it on by following these steps:

1. **Open the settings panel on the shelf and click the Wi-Fi icon.**

2. **In the menu that appears, click the Wi-Fi icon.**

   Your wireless adapter turns on and the Wi-Fi logo turns from gray to blue, giving you the option to select from all available Wi-Fi networks.

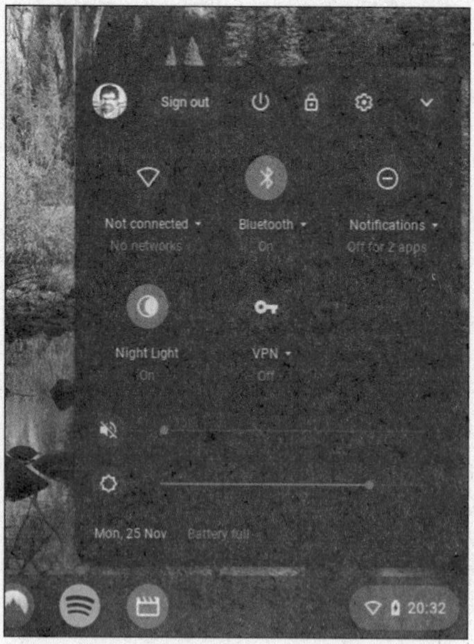

FIGURE 19-1:
The wireless adapter is turned off.

>> **Make sure that your Chromebook is connected to a Wi-Fi network.** Look at the Wi-Fi indicator that appears in the Settings area of your shelf. If you

have bars and no *X* and you still can't connect, verify that you're connected to the correct network by following these steps:

1. **Click anywhere in the settings panel on the shelf.**

   The settings menu appears, revealing several options. Just below the Wi-Fi logo is the name of the network to which your Chromebook is connected.

2. **If the connected network isn't the network you want to connect to, click the text just below the Wi-Fi icon.**

   The Wi-Fi Network menu appears.

3. **Scroll through the list, shown in Figure 19-2, to find the desired network, and then select it.**

If your wireless controller is turned on and you're connected to a network but you still can't connect to the Internet, try restarting your Chromebook. This restart flushes your Chromebook memory, power cycles all of your Chromebook hardware, and restarts the Chrome OS operating system, giving everything a chance to start fresh. Restarting devices is the easiest and most common fix for glitches like connecting to a network or the Internet.

If you've restarted your Chromebook and you're connected to the network, but you still can't connect to the Internet, ask the owner of the network to restart the Internet gateway. The gateway may be a home Internet router, cable modem, or DSL modem. If you're in an office or school, you may want to first check with other users to see whether they are having connectivity issues.

If your smartphone can provide a mobile Wi-Fi hotspot, you might turn that on and see whether your Chromebook can connect to that and access the Internet. A word of caution: Unless you are on an unlimited data plan, you want to do this only temporarily as a test to see whether your Chromebook can reach the Internet via a different Wi-Fi access point. If you can reach the Internet through your smartphone's Wi-Fi hotspot, this could mean that the other Wi-Fi network you are trying to connect to is having problems.

Looking into Browser Issues

From to time, browsers seem to take a holiday and not work quite right. Sometimes, though, it's just the website that's being ornery. But how can you know?

Some of the problems you're likely to run into include:

>> Websites won't load, or they are "stuck"

>> Websites seem to load partially but are missing images, or pages look incomplete

>> Websites can't be reached

When I'm troubleshooting issues like this, these are the actions I try:

>> **Close the tab and then try the website on a different tab.** Believe it or not, this approach sometimes works.

>> **Close and restart the browser.** I usually configure my browser to continue where I left off, meaning that all the tabs that were open when I last used my browser will be there when I restart it (or restart the Chromebook itself). Figure 19-3 shows the Continue Where You Left Off setting, which is under On Start Up on the Settings window.

>> **Try another browser.** On every device that I use for Internet access, I have the browser that the system came with (Safari on iPhones, iPads, and Macs; Chrome on Android phones and Chromebooks), and I have at least one other browser. I usually have two spare browsers, as follows:

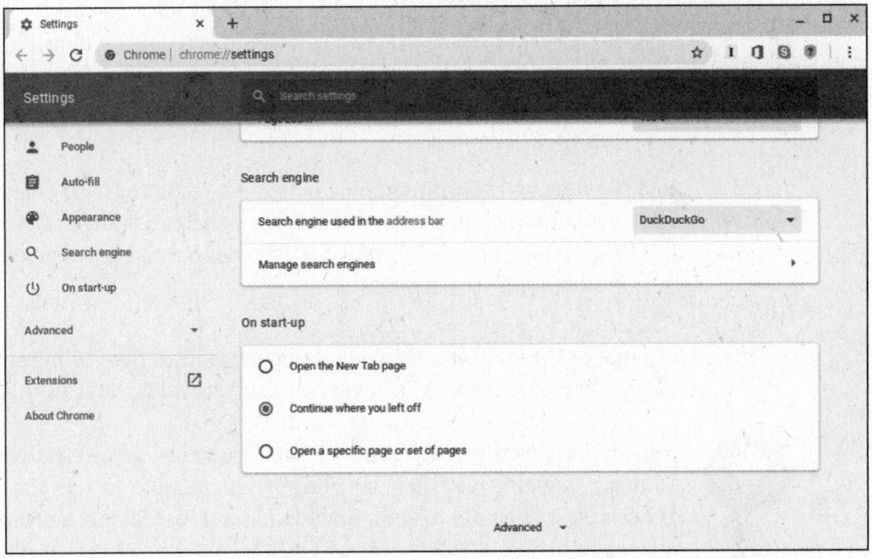

FIGURE 19-3:
Configuring Chrome to restart where it left off.

- **Firefox:** This is a very secure and user-friendly browser that is popular and has been around for a long time. Get a copy at `www.mozilla.org/firefox`.

- **Brave:** This browser is very much like Chrome itself, so much so that it will run most — if not all — Chrome browser extensions. In every way that matters, Brave is like Chrome except that it does not send tracking information to Google.

  If your website was reachable and behaved as expected with an alternative browser, either the website itself has a problem, or the Chrome browser may need to be restarted. If you followed these steps in sequence, you have probably already restarted it.

  Brave and Firefox are available in the Google Web Store. Click the launcher, click Google Web Store, search for Firefox or Brave, and install it.

>> **Disconnect Wi-Fi and then reconnect to it.** I cover this suggestion earlier in this chapter. It just might help!

>> **Sign out of your Chromebook.** Signing out and then signing back in might fix things. Figure 19-4 shows the Sign Out icon in the upper-left corner.

» **Try browsing as Guest.** To see whether you have an issue with your user account on the Chromebook, try signing out and then signing back in as Guest. Remember, though, that as a Guest, you can't save any files or access or save a bookmark.

» **Restart your Chromebook.** Sometimes, restarting (also called rebooting) your Chromebook is the only action that helps. Click Shut Down (refer to Figure 19-4) and then, after your Chromebook has powered off, press the Power button to restart it.

If none of these efforts fix your problem, skip to the, "Finding Help Online" and "Using the Chromebook Recovery Utility" sections, later in this chapter.

TIP

You should download and run — at least once — an alternative browser today. If Chrome is giving you fits, you might not be able to use the Google Web Store (which uses Chrome) to find, download, and install another browser.

Sign Off   Shut Down

FIGURE 19-4:
The Sign Off and Shut Down icons.

GOOGLE AND PRIVACY

Google has a marvelous ecosystem of computers (Chromebook, Chromebase, Android) and online services (Gmail, books, movies, chat, video chat, and so many more) that work well to enrich users' Internet experience. Sometimes, though, it seems as though Google (and others, which I won't name here, but you know who they are) knows a little too much about its users. I've heard anecdotal stories that make some people feel creepy, like, "We were talking about getting a new pressure washer today, and now I'm seeing ads for pressure washers online."

If you feel that your privacy is being invaded, you can take a couple of actions on a Chromebook to reduce that sense. First, configure the Chrome browser's Do Not Track feature. Or, go further and stop using Chrome altogether. Use Firefox or Brave browsers instead. (You should configure Do Not Track on those browsers also). Although you would still be using a Google-powered computer, the feeling of improved privacy is sure to improve your peace of mind.

Resolving Power Problems

Sometimes batteries go bad. Sometimes they even go out in a literal blaze of glory. Don't worry: The odds of such happenings with your Chromebook battery are lower than your chances of winning the lottery. However, Chromebooks — same as other brands of laptops — can have power problems like the following:

>> **Your battery's charge doesn't last nearly as long as it should, or its capability to stay charged decreases with each use.** Refer to your device manual or look online to identify estimated battery life based on your level of device usage. Then verify your Chromebook's battery consumption by following these steps:

1. **Plug your Chromebook into the power charger until you reach a 100-percent charge.**

2. **Verify the charge level of your battery by opening the Settings panel on your shelf and examining the battery indicator at the bottom.**

3. **Verify that the battery indicator says Battery Full before disconnecting your power charger.**

Take note of the time and begin working with your Chromebook. Check the battery indicator again to monitor how quickly it reduces in charge. When the battery is low enough to justify plugging it in, take note of the time again to see how long the battery lasted. If it's within normal usage limits as defined by the manufacturer of your Chromebook, you may want to adjust your usage. Maybe your screen is a bit on the bright side, for instance. Reducing the brightness level also reduces battery usage.

On the other hand, if your battery loses charge faster than your manufacturer's specifications, follow these steps before returning to the manufacturer or point of purchase:

1. **Plug your Chromebook into a power source and charge the battery to 100-percent full.**

2. **When the Chromebook has reached 100 percent, unplug it and use the device until power dwindles to 5 percent or less but not until it shuts off.**

3. **Repeat this process at least ten times before testing to see whether the battery life has extended.**

If your battery still won't maintain a charge, return to the point of purchase or contact the manufacturer for service. If your Chromebook is no longer under warranty, you may be able to have a local computer repair shop replace the battery.

Another influence on battery life to consider is your browser. One of the tabs on your browser may be running code on your computer nonstop. Unfortunately, no easy way exists to confirm this suspicion. Closing specific browser tabs, or exiting the browser altogether, might help you to isolate the problem to excessive CPU usage. Another app running in the background can also be the culprit: Try exiting all the other apps running on your Chromebook to see whether doing so helps at all.

» **The battery won't charge at all, so your Chromebook must stay connected to the power adapter, or your Chromebook won't turn on when plugged in**. Attempt to use another power adapter. If the symptoms persist with the other power adapter, your battery is likely toast. If the other power adapter rectifies the situation, you likely have a faulty power adapter.

If your Chromebook is one of the newer models with USB-C power (see Figure 19-5 for an example), you might be able to easily find another power adaptor to try. USB-C is becoming the new standard for laptop power plugs. If, on the other hand, your power cord is the "metal tip" variety like the one shown in Figure 19-6, you'll probably need to obtain another battery from the manufacturer.

TIP

I suggest that you get a good surge protector for your Chromebook. I don't mean a cheap power strip, but a decent surge protector — the kind that comes with a "we'll replace your damaged equipment" guarantee. Dirty power, with spikes, dips, surges, and so on, takes a toll on a laptop's power supply.

FIGURE 19-5:
A USB-C style
power adaptor.

FIGURE 19-6:
A "metal tip" style
power adaptor.

Finding Help Online

If you ever find yourself in a situation that you can't solve with this book or with your Chromebook's help manuals, try the Chromebook Help Center online. You can visit the Help Center, shown in Figure 19-7, at `https://support.google.com/chromebook`. The Help Center provides answers to some of the most common Chromebook questions relating to setup, connecting a Chromebook to the Internet, printing, working with media, and more. If your question is a little more refined and technical, you also have the option to explore the Chromebook Help Forum, where you can ask questions and receive helpful answers — or find others who have had the same issues, with helpful answers waiting to be found.

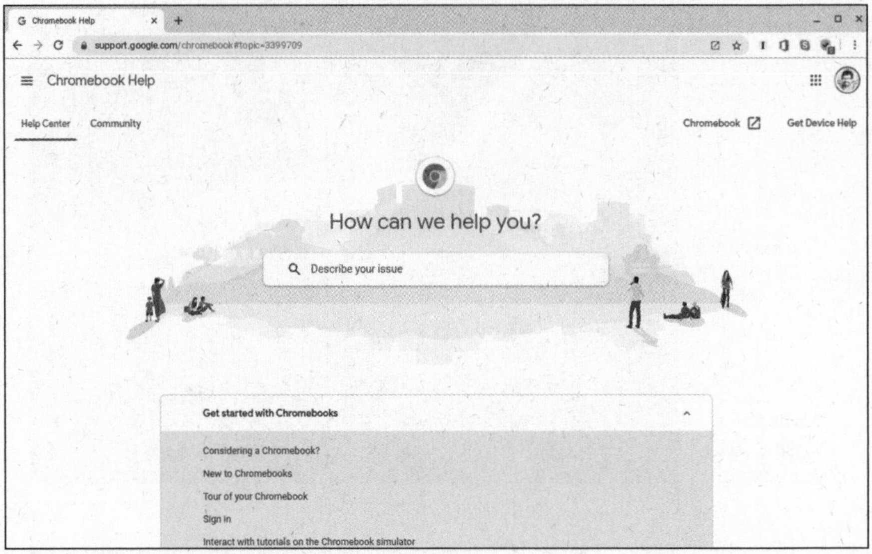

FIGURE 19-7:
The online
Chromebook
Help Center.

After you arrive at the Help Forum, you can either search or browse topics. The easiest way to get started is to type your problem or issue in the Search bar and press Enter. For example, if you're having issues with the battery in your Chromebook, search with the following query: **Chromebook battery problem**. Or you can get more specific: **Chromebook battery will not hold a charge**. Several results will appear for you to browse through.

TIP

If you have a question you want to post, make sure to do a thorough search through the Forum before posting your question. Forums are websites in which the general public can converse on a specific topic or range of topics. Although the Google forums (including the Chromebook Help Forum) are moderated to ensure that everyone is playing nicely, you may still rub people the wrong way if you post a question that has already been asked and answered.

TIP

If your problem seems to be more related to your Chromebook's hardware than its software, you can contact the manufacturer's website for help. Fortunately, the Chromebook Help Center can guide you to it. On the main page of the Chromebook Help Center, scroll down and click Device Support. Then click Get Help From Your Chromebook Manufacturer. There you see a page with all the Chromebook manufacturers, along with support telephone numbers and links to support websites.

Using the Chromebook Recovery Utility

Chrome OS is great, but it's not an infallible operating system. Things can go awry with your Chromebook. If your Chromebook ever gives you a message saying that Chrome OS Is Missing or Damaged, you may have to reinstall the operating system. Reinstalling the operating system removes all locally-stored data from your Chromebook, but if you're getting the missing-or-damaged error, chances are you've already lost your data anyway.

Google has provided a way for you to recover your Chromebook. The process is relatively simple; it involves downloading a recovery program and storing it on an external USB drive or SD card. If your Chromebook is already dead or dying, chances are you can't use your Chromebook to do this. But the good news is that you can create a recovery program using another computer, even a Windows or a Mac.

Reinstalling the Chrome OS operating system requires a recovery drive (like a USB jump drive or an SD card) to get you back up and running. To create a recovery drive, follow these steps:

1. **Do one of the following:**

    a. **If you are on a Chromebook, open the Chrome Web Store and search for Chromebook Recovery Utility.**

    b. **If you are on a PC or a Mac, open the Chrome browser and go to the Chrome Web Store at** `https://chrome.google.com/webstore`. **Search for Chromebook Recovery Utility. You need to log in to your Google account as well.**

        If the utility is not found, try this link: `https://chrome.google.com/webstore/detail/chromebook-recovery-utili/` or perform a Google search for Chromebook Recovery Utility.

2. **Add the extension to your browser.**

    Figure 19-8 shows this app. As the figure shows, I did this on my Mac to show how you can use another computer to jumpstart your Chromebook.

3. **When the browser extension has been added, launch the utility, as shown in Figure 19-9.**

    The Chromebook Recovery Utility launches.

4. **Follow the prompts until you're asked to enter the model number of your Chromebook.**

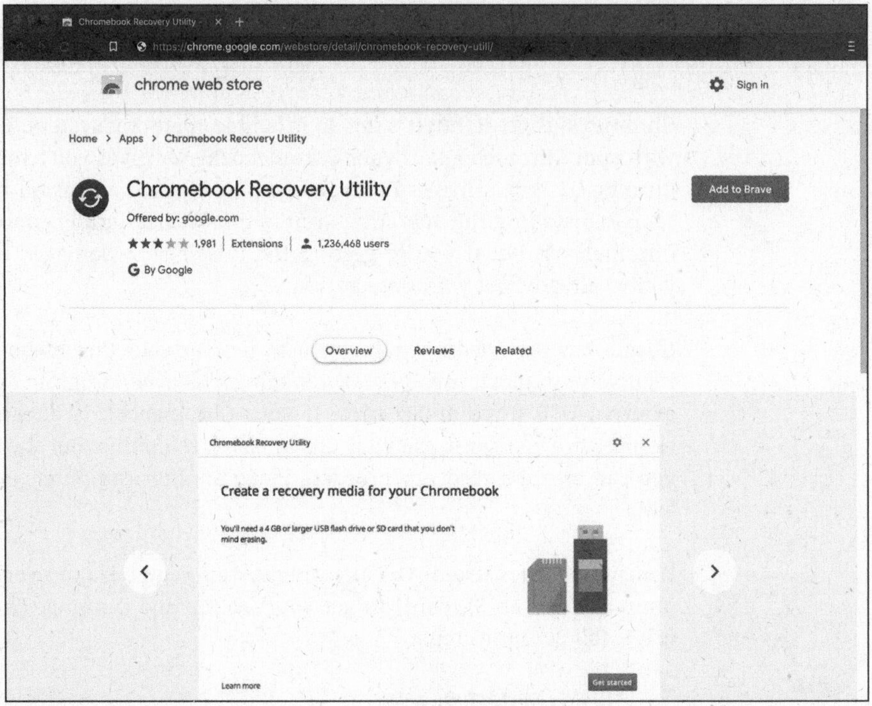

FIGURE 19-8:
Installing the
Chromebook
Recovery Utility.

FIGURE 19-9:
Launching the
Chromebook
Recovery Utility.

5. **Click Continue.**

   The Utility asks you to insert a USB drive or SD card, as shown in Figure 19-10.

6. **Select the media that you want to use as your recovery drive and click Continue.**

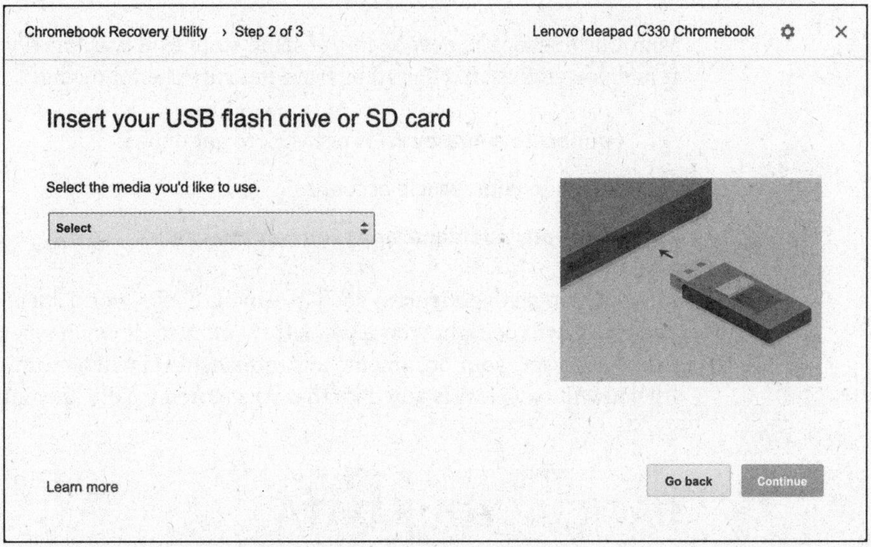

Insert your USB flash drive or SD card

Select the media you'd like to use.

Select	⇕

Learn more   Go back   Continue

FIGURE 19-10:
Insert your USB
drive or SD card.

WARNING

Anything still on your USB drive or SD card will be deleted after you create the recovery image. Now is the time to ensure that you used the right media.

7. **Click Create Now.**

Your Chromebook begins downloading and installing the software needed to make your recovery drive.

TIP

Right about now, you should be getting a cup of coffee and reviewing your stocks because this process takes the better part of ten minutes.

Chromebook notifies you when your recovery media has been successfully created.

8. **Remove your SD card or USB drive from your Chromebook and click Done.**

To recover your Chromebook by reinstalling Chrome OS, follow these steps:

1. **At the Chrome OS Is Missing or Damaged screen, insert the recovery media into your Chromebook's USB or SD slot.**

Your Chromebook automatically detects the recovery media.

2. **Wait for the operating system to install the OS automatically.**

The Chromebook begins its recovery.

3. **After Chromebook finishes recovering your system, remove the recovery media.**

Your Chromebook reboots automatically.

Your Chromebook is now be in the same state as it was when you first purchased it and powered it on. Your steps from here are the following:

1. **Connect to a nearby Wi-Fi network to get online.**

2. **Sign in to your Google account.**

3. **Install any additional apps you want to use.**

All your Google experiences, such as Gmail, books, docs, sheets, photos, movies, and chats, will be right where you left them. Also, if you happen to be a Microsoft Office 365 user, your documents and spreadsheets will be waiting for you as well. All you will have lost is any data that was stored locally on your Chromebook.

BACK UP YOUR DATA

Although most of the data you work with on your Chromebook is already online, data that is important to you can still be stored locally on your Chromebook. If this is the case, copying this data to Google Drive or to a local storage device, whether to a hard drive or SD card, is essential. If your Chromebook suffers a Chrome OS malfunction that requires you to recover your Chromebook, or if your Chromebook is lost, stolen, or develops a serious hardware problem, chances are that any data that resides *only* on your Chromebook is gone forever, unless you first took the time to make a copy.

If you're reading this, hoping against hope that there may be a way to recover data that was only on your dead or dying Chromebook, I'm sorry, but you may be out of luck. If you're not in such dire straits at the moment, remember: The time to back up your data is today, while you still can.

5

The Part of Tens

Chapter **20**

Ten Hardware Features to Consider When Buying a Chromebook

I f you haven't purchased a Chromebook yet and want to, the tips in this chapter makes you a better and smarter consumer. If you already own a Chromebook, this chapter helps you better understand the hardware in your Chromebook and how it contributes to your Chromebook experience. I point out the most important features to most users so that you can choose wisely and get the best Chromebook for your money.

If you're a serious, detail–oriented shopper, write down the features that are most important ("have to haves"), and those that are less important ("nice to haves"). Then, as you read this book, you should have a good idea of what activities you expect to use your Chromebook for, which should make the more critical features evident to you.

If you live in a city or town with one or more stores that sell computers, I recommend that you shop for Chromebooks in person so that you can become familiar with the *feel* of Chromebooks, particularly with the size of the screen and keyboard. In this chapter, I tell you about important features that are sure to make a difference in the usefulness and enjoyment of your Chromebook.

Screen

When it comes to Chromebook specifications, it's all about the screen. Through the screen, you see the world on your Chromebook, whether you're working or running your business, viewing vacation pictures, chatting with friends over video, checking your banking transactions online, or watching cat videos.

Here are the four primary aspects of the screen that are important to understand:

>> **Size:** Measured diagonally from one upper corner to the opposite lower corner, the size of the screen directly translates into your viewing experience. Generally, the larger, the better — to a point. A larger screen makes for a larger Chromebook. I prefer nothing smaller than 13 inches, but your needs may be different.

>> **Resolution:** This specification is all about the level of detail you want to see on the screen. You want at least HD quality, which requires a resolution of 1920 x 1080, meaning 1,920 pixels (dots) in width and 1,080 pixels (dots) in height. This pixel count is the resolution of a standard movie you view on DVD, Netflix, Hulu, or Amazon Prime. Bigger numbers mean that images will be even more detailed.

>> **Touchscreen:.** Many Chromebooks are equipped with a touchscreen. The touchscreen makes your Chromebook's screen perform like a tablet or smartphone: You can touch it to launch apps, scroll in windows, draw, and even type. Some touchscreen Chromebooks have an additional feature, described in the next point in this list.

>> **Convertible:** Some touchscreen Chromebooks are convertible, which means that the screen pivots around to the back, thereby turning your Chromebook laptop into a tablet computer. My Lenovo C330 Chromebook does this, and it's like having two computers in one: You have a laptop when you want it, and you have a tablet when you want it. It gives you the best of both worlds.

One crucial point about screen size: Chromebooks with screens that are smaller than 13 inches have a keyboard that may seem small and crowded. If you type a lot, you may be dissatisfied with an 11 -inch Chromebook; the keyboard may seem awfully cramped. You could, however, get an external keyboard, but for the money you would spend on that, you could also just get a Chromebook with a larger screen — 13 or even 15 inches.

Processor

Also known as the CPU, the *processor* is the brain of every computer. Here are the two main factors to know about the CPU:

>> **Processor speed, measured in gigahertz (GHz):** This rating indicates how fast your processor can perform calculations. The higher the number, the faster the calculations.

>> **Number of cores:** Each core can perform one operation at a time. Multiple cores means that multiple processes can happen simultaneously. Hence, having more cores equals a faster processor.

These two components are key drivers in overall processor performance, and more, in this case, is better.

The faster the processor and the more cores it has, the more expensive the processor, and the more electricity it consumes, which shortens battery life. Chromebooks don't need much power, so the processor doesn't need to be over-the-top fast!

Memory

Another critical factor in the performance of a Chromebook (and any other computer) is the quantity of memory present. *Memory* is high-speed, short-term storage, which is often referred to as RAM. When you open a program, the program is loaded into memory so that it can be run. Naturally, the more memory you have, the more browser tabs you can open and the more apps you can run simultaneously. Chromebooks, however, don't load many programs into memory. Therefore, a large amount of memory is not necessary. The amount of memory in a computer is measured in gigabytes (GB), and your Chromebook should have anywhere from 4GB to 16GB. Four gigabytes (4G) will be adequate for the average user. Avoid Chromebooks with 2G of RAM.

Storage Capacity

Formerly called the *hard drive*, a computer's ability to store data is often just called its storage capacity.

Look for at least 32GB of storage. If you plan to store a lot of photos and videos directly on your Chromebook, look for 64GB or more. This will seem tiny in comparison with Windows and Macs whose storage capacity ranges from 250GB to 1,000 GB and even more! But remember, a big part of the Chromebook experience is the fact that the Chrome OS itself is very small, and most of your content is stored online. (See Chapter 7 for the skinny on using online content on Google Drive.)

REMEMBER

Be sure to find out whether your Chromebook's storage is an SSD (solid-state drive; it has no moving parts) or an HDD (hard disk drive; it has a spinning drive). Most newer laptops come with an SSD, which is a whopping 1,000 times faster than an HDD, and it lasts longer, too. A computer with an HDD is far slower in almost every respect and should be avoided.

Webcam

Most Chromebooks come with webcams. If you are interested in video chats with coworkers, friends, or family, a webcam built into your Chromebook is a must; otherwise, you need to buy one and plug it into a USB port.

If high video quality is important to you (in the case of a webcam, this means the image quality of *you* that people view on *their* computers), look for a webcam that is at least HD (1920p) quality. Most, though, are lower — 720p, for instance — and adequate for most purposes.

Internet Connection

To be fully useful, Chromebooks require an Internet connection. The connection can come in three forms:

>> A built-in Wi-Fi to connect to wireless networks. All Chromebooks have this.

>> A hardwired connection to an Ethernet cable which, for virtually all Chromebooks, requires an adaptor that typically plugs into a USB port.

>> Cellular options that you use to activate a wireless Internet data plan with a national provider such as Verizon or AT&T. Some Chromebook models come with these options.

If you expect to frequently visit locations that have no accessible Wi-Fi, and you don't have a mobile hotspot or a phone that can produce a mobile hotspot, you should consider purchasing a Chromebook with the cellular option built in.

Many Chromebooks are listed as having "faster Wi-Fi," or Wi-Fi with the latest high-speed standards such as 801.11ac. For the most part, this claim will mean nothing if most of your Chromebook work involves visiting websites. That's because if you have a 15 Mbps Internet connection, web pages will load no faster than that no matter how your Wi-Fi is — even if it's just as fast or 50 times faster. Ultra-fast Wi-Fi matters only if you are doing advanced work such as connecting wirelessly to a storage server and transferring large amounts of data.

Battery

Battery life, which is usually a big deal with portable devices like laptop computers, smartphones, and hoverboards, is an essential feature of the Chromebook. If you compare the specifications of different devices, you find that the battery life of more powerful devices is typically shorter. Although this situation is also the case with the Chromebook, a Chromebook tends to have a *longer* battery life because its operating system is streamlined and doesn't run much software or require ultra-powerful hardware.

If battery life is important to you, the only battery-centric specification that matters is the number of hours of battery life you can expect to get. However, as with fuel economy in an automobile, *your mileage may vary*. On a laptop, you can greatly influence battery life by adjusting the brightness of the screen, and by turning off Wi-Fi and Bluetooth when you're not using them.

SD Card Slot

An *SD card* is a tiny, inexpensive storage device that you typically find in digital cameras, security cameras, and dashcams. Some Chromebooks come with an SD card slot, which enables you to easily view content from these devices. SD cards are also handy for storing and transferring photos and videos, among other file types, between computers. Having the ability to add external storage with a collection of SD cards quickly is valuable, especially if you have an extensive library of photos, videos, movies, or other files that you want to access quickly.

HDMI Port

HDMI, which stands for High-Definition Multimedia Interface in case you're curious, is a type of interface primarily used for high-definition video and audio. If you want to connect your Chromebook to a high-definition external monitor or a flat-screen TV, you should make sure that your Chromebook comes with an HDMI port.

TIP

HDMI ports enable you to use your television as an external monitor. Connecting your Chromebook to your TV via HDMI turns your Chromebook into a portable media center!

USB Ports (Including USB-C)

USB is the standard for attaching all kinds of devices to laptops and desktop computers. It has also become the standard for digitally powering and charging electronic devices. The question you need to ask yourself when selecting a Chromebook is not *whether* it has a USB port, but *how many* USB ports it has. If you use a USB mouse and need another port for a USB keyboard or external storage device, you should ensure that your Chromebook has more than one USB port. (Many people opt for a wireless mouse and keyboard to save their USB ports for other uses, such as external hard drives.)

You want to be sure that your Chromebook is USB 3.0 instead of the older USB 2.0. If you connect an external hard drive to your Chromebook to copy data into or from your Chromebook regularly, you immediately see the difference between the newer and older USB: Data transfers about ten times faster with USB 3.0 than with USB 2.0.

USB-C is becoming a standard on laptop computers, including Chromebooks. My Lenovo Chromebook has a single USB-C port used for charging the Chromebook's battery, but it can be used to connect external devices using a USB-C cable or connector. If you have any USB-C–connected devices that you want to use with your Chromebook, you may want to look for a Chromebook that has at least two USB-C ports.

Chapter **21**

Ten Handy Chromebook Shortcuts

A Chromebook is made to be easy to use right out of the box. It's not a self-driving car, but it's almost as easy. Get it out, plug it in, turn it on, and follow the prompts: You'll be up and running in minutes. Still, even though Chromebook is very usable, you may want to do some further customization. This chapter contains ten tips, tricks, and shortcuts to make your Chromebook experience more productive — or at least a little more fun.

Search from the Launcher

The Google platform is baked into the Chromebook and Chrome OS through and through. That was the point when Chromebook was created: Create a tool that's powered by — and showcases — the extensive Google ecosystem of applications. One way in which the Google platform is integrated into Chrome OS is the Chromebook Search feature. When you open the Launcher or press the Search button on your keyboard, a Search bar is revealed. Type a search query into the bar and press Enter. Chromebook serves you Google search results, as though you had first opened a browser and gone to Google.com to find something.

Do a Quick Reboot

No computer is perfect, and although some manufacturers like to make you think that you'll never need to reboot your computer, you almost always will at one point or another. The longer you use your Chromebook, the more gunked up the memory becomes with remnant websites, applications, data, and so on. You can reboot your computer a few ways, but the fastest way to reboot is to press the Power button and Refresh button simultaneously. Like a flash of light, your Chromebook restarts with fresh memory in just a few seconds.

Note, however, that when you start the Chrome browser after a reboot, it picks up where you left off if you configured Chrome to do so (as described in Chapter 3). But when you do a quick restart, Chrome asks whether you want to restore pages," meaning just that: It will pick up where you left off, or you can just select that little box and start anew. Figure 21-1 shows what I'm describing.

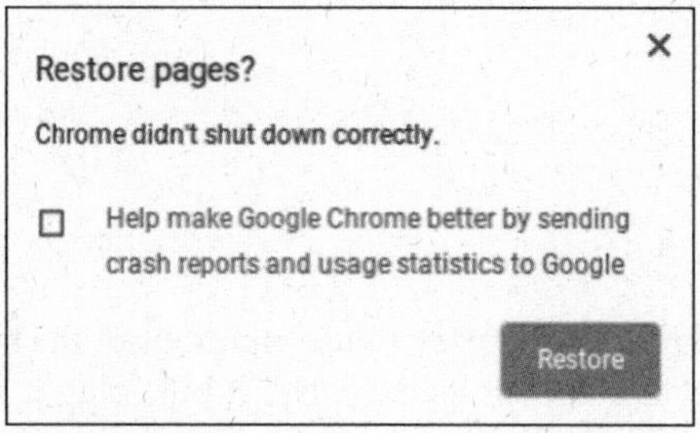

FIGURE 21-1: The Chrome browser asks whether you want to continue from where you left off before your reboot.

Restore pages?

Chrome didn't shut down correctly.

☐ Help make Google Chrome better by sending crash reports and usage statistics to Google

Restore

Control Chromebook with the Omnibox

If you're familiar with Chrome from using it on devices other than your Chromebook, you may already know that Chrome has several high-powered features that you can access by entering Chrome shortcuts into the Omnibox (the search or URL field). Naturally, Chrome on Chromebook has the same set of features. Following are some of the shortcuts you might find the most helpful:

» **chrome://power:** View how much charge your Chromebook has and how much power you're using.

» **chrome://settings:** Load your Chromebook settings.

» **chrome://extensions:** See and manage all your Chrome browser extensions.

>> **chrome:// quota-internals:** Quickly view how much storage space you have on your Chromebook.

>> **chrome://chrome-urls:** A complete list of all these Chrome URLs.

Lock Your Screen

Ever been in a public place working on your computer and need to get up to go to the bathroom in a hurry? Or maybe someone is barging into your room, and you don't want him or her to get into your business and see what you're doing on your Chromebook? You can lock your screen by holding down your Power button for 400 milliseconds and then clicking Lock. But sometimes you need to lock your screen in 1 millisecond. Never fear: Press the Lock key (shown in Figure 18-14 in Chapter 18) to lock your screen in an instant!

Launch Apps in the Shelf

One way that you can save time on your Chromebook is by pinning frequently used apps to the shelf. In doing so, you save yourself the extra click, as well as the scrolling through pages of applications to find the one you want. If you're serious about keyboard productivity, you can save yourself the need to even click: Load a pinned app by pressing Alt and the number corresponding with the placement of the application in your shelf (counting from left to right or top to bottom). No longer will you be bogged down by the long journey of a mouse pointer to a click.

Do a Barrel Roll

Sometimes, you just need to have a little fun with your day. Google has hidden a few Easter eggs in your Chromebook. Make your screen do a barrel roll. That's it. No productivity, usefulness, or work-changing functionality here. It's just fun to make your screen go bananas for a brief moment. Press Ctrl+Alt+Shift+Refresh to make your focused browser window roll around and then snap back to normal. (If all apps are minimized and you see only your wallpaper, nothing will happen.)

View Chrome Browser Tasks

Have you ever wondered why your Chromebook has slowed down but weren't sure which tab was responsible? Find out by going to the Chrome browser, clicking the menu button (just under the X used to close the window), clicking More Tools, and then clicking Task Manager. A new window opens, showing the tasks running on your Chromebook. Click CPU, and Chrome sorts the list, showing the biggest users first.

Further, if you think a tab is causing browser problems, fix it by clicking the corresponding row in Task Manager and then clicking End Process.

See All Your Open Windows

If you've been using your Chromebook for a while and doing a lot of different things with it, you might have a lot of apps open. Press the Show All Open Windows key to immediately show all the apps and windows that are open on your Chromebook. (See Figure 21-2.)

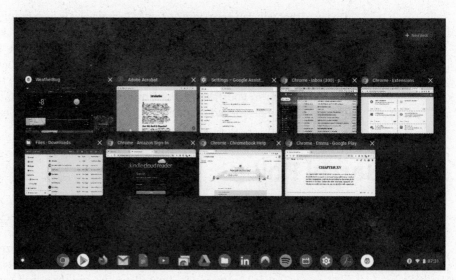

FIGURE 21-2:
Press the Show All Open Windows key to view all open windows.

What to do from here? Press the Show All Open Windows key again to return to what you were doing before. Or, click any of the open windows to switch to the one you want.

Perform Math, Conversions, and Definitions with Search

Google Search is a major feature that's available on a Chromebook. Have you ever used Google to perform conversions or calculations for you? If you haven't, you should. Your Chromebook will give you the same service through the Search bar. Give it a try with these steps:

1. **While logged into your Chromebook, click the Launcher.**

The app menu opens, and the Search bar appears.

2. **Enter your math problem or search query into the Search bar.**

For example, type **4+4**. The second result will be the answer: = 8. You can even ask for conversions: Type **15 ounces to grams**. The second result is = 425.2428 grams.

3. **Enter a word to define into the Search bar.**

For example, type **define cello**. The result is "the bass member of the violin family tuned an octave below the viola."

Google Translate is also available on Chromebook through the Chrome browser. Go to `https://translate.google.com/`, and Google can translate words and phrases from one language to another.

Use A Proxy for the Delete Key

It's true: Your Chromebook doesn't have a Delete key. It has a Backspace key, but no Delete key (unless you're one of the fortunate few). Here's the difference between these two keys: Delete removes the character to the right of your cursor, whereas Backspace removes the character to the left of your cursor. This is handy if you are typing an email message or composing or editing a document.

To delete characters to the right of your cursor, press Alt+Backspace. Characters to the right are deleted one by one.

You can also delete entire words to the left of your cursor by pressing Ctrl+Backspace. The words start to vanish one by one.

Chapter 22

Ten Great Chrome OS Apps

Apps are all people hear about today. Apple, Android, and Google all have application stores. With literally millions of apps available, we are in application overload. Still, many beneficial apps are available for Chromebook users. In this section, you get a brief overview of ten apps that make your life on Chromebook more enjoyable, productive, and entertaining.

Skype

Skype is the original killer app for texting and video chatting. With millions of users worldwide, Skype is the app that works on all platforms: Chromebooks, Android, iPhone, PCs, Macs, and even Linux systems.

Skype became popular when it was a great way to communicate for free, helping users avoid costly international calling fees. Another cool Skype feature is that you can call a landline phone with Skype if you want. Unfortunately, that *does* cost you a per-minute charge because a landline is involved.

WeVideo

Not having a lot of storage or resources on your Chromebook doesn't mean that you can't have a lot of fun working with video. WeVideo is an excellent app for editing video anywhere in the world. You can work in multiple editing modes (storyboard, timeline, or an advanced mode) and connect with your Facebook, Google Drive, or Dropbox to make dragging and dropping video files and photos easy. Add effects, text, transitions, and subtitles, along with background music or recorded voiceovers to bring your videos to life. You can export WeVideos to various web services in standard definition and high definition. Video is a serious business on the Chromebook with WeVideo.

WeVideo has been around for years and is still popular, as evidenced by its millions of users and high ratings. WeVideo is free to use, but with a paid subscription, you unlock more features like a vast library of stock images, videos, and audio.

Lexulous Solitaire

Lexulous Solitaire is a word game that's a mix between Solitaire and Scrabble. You start with a game board and seven letter tiles, and you try to think of words with your tiles and place them on the board. If you love Scrabble but don't have an opponent, Lexulous Solitaire is just the ticket. I'm a fan of word games; I like to think it keeps me young, but maybe I'm just fooling myself . . .

You can also play against others, making the game similar to Scrabble. You can't cheat like you can in the board game, though (snicker!).

Angry Birds

You've been living under a rock for the past decade if you haven't heard of *Angry Birds. Angry Birds* is a fun way to kill time with your Chromebook. Essentially, the premise of the game is to fling birds at the evil pigs and make their makeshift towers fall with a spectacular crash. Quite a bit of strategy is involved, especially in the more advanced levels, because you have to toss birds that can smash through different materials to get to the evil green pigs. The one thing that makes the game genuinely remarkable, aside from the hilarious audio, is the fantastic physics engine that calculates trajectory, velocity, and the force and sound of impacts. But don't kid yourself: This a game doesn't develop mental strength.

Still, *Angry Birds* is one of the most popular computer games ever, with over 100 million downloads.

Today, you have many different *Angry Birds* games to choose from: *Angry Birds 2, Angry Birds Friends, Angry Birds Evolution 2020, Angry Birds Transformers,* and many more!

Chrome Remote Desktop

Sometimes you may need to get work done on a machine other than your Chromebook. Or maybe you have some files that reside on another device that's miles and miles away. Remote Desktop is a great way to remotely access your other computers without having to be in the same room, or even in the same city. The Remote Desktop client must be installed in the Chrome browser of each machine that you want to control. You also have to make sure that the other computers are connected to the Internet and the Chrome browser is open.

You can also remotely access, and even control (with the owner's permission), someone else's Chromebook. You can control your friend's Chromebook, or your own, from a Mac, PC, or another Chromebook. My mother has a Chromebook, and sometimes when she has a question, I can access her Chromebook and remotely control it to show her how to do something. This type of access is a great way for someone to be the IT department for relatives and friends.

PicMonkey

PicMonkey is a powerful photo editor that works great on a Chromebook. Technically a Chrome browser extension, PicMonkey is chock full of filters and other special effects to make your photos really dazzle. You can fix exposure problems, crop and resize photos, touch up photos to take the years off those family portraits, and add graphics, icons, text, and more. PicMonkey is a great app if you are into serious photo and image editing.

PicMonkey offers a free trial, Try it— if you love it, you'll want to buy it!

Sketch The Best

This app is the Adobe Photoshop Sketch app for Chromebook. The ultimate in sketch tools, Sketch The Best lets you create digital art, whether you're just starting out with art or are a modern master. With Sketch The Best, you draw with different pencils, pens, brushes, watercolor, acrylic, ink brushes, and more — all digital. Create your art in different layers and then edit, combine, and manipulate the layers and even name and save them.

Sketch The Best is a Chrome browser extension and works on not only your Chromebook but also the PC and Mac.

Pandora

Google Play may be a bit much for those of us just looking for a little background music while we work or play. Enter Pandora, a wildly popular Internet radio platform that lets you create stations from songs, performers, and albums. Pandora uses a combination of algorithm and user feedback to ensure that songs that load into your radio station fit the sound you're looking for. Pandora is a free service, like Google Play — and that should be music to your ears!

Like a lot of free apps, you hear commercials on the free version of Pandora. For a modest monthly fee, the ads disappear forever, and you discover even more great features.

Microsoft Word Online

Google Docs, the word processor from Google, is impressive. But if you come from a lifelong career working in Microsoft Word, Word Online may be the right option for you. Create documents of all sorts, from letters to research papers and autobiographies. Word Online is a near replica of the desktop experience, just online. Share your documents and invite collaborators to participate in the editing of documents with Word Online; then save your documents in OneDrive or download them for storing elsewhere. Word Online is an excellent option if you aren't ready for Google Docs.

Do note that you need to have an Office 365 account to use Word Online.

Weatherbug

The makers of Weatherbug touts that it's the fastest, most accurate weather application currently available. Weatherbug is a ray of sunshine in your Launcher menu. Save multiple locations in your Weatherbug for quick referencing. Check current conditions or long-term forecasts. The virtual window gives you a pleasant visualization of the forecast. Weatherbug also funnels out real-time weather alerts to make sure that you're in the know when severe weather is moving into your area. Also, check out local or national radar and plan a long trip with a precise weather forecast.

I especially appreciate Weatherbug's lightning strike detector. For me, as a frequent air traveler, thunderstorms near airports matter because ramp operations are suspended when storms are too close, which translates into delayed or canceled flights. No planes can come or go, and when you're trying to make tight connections, having this information can make all the difference when it comes to getting home on time.

authentication

» **Improving network security**

» **Preventing theft of your Chromebook**

» **Keeping prying eyes away with a privacy filter**

Chapter **23**

Ten Chromebook Security Tips

C ybercriminals are making good money, but I want to make sure that they don't get any of yours! Having a Chromebook is a great start because the design of Chrome OS — the heart and soul of a Chromebook — has security strongly in mind. The nature of cybercrime makes it necessary for you to be vigilant, even when using the most secure laptop available. The tips in this chapter can help keep you and your data safe.

Lock Your Chromebook when You're Away

Whenever you're working on your Chromebook where other people are around, an excellent habit to get into is to lock it when you step away, even for a minute or two. You can easily lock it; Chromebooks give you not one, not two, but three ways, as follows:

» Briefly press the Power button and then click Lock.

» Open the Settings window and click the Lock symbol.

» Press the Lock key on your keyboard.

Use Strong, Complex Passwords

The top ten passwords in use in 2019 are 123456, 123456789, qwerty, 12345678, 111111, 1234567890, 1234567, password, 123123, and 987654321. The next ten are just as lame.

Using such passwords is just laziness, and user accounts with weak passwords like these are broken into a lot. Using stronger, complex passwords isn't difficult. Here are some examples of better ones (but don't use these because they're in a published book now):

>> ST4R.wars (Star Wars)

>> Loosie.IN.the.sky-withDiamonds (Lucy in the Sky with Diamonds)

>> Run-Forr35t-Run! (Run Forrest Run!)

>> Sea-Sp00t-Run (See Spot run)

The idea is to think of a phrase and then devise some consistent way of misspelling it that you can remember.

You need to use a different password on each site you use. Here's why: If cyber-criminals can successfully break into a website's user IDs and passwords database (which happens often), and if you use the same user ID and password everywhere you go, the cybercriminals who stole these credentials can easily log in to all the websites you use frequently. If this includes online banking or other sites on which you buy or sell, you're in big trouble.

Use complex passwords on your websites, and a different password on each site, is a lot to remember — so read the next tip.

Use a Web-Based Password Vault

Maintaining security isn't easy. Using different passwords on each site is definitely the way to be more secure, but remembering all those passwords can be challenging. The good news is you don't have to.

Some trusted, high-quality password vaults are available. These securely store your login credentials so that you don't need to remember them all. Some of these vaults can even automatically enter your login credentials when you log in. How cool is that!

The best password vaults are LastPass (at www.lastpass.com), Keeper (at www.keepersecurity.com), and Dashlane (at www.dashlane.com).

Use Multifactor Authentication Everywhere You Can

One of the biggest threats on the Internet involves the theft of login credentials for popular websites. Even if Chrome OS is resistant to attack, hackers use malicious browser extensions that are designed to steal user IDs and passwords when you type them in. Also, cybercriminals directly attack popular website databases and, if they can break in, often they go for encrypted password databases and attempt to decrypt them. If they do, they have the user IDs and passwords for many — or all — of the site's users!

Using multifactor authentication is generally pretty easy. When you log in to a website, the website sends a code to your smartphone, and you type in that code to log in. Even if hackers can obtain your user ID and password, they can't log in because they don't have your smartphone as well.

Be on the lookout on your social media, financial services, medical, and other websites where sensitive information about you resides. When you see information about activating multifactor authentication (sometimes called two-factor authentication), please consider enabling it. You'll thwart cybercriminals, and your data will be a little bit safer.

Get a Screen Privacy Filter

If you work with confidential information on your Chromebook, and do so frequently in public places, you might consider getting a screen privacy filter. It helps to keep prying eyes that glance at your screen from seeing what you're up to. When using a privacy filter, you can clearly see the screen, but people to your left and right just black when they look at your screen. Keep your business information, or those cat videos, to yourself!

Block Malicious Websites with an Antimalware Program

Chrome OS is quite robust and resistant to the kinds of attacks that have plagued Windows computers for decades. Still, hazards are out there, and most of the attacks you face are attacks on your browser in the form of malicious extensions and websites that attempt to steal your data.

Security programs like AVG Online Security or McAfee Endpoint Security are available from the Google Web Store. They are purpose-made for Chromebooks and help protect you from known malicious websites and other threats.

Update the Security on Your Wi-Fi Access Point

You're only as secure as the Wi-Fi network you usually use. If you have a new Chromebook and your Wi-Fi access point (which might be doing double-duty as your cable modem or DSL modem) is old, you might consider replacing it with a newer one.

The two most important security settings to look at on your Wi-Fi access point are the type of encryption (which is usually none, WEP, WPA, or WPA2 — pick WPA2!) and the default password. Be sure to read the instructions for your Wi-Fi access point carefully. Visit the Wi-Fi access point manufacturer's website for help. You might also pick up a copy of *Networking For Dummies*, 11th Edition, by Doug Lowe (Wiley) for more information on securing and customizing your home Wi-Fi network.

Back Up Your Local Data

With ordinary use of your Chromebook, most of the data you create and deal with is stored by Google "in the cloud," where it is available on all of your Google-enabled devices. Still, you might have local data that matters to you. The best way to find out is to open the Files app and see what data is stored locally. Anything in the Downloads, Images, Audio, or Video folders might exist only there and nowhere else. If this is the case, *and* you care about any of these files, it's best to copy them to your Google Drive: Just drag and drop your files to it — into separate folders if you want.

Alternatively, you can back up these files to an external hard drive or SD card if you prefer to maintain complete control over this data. Either way, backing up your local data is easy and takes only moments.

Use a VPN If You Use Public Wi-Fi Routinely

If you frequent Wi-Fi networks at coffee shops, hotels, airports, and other public places, I recommend that you subscribe to a VPN service. As discussed in Chapter 18, getting a free VPN service is likely to do more harm than good. Instead, go with one of the leading VPN services, such as Nord VPN, Encrypt.me, ExpressVPN, or Cyberghost VPN.

VPN software encrypts all your Wi-Fi network communications so that snoopy people can't eavesdrop on any of your communications on a public Wi-Fi network. This issue is less important at home where, hopefully, your Wi-Fi access point is configured to use WPA or, better yet, WPA2, which encrypts your network traffic at home.

Keep Your Chromebook Up to Date

I'm saving the best — and most important — security tip for last. Keeping your Chromebook's Chrome OS up to date is vital for your security, as well as for the stability of your Chromebook. Be sure to watch your notifications and act promptly to update Chrome OS as well as all the apps you've downloaded from the Chrome Web Store and the Google Play Store.

Although some of the updates fix software bugs, you can be sure that many of the fixes improve the security of your Chromebook and the apps you run. When these security bugs are fixed, criminals have a harder time breaking in and stealing your data.

Index

About the Author

Peter H. Gregory is a life-long technologist, having worked on old-school mainframes, supercomputers, minis, micros, PCs, Macs, Chromebooks, smartphones, and more, up to the present day. Since early in his career, Gregory has been helping others understand how to use computers and software through seminars, university courses, on-site training, and by mentoring friends and family. He taught a cybersecurity course for IT professionals for ten years at the University of Washington, and he is also adjunct faculty for the University of South Florida's Cybersecurity for Executives program. Gregory was also an instructor of motorcycle riding for a few years until a new job with heavy travel made him hang up his motorcycle-instruction spurs for a time. Currently, Gregory is an executive cybersecurity advisor for Optiv Security, where he helps business executives and board members understand cybersecurity issues in business terms. He holds several cybersecurity certifications (CISA, CISM, CRISC, CISSP, CIPM, CCISO, CCSK, and PCI-QSA), which for Chromebooks means only that he knows information technology, privacy, and cybersecurity inside and out. In his spare time, he enjoys motorcycling, woodworking, and metalworking.

Dedication

To people everywhere who are just looking for a simpler and safer way to get online.

Acknowledgments

I am grateful for my wife, Rebekah, who inspires me to greatness, and who put up with a lot of early mornings, late nights, and weekends when I was there at home but still far, far away. Many thanks to Katie Mohr at Wiley for responding to numerous emails as well as for helping to drive this project to completion. Thanks also to Russ Mullen, our technical reviewer, for great and constructive feedback, even before he saw a single written page. Thank you, Susan Christophersen, for helping to organize, refine, and copy edit all this content. Also, thanks to Wordsmith Editorial, Inc. for proofing and the Wiley production team for the layout. Thank you, Gio G. and Rich S. for being live test subjects. My gratitude also goes to Rebecca Steele, my faithful business manager and research assistant, for being an excellent Chromebook test subject. And finally, thanks to my agent, Carole Jelen, for pursuing this opportunity. Writing a book is not a solo act but a team sport, and I'm grateful for everyone mentioned here and others I'm not aware of. Thanks to Ralph Pratt (God rest your soul) for inspiring and coaching me for my first classroom instruction gig, where I taught programmers, department heads, and business leaders how to use a new computer program known as Mapper, which is a bit like modern-day spreadsheets. Mind you, this was in the early 1980s, before Excel, Lotus 1-2-3, Multiplan, or even Visicalc. Ralph's patient coaching set me on a path that would change my career and lead to my writing dozens of books, helping thousands better understand the great complexity of information technology.

Publisher's Acknowledgments

Associate Publisher: Katie Mohr

Project Manager and Copy Editor: Susan Christopherson

Technical Editor: Russ Mullen

Author's Research Assistant: Rebecca Steele

Production Editor: Siddique Shaik

Cover Image: Screenshot provided by Peter H. Gregory

Leverage the power

Dummies is the global leader in the reference category and one of the most trusted and highly regarded brands in the world. No longer just focused on books, customers now have access to the dummies content they need in the format they want. Together we'll craft a solution that engages your customers, stands out from the competition, and helps you meet your goals.

Advertising & Sponsorships

Connect with an engaged audience on a powerful multimedia site, and position your message alongside expert how-to content. Dummies.com is a one-stop shop for free, online information and know-how curated by a team of experts.

- Targeted ads
- Video
- Email Marketing
- Microsites
- Sweepstakes sponsorship

20 MILLION PAGE VIEWS EVERY SINGLE MONTH

15 MILLION UNIQUE VISITORS PER MONTH

43% OF ALL VISITORS ACCESS THE SITE VIA THEIR MOBILE DEVICES

700,000 NEWSLETTER SUBSCRIPTIONS TO THE INBOXES OF *300,000* UNIQUE INDIVIDUALS EVERY WEEK

# of dummies

Custom Publishing

Reach a global audience in any language by creating a solution that will differentiate you from competitors, amplify your message, and encourage customers to make a buying decision.

- Apps
- Books
- eBooks
- Video
- Audio
- Webinars

Brand Licensing & Content

Leverage the strength of the world's most popular reference brand to reach new audiences and channels of distribution.

For more information, visit dummies.com/biz

PERSONAL ENRICHMENT

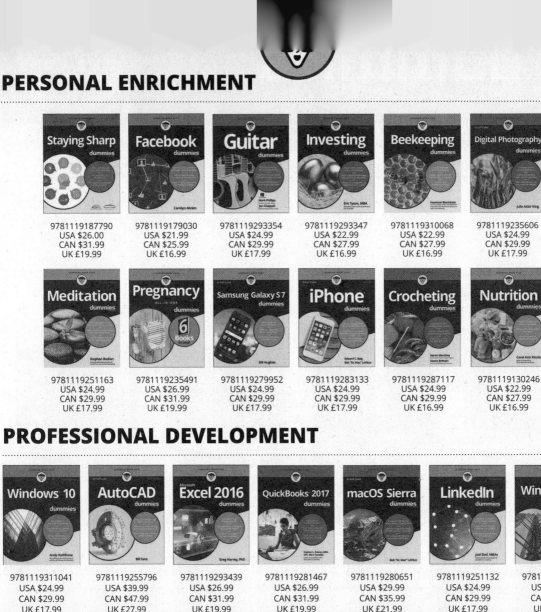

Staying Sharp
9781119187790
USA $26.00
CAN $31.99
UK £19.99

Facebook
9781119179030
USA $21.99
CAN $25.99
UK £16.99

Guitar
9781119293354
USA $24.99
CAN $29.99
UK £17.99

Investing
9781119293347
USA $22.99
CAN $27.99
UK £16.99

Beekeeping
9781119310068
USA $22.99
CAN $27.99
UK £16.99

Digital Photography
9781119235606
USA $24.99
CAN $29.99
UK £17.99

Meditation
9781119251163
USA $24.99
CAN $29.99
UK £17.99

Pregnancy
9781119235491
USA $26.99
CAN $31.99
UK £19.99

Samsung Galaxy S7
9781119279952
USA $24.99
CAN $29.99
UK £17.99

iPhone
9781119283133
USA $24.99
CAN $29.99
UK £17.99

Crocheting
9781119287117
USA $24.99
CAN $29.99
UK £16.99

Nutrition
9781119130246
USA $22.99
CAN $27.99
UK £16.99

PROFESSIONAL DEVELOPMENT

Windows 10
9781119311041
USA $24.99
CAN $29.99
UK £17.99

AutoCAD
9781119255796
USA $39.99
CAN $47.99
UK £27.99

Excel 2016
9781119293439
USA $26.99
CAN $31.99
UK £19.99

QuickBooks 2017
9781119281467
USA $26.99
CAN $31.99
UK £19.99

macOS Sierra
9781119280651
USA $29.99
CAN $35.99
UK £21.99

LinkedIn
9781119251132
USA $24.99
CAN $29.99
UK £17.99

Windows 10
9781119310563
USA $34.00
CAN $41.99
UK £24.99

SharePoint 2016
9781119181705
USA $29.99
CAN $35.99
UK £21.99

Fundamental Analysis
9781119263593
USA $26.99
CAN $31.99
UK £19.99

Networking
9781119257769
USA $29.99
CAN $35.99
UK £21.99

Office 2016
9781119293477
USA $26.99
CAN $31.99
UK £19.99

Office 365
9781119265313
USA $24.99
CAN $29.99
UK £17.99

Salesforce.com
9781119239314
USA $29.99
CAN $35.99
UK £21.99

Coding
9781119293323
USA $29.99
CAN $35.99
UK £21.99

dummies.com

dummies
A Wiley Brand

Learning Made Easy

ACADEMIC

Algebra I dummies
Mary Jane Sterling
9781119293576
USA $19.99
CAN $23.99
UK £15.99

Basic Math & Pre-Algebra dummies
Mark Zegarelli
9781119293637
USA $19.99
CAN $23.99
UK £15.99

Calculus dummies
Mark Ryan
9781119293491
USA $19.99
CAN $23.99
UK £15.99

Chemistry dummies
John T. Moore, EdD
9781119293460
USA $19.99
CAN $23.99
UK £15.99

Physics I dummies
Steven Holzner, PhD
9781119293590
USA $19.99
CAN $23.99
UK £15.99

SAT dummies
1,001 Practice Questions
Ron Woldoff
9781119215844
USA $26.99
CAN $31.99
UK £19.99

Organic Chemistry I dummies
Arthur Winter
9781119293378
USA $22.99
CAN $27.99
UK £16.99

Statistics dummies
Deborah J. Rumsey, PhD
9781119293521
USA $19.99
CAN $23.99
UK £15.99

2016/2017 ASVAB dummies
Rod Powers
9781119239178
USA $18.99
CAN $22.99
UK £14.99

Praxis Core dummies
1,001 Practice Questions
Includes Online Practice Tests
Carla Kirkland
Chan Cleveland
9781119263883
USA $26.99
CAN $31.99
UK £19.99

Available Everywhere Books Are Sold

dummies.com

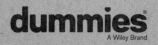

dummies
A Wiley Brand